Science Fiction Literature
in East Germany

East German Studies/ DDR–Studien

Volume 15

Edited by Richard A. Zipser

PETER LANG
Oxford · Bern · Berlin · Bruxelles · Frankfurt am Main · New York · Wien

Science Fiction Literature in East Germany

Sonja Fritzsche

PETER LANG

Oxford · Bern · Berlin · Bruxelles · Frankfurt am Main · New York · Wien

Bibliographic information published by Die Deutsche Bibliothek
Die Deutsche Bibliothek lists this publication in the Deutsche
Nationalbibliografie; detailed bibliographic data is available on
the Internet at ‹http://dnb.ddb.de›.

British Library and Library of Congress Cataloguing-in-Publication Data:
A catalogue record for this book is available from *The British Library,*
Great Britain, and from *The Library of Congress,* USA

ISSN 1072-0626
ISBN 3-03910-739-9
US-ISBN 0-8204-8001-0

© Peter Lang AG, International Academic Publishers, Bern 2006
Hochfeldstrasse 32, Postfach 746, CH-3000 Bern 9, Switzerland
info@peterlang.com, www.peterlang.com, www.peterlang.net

Printed in Germany

To my parents, Nan and Dave Fritzsche,
and to my sister, Tanya Losey

Contents

Acknowledgements

All projects are the sum of the work of many people behind the scenes. Throughout the research and writing process, I have benefited from the advice and moral support of numerous individuals, all of whom I cannot name here, but whom I wish to thank nonetheless. First of all, I wish to extend my appreciation to Jack Zipes, Arlene Teraoka, Rick McCormick, Mary Jo Maynes and John Mowitt, who have been patient and forthcoming with extensive resources and critique. Thomas Kramer and Vibs Petersen also provided valuable commentary. I would like to thank the German Academic Exchange Service (DAAD), the Office of External Affairs at the Freie Universität, Berlin, the Department of German, Scandinavian and Dutch at the University of Minnesota, the University of Minnesota Graduate School and Illinois Wesleyan University for financial support that proved invaluable for the completion of this project.

For their time and insight into the world of East German science fiction, I would like to thank authors Johanna and Günter Braun, Alexander Kröger and his wife Susanne Routschek, Carlos Rasch, Karlheinz and Angela Steinmüller, Michael Szameit and editors Ekkehard Redlin and Erik Simon. Many contacts and opportunities would have passed me by if it had not been for the industrious members of the Andymon science fiction fan club, including, among others, Wolfgang Both, Siegfried Breuer, Ronald Hoppe, Hardy Kettlitz, Hans-Peter Neumann, Klaus Scheffler, Ingolf Vonau, and Anita Winkler. We miss collector Hans-Jürgen Erich. The staffs of the Bundesarchiv–Berlin, Staatsbibliothek Berlin, Amerikanische Gedenkbibliothek–Berlin, and Phantastische Bibliothek Wetzlar have been invaluable. In addition, I wish to acknowledge the Das Neue Berlin/ Eulenspiegel Verlag, which furnished and granted permission to use the original book cover artwork from Del Antonio's *Heimkehr der Vorfahren,* Johanna and Günter Braun's *Unheimliche Erscheinungsformen auf Omega XI* and Angela and Karlheinz Steinmüller's *Der Traummeister.*

For careful and consistent reading, I would like to thank Gun Edberg–Caldwell, Barbara Drescher, Rachel Huener, Beth Muellner, and Leo Riegert. Stokes Schwartz caught errors that I could no longer see. My student assistant Matt Thompson worked tirelessly at a tedious research task. Thanks are also due to Marina Balina, Kathy Brown, Robert Doebgen, Klaus Frühauf, Detlef Kannapin, Ludmila Kizer, Patrick McLane, Julie Prandi, Heidi Soneson, Nancy Sultan, Lyman Tower Sargeant, and Gerhard Wiechmann. Finally, I cannot begin to adequately thank my family, Nan and Dave Fritzsche, Tanya Losey, and Stokes Schwartz, for their unwavering moral support and painstaking reminders that there is a life beyond the book manuscript.

This book is a result of the input of many individuals. Still, this author has been the one to sift through and analyze the information provided. Therefore, any errors or oversights are my own. In addition, all English translations are my own unless otherwise indicated. If a book exists in English translation, I deferred to this translation.

List of Abbreviations

AG	Committee or interest group (Arbeitsgemeinschaft)
AK	Committee or interest group (Arbeitskreis)
BArch	German State Archive (Bundesarchiv)
BRD	Federal Republic of Germany (Bundesrepublik Deutschland)
DDR	German Democratic Republic (Deutsche Demokratische Republik)
DEFA	East German State Film Studio (Deutscher Film Aktiengesellschaft)
DSV	German Writers' Union (Deutsche Schriftstellerverband)
FDJ	Free German Youth (Freie Deutsche Jugend)
FRG	Federal Republic of Germany
GDR	German Democratic Republic
HVV	Office of Publishing and Book Sales (Hauptverwaltung Verlagswesen und Buchhandel)
IM	Unofficial Informant (Inoffizieller Mitarbeiter)
KPD	Communist Party of Germany (Kommunistische Partei Deutschlands)
KPdSU	Communist Party of the Soviet Union (Kommunistische Partei der Sowjet Union)
MfK	Ministry of Culture (Ministerium für Kultur)
SAPMO	Archival Foundation for Party and Mass Organizations of the GDR in the German State Archive (Stiftung Archiv der Parteien und Massenorganisationen der DDR im Bundesarchiv).
SED	Socialist Unity Party (Sozialistische Einheitspartei Deutschland)
Stasi	Ministry for State Security (Staatssicherheitsdienst)
WTR	Scientific Technical Revolution (Wissenschaftliche-technische Revolution)
ZK	Central Committee of the SED (Zentralkomittee)

Chapter One
Introduction

The fall of the Berlin Wall on November 9, 1989 signaled the political and geographical demise of the German Democratic Republic (GDR). This collapse became official with the reunification of the two Germanies on October 3, 1990. Germans on both sides euphorically tore down the wall that had separated them since 1961. Although it has been more than fifteen years since the removal of this physical obstruction, mental barriers between eastern and western Germans, formulated during the Cold War, have proven more difficult to dismantle. The various social, cultural and political discourses that shaped the identities and experiences of East and West Germans persist. They are reinforced by new prejudices and assumptions that often lead to misunderstanding and resentment.

Despite reunification, the persistent mentality of division in Germany demonstrates that 1990 can by no means be termed a "Stunde Null" or zero hour from which Germany started anew. To consign GDR culture to the past would leave intact an interpretation shaped by the Cold War and limited by inadequate access to extensive documentation. Moreover, many of today's Germans experienced and participated in the GDR's challenges, successes, and offenses. Although the everyday reality of political oppression is central to an understanding of life in East Germany, this multifaceted society constantly changed and transformed in response to a variety of international and domestic influences. The continued study of East Germany, therefore, contributes to a more comprehensive depiction of the country and its inhabitants. If Germany is to overcome the deep divisions that contribute to today's political, economic and cultural instability, each side must attempt to understand the "other."

The study of the country's science fiction is one way in which to access the "alien" world of East Germany. Anita Mallinckrodt observes that popular literature holds "many keys to understanding another people" (9). In her study of East German dime novels, she describes the necessity to look beyond "dissident" writing to gain a view of life there from diverse sources. Frederic Jameson has expressed a similar belief regarding East German science fiction, more specifically. He writes, "[A]part from the literary merits of individual texts – [it] has great value as a cultural symptom, as one privileged way of taking the temperature of a social system at a particular historical moment" ("Science Fiction and the GDR" 199). A literature concerned with contemporary events, science fiction is integrally related to its historical context and, therefore, provides a unique view into East German cultural practices. An analysis of this science fiction literally constructs a path, which leads to alternative socialist worlds and times. At the same time, through an examination of the texts and their reception, we begin to see how the contributors to this discourse understood their surroundings and themselves.

GDR science fiction is of special interest, since it developed in relative isolation from the discursive conventions in and about Anglo-American science fiction. It took its cue from Jules Verne and selected German, Polish, Czech, and Soviet science fiction publications. In addition, GDR science fiction contributed a great deal to the satirical tradition started by Polish author Stanislaw Lem in the mid-1960s. Banned under the National Socialists, limited Anglo-American texts first became available in the GDR in the late 1970s and 1980s. A predominance of translated, Anglo-American science fiction excluded any notable parallel development in West Germany.

The popularity of science fiction in East Germany also makes it worthy of greater scholarly attention. The GDR possessed a significant science fiction tradition, more so than that of the BRD due to the fact that it was artificially shielded from competition with the Anglo-American translations.[1] Like detective and adventure novels, all East German science fiction titles consistently sold out (Kruschel, "Zwischen" 155, Klotz and Matzer 106). By 1990, some 151 novels appeared, which was by far the dominant form of science fiction in the GDR. Furthermore, over six science fiction anthologies, twelve

---

1   Some science fiction writers were able to live for one year from the proceeds from one book (Klotz and Matzer 107).

children's books, fifty-four dime novels, fifty-six short story collections, and countless other short stories in magazines and journals appeared as well.[2] Additionally, the East German film studio, *Deutsche Film Aktiengesellschaft* (DEFA), produced six, feature science fiction films.[3] Furthermore, unlike those interested in detective and adventure novels, science fiction readers in the East formed a number of clubs in which to discuss and swap books. These clubs are but one facet of what was to become a self-selected, science fiction "niche" or "ghetto" in western terms.

While the publications of East Germany's literary avant-garde are well documented in the United States, little is known of the popular literature that prospered behind the wall. The availability of GDR popular literature restricted its study in both the United States and in the Federal Republic of Germany (FRG). Writing by more distinguished East German authors often appeared in West German editions and was discussed, not only by academics, but also in prominent newspapers and magazines. In contrast, the occasional detective or science fiction novel that did appear in the West attracted much less critical interest.

This book sets out to identify several historical, methodological, and literary gaps in the study of GDR science fiction. First, it introduces the English-speaking reader to this tradition, and, in doing so, locates it both aesthetically and historically. As some might not be familiar with East Germany, I include details with which the expert is already familiar. To this end, my project analyzes cultural policy

2   The dime novel series "BASAR" from Verlag Neues Leben and "SF-Utopie" from Verlag Das Neue Berlin both regularly appeared in circulation rates of 50,000 copies and "Das Neue Abenteuer" from Verlag Neues Leben appeared in a rate of 100,000 copies per publication. Most novels in the series "Spannend erzählt" from Verlag Neues Leben, for instance, started with 20,000 and were often brought out in subsequent editions (Steinmüller, *Vorgriff* 10, 12 and Neumann, *Bibliographie* 888–930).

3   These include: *Besuch bei Van Gogh* (Dir. Horst Seemann, 1985), *Eolomea* (Dir. Hermann Zschoche, 1972), *Im Staub der Sterne* (Dir. Gottfried Kolldiz, 1976), *Der Schweigende Stern* (Dir. Kurt Maetzig, 1959), *Signale* (Dir. Gottfried Kolldiz, 1970) and *Der Mann mit dem Objektiv* (Dir. Frank Vogel, 1961). In addition, a made-for-television film *Abenteuer mit Blasius* (Dir. Egon Schlegel) also appeared in 1975.

pertaining to science fiction and provides an overview of major thematic developments in the genre in the GDR. In the process, it concentrates on the novel in an effort to provide a broad, yet focused, look into the development of GDR popular literature over the course of the country's forty-year existence. The book's chronological organization is not designed to construct a linear narrative of a national genre. It provides a unique view of major events in GDR history and conveys particular German practices in the writing of science fiction.

Second, my study raises key theoretical issues that affect the broader field of GDR literature. It questions the notion of the "subversive," which has driven studies of East Germany through the Cold War and beyond. In doing so, it interrogates assumptions surrounding categories of "high" and "low" literature as well as center and periphery by contextualizing their application. Drawing upon a variety of original sources, I assume a gradation of participation within the system and demonstrate how a number of science fiction authors and editors were able to influence policy to their own ends. In the process, I present a model of interactive relations between elements of GDR state and society.

Finally, this project defines GDR science fiction as a literature of both affirmation and subversion. It looks at the ways in which authors employed the genre's qualities of estrangement, both in terms of utopian literature and as a literature of the fantastic, to strengthen and criticize GDR socialism. To do so, my study takes an in-depth look at novels by three authors, whose writing resonated with a large number of GDR science fiction enthusiasts. These publications are: Eberhardt Del Antonio's *Heimkehr der Vorfahren* (Return of the Forefathers, 1966), Johanna and Günter Braun's *Unheimliche Erscheinungsformen auf Omega XI* (Uncanny Manifestations on Omega XI, 1974), and Angela and Karlheinz Steinmüller's *Der Traummeister* (The Dream Master, 1990).

Scholarship on East German Popular Literature

While studies in science fiction flourished in both Great Britain and in the United States during the seventies and eighties, primary literature in the German language has garnered sporadic attention.[4] West German literary scholars have shown interest in the critical study of science fiction only recently. This lack of interest can be attributed to a general mistrust of popular literature, an attitude, which can be traced back to the Enlightenment.[5] In the sixties, seventies and eighties, many West German sociologists concentrated on the potential for escapism and conformism among readers of popular genres.[6] Nevertheless, several calls for a critical study of the aesthetics of this literature in both Germanies surfaced in the West.[7] In 1970, Hans

4   Much science fiction discourse of the twentieth century in the West has centered on the Anglo–American tradition. Foreign publications remain isolated to their country of origin. The majority of foreign/non-western science fiction stays untranslated or unavailable, as in the case of many authors from the former East Bloc. Publications in English on East German science fiction include Frederic Jameson "Science Fiction and the German Democratic Republic," Werner Förster "Time Travelling into the Present: Science Fiction Literature in the GDR," Barbara Mabee "Astronauts, Angels, and Time Machines: The Fantastic in Recent German Democratic Republic Literature," J.H. Reid "En route to Utopia. Some Visions of the Future in East German Literature," William Walker "Contemporary GDR Science Fiction: The Example of Johanna and Günter Braun," as well as Darko Suvin's article on Johanna and Günter Braun "Playful Cognizing" and anthology of Eastern European science fiction *Other Worlds, Other Seas*. Förster's article is the only one by an East German to appear in English.

5   See Schulte-Sasse, Die Kritik an der Trivialliteratur seit der Aufklärung.

6   See Michael Pehlke and Norbert Lingfeld's Roboter und Gartenlaube: Ideologie und Unterhaltung in der Science-Fiction-Literatur and Walter Nutz Der Trivialroman.

7   See Jörg Hienger *Unterhaltungsliteratur. Zu ihrer Theorie und Verteidigung,* Richard Albrecht *Das Bedürfnis nach echten Geschichten,* and the useful bibliography by Ludwig Fischer, Dietger Pforte, Kristina Zerges and Hella Dunger, eds. *Zur Archäologie der Popularkultur.* See also Barbara Gentikow "'Spannungs- und Unterhaltungsliteratur' der DDR" and Manfred Nagl "Neu in der DDR." Austrian Franz Rottensteiner made significant contributions to the

Friedrich Foltin lamented a widespread presumption that this type of literature fails to contribute to the broader understanding of the human condition or push aesthetic boundaries (3).

East German science fiction remained doubly marginalized. In the West, "German science fiction" referred to publications from the Federal Republic only. Very few works on the subject acknowledged the GDR's tradition or granted it more than an ancillary role.[8] Many assumed GDR science fiction to be an instrument of the Socialist Unity Party (SED).[9] One notable exception is Anita Mallinckrodt's sociological study of East German dime novels that includes a well-researched history of GDR popular literature with reference to science fiction. In addition, Horst Heidtmann completed a structuralist analysis of East German science fiction in 1982.

A considerable amount of documentation existed on the eastern side of the wall. Academics and literary critics initially saw popular literature as a bourgeois tool of class warfare. Many remained opposed to the creation of a "socialist alternative" to compete with the West.[10] Consequently, they left the theorization of early GDR science fiction to the authors, editors, and party functionaries directly concerned.[11] In the seventies, East German pedagogues conducted an

study of German science fiction in his science fiction journal *Polaris* and his article "Die 'wissenschaftliche Phantastik' der DDR."

8   See Manfred Nagl *Science Fiction in Deutschland* and Hans-Joachim Schulz *Science Fiction.*

9   See Sven-Aage Jorgensen's "Valium des Volks? Die utopische Science-Fiction in der DDR." Gerd Henning equates GDR mass culture with propaganda in "'Mass Cultural Activity' in the GDR. See also Reinhold Krämer's *Die gekaufte "Zukunft."*

10   See Fritz Lange "Schund und Schmutz – ein Teil imperialistische psychologischer Kriegsführung" and Arno Hochmuth and Hinnerk Einhorn "Geschäft mit der Zukunftsangst."

11   See for instance Erich Sielaff "Zur Frage des Unterhaltungromans," Eberhardt del Antonio "Für oder wider utopische Literatur" as well as a policy brief of the HR Jugend- und Kinderbuch "Hinweise für die Diskussion der Themenpläne 1956 und der Perspektivepläne bis 1960 auf der Planungsgemeinschaft Kinder und Jugendbuch Ende November 1954."

historical survey of East German popular literature.[12] The first comprehensive, Marxist–Leninist theory of science fiction in East Germany appeared in 1977.[13] A series of dissertations in the eighties analyzed specific themes, for example, as the portrayal of women and of the alien, as well as elements of utopia and dystopia.[14]

Over the past fifteen years, a new generation of German and American literary scholars has begun to address the significant number of romance, science fiction, detective, adventure, and war novels that appeared in the GDR. Recent approaches to GDR popular literature outline ways in which it, while limited in scope by censorship, nevertheless provided the reader with entertainment, excitement, relaxation, education, and, in some cases, criticism of an authoritarian regime. In the area of GDR science fiction, Thomas Kramer provides an in-depth look at the influences of Karl May and Hans Dominik on the comic book *Mosaik* in *Micky, Marx and Manitu*. Michael Grisko, Detlef Kannapin, Stefan Soldvieri, and Gerhard Wiechmann all have published on GDR science fiction film.[15]

12   See Schröder, Gustav ed. *Potsdamer Forschungen. Untersuchungen zur sozialistischen Unterhaltungsliteratur.*

13   See Adolf Sckerl "Wissenschaftliche-phantastische Literatur. Überlegungen zu einem literarischen Genre und Anmerkungen zu seiner Entwicklung in der DDR."

14   See Mikaela Blume *Untersuchungen zur Rolle der Frau in der Science-Fiction Literatur der DDR seit 1970*, Annette Breitenfeld *Die Begegnungen mit außerirdischen Formen. Untersuchungen zur Science-fiction-Literatur der DDR.* and Karsten Kruschel *Spielwelten zwischen Wunschbild und Warnbild.* See also Werner Förster "Realität und Entwurf. Zu einigen Aspekten des Genres Phantastik in der DDR-Literatur der siebziger Jahre," Thomas Hartung *Die Science-fiction Literatur der DDR von 1980–90* and Sabine Vollprecht *Science-Fiction für Kinder in der DDR.* These dissertations were written in the GDR and published in the years immediately following unification.

15   See also Brigitte Kehrberg *Der Kriminalroman in der DDR 1970–1990*, Dorothea Germer *Von Genossen und Gangstern*, Reinhard Hillich and Wolfgang Mittmann *Die Kriminalliteratur der DDR*, Catrin Gersdorf "The Digedags Go West" and Thomas Beutelschmidt and Henning Wrage on literary adaptation in GDR television. More general reassessments of German popular literature include: Walter Nutz' more recent publication *Trivialliteratur and Populärkultur* and Helmut Schmiedt *Ringo in Weimar. Begegnungen zwischen*

Authors, editors and fans from the former East Germany have also made a substantial contribution to the study of East German science fiction. Udo Klotz, Michael Matzer, Karsten Kruschel, Erik Simon, Olaf Spittel, Angela and Karlheinz Steinmüller, and others published reflective articles on East German science fiction after reunification. In 1995, Angela and Karlheinz Steinmüller examined the social and political context of GDR science fiction through the late 1960s, in a perceptive, inside commentary on writing during this time period. More recently, a detailed account of the East's science fiction fandom appeared. Entitled *Geschichten aus der Parallelwelt* (Stories from a Parallel World, 1998), it was written and edited by former fan club members Wolfgang Both, Hans-Peter Neumann, and Klaus Scheffler. Their account provides a valuable view into the structure and activities of one popular cultural niche.[16]

Science Fiction as Popular Literature

The notion of popular or mass culture has long been equated with forms of "low" societal value. Horkheimer and Adorno reinforced this assumption through their influential definition of this literature's "manipulative capacities" when produced by the culture industry (148). David Bathrick, however, has described a shift in Western thought away from Horkheimer and Adorno's definition. This new approach focuses on the potential for political activism in mass culture through a Brechtian revolutionary aesthetic in a bourgeois socio-economic structure that is full of gaps and fissures, rife with contradiction and the potential for change (Bathrick, "Reading" 246). Indeed, theories from alternative Marxists such as Brecht, Walter Benjamin and Stuart Hall, Richard Hebdige, and Richard Hoggart of

*Hochliteratur und Popularkultur.*See also my article "Auf dem Weg zur Venus. Die Entdeckung ostdeutscher Populärkultur: *Der schweigende Stern.*"

16   Both Neumann and Scheffler recently came out with a bibliography of East German fanzines.

the Birmingham school provided the methodological foundation for many of the recent cultural studies of reader agency in popular culture.[17] Feminist scholars, including Janice Radway, Tania Modleski, and Constance Penley, unearthed emancipatory uses of so-called "low" literature.

Former understandings of high and low literature still shape studies of GDR literature and must be re-examined to correctly describe their function in that context. Marxist–Leninist theory held items mass-produced under capitalism to be a type of commodity fetishism, similar to the Horkheimer–Adornian interpretation of products of the culture industry. However, this definition of mass culture and the definition of mass culture in East Germany differed in the SED's embracing of technology. Horkheimer and Adorno could not find emancipatory power in the mass-produced item as it lost what Benjamin termed the artwork's "aura" (152). Leading East German cultural officials perceived mass literature to be a revolutionary tool for the greater emancipation of the proletariat in the hands of the appropriate producers. Furthermore, mass production increased the availability of culture through greater distribution and lower prices. More importantly, it was not a bourgeois mass literature but a proletarian one that could bring about the "German cultural renewal" called for by cultural official Anton Akermann at the end of World War II. However, orthodox party members felt "genre" literature had no place amongst the new "high" literature of the working class. This view influenced policy on popular literature throughout the GDR's existence.

In the United States, the study of popular literature often equates its production and reception with locations on the center and periphery of society, respectively. Due in part to Cold War tension, East German Studies in the United States has traditionally focused on acts of dissidence. While this is a valuable approach, the resultant assessment of East German literature is incomplete and restricted to a narrow set of

---

17   See for instance "Benjamin's Passagen-Werk: Redeeming Mass Culture for the Revolution" by Susan Buck-Morss, *Bond and Beyond* by Bennett and Woollacott and Fredric Jameson "Reification and Utopia in Mass Culture" among numerous others.

publications. Adele Marie Barker, in her study of Soviet popular culture, acknowledges that analytical distinctions often depend upon an observer's location within a society or without (20). The same is true for American and West German students of East German literature, who focused on the publications at the "margins of acceptability" and canonized those who were critical of the Party. On the outside, this process created a type of elite determined by the category of subversion. In the case of canonical authors, like Christa Wolf and Heiner Müller, for instance, the distinction between margin and center becomes less clear. Despite their controversial stance, they still possessed economic, cultural, and social capital internally as international representatives of a new East German cultural tradition. Indeed, in the early 1990s, the field of East German Literary Studies experienced a crisis, when it was alleged that Wolf and Müller had been informants for the East German secret police.[18]

To approach GDR popular literature solely with the intent of identifying aspects of dissent inadequately describes East German conditions of culture. A focus merely on the subversion of this hegemonic ideology fails to recognize Bathrick's contention that few individuals in the GDR lived completely outside of the system. Rather, East German life was characterized by the negotiation of everyday life both inside and outside the Marxist-Leninist ideology that informed existence within the GDR (*Powers* 1–25). Furthermore, my study acknowledges various *degrees* of subversion in the GDR, and, in addition, sheds new light on the intricacies and complexities of state and societal relations within that country. In the words of Mary

18   The degree of Wolf and Müller's individual involvement with the East German secret police (the *Staatsicherheitsdienst*) differed. Müller was a registered "unofficial informant" (IM) under two separate code names and also admitted to speaking with the Stasi. However, no IM file has been found on Müller. Christa Wolf's IM file primarily contains records of conversations that took place between 1959 and 1962. At the time, she was a committed member of the SED and was moving swiftly up in the party ranks. Three years later, she broke with the party. By 1968, the Stasi had begun to observe her. Neither Wolf's nor Müller involvement with the Stasi compares to the allegations made against Prenzlauer Berg poets Sascha Anderson and Reiner Schedlinski. However, it threw assumptions regarding the role of the GDR public intellectual as dissident into question. See Bathrick *Powers*, 21–22, 221–225.

Fulbrook, it is important to rethink not the "'relations' between, but rather the '*inter*-relations' between, the overlapping and mutually informing elements of state and society" (Fulbrook's emphasis 289). This new method reveals a much more complex and interconnected process of production and reception.

Science Fiction Discourse in the GDR

Recent contributions to East German Studies have focused on language as a means to shed new light on subversive acts in culture and society. Based in part on Michel Foucault, these studies have sought to examine the manner in which "the production of discourse [was] at once distributed, selected, organized and redistributed" in East German society and the role in which such discourses shaped practices of exclusion and inclusion ("Order" 52). Yet, as David Bathrick points out, many semiotic and cultural studies of East German ideological constructs theorize them in terms of black and white (Powers 15–17).

Such studies describe an exclusionary system that operated according to a framework of binary opposites, through which all cultural and social norms were evaluated and encoded. Determining what was "right" and "wrong," "true" and "false", "progressive" or "reactionary," these values excluded or outlawed all those who did not operate within them. Designed to enforce a "singleness of meaning" in cultural understanding and interpretation, censorship then did not simply exist on a governmental level, but throughout all levels and facets of life in the public sphere. It created a total discursive system and determined the aesthetic norms implemented through official cultural policy. Those who chose to speak publicly, regardless of the form, had to demonstrate their *Parteilichkeit (*commitment to the Party). They not only complied with, but also internalized it in order to insure communicable meaning (Bathrick, *Powers* 15–17).

This model is on the whole very useful in understanding the discursive practices in East Germany. Still, the totality of this model is an ahistorical, theoretical construct, which becomes less accurate

23

when applied to a specific individual or societal context. Generational difference, shifts in political and ideological thought, combined with multiple levels of ideological compliance within state institutions, created degrees of totality and variation in meaning over time and space. Numerous discourses existed within this ostensibly total discursive system. Bathrick's own analysis of the complex political and cultural roles of GDR literary intellectuals demonstrates the manner in which these authors sometimes "rewrote the master code from within the code itself" (*Powers* 19). My study of GDR science fiction continues to question the existence and nature of this master code. In addition, it reveals the gaps and fissures that resulted from the overlapping of discourses on popular culture, literature and utopia that comprised official efforts to create and enforce that very master code.

Science fiction, itself, is a form of popular literature that blends the fields of science and technology with literature in an uneasy synthesis. This tension permeated the discourse on science fiction as it incorporated two foundational tenets of the SED's Marxist–Leninist ideology: technological determinism and reeducation through literature. The primary focus of this evolving discourse concentrated on the role of science fiction within socialism and the instrumentalization of the genre's utopian function. An analysis of this discursive focus makes up the core of this investigation. It makes visible the power relations present in the repeated redrawing of barriers around science fiction's location in an "openly interrogative space" (Armitt 81). Party functionaries continually tried to contain science fiction within a Marxist–Leninist discourse built upon ideologically defined scientific or literary forms.

GDR cultural policy was constantly evolving to meet the needs of the current economic and political situation. Carol Anne Costabile-Heming writes, "concepts such as 'socialist realism' and 'critical' changed over time, often in response to the kinds of texts that writers were submitting for publication." Consequently, "[n]egotiation constantly occurred as the borders of censorship were regularly redefined" (57). Certainly, the power to determine the ultimate course of cultural policy lay with the Central Committee of the SED. Many critical authors had their careers and personal freedom unjustly curtailed under the Walter Ulbricht and Erich Honecker regimes. Still,

24

the government's actions were not always systematic. Particularly in the first decade of the GDR, overarching policy remained vague with regard to science fiction. In a sense, the primary agents of science fiction policy were the genre's editors and authors who constantly navigated the boundaries of a programmatic literary policy. Their efforts point to the presence of diverse ideas concerning the nature and purpose of science fiction in East Germany.

For science fiction authors and publishers, the negotiation process was particularly complex, since GDR science fiction occupied a curious combination of discursive locations. It lay on: 1) the margins of literary policy and discourse; 2) the margins of institutional discourse on scientific and technological progress, but at the center of a popular fascination with this same subject; 3) the center of a pedagogical discourse on reeducation; and, in the latter half of the GDR; 4) the center of the discourse by authors and fans in the science fiction niche. These various discourses overlapped, conflicted with, and informed each other. Where the censor did determine the parameters of the discussion, individuals with an interest in improving the quality and diversity of science fiction in the GDR were able to work the codes of the GDR system to bring about small, yet significant changes. Furthermore, there is substantial evidence that the censor failed to take science fiction seriously and often overlooked critique that might have otherwise been targeted had it appeared in a manuscript of a more well-known, dissident writer (Kruschel, "Zwischen" 158–9).

My project analyzes the formulation of policy by the Socialist Unity Party (SED) on popular literature as it related to science fiction. Yet, it also compares and contrasts the arguments of prominent individual voices, which influenced the shape of this plan over time. The science fiction that resulted was not mere party propaganda. Of the over 150 science fiction novels published in East Germany, some aligned more than others with the doctrine of socialist realism. Many stories, however, also contained a subtext. For others, the mere act of imagining a socialist future pushed the boundaries of party policy that had not yet considered or proclaimed the exact nature of that future.

Chapters two, three, four, six and eight cover the role of East German science fiction in society. Chapter two focuses on German science fiction before 1949 and has two primary goals in mind. One is to establish a pattern of both continuity and change prior to the creation of two Germanies. To this end, it provides a brief introduction to the three most influential German science fiction writers up to the end of World War II: Kurd Lasswitz, Hans Dominik and Thea von Harbou. Second, the chapter surveys the science fiction of the Left in the Weimar Republic. Third, although the Soviet presence ensured the dominance of a Stalinist model, German communists also made their own contributions to the discussion on popular literature in the Soviet Occupational Zone (SBZ). Only two original German science fiction novels appeared during this period: Ludwig Turek's *Der goldene Kugel* (The Golden Sphere, 1949) and Fritz Enskat's *Gefangen am Gipfel der Welt. Im Nordmeer verschollen* (Imprisoned at the Top of the World. Missing in the North Sea, 1949). An examination of the utopian aspects of these two books provides insight into German Marxist–Leninist science fiction in a period before the foundation of the GDR.

Chapter three examines the early formation of GDR science fiction during a pivotal period from the founding of East Germany in 1949 up through the construction of the Berlin Wall in 1961. The first half outlines three important debates surrounding science fiction that were to influence its shape in the coming forty years. One concerns the genre's conflicting status as both popular culture and as literature. In the fifties, debate on science fiction took place within the broader dispute concerning socialist popular literature. The chapter scrutinizes the manner in which select authors, editors and party functionaries established a place for science fiction in two separate phases: 1949–1957 and 1957–1961.

Closely associated with the dichotomy of popular culture/literature is a second juxtaposition: the distinction between reality and fantasy. These two terms represent the core of the Socialist Unity Party's power as it reserved the right to determine truth and falsehood. In the fifties, the party required all publications conform to socialist realism, a politically driven construct. This literature was intended to educate the worker of the future where fantasy remained a dangerous fascist form of the past. An analysis of debates concerning the real and the fantastic in early science fiction novels reveals how room was made for their publication from the beginning of the GDR.

The second part of chapter three introduces the term "utopian realism" to describe the narrative and formal tension present in early GDR science fiction. The "utopian" implies a critique of the existing system and a vision of a more perfect future, where the "real" refers not only to what is scientifically possible but also to the "real" communist future of Marxism-Leninism's scientific socialism. A closer look at two science fiction novels of the period, Heinz Vieweg's *Ultrasymet bleibt geheim (*Ultrasymet Remains Secret, 1955) and H.L. Fahlberg *Ein Stern verrät den Täter* (A Star Betrays the Culprit, 1955) further defines the term. The chapter then examines secondary material, including book reviews, applications for publication, editorial reviews, author letters, and official literary proclamations as well as information from personal interviews, to show that this tension existed on the level of both production and reception.

Two events shape the course of chapter four: 1) the imposition of cybernetic theory on science fiction policy in the early sixties and 2) early signs of a "new wave" in science fiction theory in the late sixties. This chapter describes how science fiction policy reflected Walter Ulbricht's renewed emphasis placed on industrialization at the German Writers' Union first conference on literature of the future in 1962. It then surveys a number of novels to show how their authors displaced "space age" adventures on a distant planet to gain greater narrative leeway. These publications soon gave way to a new kind of literature that further exploited estranged settings and times to correct East Germany's path towards communism: the ambiguous utopia. Influenced by German Romanticism and the satirical science fiction of Stanislaw Lem, it began in the late sixties and dominated the seventies and eighties. *Reise zum Stern der Beschwingten (*Trip to the Planet of the Exhilarated, 1968*)* by Gerhard Branstner and three poems by Günther Kunert are early examples of this science fiction that came about primarily through the efforts of editors at the Verlag Das Neue Berlin.

Several literary, social, and economic developments, discussed in chapter six, fundamentally reshaped science fiction in the seventies. Officially incorporated by the Writers' Union in 1973, the genre became an established method with which to anticipate false paths on the way to communism and dream of solutions. As a result of Honecker's new cultural policies, the availability and diversity of science fiction steadily increased. Even internationally known writers such as Günther Kunert, Anna Seghers, Christa Wolf and Franz Fühmann turned to science fiction to experiment with new narrative techniques. Stories by Seghers, Wolf, Johanna and Günter Braun, Klaus Möckel, Gerd Prokop, Heiner Rank, and Bernd Ulbrich all represent examples of ambiguous utopia.

The second half of this chapter focuses on the emergence of a science fiction niche in East Germany. It examines the function of this niche and identifies some of its members, which included prominent science fiction authors as well as devoted fans. Similar to the science fiction "ghetto," this niche provided its members with a greater degree of trust and privacy, and contact with others interested in similar issues, as well as broader access to international science fiction. While not an overtly subversive set of communities, the niche nevertheless became the object of intense political scrutiny, since its participants easily strayed from the SED's narrow ideological parameters. In the early seventies, the Kulturbund and the German Writers' Union attempted to contain science fiction and supervise the activities of the niche.

Chapter eight demonstrates that the center of meaningful discourse on science fiction gradually shifted from the Kulturbund and the German Writers' Union to publications that were associated with the niche discussed in chapter six. In the eighties, science fiction authors Angela and Karlheinz Steinmüller, as well as the critic and editor Hartmut Mechtel, formulated literary theories of science fiction. Both stressed that the fantastic provided a more legitimate way to access the "real" in socialism. One author who purposely distanced himself from the science fiction niche was Franz Fühmann, who published his satire *Saiäns-Fiktschen* in 1981. Much science fiction in the eighties satirized the reality of the GDR and continued to explore notions of individual identity within the community. Science fantasy produced by the Steinmüllers and Michael Szameit, along with dystopias by Reinhard Kriese and Peter Lorenz, betrayed the further influence of international science fiction.

What is Science Fiction?

Western literary criticism traces the roots of science fiction to works by authors as diverse as Plato, Thomas More, Mary Shelley, Edgar Allen Poe, and E.T.A. Hoffmann. The genre is said to contain elements of the fairy tale, myth, utopia, adventure story, and the science experiment.[19] Initially a literature of the modern period, the genre's first authors included Jules Verne, Kurd Lasswitz and H.G. Wells, whose stories were not so much driven by science, but more precisely governed by the search for truth and the real, a basic assumption of the scientific method.

The science fiction story itself takes the form of a scientific experiment. It often combines some form of utopian (or dystopian) narrative with technological innovation in a rationally explained setting and time. The author recreates a world for the most part similar to our own on another planet or in another space and time. Then, she isolates an experimental factor by introducing it in a new or strange form, and, in doing so, places the universality of this factor in our world into question. As many an author, critic, or fan has expressed, science fiction is a literature that poses the question: "What if?"

In East Germany, the term science fiction originally indicated what was considered to be western trivial literature, where *wissenschaftliche-phantastische Literatur* (scientific fantastic literature) came to designate the socialist tradition. This second term was based theoretically on the Soviet tradition of *nautia-fantastica*. In literary and publishing discourse, science fiction and scientific fantastic literature coexisted with other generic labels in East Germany, including "technical literature," "utopian literature," "scientific utopian literature," and others.

In order to gain distance from the ideological term "scientific fantastic literature," I use "science fiction" to refer to the East German tradition. This designation allows for greater analytical leeway, when discussing the specific connotations of various terminologies in con-

---

19   See Scholes and Rabkin 113–162, 165–174; Janice Antczak, Steven Kagle 225, and James 12–27.

text. Due to the widespread reintroduction of the "science fiction" label by East German fans, authors, and editors in the 1980s, this convention is a valid one. Where some eastern fans and authors still use "science fiction" to refer solely to the Anglo–American form, others did and do understand science fiction to have a broader meaning.

Science fiction and Utopia

Science fiction has much in common with its close relative and predecessor the utopian novel. The classic literary utopia is characterized by the discovery of an ideal society, which remains closed off and unknown to the outside world. Often appearing in discursive form, the narrator acts as discoverer, explaining and evaluating the advanced society for the benefit of a contemporary reader. Through this evaluation, Thomas Moylan writes, "utopia negates the contradictions in a social system by forging visions of what is not yet realized either in theory or practice. In generating such figures of hope, utopia contributes to the open space of opposition" (*Demand* 1–2). Philosophical-political projections of a perfect society appeared as early as Plato's *Republic* and included More's *Utopia* and Gilman's *Herland* to name a few. These writings reflected upon the present in a corrective manner and suggested means for improvement in the quality of society.

The formal elements of the fantastic in science fiction enhance the critical function of any utopian narrative. Stucturalist Tzvetan Todorov incorporated science fiction in his landmark study of the fantastic in the category of the scientific wonderful. In this category, he presents the fantastic as an irrational element that is then logically explained. Todorov describes its ability to rupture perceived limits of the real: "The fantastic permits us to cross certain frontiers that are inaccessible so long as we have no recourse to it" (158). As a result, the progression from irrational to real creates a dialectic between the "moment of uncertainty" of the fantastic and the resulting "reality," which destabilizes an implied reader's notion of the real (33). It is this dialectic between the fantastic and the "real" that allows for a more precise analysis of science fiction's inherent potential to trangress existing notions of reality. In a societal context, Todorov extrapolates the potential subversive function of the fantastic as "a means of combat against [...] censorship" (159) whatever form this censor might take.

In a manner similar to Todorov, Brecht scholar and science fiction expert Darko Suvin developed a Marxist definition of science fiction in the early seventies based on estrangement theory. By transporting the reader into another time and place, he believed that science fiction does not predict the future, but rather addresses the present. Suvin described science fiction as "a literary genre whose necessary and sufficient conditions are the presence and interaction of estrangement and cognition, and whose main formal device is an imaginative framework alternative to the author's empirical environment" (*Metamorphosis* 8). He drew upon the concept of estrangement, which was originally developed by the Russian Formalists and adopted by Bertolt Brecht in his *Kleines Organon für das grosse Theater*. Here, Brecht defines the effect of estrangement (*Verfremdungeffekt*) as "one which allows us to recognize its subjects, but at the same time makes it seem unfamiliar" (quoted in Suvin 6). In this respect, Suvin's theory likens theoretical developments in the GDR regarding science fiction. Engaged editors and authors perceived science fiction first as a way to rejuvenate the communist revolution in the late sixties and seventies, and then later as a method in which to unmask the "real."

Suvin also incorporates the theories of Ernst Bloch, another figure important to East German utopian discourse, into his own thinking. Bloch's writings aptly describe the hope and aspects of revolutionary utopia present throughout the East German science fiction tradition. He postulates that the estranged aspect of the science fiction narrative can be attributed to the presence of the *novum*, a term which Bloch defines as a "totalizing cognitive innovation" that deviates from "the author's and implied reader's norm of reality" (quoted in Suvin 64).

According to Suvin's definition of science fiction, the effect of estrangement, set into motion by the presence of a novum, leads to and interacts with what Bloch conceived to be the process of cognition on the part of the reader. In this way, the implied reader "reflect[s] on reality" in a rational manner and sees the present in a different light. Resulting observations are perceived to be more real or true and contain an innately progressive element. According to Suvin, the act of reading science fiction simultaneously distances the reader from her empirical environment, and invites comparisons between an alternative world and the real world (6). For clarification, Suvin insists on a rational scientific process of estrangement for science fiction that he juxtaposes with the less "rational" world of fantasy literature.

Where Suvin's definition was influential in the establishment of science fiction as a literary genre within the academy, it fails to adequately articulate the genre's estranged location within a particular society. The sizable amount of feminist science fiction written over the past thirty years in the United States and Great Britain provides one example. Taking advantage of science fiction's fantastic qualities, authors such as Ursula K. Le Guin, Johanna Russ, Marge Piercy, and Octavia Butler have used the genre to explore the alternative realities of gender and racial difference. They thematize what Lucie Armitt describes as science fiction's general preoccupation with "the precariousness of apparently fixed structures, their transgression and the problem of the small-scale individual who finds herself amid large-scale circumstances beyond her control" (72). According to Armitt, science fiction is an ideal medium with which to subvert hegemonic systems and values, while simultaneously contributing to the articulation of a voice specific to that difference. Figures such as Donna Haraway's cyborg and Sigourney Weaver's Ripley have come to symbolize the feminist struggle for, and possibility of redefining reality from both inside and outside the existing social matrix.

Based in feminist and postmodern theories, Lucie Armitt writes of science fiction's dynamic position on the "frontier" between high and low culture in her book *Theorizing the Fantastic* (72). Blurring the boundaries between both, science fiction thus functions as an ideal site from which to gain a better understanding of these categories in the East German context. GDR science fiction occupied not only frontiers between high and low, but also those gaps between state institutions with inconsistent mandates and policies. In this way, science fiction remained, as David Bathrick has described, simultaneously inside and outside of the system.[20] As discussed in the following chapters, a number of its authors wrote both in affirmation and dissent of the existing regime. For that reason, the study of science fiction complicates the common academic perception of GDR literature as either hegemonic or subversive.

Similarly, Armitt discusses science fiction's predisposal to transgress the generic frontiers, to mix with other forms, and create "mongrel or heteroglot texts" in which "the repressed or excluded meanings of popular culture become most intelligible" (72). The use of text in this manner refers not only to inner-textual tension and rupture, but also extra-textual transgression of societal generic codes and discourses defined by the hegemonic ideology of East Germany. By examining these codes and discourses in East German science fiction more closely, I define the genre and also reveal the everyday transgressions and repressions present in one subsection of GDR society. As will be shown, the fantastic elements of science fiction, the displacement of its setting in another time and space, and the utopianism of that more perfect time and space inherently contained the potential to provide a vision of a socialist future, which was either at odds with, or beyond, that of the SED.

The prevalent literary historical narrative of GDR literature characterizes it as an initial return to an older style of realism of the 19th century that then progressed to a late development of modernism in the seventies and eighties. In her study of the post-fascist familial narrative, Julia Hell challenges this portrayal and asserts that some early East German literature was modern (15–16). I am inclined to agree with Hell and point to the early works of science fiction covered in this book as an example. Science fiction was, in its first stages, a modern literary form. The genre first developed in the late 19th century and came into its own at the beginning of the 20th century as the pace of technological development continued to progress at lightening speed. The same faith in technological progress existed in

---

20   See *Powers* 13. Foucault also observed that, in instances of discursive control, effective formation of competing discourses can occur "within the limits of this control, or outside them, or more often on both sides of the boundary at once." See "Order" 73.

East Germany from the beginning, redirected from its fascist version to a communist one. Furthermore, science fiction allowed East Germans to respond to anxieties concerning the new and different in their own time.

Chapters five, seven, and nine each cover one of three novels. Chapter five looks at Del Antonio's *Heimkehr der Vorfahren (*Return of the Forefathers, 1966) as utopian realism. This particular work provides a comprehensive vision of a communist future, which was not isolated or unreachable, but was believed to be instructive in demonstrating the dialectical path to such a possibility. Through his science fiction, Del Antonio strove to recreate and redefine a German national pride based on technological superiority. Influenced by Soviet science fiction author Ivan Efremov and classic German science fiction author Hans Dominik, Del Antonio's fourth book outlines a vision of future communist society. The novel contains far-reaching extrapolations of both the social and scientific applications of cybernetics on Earth. Del Antonio affirms official cultural policy in this manner. Yet the utopian quality of his Earth setting also transgressed the boundaries of defined ideological reality. What sets this text apart from others was its female protagonist, Vena Rendhoff, and a discourse on the "other" set in an imperfect communist society. Although officially emancipated by Marxism–Leninism, women experienced a different reality from that of men in East Germany of the 1960s. Del Antonio not only problematized the inadequate extension of economic rights under both the "capitalist" and "communist" umbrellas in the area of gender, he also examined the category of difference through the reintegration of a 300-year old crew to a more advanced Earth.

Chapter seven examines Johanna and Günter Brauns' *Unheimliche Erscheinungsformen auf Omega XI* (Uncanny Manifestations on Omega XI, 1974) as ambivalent utopia. This particular novel contains a cautionary, often satirical, social commentary with corrective systemic suggestions modeled in the story itself. The feature helps to retain an encouraging, yet tempered outlook. The title betrays the Brauns' literary background. Influenced by E.T.A. Hoffmann, they incorporated romantic elements of the uncanny, the grotesque, and a critique of the Enlightenment to comment on the development of East

German society. Their second science fiction novel, the book underscores the importance of the genre as *Gedankenspiel* (critical thought game). The Brauns' employed the notion of play and of the game, a theme found throughout much of their writing, as a way of revealing the "real," in order to address pressing problems of society at large. In this manner, their narrative transcended the East German paradigm and warned of false steps in both the East and West from within the moral framework of Marxism–Leninism.[21]

Chapter nine analyzes Angela and Karlheinz Steinmüllers' *Der Traummeister* (The Dreammaster, 1990), treating it as socialist apocalypse. The novel represents a critical rejection of what I term collective, static utopia, with hope placed in a future society based on dynamic utopia(s) made up of individual dreams. The first-person narrative follows the maturation of its teenage protagonist Glauke Arnya, who through her estranged position as a woman, is able to progress from the notion of "we" to "I." She learns to dream on her own by the end of the novel. Completed in 1988, this *Wendetext* combines the genres of science fiction and fantasy to highlight the uncertainty of the "real" in both western and eastern political systems. Although largely allegorical, the ambiguity of the text is maintained throughout. In this manner, the Steinmüllers not only bypassed the censors successfully, but they also underscored the importance of both the rational and the irrational in an ever-present struggle to perceive the "real."

Methodological Challenges

There are a number of methodological challenges present in this study. In my analysis, I present various readings of science fiction in East Germany. For the most part, I focus on material from the public sphere, primarily on articles in various journals and magazines as well

---

21   The concept of voice and the co-mingling of voices of different gender in team writing presents an interesting theoretical conundrum. In my present analysis, I do not try to separate one author's voice from the other, as it would prove almost impossible even for the authors themselves.

as meeting protocols and documentation from numerous applications for publication submitted by the publisher for each book. When analyzing such literature, it is important to recognize the ground rules for the publication of an article in the GDR, namely that it had to correspond to the orthodox interpretation of the Marxist–Leninist worldview by the Socialist Unity Party. However, the degree and manner of ideological interpretation proved highly unpredictable. It varied with each political shift and, to a varied extent, with each individual. Many policies were shaped by personal conviction, as well as institutional affiliation and degree of power within that institution. Consequently, it is useful to look closely at the way in which the GDR media read science fiction and influenced reception.

In addition, I have conducted a number of author and editor interviews, but refrained from holding interviews with readers on a broad scale. My discussions with authors and editors aided greatly in ascertaining how writers perceived their work and how the publisher received it. Ascertaining actual reader reception was more difficult for several reasons. To begin with, the limited number of first-person reader accounts from the 1950s and 1960s proved unreliable. Although readers' accounts appeared in a series of letters to the editor in the journal *Jugend und Technik* in the late 1960s, there is no way to verify the legitimacy of these opinions. In addition, any reader interviews conducted after 1989 are necessarily compromised by the reactions to the events since then. How a reader remembers their reading today might differ greatly from the reactions they had when East Germany still existed. For the time being, such readings are the material for a future study.

I do not give a detailed thematic overview of GDR science fiction, since Horst Heidtmann and Thomas Hartung have done this already. Their approach is useful in that it grants an overall understanding of what was possible in a socialist society under censorship. Conversely, I choose to deal with three science fiction novels in depth. It is important to recognize these science fiction novels as individual texts that each had their own particular commentary and future vision. At the same time, each serves as an example of the major developments within the respective decades.

For this reason, I have chosen to analyze texts by authors, which were either recommended to me as outstanding in my extensive contact with both active and non-active fan club members in Berlin, Leipzig, and Dresden, or were among the favorite science fiction authors documented in reader surveys taken in 1967 and 1989. Of course, this does not mean that other authors and novels were neither well liked nor well written. However, large numbers of readers responded to works by Del Antonio, the Brauns and the Steinmüllers. I am not able to demonstrate how East German fans and others read these texts at the time of the original publication. At the same time, my reading accesses what Raymond Williams believed science fiction could demonstrate, namely that "contemporary structure of feeling" which reverberates among its readers and strikes a common chord.[22]

---

22   See Williams, "Science Fiction" 356. In *Problems* 22–23, Williams defined a "structure of feeling" as that "organizing principle by which a particular view of the world, and from that the coherence of the social group which maintains it, really operates in consciousness."

Chapter Two
German Science Fiction before 1949

Science fiction is itself a comparatively young genre, emerging as a distinct form during the mid-19th century. The creator of *voyages extraordinaires*, Jules Verne's (1828–1905) mixture of the fairy tale with exotic adventure lent itself easily to the addition of new scientific inventions. Literary scholar Roland Innenhofer describes Verne as a modern writer, who incorporated a veritable encyclopedia into his stories and created a new genre for mass consumption (31). Such classics as *Around the World in Eighty Days* (1873) combined the new technology of the hot air balloon with the genre of travel literature. In other publications, including *From the Earth to the Moon* (1865) and *20,000 Leagues Under the Sea* (1869), Verne envisioned the airship, the submarine, the automobile and many other future inventions.

Verne's writing played a key role in the development of German science fiction. He became extremely popular in Germany and appealed particularly to young readers who also favored Karl May (1842–1912), an author of German westerns and adventure novels. Verne's success helped to establish science fiction as a commercially viable genre in Germany. The generic designation "story in the style of Junes Verne" or "the German Jules Verne" appeared on the cover of early German science fiction publications (Innenhofer 13).

Kurd Lasswitz is credited with writing the first German science fiction.[1] Born in Breslau on April 20, 1848, he taught philosophy, math and physics at a preparatory school in Gotha, Germany. A scholar by training, Lasswitz turned to writing what he called "modern fairy tales" when he failed to attain a university professorship. Yet it

---

1   Darko Suvin lists E.T.A. Hoffmann's *The Sandman* as a proto-science fiction story (*Metamorphosis* 132). Science fiction by German women at this point was very rare. See for instance, the Austrian peace activist Bertha von Suttner (*Das Maschinenzeitalter*, 1889 and *Der Menschheit Hochgedanken*, 1911). German feminist Rosa Voigt wrote utopian fiction (*Anno domini 2000*, 1909).

was his interdisciplinary academic training that enabled him to evolve a theory that brought together both science and literature.

Studies of Lasswitz emphasize the manner in which he incorporated fantasy with the concept of reason from Germany's rich Enlightenment heritage. William Fischer explains that Lasswitz, as a Neo-Kantian, "conceive[d] of space and time as subjective modes of perception." (62) The writer believed that both space and time could be articulated in a rational and quantifiable manner through scientific study or in a creative manner through art. For Lasswitz, the combination of science and literature provided the ideal method with which to explore a future on the basis of science but in a manner of which science could not yet conceive. The sciences are dependent upon the past and the present as their sources for comprehending the natural world. Through his modern fairy tales, Lasswitz believed he could enable the writer to see into the science of the future (Fischer 64–68).

Lasswitz is perhaps best known for the socialist utopian epic *Auf zwei Planeten* (Two Planets, 1897) that chronicles the first contact between a Martian civilization and humanity. During a hot air balloon expedition, explorers discover an alien colony at the North Pole. The colony turns out to be a research station manned by peaceful Martians, who hope to exploit Earth's energy resources. The novel takes the form of an encounter between these two cultures, the Martian civilization having long since reached a social and technical level far beyond that of Earth. This apparently utopian civilization shares its knowledge with humanity. However, the encounter reveals aspects of the Martian civilization that conflict with the aliens' universal code of ethics. The collision between the two cultures leads to a critique of the method in which the Martians "enforce" their humanist model upon the inhabitants of Earth. In the context of the day, the novel questioned Germany's colonial and industrial aspirations.[2]

---

2   Kurd Lasswitz' novels were banned by the Nazis (Fischer 80). His works did not appear in East Germany until the late seventies and eighties. In his dissertation, Adolf Sckerl attributed this to the difficulty and relatively small number of Lasswitz' publications (34). The Verlag Das Neue Berlin first published *Bis zum Nullpunkt des Seins*, a collection of his short stories in 1979. See Olaf Spittel "Gutachten zu Kurd Lasswitz *Bis zum Nullpunkt des Seins*."

At the turn of the century and up to the end of the Weimar Republic, Germany had a number of science fiction writers whose stories varied both in quality and political conviction.[3] However, none of them published as many novels nor were as successful as Hans Dominik (1872–1945).[4] Born on November 15, 1872 in Zwickau, he spent the majority of his life in Berlin. Dominik lived for a period of time in the United States as a student in 1895 and then as an electrical engineer, before he found employment as a technical writer for Siemens. Beginning in 1924, he dedicated himself entirely to writing. Like Jules Verne, Dominik relied on his popular novels as his only source of income and published almost one novel a year between 1922 and 1939 with the Scherl Verlag. Many stories appeared first in serial form in the popular science magazine *Das neue Universum* (The New Universe). Several of his best-known novels include *Die Macht der Drei: Ein Roman aus dem Jahre 1955* (The Power of the Three: A Novel from the Year 1955, 1921), *Die Spur des Dschingis-Khan: Ein Roman aus dem 21. Jahrhundert* (The Trail of Genghis Khan: A Novel from the Twenty-first Century, 1923) and *Der Wettflug der Nationen* (The International Airplane Race, 1933).[5] Dominik's name also dominated the narrow range of right wing science fiction published from 1933 to 1945. He was so popular that, by the end of the World War II, his name had become synonymous with German

3   In 1929, Hugo Gernsback, a German immigrant to the United States, coined the term "science fiction" to describe the type of stories to appear in his newly founded magazine *Amazing Stories*. He wrote, "I mean the Jules Verne, H.G. Wells, and Edgar Allan Poe type of story – a charming romance intermingled with scientific fact and prophetic vision" (Clareson 15}. Gernsback had problems finding German authors to publish in his American magazine *Amazing Stories* in 1926 (William Fischer 6). Still, although German science fiction was still in its infancy, Manfred Nagl notes that many more German science fiction novels were translated into English between 1920 and 1933 than the reverse (171). For more information on early German science fiction, see also Roland Innerhofer *Deutsche Science Fiction 1870–1914*.

4   There is, in fact, an ironic connection between Lasswitz and Dominik. A student at the high school where Lasswitz taught, Dominik admired this teacher for his science fiction (William Fischer 180).

5   All English translations of novels by Lasswitz and Dominik come from William Fischer.

science fiction.[6] Numerous post-war editions of Dominik's works brought out by the Gebrüder Weiss Verlag and the Heyne Verlag attest to the author's enduring success in West Germany. Only *Perry Rhodan*, the most successful post-war West German science fiction series, can compete.

Dominik's works belong to a type of German science fiction that initially reflected the country's imperial and colonialist ambitions at the turn of the century. These goals were politically conservative, nationalistic, and often racist. During the Weimar Republic, this kind of science fiction became even more reactionary as economic and political tensions heightened. Its militaristic fantasies and technocratic futures formed an "ersatz" utopia (Manfred Nagl) for those whose irrational, völkisch aspirations of German world dominance remained unfulfilled at the end of World War I. Such science fiction easily integrated the legend of the "stab in the back" that developed among those who refused to accept the conditions of the Treaty of Versailles. Nagl argues that the revisionist, fascistic utopias imagined by authors such as Alfred Reifenberg and Pierre Lhande provided fertile ground for and even foretold of Hitler's *Mein Kampf*.[7]

Nagl includes Dominik as a leading figure within right wing science fiction circles, who contributed greatly to the fantasies of German domination through technological superiority (159). Not all critics, though, are willing to associate Dominik as closely with National Socialism as does Nagl. For instance, Alfons Höger emphasizes the differences in Dominik's nationalism of the Bismarck era and that of National Socialism (387). William Fischer finds that his "racist and chauvinist [...] attitudes and works easily lent themselves to the aims of National Socialism" (179). These ideological overtones notwithstanding, it is important to look at Dominik's writing form and content, since it influenced German science fiction in both East and West for years to come.

6   This was in part due to his dominance of the science fiction market under the National Socialists.

7   See Nagl, *Science Fiction in Deutschland* 155–163. For further information on science fiction in the Weimar Republic, see also Rolf Tzschaschel *Der Zukunftsroman der Weimarer Republik,* and Peter Fisher *Fantasy and Politics: Visions of the Future in the Weimar Republic.*

Fischer juxtaposes Lasswitz and Dominik politically, so that they underscore the theory of the German *Sonderweg*. For Fischer, Lasswitz' science fiction reflects a side of Germany that still considered itself to be a "land of poets and thinkers" (61). Conversely, Dominik's writing reveals a new German national image as the land of scientists and technologists. However, Fischer himself recognizes that this presentation fails to mention the variety of science fiction written by many other less-prolific writers of the era.

Fischer's characterization of the individual style of both writers is accurate. In contrast to Lasswitz' often playful and self-reflective stories, Dominik pioneered the more formulaic "technical novel of the future" (*technischer Zukunftsroman*). Heavily focused on the superiority of German technology, his stories contained tales of nationalist intrigue and industrialist competition for new technical innovations and natural resources. Intended primarily for young men, Dominik hoped to inspire a new sense of national identity through his fiction as well as educate his readers in science and technology, particularly in the areas of electrical engineering and rocket science. The novels themselves combined elements of melodrama, romance, and adventure fiction with Dominik's experience from his days as a popular science journalist. His primary models included Jules Verne, Rudyard Kipling, Karl May, as well as Alexander Dumas (Fischer 179–196 and Höger 387).

The content and form of all sixteen of Dominik's novels are remarkably similar. Each relies on the basic structure of conflict between good and evil. At the center of the story is a heroic German scientist. Inherently a man of action, this morally upright male is fearless and fanatically devoted to his work. He intends to use his superior knowledge of science for the greater good of humanity and is an unwavering German patriot (Höger 390). Moreover, he is aided by a number of lesser, but as equally devoted individuals, including some women. However, these Teutonic women, although often portrayed as having superior scientific knowledge, take on the role of damsel in distress or wait at home for their hero to return (Fischer 205–206).

On the side of evil, the reader finds an array of characters, which supposedly endanger a modernizing yet conservative Germany. A primary example is the (sometimes Jewish) industrialist from the

United States who jeopardizes German or world stability for personal gain or out of envy. In a series of novels published in the late twenties, Dominik developed a German-European confederation that fought off the dangers of capitalism, the Bolsheviks, the "yellow danger" the Morrocans, the Arabs, and the Africans.[8] Interestingly, Dominik's stories contain no female villains. He also employed neither aliens, nor robotic beings, nor the *femme fatale*, unlike the Anglo–American science fiction of the time (Fischer 206).

A final influential German science fiction author was, of course, Thea von Harbou (1888–1954). Unlike most of her contemporaries, von Harbou composed directly for the new medium of silent film. She later developed scripts for "talkies" under the National Socialists and in the Federal Republic of Germany.[9] Von Harbou's screenplays *Metropolis* (1927) and *Frau im Mond* (Woman in the Moon, 1929) provided the basis for Fritz Lang's classic science fiction films of the same name. *Metropolis* has been read by German cinema's most famous film critic, Siegfried Krakauer, as a quintessential example of the period's cultural affirmation of German absolutism (*Caligari* 162–163). Where, Freder, the son of an autocratic industrialist, rebels against his father, he eventually rejoins him at the end of the film. "The mediator between brain and muscle must be the Heart" (Harbou 2). Although Freder, the heart, represents the interests of the working classes shown to him by Maria, the head-hand hierarchy remains intact. More recent scholarship points to the paradoxes of modernity as portrayed in Metropolis' vision of the city, class, religion, and gender. Such analyses demonstrate how the screenplay and the subsequent film, which are rarely studied separately, captured the anxieties of an age of rapid technological advancement in a manner that has influenced film making ever since. Von Harbou's subsequent screen-

8   These titles were *Die Spur des Dchingis-Khan* (The Trail of Genghis Khan, 1923), *Atlantis* (1925), *Der Brand des Cheopspyramide* (The Burning of the Pyramid of Cheops, 1926), and *Das Erbe der Uraniden* (The Legacy of the Uranids, 1928), see Höger 388.

9   Thea von Harbou stayed in Germany after 1933. Propaganda Minister Joseph Goebbels infamously asked Fritz Lang to stay and make films for Hitler. Lang chose to immigrate to the United States (Nagl, *Science Fiction in Deutschland* 167).

play, *Frau im Mond,* glorified recent advances in German rocket technology and was meant as a continuation of the story presented in *Metropolis.* The majority of film critics attacked its rather thin plot, while the reactionary press praised its fantasy of progress among the German *Volk* (Keiner 104–106). This film has not endured in the same manner as its predecessor.

Socialist Science Fiction in the Weimar Republic

During the 19th and early 20th centuries, Russia developed a substantial tradition in leftist utopian literature and science fiction. A similar tradition of socialist science fiction began to appear in the Weimar Republic. As Peter Fisher writes, however, these authors were often socialist outsiders and wrote in "critical relation" to the two organized parties, the SPD and the KPD (157). For instance, the disillusioned Konrad Loele was unable to predict a bright communist future in his antiutopian *Züllinger und seine Zucht* (Züllinger and his Generation, 1920) following the failed revolution of 1918–1919. Several pacifist dystopias warned of a coming war and criticized rampant German militarism (Arthur Zapp *Revanche für Versailles!* [Revenge for Versailles, 1924] and Hanns Gobsch *Wahn-Europa 1934* [Insane Europe 1934, 1931]).

One exception to this trend was *(CHC1-CH)3 As (Levisite) oder Der einzig gerechte Krieg* (Levisite, or The Only Just War, 1926) by Johannes R. Becher. He was very active in the KPD during the Weimar era. Due to the publication of *Levisite* and several other works, Becher was accused of treason. Although German authorities confiscated his literature and jailed two Communist book dealers, Becher himself escaped prison (Fisher 160). After 1933, he went into exile, first to Prague, then Paris and finally, in 1935, to Moscow. Following World War II, Becher became the head of the Kulturbund in the Soviet Zone, as well as East Germany's first Minister of Culture from 1954–56. Interestingly, Becher's novel was not reprinted in the GDR until 1969.[10]

According to Becher, *Levisite* was intended as a call to arms for the proletariat (Fisher 160). It follows the experiences of soldier Peter Friedjung from his return home after World War I to his death during a future class war in Germany. The novel focuses on Friedjung's conversion to Communism, when he rejects the revanchism of his family and friends. It also justifies the need for an immediate, preemptive communist revolution that would wipe out the class system in Germany and, therefore, avoid another world war. Friedjung is ultimately wounded in a street skirmish and tortured by police before he dies.

Becher's novel is typical of the millenarianism on both sides of the political spectrum in the latter half of the Weimar Republic. As Fisher emphasizes, Becher's protagonist represents the martyred comrade who attains transcendence through his act. Friedjung's own identity has been absorbed into the mass that gives it strength, meaning and purpose (Fisher 160–162). This characterization is not unlike similar portrayals in ultranationalist writings of the time.

In 1930, the Malik Verlag published Walter Müller's alternate history *Wenn wir 1918...* (If we in 1918...). In a series of fictitious articles from the SPD newspaper *Vorwärts*, it replayed the events of the Weimar Republic and envisioned a working class united with the radical left. In the story, the "pseudo-Marxist" SPD loses power immediately and a Soviet-style revolution takes place in Germany under Lenin's guidance. As Fisher notes, the novel received mixed

---

10 By contrast, Bernhard Kellermann's novel *Der Tunnel* (1912–13) appeared in 1950. Kellermann was active in the Kulturbund in the Soviet Zone (Heidtmann, *Utopische* 226). Soviet editor of the *Tägliche Rundschau* and later head of the cultural section of the Soviet Military Administration in Germany, Alexander Dymschiz remembered meeting Kellermann after the war: "For this reason, I met Bernhard Kellermann in Werder. He was full of mental energy, completely obsessed with his work and thoughts to blaze the trail to a better future for his people." See Dymschiz's memoir: *Ein unvergeßlicher Frühling* quoted by Jäger 9. Upon Kellermann's death Johannes Becher commemorated his role as a founding member of the Kulturbund at a meeting of that organization in 1951. See "Protokoll der Präsidialratssitzung des Kulturbunds" 169.

reviews in the socialist press. The *Neue Revue* (The New Revue), *Die Literatur*, *Die rote Fahne* (The Red Flag), and *Die Linkskurve* (The Left-hand Curve) all recommended it to its readers with minor reservations. *Vorwärts* accused Müller of avoiding reality in favor of idealized dreaming and rejected the novel as a simplification of the present (Fisher 202). Moreover, a somewhat critical review in the communist newspaper, *Die Internationale*, pointed to the danger of utopian thought to Marxism. This argument echoed Friedrich Engel's prohibition of utopian socialism in favor of scientific socialism (Stites 225–241). Opponents of science fiction repeatedly quoted this proclamation in the GDR.

Encouraged by the Social Democratic book club and publisher, *Der Bücherkreis* (The Book Circle), Werner Illing, wrote *Utopolis* (1930) with the intent of creating a socialist alternative to the right-wing *Zukunftsroman*. It was received very favorably in SPD circles (Fisher 188). The first portion of the novel consists of a socialist utopia, rare to Germany of the inter-war years. The remaining portion relates the war between the city of Utopolis and the capitalist dystopia U-Privat. The capitalists in U-Privat keep the working class from revolting by offering them cheap goods and free cocaine. U-Privat slowly gains the upper hand among the citizens of Utopolis through the use of secret rays, which destroy their class-consciousness. It seems Utopolis is doomed, in much the same way as socialists of the Weimar Republic lost targeted supporters to the right wing parties. The city is ultimately saved by a socialist dictator, but only after it has sunk into chaos. With this finale, Illing expresses his political frustrations with Germany's unstable democracy that continued to be influenced by conservative industrialists and was unable to ward off increased right-wing reactionaries. He supports the establishment of a temporary dictatorship of the proletariat that will be followed by a "true" democracy (Fisher 193–200 and Tzschaschel 98–101). *Utopolis* did not appear in the Soviet Zone or in the GDR.

The relatively small number of socialist science fiction titles in the Weimar Republic is in part due to the contentious status of socialist popular literature. The debate concerning popular literature in the Communist Party of Germany (KPD) involved controversies that also were key to the formulation of the party's literary policy. Soon after the revolution of 1918–1919, the newly founded German communist organization, the *Unabhängige Sozialdemokratische Partei* (Independent Social Democratic Party, USPD), called for the creation of a proletarian culture modeled on the Soviet *Proletkult* movement. In 1920, an article in this organization's newspaper, *Die Internationale*, maintained that ascendancy to cultural power could only occur when the working class had developed its own "cultural confidence" (quoted in Trommler 432). The creation of a proletarian literature became one of the central tenets of KPD cultural policy when it merged with the leftwing of the USPD in 1921. The KPD leadership saw culture as a crucial revolutionary tool in the unstable economic and political conditions of post-World War I Germany. They felt that literature should not contain the values and morals of an elite-upper class, but rather should reflect the experiences and everyday life of the working class. However, two central question remained: 1) Which would come first – communism or a literature of the proletariat? 2) How much continuity should exist between literary forms developed in a bourgeois society and those of the envisioned communist society? (Trommler 431–436).

Many in the KPD considered popular literature to be "Schund" (trash) and "Schmutz" (smut) literature and therefore unusable in a socialist society. In the Weimar Republic, these terms were often used to refer to the substantial number of dime novels and lending library editions that appeared and were read primarily, but not exclusively, by the lower classes. Broadly, "Schund" designated literature believed to be of a bad quality. "Schmutz" on the other hand referred to literature that was deemed to be morally dangerous (Beissel 6–8). The pejorative "Trivialliteratur" also appeared in this context, to indicate all popular literature of which "Schund" and "Schmutz" made up one part. In 1926, the German parliament passed a law designed to protect children and young adults from "Schund" and "Schmutz" literature. In a 1928 ruling on the definition of "Schund," the Upper Inspection Office (*Oberprüfstelle*) determined that a work falls under this category, "if the story plays either on the unsuspecting reader's base instincts or naïvité" (quoted in Beissel 8). As can be expected, the definitions of "Schund" und "Schmutz" remained controversial through 1933.

Many in the communist party in the twenties adapted the terms "Schund" and "Schmutz," as well as "Trivialliteratur," to refer to mass-produced literature under capitalism. They believed such literature to be a tool of the upper classes used to pacify the proletariat. Wieland Herzfelde, the head of the Malik Verlag, an early communist publisher, described the so-called "trash and commercial writers" as authors that are motivated by profit alone. Herzfelde acknowledged that popular literature did constitute the only existing literature of the masses. In his opinion, however, until the real needs of the working class were met, there would still be a demand for bourgeois popular literature or what he called "Schundliteratur" (quoted in Mallinckrodt 16).

There was also active support for the creation of socialist popular literature. In 1922, an anonymous article in *Die Rote Fahne* appealed for lighter fare that would supplement political reading. As political conflict heightened in the late twenties, emphasis on the pedagogical effectiveness of literature increased. At the Eleventh Party Congress of the KPD in 1927, there were calls for a "red cultural front" as well as the production of cheap literature for the masses (Mallinckrodt 17–18). Furthermore, Johannes R. Becher fully supported the production of socialist popular literature. In an article in *Die Linkskurve* from October 1931, he complained that an "avant garde attitude" was underestimating the effectiveness of "socialist mass literature." Despite his support, Becher believed the existing methodology was insufficient and consisted of the following: "Trash and offensive material, colored red – and we have, what we want" ("Unsere Wendung" 417). He stressed that authors needed to work harder to create truly socialist popular literature.

As discussed above, a number of communist-sponsored popular publications did materialize in the Weimar Republic. First was the Malik Verlag's "Red Novel" series, which appeared from 1921 to 1924 and contained thirteen titles by such authors as Upton Sinclair, Anna Meyenburg, and Oskar Maria Graf. Moreover, this publisher printed a series of twelve dime novels between 1920 and 1923 entitled the "Little Revolutionary Library." These booklets contained poems, essays and various documents. In 1928, the newly founded *Bund Proletarisch-Revolutionärer Schriftsteller* (League of Proletarian

Revolutionary Writers) started its own magazine, *Die Linkskurve*. Kurt Kläber, the editor of this magazine, also published the one-mark novel starting in 1930 as an alternative to the offerings of Verlag Ullstein and Scherl. The *Internationaler Arbeiterverlag* (International Workers Publisher, IAV) initiated its series "The International Novel" in 1929. Anita Mallinckrodt notes that the production of socialist popular literature increased rapidly in the years immediately preceding 1933, yet also confronted increasing efforts at censorship on the part of the government (16–20).

Science Fiction in the Soviet Occupational Zone

At the end of the World War II, the Allies divided Germany into four parts: the French, British, American, and Soviet sectors. On August 2, 1945 at the Potsdam Conference, the Allies had agreed to the following guiding principals in an effort to coordinate policy-making in the respective zones: the demilitarization, denazification, democratization and decartelization of Germany. Almost immediately, it became apparent that the Soviet interpretation of these principals in their reeducation and reconstruction efforts differed greatly from those of the other three Allies. Allied administration in the western sectors began to instill the economic, political, and social values of western, free market democracy. In contrast, the *Sowjetische Militäradministration in Deutschland* (Soviet Military Administration in Germany or SMAD) adapted the ideals and methods of Marxism–Leninism to the German context. Where a common German enemy had allowed the Allies to put aside their ideological differences for a time, these modes of thought quickly resurfaced and hindered initial efforts at German reunification. Consequently, in 1949, the French, British, and American zones became the Federal Republic of Germany (FRG) and the Soviet Occupational Zone (SBZ) the German Democratic Republic (GDR).

Cultural historian Manfred Jäger emphasizes the Soviet's desire to establish continuity between the Germany before 1933 and the post-war period. He also points to a long-standing respect in the Soviet Union for the classical heritage of the German Enlightenment, of which Marxism–Leninism considered itself an heir (19). Based on the Communist International's declaration of a Popular Front (*Volksfront*) in the thirties, SMAD initially focused on a policy of "antifascism" and "democracy" in the SBZ. The central element of this effort remained the reeducation of the German people to rid them of fascist tendencies and instruct them in the redemptive qualities of the German Enlightenment. Both the head of the Cultural Office of SMAD, Alexander Dymschiz, and the head of its Information Office, Sergei Tulpanov, intended to emphasize the existence of great authors not only in Germany, but also in various world literatures. In Tulpanov's opinion, as German society transformed into a more democratic form, it would too be able to create its own socialist literature. However, this would take some time ("Zeit des Neubeginns" 9).

The newly reformed KPD lost no time in creating a cultural infrastructure with which to begin the process of denazification and reeducation processes demanded by the Allies. In August 1945, former KPD member Johannes Becher helped to found the *Kultur-bund zur demokratischen Erneuerung Deutschlands* (Cultural Alliance for the Democratic Renewal of Germany) with this in mind:

> We must give decisive, powerful, convincing, and radiant expression to the rich heritage of Humanism, the Classical Period, and the rich heritage of the Workers' Movement in the political and moral stance of our people once more. (*Manifest* 39)

In accordance with SMAD's support of "bourgeois humanist" and "socialist literature," the Kulturbund's press, the Aufbau Verlag, published works by Goethe, Schiller, and Heine. Such writers were deemed to represent the enlightened, rational period of Germany's history in a time before the introduction of the irrationalism of the Romantic era, which was linked increasingly to fascism (Feinstein 19–27).

Most existing German popular literature proved unsuitable to the current political situation and new manuscripts were rare. This circumstance was due in part to the Allied prohibition on September 16,

51

1945, of any national socialist or militaristic material. Much of the German spy, science fiction, and detective novels written prior to 1945 contained one of the following: fascist propaganda, racial theories, references to the conquest of other countries, comments directed against the Soviet Union and its Allies, or scientific and technical references that dealt with war ("Ausschaltung der nazistischen und militaristischen Literatur" 1). An essay by Hans Dominik appeared in the 1946 and 1948 editions of the *Liste der auszusondernen Literatur,* a list of banned books in the Soviet Sector. By 1953, four of Hans Dominik's works, including *Der Wettflug der Nationen* appeared on a revised version of the list.[11]

It was also difficult to find authors who were able to produce the kind of science fiction novel desired by the KPD elite in the tumult of post-war Germany. Walter Ulbricht along with other German returnees, who had spent the war in exile in Moscow's antifascist schools, brought the Stalin-cult to the SBZ. Their planned "Sovietization" of Germany maintained only a pretense of democracy. In the cultural sphere, this meant an orthodox adoption of Stalin's socialist realism. Authors took on the role of "engineers of the soul" (Stalin). Literature existed to underscore party policies, leaving little room for individual initiative or experimentation (Staritz 70–71).

Furthermore, any publication by German-controlled publishing houses required SMAD approval in the form of a license. Both political appropriateness and the availability of paper in a time of extreme shortage determined priority when granting a license. Despite a desire on the part of the German committee of publishers (*Kultureller Beirat*) to increase the availability of inexpensive, socialist literature for the masses, the Soviet control of paper rations kept this capability in the hand of SMAD ("Protokoll der internen Besprechung" 5).

---

11   Gustav Schröder claims that two editions of Dominik's *Wettflug* appeared in the Soviet Zone ("Zur Geschichte" 33). I have found no information to corroborate this claim and find it unlikely. Editions of this Dominik novel did appear in the western sectors with the Gebrüder Weiss Verlag and also are listed in the microfiche of the East German National Library.

Despite a similar licensing procedure in western zones, science fiction there returned to its pre-war boom levels almost immediately. In 1948, the Gebrüder Weiss Verlag reissued Dominik's *Atomgewicht 500* (Atomic Weight 500, 1935). At least twenty new science fiction titles appeared in the French, British, and American sectors between 1946 and 1947 and approximately eighty-four between 1948 and 1951. A number of these authors had been successful previously in Nazi Germany.[12] According to Nagl, the science fiction published in West Germany focused on the frustration with the national defeat of Germany. Readers remained uninterested at first in foreign science fiction, particularly in stories from Allied countries (*Science Fiction in Deutschland* 195–196).

In an effort to compete ideologically with these publications, SMAD brought out a highly selective and limited list of science fiction novels in its own SWA Verlag. Translated Russian novels by the popular and influential Ivan Efremov as well as Sergei Belyayev, Lasar Lagin, and Valentin Ivanov appeared both in this publishing house and in the German Verlag Volk und Welt. During this time, these writers wrote adventure science fiction set in a communist world of the near future. This future demonstrated the technological superiority and peaceful intentions of communism in which the Socialist Personality, or the ideal communist person, starred. These novels provided one model for East German writers of the fifties, who searched for a politically viable style for their prose.[13] Science fiction scholar Horst Heidtmann links the approbation of this genre to the

12   Paul Alfred Müller, Kurt Walter Röcken, Fritz Mardicke, Paul Eugen Sieg, Erich Dolezahl and Axel Berger all continued to publish, many under numerous pseudonyms. See Nagl, *Science Fiction in Deutschland* 195–196. Interestingly, I could not find their names or their pseudonyms in the SBZ list of banned books. In addition, I could find no reference to their publication in the SBZ itself. Their works were also banned later in East Germany.

13   During this time Ivan Efremov's *Ten' minuvshego* (The Shadows of the Past, 1945, Soviet Sector 1946), Sergei Belyayev's *Desiataia planeta* (The Tenth Planet, 1945, Soviet Sector 1947), Lasar Lagin's *Patent AV* (1947) and Valentin Ivanov's *Energia podvlastna nam* (Energy is Our Servant, 1949) appeared (Simon and Spittel 21; Schröder 32). I have anglicized the spelling of these Russian names from the German spelling: Iwan Jefremow, S. Beljajew, Iwanow.

ideological parallels between the Soviet occupational authority and Russia's own science fiction tradition, which can trace its roots back to "non-trivial traditions and tendencies that include a broad spectrum of humanistic and socialist thought" (*Utopische* 47).

Other Soviet science fiction of this era was more dystopian in nature. For example, Sergei Belyayev's *Desiataia planeta* (The Tenth Planet, 1945, Soviet Zone 1947) provides a contemporary look into the more technologically perfect society of the Solar System's tenth planet, Syalme.[14] The Syalmeans possess advanced architectural techniques, travel in air cars, and possess the ability to become invisible. They are, in many ways, identified as a communist society. Nonetheless, this enchanting society was not always so peaceful. They had fought their own world war three hundred years before against an aggressor race of ape-like beings. Transformed by successive "Führers," this race

> retained certain elements of their earlier appearance, but the keen, primitive instincts of the original thieves began to control their entire inner being. They ceased to be harmless; they became subhuman. (112)

These opponents attacked and succeeded in conquering and destroying everything and everyone they touched in an exceedingly violent fashion. Here, Belyayev's narrative takes a violent turn away from its similarities with contemporary Earth history. The Syalmen chose to annihilate their opponent. As one Syalme demonstrates to the visiting Russian professor: "Look, the [Syalmen] people are cleansing the air of these freaks" (115). Such violence on the part of communist societies remained taboo in East German science fiction.

Several American and British titles also appeared in the Soviet Zone. One such author was Jack London, who had many works published in the GDR. Of particular interest is his book *The Iron Heel* (Soviet Sector 1948), which predicted the development of a fascist America in much the same manner that fascism had taken over Germany (Heidtmann, *Utopische* 47). London's story fit into the SBZ's self-legitimation as "anti-fascist" and "anti-imperialist" precisely by

---

14   To the best of my knowledge, this book does not exist in English translation.

drawing a connection between a "fascist" West and the United States.[15]

In an effort to provide a counterweight to this "late bourgeois" literature, SMAD also approved the publication of a number of early science fiction and utopian classics. Such classic Anglo-American literature included Thomas More's *Utopia* and Edward Bellamy's *Looking Backward*, one of the GDR's first publications in 1949. In 1914, feminist and socialist activist Clara Zetkin translated this book as *Ein Rückblick aus dem Jahre 2000* as a protest against World War I. The East German editor included her introduction, believing it was still relevant at the end of World War II. Zetkin wrote:

> Although the depth and clarity of scientific socialism is missing from *Looking Backward*, the book is still rich in suggestions, critical and fruitful thoughts about the society of today and tomorrow. [...] Today *Looking Backward* also has much to say to the working masses. [...] Yes perhaps today more so than ever, where the world war also has torn away the last veil of cognition that the construction of a socialist society must be the work of the fighting proletariat (Zetkin 10–11).

Zetkin's own words provided the necessary justification for the book's publication in the early GDR and also provided post-humous legitimation of the East German socialist alternative.

The First German Science Fiction in the Soviet Sector

By 1948, as the Cold War began to heat up and the reunification of Germany seemed less likely, the newly founded Socialist Unity Party (SED) proclaimed its intention to establish the "foundations of socialism" in the Soviet Sector. At the party's first cultural congress in May 1948, it announced its intention to develop a close relationship between the worker and a "new culture." Similarly, all work in the

15   The Malik Verlag, a publisher for the KPD, also published *The Iron Heel* in 1922 (Mallinckrodt 18).

sciences and arts would be created according to the "needs of the working class" (quoted in Mallickrodt 25.) In that same year, SMAD also turned the publishing houses over to the Germans. The Aufbau Verlag, Dietz Verlag, Verlag Neues Leben, and other existing publishers fell under control of the SED and its supporters ("Regelung der Tätigkeit von Verlagen" 1).

In an article printed in Leipzig's *Börsenblatt* in 1947, Hans Friedrich Lange spoke out in favor of resuscitating the efforts of the Malik Verlag and *Die Linkskurve* to publish socialist popular literature. He suggested establishing a prize-competition to encourage new and old writers in this regard (235). Whether this competition actually took place is uncertain. However, in 1949 the Verlag Neues Leben inaugurated its successful series *Das Neue Abenteuer* (New Adventure) and published eleven issues.[16] One year later the Verlag Vorwärts began the series *Geschichten, die das Leben schrieb* (Stories That Wrote Life*)*, which only existed for a short time. The former started up again in 1952 and would publish adventure, detective, and science fiction stories through 1990 (Neumann, *Bibliographie* 884–885).

Two science fiction novels also appeared in 1949 shortly before the founding of the German Democratic Republic (GDR).[17] One was Ludwig Turek's *Die goldene Kugel* (The Golden Sphere), a full-length novel set in the near future. The other, Fritz Enskat's *Gefangen am Gipfel der Welt. Im Nordmeer verschollen* (Imprisoned at the Top of the World. Lost in the North Sea), consisted of two short stories designed for young adults. Both appeared under license from the Soviet Military Administration.

Turek's novel used science fiction's interrogative space to address the immanent danger of nuclear war and educate the eastern reader about the alleged threat posed by western powers. His story set a precedent in content and form, because it represented the first

16   The Verlag Neues Leben originated as the Verlag für Jugendliteratur in July 1946 (Mallinckrodt 26).

17   According to the Neumann bibliography, Albert Sixtus' *Das Geheimnis des Riesenhügels. Ein Abenteuerbuch für die Jugend* originally appeared in Germany in 1941 and in the Soviet Zone in 1949. To date, I have been unable to find a copy of the 1949 edition.

science fiction novel that conformed to the directives of an evolving SED censorship apparatus. Consequently, the publication of this novel signaled that science fiction was a viable socialist literary form in East Germany. Since censor restrictions made the representation of Germany's present difficult, the majority of novels and films produced in the SBZ at this time were set in the Germany's past. Contrary to this general trend, Turek instead attempted to involve Germans in the creation of East Germany by illustrating his vision of the future that awaited them. Turek's novel is also unique in that it draws upon the writings of Kurd Lasswitz and is similar in its portrayal of the American capitalist to those of Hans Dominik.

Turek himself was active in the *Sozialdemokratische Arbeiterjugend* (Social Democratic Worker Youth) beginning in 1912 and later in the KPD during the Weimar Republic. His 1929 autobiography *Ein Prolet erzählt* (A Proletarian Narrates, 1929) remains a leading example of German communist *Arbeiterliteratur* in which the worker, rather than the literary intellectual, narrates his or her own life experience. Turek also co-wrote the screenplay to Slatan Dudow's film *Unser tägliche Brot* (Our Daily Bread, 1950) for DEFA.

The impending threat of a global nuclear war is the primary focus of *The Golden Sphere*. Within this novel, the status of aggressor nation was displaced from Germany onto West Germany and the United States. This particular rhetorical strategy became part of the foundational narrative used to establish the political legitimacy of the GDR. At the time Turek's novel appeared, however, the creation of two Germanies was not yet a certainty. Although the story is set in New York City, the narrative voice is neither American, nor East nor West German, but rather European. This figure identifies the cause of the war as the greed of the capitalist and military concerns, which control the United States. Such

> human children play with dangerous weapons and munition. In Europe, where one generally is fed up from the last time, those people, who upon first glance viewed the coming new massacre with hope for the improvement of their own position, are now quaking in their boots (10).

The identification of the capitalist as villain is a quality shared by both Dominik's science fiction and the socialist science fiction from the Weimar Republic. In Dominik, the foreign (often Jewish) capitalist threatened German *völkisch* nationalism. In Becher's *Levisite*, both German and foreign capitalist forces enslaved the German worker and intended to reenlist him in yet another destructive world war. As many more readers in the SBZ were familiar with Dominik, Turek's novel attempted to redirect existing National Socialist prejudices regarding the foreign capitalist in favor of communism. Although the novel itself is not overly anti-semitic, it is likely that some readers linked its repeated connections between capitalism and novel's portrayal of the head of Bethlehem Steel in this manner.[18]

Thomas Fox observes East Germany's placement of responsibility for the Holocaust on the West "did not encourage much thinking about [it] in the GDR" (12). These policies had begun to crystallize by 1949. The erasure of German guilt and subsequent transformation into the upstanding, socialist victim was a highly problematic, yet common, strategy in a Soviet Zone that needed to recruit Germans to reconstruct a devastated country. In early East German science fiction, there was a distinct split between East and West Germany, the West as the warlike, fascist past and the East as the peaceful, communist future. Like select Dominik novels, Turek's narrator speaks as a European, yet any trace of a German voice has now disappeared. Rather than identify exclusively with Moscow, Turek's novel substitutes Germany with a Europe that is caught between two world powers – the Soviet Union and the United States.

The title *The Golden Sphere* refers to a space ship from Venus that lands in New York City in order to avert an impending global nuclear war. The reader, along with the novel's main character, journalist Bill Larsen of the *New York Herald Tribune*, discovers the nature and purpose of the space ship. Larsen witnesses the arrival of the Venusians and, increasingly, becomes a convinced representative of the message of peace brought by aliens. He watches their transformation of those responsible for the dangerous world political

---

18   In actuality, Bethlehem Steel was named after Bethlehem, Pennsylvania in the United States and was founded in the 1863 by Asa Packer, Robert Sayre and John Fritz. The company would later become a major supplier of the U.S. Navy during World War II. See "Forging America: The Story of Bethlehem Steel."

situation, certain American capitalists and the country's defense minister, into adults with the minds of children. When the general director of Misanto Chemical, Richard Worlton, votes to "nuke" the golden sphere, he becomes green and infantile. In addition, the aliens broadcast the thoughts of the head of Bethlehem Steel, Robert Sheffield, and the head of Hearst Publishing, Fernand Allain, worldwide. This process reveals their complicity in the plans for a war that is inexorably associated with their greedy and criminal natures.

With the enemy neutralized, the Venusians appoint five Americans to act as their message bearers and orchestrate a peaceful revolution on Earth. Those selected include Bill Larsen and his female, Greek-American co-worker, Sinjossoglough or "Sin." At this point, author Upton Britten is revealed to be a communist writer, who was banned in the United States.[19] As the valued literary intellectual, his becomes the voice of the impending socialist revolution. American General Appels, who has seen the error of his militaristic ways, takes part. And finally, James Westerland enters the story as a miner and union member, imprisoned in Sing Sing for his participation in a failed strike.

In many ways, the aliens represent an idealized rendering of the Soviet Union. Turek's novel transforms the hostile Martians of H.G. Wells' *The War of the Worlds* (1898) into peace-loving Venusians. In a famous radio broadcast of this story by Orson Welles in 1938, American radio listeners panicked at what they believed was a real attack. Turek's visitors use their human emissaries to calm the panic-stricken. The Venusians destroy the aggressive factions and provide the world (particularly the Germans/Europeans) with the ability to carry out a communist revolution successfully. In *The Golden Sphere*, humans, not the Venusians, advocate for a communist revolution. Rather the Venusians represent a highly advanced society that has many values in common with a Marxist–Leninist utopia, including the emancipation of women. It is the redemptive nature of the Venusian technology, which they share with Earth that will bring about a new era.

19   This is a reference to author Upton Sinclair.

Interestingly, *The Golden Sphere* introduces the aliens in redemptive terms with Christian overtones. For instance, the masses that gather in front of the space ship are described at several points as "pilgrims" (42). Fernand Allain, the head of Hearst Publishing, is not only a capitalist, but also a blasphemer. In order to combat the mind-reading device of the Venusians, he turns to the Bible.

> Where is my father's Bible? It has lain unused by me for thirty years. Bring the Bible here! I will read and throw my own thoughts off course. Simply start here (134).

As he reads, he criticizes each passage. Yet, simultaneously, the scene grants not only the feeling of a higher judgment passed on Allain himself, but also Allain's realization of his impending loss of power. Additionally, the Venusians have God-like capabilities to interrupt all communication on Earth at once. They speak to the entire world in one commanding voice. Analogous religious references would later disappear from science fiction in East Germany, due to the official atheist stance of Marxism–Leninism. Here, they provide the promise of collective transcendence similar to that guaranteed by National Socialism, but now to those who are making the transition to the socialist cause.[20]

Unlike Becher's novel from 1931, post-war Germany partakes in a peaceful, international socialist revolution upon the arrival of the Venusians. Their society itself is not described in terms of class warfare, but rather in humanist terms. Their laws are based upon the concepts of honesty, reason, and equality and are, in the Venusian Ereaya's words, "the true laws of Nature, which are all encompassing" (107). If humanity adopts the new technology, the complete visibility of all individual thought will render war impossible. Protests as to the anti-democratic nature of such measures are rendered inconsequential as they come from the mouth of the American Defense Minister (135).

---

20 God-building was not a new phenomenon to Marxism–Leninism, but rather existed among a number of the Russian avant garde movements in the early 20th century. Particularly during and immediately following the Russian revolution, intellectuals such as Mayakovsky and other Futurists imagined the creation of a New Jerusalem in Moscow. (Stites 101–123)

The Golden Sphere stresses that the individual benefits brought by the Venusian technology outweigh any loss of personal freedom.

With the introduction of new technology come several intertextual references to Kurd Lasswitz' stories "Bis zum Nullpunkt des Seins" (To the Zero Point of Existence, 1871) and "Gegen das Weltgesetz" (Against World Law, 1871). A central characteristic of "To the Zero Point of Existence" is the *Ododion* or *Geruchsklavier* (Scented Piano). The harmonious music coming from the scented piano engages its listener, not only with sound, but also with smell. The ever-playful Lasswitz included a similar instrument, the "brain organ" (*Gehirnorgel*) in his second story "Against World Law". The music emanating from the Venusian ship has a similar effect to Lasswitz' musical inventions. Its soothing, hypnotic qualities are emphasized at several points, particularly during a concert inside the ship itself. Much like Lasswitz' stories, the magical and mysterious qualities of music remain unexplained as opposed to the lengthy technical descriptions of Dominik and early GDR science fiction. Likewise, the inclusion of music and literature in *The Golden Sphere*, echo Lasswitz' emphasis of the role of critical literature to the development of humanistic values. The fine arts rarely found a place in early GDR science fiction.

In addition, the premise of Turek's novel resembles that of Lasswitz' *Two Planets*, but provides a more positive outlook. In *Two Planets*, two cultures come together, one alien and one human. However, the humans are unable to handle the advancements that have been shared with them. Conversely, the socialists in Turek's novel adopt the alien ways and incorporate them successfully into the Earth context. East German literary critic Hans Schlösser describes the manner in which Turek adapted Lasswitz.

> Ludwig Turek consciously referred to Lasswitz' "Two Planets" critically, which he relayed to this author in a conversation in October 1972. Lasswitz and Turek have their sense of humor, satire, and liberating laughter in common, despite the seriousness of their statements. Each in his own way and according to his own class standing, each corresponding to his own time period. (1)

Ironically, in this review, Schlösser uses Turek's reputation as a socialist writer to justify the rehabilitation of Lasswitz in the GDR in 1982.

Looking to the novel's limited reception, two positions on Turek's book become visible in an article that appeared in the *Bibliothekar* in 1950. This is one of the first references to science fiction in the GDR. The first librarian commented that *The Golden Sphere* filled a gap in available literature. The second librarian's reading articulated his opinion in ideological terms. Despite the postscript, the latter reviewer believed that the novel provided too passive an example. Instead, it relied on the outside force of an alien race to discover the "capitalist" danger and cause a planetary revolution. To lead to a reading in accordance with GDR goals, this librarian suggested that such literature needed to focus on the solution to problems in the contemporary world by socialist *human* beings ("Wir stellen" 46–47).

Interestingly, the objection did not refer to the fantastic alien presence nor was it concerned with the technical magic of the golden sphere. Rather the critique betrays the preoccupation with class conflict in a highly unstable, divided Germany. In what is labeled the novel's "necessary postscript," Turek explains the intended meaning of the "unreal" elements. He advises the reader to take an active role in the fight for peace and progress in post-war East Germany.

> After reading this book, do not set yourself down on the roof of your house and stare into space waiting for the "golden sphere." [...] The only things that can fall from heaven unexpectedly as a result of such an unproductive dreamless "activity" are atom bombs (171).

Whether the censor required this postscript, as was so often the case in GDR science fiction, is uncertain. Turek touches on the perceived danger of escapism, so often a critique of science fiction. By defining distinctly between what was "real" and what was "fantasy," he attempts to clarify any assumed confusion and avoid any alternate, undesirable reading.

Enskat's *Imprisoned at the Top of the World. Lost in the North Sea*, consists of two short narratives published in one volume. The first relates the story of young Berthold Heinle, an apprentice at the machine factory in Jena. He is about to embark on a brilliant career as an engineer, when he receives a mysterious SOS from his missing brother, Andreas Heinle. A leading engineer at the same firm, Andreas disappeared on a climbing expedition to Mount Everest over a year before. Thanks to the discovery of his brother's secret long-distance communication device, Berthold receives the message and accompanies the ensuing search and rescue attempt to the Himalayas. In the end, due to Berthold's technological ingenuity, he and his brother make it back to Germany safely.

The second story, *Lost in the North Sea*, includes three main protagonists. The first, Paul Gartz, accompanies his German mother in September 1943 on a risky sea voyage from the United States to visit his father in Moscow. On the way, the German navy attacks the ship. Paul ends up floating aimlessly for ten years in the artic ocean on a vessel abandoned during the attack. The second protagonist, Alexander Oskin, attends a school for young airplane mechanics and pilots in the North Siberian Taiga. He is fascinated with the unexplored territory beyond the artic circle and hopes to become a pilot in the Soviet coast guard. After he accomplishes this goal, he works together with a former schoolmate to develop an airplane capable of flying to the North Pole. The third character, American William West, wants to stay in Maine and study Physics. His father, a successful businessman, insists that William follow in his footsteps. In the end, William does go to New York City, but secretly pursues a degree in the natural sciences. He later accepts a position at an observatory in Denver, Colorado. A successful inventor, William creates a communication device, much like a shortwave radio, that can send messages very long distances. He invents a human homing signal that functions all over the world. Inevitably, William detects Paul's boat in the arctic in 1953. Paul is then rescued by Alexander's frosty airplane.

Enskat's stories are significant in that they continue the tradition of the *technischer Zukunftsroman*. He himself published *Marso der Zweite* (Marso the Second) in 1936 with the Fritz Mardicke Verlag.[21]

---

21   Fritz Mardicke was a successful science fiction writer under the National Socialists and also published under the pseudonyms Wolfgang Marken and Ludwig Osten (Nagl, *Science Fiction in Deutschland* 196).

A second edition appeared in Berlin in 1941 under the name *Welt-raumschiff Unimos* (Spaceship Unimos). Although little survives of this novel, his later two stories are similar to Hans Dominik in style. Enskat's protagonists are industrious, stalwart youths with great talent and dedication to science and technology. They are not yet the model socialist personality, whose hard work originates with the brigade and whose rationale is the collective. Instead, like Dominik's main characters, these individuals develop their innate talents on their own initiative and through their own personal will. Unlike Dominik's protagonists, though, they are not nationalists nor are they openly racist.[22] Enskat's socialist project is not as overt Turek's. His stories suggest an author who is in the process of transisting from publication under a National Socialist censor to that of the censor in the SBZ. Enksat's figures are most interested in helping humanity reach a destiny of technological superiority, an element common to both ideologies. The establishment of socialism in the present is a secondary concern.

Both *Imprisoned at the Top of the World* and *Lost in the North Sea* share other similarities that indicate a transition from National Socialist science fiction to its communist counterpart. Many of Dominik's novels included the creation of one or two inventions to further the plot, but relied primarily on political and economic espionage to create tension. Enskat's two stories also employ timely technological innovation to advance the action, yet focus primarily on the personal successes of each individual. Enskat glorifies the communal feeling present amongst those on the Mount Everest expedition. However, such camaraderie is common in life/death situations. Although pu-blished in the SBZ, *Imprisoned at the Top of the World* equally draws on the collective of the German Volk. This is particularly the case due to the association of National Socialist culture with mountain settings. In addition, the hierarchy of the expedition remains intact. The Nepali chirpas are subordinate and in one scene also subhuman in relation to their German counterparts. Finally, Enskat's settings in distant areas of the globe, like the Himalayas and

---

22   For more on Dominik's character types see William Fischer 203–213.

the North Pole, echo the travel adventures of Dominik, Karl May, and Jules Verne.

Officially, socialist realist science fiction was to establish a clear break with the past and outline the new Soviet-style future in the Soviet Zone. However, both examples of German science fiction from this period draw upon the existing science fiction tradition in Germany. They incorporate aspects of two of the most popular and well-known writers, Lasswitz and Dominik. In addition, they continue the mission of early communist science fiction of the Weimar Republic, yet in a very different time and place. Both Turek and Enskat's work represent a renewed interest in science fiction present in the Soviet Zone despite the long shadow of the genre's National Socialist history.

Chapter Three
Reconciling Science Fiction with Socialist Realism (1949–1960)

> In the past, people paid more attention to famous singers, film stars, and sport greats. Then everything changed [...]. And the whole course of mechanization and civilization assumed a different path through the positive participation of people from all walks of life in the life and work of the scholars, engineers, and technicians. (Fahlberg, *Erde ohne Nacht* 266)

> For us, the future is not utopia, but socialism, and we are in the lucky position to be able to learn from our own future, namely the Soviet Union, 'where tomorrow is already history.' (Hauswald, "Propheten" 8).

With the founding of the GDR in 1949, the Central Committee of the SED officially aligned East Germany with the Soviet Union. It hoped to insure a quick revolution and rapid transition to communism, and adapted Stalinist socialism as a model for its cultural policies and organizational structure. Accordingly, the SED established a cultural infrastructure made up of several institutions designed to regulate cultural production and discourse in East Germany. The Academy of Arts (*Akademie der Künste*), which had done much to support democracy in the Weimar Republic, was reestablished in 1950 to serve the cultural policies of the SED. The German Writers' Union (*Deutsche Schriftstellerverband*, DSV) originated on June 4, 1950 as a part of the Kulturbund. In 1952, it became a separate entity and reported directly to the Cultural Section of the SED's Central Committee (Emmerich 44–45). In August 1951, the Office of Literature and Publishing (*Amt für Literatur und Verlagswesen*) began to centrally manage the publishing industry and facilitated the appearance of those texts commensurable with cultural policy. All books published in the GDR had to be approved by this office.

At the same time, the SED began to formulate its national cultural policy. At issue were the same two theoretical questions that had dominated similar discussions in the Weimar Republic. One was the question of cultural heritage. In the wake of World War II, which German literary traditions were appropriate to the newly proclaimed communist state? Second, what was the best way to create a "literature of the proletariat" within communism? What resulted was a politically motivated, public campaign against cosmopolitanism (*Kosmopolitismus*) and formalism (*Formalismus*) that was designed to aid in East Germany's process of nation building.

The so-called Formalism debates originated at the Third Party Congress in July 1950 when the SED announced its first Five-Year Plan. Cultural policy remained subordinate to economic interests. It was to help increase worker productivity and continue reeducation efforts. Concerned solely with the ideological content of cultural production, Walter Ulbricht instructed artists to create cheerful and self-sacrificing protagonists, whose only purpose was the construction of socialism (Jäger 34). Ulbricht maintained,

> We need neither pictures of *moonscapes* nor of foul fish and the like [...]. The gray on gray art of painting [...] stands in stark opposition to the new life in the German Democratic Republic (Schubbe 214, my emphasis).

Essentially, the SED expected GDR artists to mirror its policies and portray the "reality" it envisioned. Ulbricht's pronouncement sheds light on the plan-mentality behind the formulation of socialist realism as the SED's official literary form.

The Formalism debates from 1951 to 1952 took the shape of similar debates held in the Soviet Union and underscored the inexorable link between politics and aesthetics (Staritz 71–72). They proved to be the crux of a number of key issues in emerging cultural policy and contributed to the construction of a national identity and to the legitimization of the existence of the GDR as the self-defined, only true German alternative in the Cold War context. Central to the debate was the manner in which the Socialist Unity Party adopted Soviet socialist realism and adapted it to German context. Up to the end of the Weimar Republic, a variety of socialist styles had existed in Germany, most notably that of Bertolt Brecht. The definition of socialist realism that resulted from the debates on Formalism was intended to silence alternative paths to socialism and communism present in the GDR immediately after the end of World War II, and to consolidate the power of the Socialist Unity Party.

In their interpretation of Soviet socialist realism, SED cultural officials drew heavily on the writings of Hungarian literary critic György Lukács. His concept of realism replaced that of Brecht's estrangement method (*Verfremdungstechnik*), which they now labeled formalist. In *The Destruction of Reason* (1952), Lukács bases his definition of socialist realism theoretically on Hegel and aesthetically on the German Classical period and on 19th-century bourgeois realism. Through the use of mimeticism, literature functions as an educative tool. Its ideal socialist reality sets an example for the reader. Lukács argues that art and literature should represent the "totality of life" in a manner that presents the reader with a totality of meaning. This premise stands in stark contrast to the Brechtian theory of alienation, which had relied on gaps in meaning that force the audience to reflect critically upon reality. Conversely, Lukàcs believed literature should reflect the commonality, the essence, and the legal legitimacy of a socialist reality in an organic and closed form that left no room for questioning (Emmerich, *Kleine Literaturgeschichte* 120). In many ways, Lukács socialist realism resembled the classic utopia in its presentation of socialism as an ideal yet closed system.

At its fifth conference in March 1951, the Central Committee of the SED reiterated its support of Lukács' concept of socialist realism. In applying his aesthetic theory to the post-war context, Lukács bifurcates the interpretation of cultural and political history into the categories of Enlightenment and anti-Enlightenment. He holds the former to be rational and progressive and the latter irrational and destructive. The SED leadership adopted this rationale and equated charges of "formalism" or "kitsch" with "regressive" Romantic influences, which it believed had led to fascism and continued to dominate western culture. It announced that a literary form other than socialist realism contradicts "objective reality" and does not transmit an awareness of that reality. Such art endangered the foundation of a new German national culture and supporting the "cosmopolitanism" and the "war-like policies of American imperialism" (*Dokumente* 431).

The SED's support of socialist realism had powerful literary and political implications. Its implementation as state cultural policy established an institutional link between an objective, totalizing representation of existence and the socioeconomic policies of the Socialist Unity Party (SED). In many cases, socialist realism became a propaganda mechanism with which to convince the populace to aid in the centrally orchestrated reconstruction and reorganization of East Germany. SED officials also accused West Germany of failing to implement effective denazification procedures. The party maintained that it had eradicated fascist influences from East German literature, by eliminating all texts that fell outside of its restrictive boundaries.

Its broad understanding of fascism targeted all formal innovation after 19th-century realism, including the utopian socialist and avant garde movements of the Weimar Republic. Those authors who chose to comply with socialist realism helped to reinforce its legitimacy. Writers who incorporated unwelcome narrative forms came to be known as decadent followers of bourgeois formalism (Emmerich, *Kleine Literaturgeschichte* 118–123). Literary genres which did not comply with the total, typical, organic and closed nature of socialist realism became politically undesirable and threatening. Such literature included forms of the fantastic (e.g. the fairy tale, the parable, the myth and science fiction) as well as other types of prose that contained an open or fragmented structure.

In his book *The Powers of Speech*, David Bathrick emphasizes that

> literary dissidence in the GDR often began *not* as a philosophical or political challenge to the ideological principles of Marxism–Leninism, but as a sometimes unintended fall into 'polysemic' modes of address and that, by virtue of their multiplicity of meaning, were perforce understood and evaluated as negative, that is, as subversive of the official, 'monosemic' mode of discourse. (16)

Similarly, fantastic literary forms were inherently subversive due to the polysemic nature of their fractured narratives. They contained the potential to challenge the unified presentation of SED policy as the historically inevitable, rational, enlightened path to a socialist future based on sound, scientific method and rapid technological advancement.

In the case of science fiction, not only did its use of the fantastic conflict with socialist realism, its incorporation of utopian or dystopian narrative did too. Lyman Tower Sargent defines utopia as a narrative that through its presentation of an ideal, implicitly criticizes the present (3). The presentation of a future other than the vision outlined by the SED challenged the party's authority. Therefore, even if the author subscribed to Marxism–Leninism, the potential for deviation from the party line lay in the act of extrapolation into the future. Indeed the very articulation of a future vision created an open structure with many potential paths leading to that future, instead of the one presented by the SED.

The potential for utopian subversion did not remain an idle threat in the eyes of the SED leadership. At this time, the influence of Ernst Bloch, who had revised Marxist theory to include the utopian as a creative impulse towards the future, cannot be underestimated. In his successive volumes of *Das Prinzip Hoffnung* (The Principle of Hope), published in 1954, 1956, and 1958, Bloch outlines his "Principle of Hope." This idea refers to the revolutionary power of hope for a better tomorrow as a decisive factor in future progress. Also central is his concept of utopia, which Bloch does not limit to the usual classic definition of a political or literary form. Instead his utopian future is determined by tendencies, which are born of and shaped by hope in the present. Bloch finds these tendencies in many places, including in all kinds of art, popular and "high" literature. He believes they can function as a type of "social daydream" and provide an important direction in the future, creative development of society. According to Bloch, the author or artist demonstrates a latent tendency towards the future in her work, which he identifies as the not-yet-conscious. This element can manifest itself in the future, if the time and place are right for its recognition and utilization. Using the methodologies of Marx, Engels and Lenin, Bloch finds his principle of hope in Marxism, believing it to be "the unity of hope and a process of cognition" (*Freiheit* 180). Where the classical utopia presents an ideal yet timeless future without showing the clear path to it, Bloch interprets Marxism as the "concrete anticipation" where utopia became accessible.[1]

Returning to the University of Leipzig in 1948, Bloch remained a controversial figure up through his decision to remain in the West after the building of the Berlin Wall in 1961. Despite the great importance of his utopian conception in artistic and literary circles of the time, his work came under open attack in the GDR. The increasing tensions of the Cold War and adoption of the Soviet model for the reconstruction of the GDR, made the presentation of alternative or multiple futures unwanted. Bloch's ideas resonated with many intellectuals of the day. In 1955, the SED declared him to be an "ideological enemy." In the later 1950s, he increasingly found his freedom curtailed and his work attacked by party hard liners as unorthodox. Participants of the 1957 "Conference on the Question of Blochian Philosophy" in Leipzig labeled Bloch a revisionist (*Ernst Blochs Revision* 7). The conference attacked Bloch from a pragmatic perspective, arguing that his "principle of hope" distracted attention from current everyday problems, by appealing to abstract ideals, wishes and desires.

Horst Heidtmann searches unsuccessfully for a direct connection between Ernst Bloch's principle of hope and the development of GDR science fiction. He provides a convincing connection through one or

---

1   "To have as the focus of philosophical deliberations speculation about the most distant future is unfruitful and distracts from life and the active participation in the formation of our present and the next future." See Schultz 61. In addition, they called him "unscientific," arguing that daydreams and utopian hopes belonged to the irrational, unscientific world of fascism, and not to the rational reality of scientific socialism. Horst Heidtmann remarks that this last point stems from a philosophical contradiction between the Socialist Unity Party's hard-line interpretation of Marx and Bloch's interpretation, in which Bloch believed that the material basis of the future should be created by the hope and wishes of the people in the present. In the eyes of the dominant SED party, any democratic-socialist hopes or other future visions already had been channeled into their pragmatic solutions to the current political situation. Only when the struggle of the everyday was completed could attention be paid to the more abstract goal of a communist future and the freedom of humanity. For a succinct and clear description of Bloch's reception in the GDR, see Heidtmann, *Utopische* 138–144.

two references, which lie "in-between the lines" (*Utopische* 138–144). As will become evident in the pages to come, there seem to be a number of indirect references to Bloch. Indeed, there is a sense of hope in the projections into the future in numerous GDR science fiction works. Its authors often described their works in terms of dreaming towards the future, a phrase that is not unlike Bloch's emphasis on the act of "dreaming ahead." In addition, future hope and creative projection into the future are common qualities of science fiction as a genre. While it is likely that his philosophy had an influence on GDR science fiction, it is certain that its concepts of "hope" and "dreaming" are a continuation of the phenomena described by Bloch.

Recently, science fiction author Karlheinz Steinmüller referred to the quandary utopian literature created for East German cultural officials. According to Steinmüller, socialist-leaning utopias (More and Bellamy) represented a respectable humanistic tradition, which was acknowledged by the Soviet Union. However, as these works criticized their own contemporary societies, further developments in the genre represented the potential for continued resistance and critique ("Ende" 166). In light of Steinmüller's comments, it would seem that the utopian elements inherent to science fiction and socialist realism would remain irreconcilable on a political level as played out in the discourse on the literary form.

Trivialliteratur or Socialist Entertainment Literature?

The discourse surrounding popular literature in the early 1950s paralleled the discussion on formalism and kitsch. Both Bertolt Brecht and Hanns Eisler represented one socialist tradition, along with Ernst Bloch, a number of expressionists, dadaists and others on the Left during the Weimar period. These artists and philosophers favored the fantastic mode and popular art forms as a means of accessing dynamic, generative forces necessary to the continued historical dialectic. As David Bathrick writes, they focused on artistic experimentation as the building block of a new socialist culture, and rejected the Enlightenment and German classicism as the only legitimate sources from which to draw material for the establishment of a progressive social society. This approach brought them into continual conflict with Marxist-Leninist historical materialism (*Powers* 183). In 1948, Bertolt Brecht outlined a model for the development of a socialist popular literature in his *Kleines Organon für das Theater* (Little Organon for the Theater). Herein, he stresses the positive effects it could have in the development of a society based on humanism and in the formation of a "scientifically" educated reader.

However, it was the adoption of Lukács' socialist realism by SED cultural officials that originally determined and shaped official policy on popular literature. Lukács' coupling of "völkisch" with irrationalism and the Third Reich led to efforts to rid popular culture's "folk character" of its "fascist" heritage and instill in it the classical-progressive traditions with "anti-fascist" morals. This position did leave room for the establishment of a socialist popular literature as a legitimate alternative to western forms.

Open support for popular literature continued through 1950. In that year, academic Erich Sielaff called for an end to the value distinction between the literary novel and the entertainment novel (*Unterhaltungsroman*) (464). Its negative influence in Wilheminian Germany and under National Socialism, he argued, does not imply that popular literature must take the form of "trivial" literature (*Trivialliteratur*). Sielaff reasoned that the "entertainment novel" should play as important a role in the GDR precisely due to its previous sociological importance. "'Entertainment' via the novel becomes 'education'" (462). Sielaff's use of the less pejorative "entertainment novel" signals its designation as socialist popular literature.

In the *Bibliothekar*, Ursula Goetz lamented the reader who was attracted solely by suspense in a science fiction novel. She emphasized, in any case, that the science fiction reader is not predisposed to escapism. More precisely, science fiction prepared this person for confronting the day-to-day challenges of life in the GDR. Goetz also stressed science fiction's ability to engender a sense of wonder and excitement in its readers about the future (261). Due to hard-line cultural functionaries in the early fifties, articles in support of science fiction disappeared until 1957.

It is important to note, too, that the Formalism debates did not completely halt the publication of science fiction. It continued to appear, despite uncertainty as to its ideological legitimacy. The first GDR titles included Arthur Bagemühl's novel *Das Weltraumschiff* (The Spaceship, 1952) and Klaus Kunkel *Heißes Metall* (Hot Metal, 1952). The Verlag Neues Leben (New Life Publishers) published science fiction in its dime novel series *Das neue Abenteuer* (New Adventure) as early as 1953. In the same year, short stories began to appear in the magazines *Jugend und Technik* (Youth and Technology), *Junge Welt* (Young World), *Fröhlich sein und singen* (Be Happy and Sing, or *Frösi*) and in *Die Schulpost* (The School Post).[2] Many stories combined adventure narratives with a heavy emphasis on popular science. They were designed to interest children and young adults in science and technology, so that they might choose careers in related fields. Although most of the stories were written for young boys, several science fiction stories appeared a few years later for girls in *Die Zaubertruhe. Almanac für junge Mädchen* (The Magic Chest. An Alamanach for Young Girls, 1955), and *Unsere Welt. Jahrbuch für Mädchen und Jungen* (Our World. A Yearbook for Girls and Boys, 1955).[3] Unfortunately, little documentation remains of this science fiction, besides the stories themselves.[4]

---

2   See Hans-Joachim Hartung, who wrote a number of short stories, including "Letzter Start von EZ-14" and "280 km/h im Blauen Blitz," and authors Siegfried Dietrich, Rudi Paschke, and Bernhard Schuster. All short stories are listed in Neumann *Die grosse illustrierte Bibliographie der DDR Science Fiction.*

3   Stories include Majoll Büttner's "Hille reist ins Jahr 2000," Heinz Mielke's "Gefährliches Ziel," and Gerhard Hardel's "Kindergericht in Blumenthal im Jahre 2455." See Neumann.

4   It is often difficult to find early titles. Many are available in private collections. In addition to these new German publications, several foreign science fiction writers also appeared at this time. See Ivan Efremov *Der Tod in der Wüste* (Rasskazi, GDR 1953), Vladimir Obrutchev *Plutonien* (Plootoiviya, GDR 1953) and *Das Sannikovland* (Zemlya Sannikova, GDR 1953), Karel Čapek *War with the Newts* (GDR 1954) and Stanislaw Lem *The Astronauts* (GDR 1954).

While science fiction appeared in the early fifties, hard-liners called strongly for its demise. Alfred Kurella, one of the earliest staunch proponents of a strict interpretation of socialist realism, argued that the need for entertainment literature disappears in a socialist society. Kurella shared the orthodox socialist viewpoint that all "trivial" literature was in reality a propaganda tool of the ruling classes used to provide an outlet for working class frustration with poor living conditions. In a classless society, he maintained, the workers' needs are fully satisfied. Their desire to escape from the real world disappears.[5] Kurella rejected the foundation of a socialist "entertainment" literature, defining it as a form of bourgeois kitsch.

However, historical events soon forced a change to this strict interpretation. Stalin's death on March 5, 1953 led the Soviets to ease their severe treatment of Germany. In June 1953, they called upon the GDR to loosen its restrictions (Jäger 71). As a result of the Workers' Revolt one week later on June 17, 1953, the SED reassessed its cultural policy in the *Neuer Kurs* (New Course). In 1954, Johannes Becher became the head of the new Ministry of Culture and consolidated the various cultural institutions by placing them under his control. He thus subdued a number of polemical and hitherto influential art and literary scholars (Staritz 137).

The change in leadership impacted science fiction as popular literature by opening up a theoretical space for its existence in Marxist–Leninist ideology in the GDR. Similar to his activities in the Weimar Republic, Becher now pressed for the creation of alternative forms of socialist popular literature. His approach was pragmatic and argued along lines similar to Lukács that entertainment literature should be used in much the same way as it was in the West, as a political tool. Rather than dismiss the need for entertainment, Becher

5   See Schubbe 471. This statement echoes a wide-spread prejudice against popular literature, which betrays a gulf between high and low culture that was to cause further problems in the future of GDR politics. In his 1964 article "Überblick über die französischen Utopien von Cyrano de Bergerac bis zu Etienne Cabet" Werner Krauss predicts the imminent end of the utopia as well, as it had lost "its actual dimension" in a socialist society. See Krauss, *Reise* 16. Krauss also comments that the existing form of GDR science fiction is an "unfavorable" prognosis that does not differentiate itself from the utopia.

acknowledged reader demand for popular literature and reiterated his opinion expressed in 1931:

> Of course, if we do not satisfy this need, the masses will find another outlet and obtain reading material from the other side. We cannot combat this reading material from the other side with criticism, with education, etc., […] we must set our own literature against it – for women, young adults, and children (quoted in Schubbe 223).

Becher's statement reflects a shifting of policy in the upper echelons of the SED. The party elite now considered East Germany to be   in a transitional period from socialism to communism, which was a revision of its previous declaration of a communist GDR in 1949. Ideologically, in a transitional state, it was still possible for the "worker" to desire forms of entertainment that existed prior to 1945.

Becher, ironically, draws upon traditional bourgeois associations between entertainment, femininity and childishness from the nineteenth century. Where the working class was then often feminized in this manner, Becher implies a gendered division in the new classless society of the GDR. Popular literature remained trivial, a form not considered to be rational, adult and masculine as is high culture, but rather irrational, naive and feminine. The new socialist literature continued to exist as a second-class or low cultural form of dubious literary value.[6]

One step in creating an official policy on socialist popular literature was the identification of its negative counterpart embodied in the creation of a campaign to rid the GDR of the influences of so-called *Schund und Schmutz* literature. Similar to KPD policy in the Weimar Republic, the SED now denounced all forms of *Trivial-*

---

6   In the GDR, science fiction was read primarily by males, often of high-school or college age, but also by older technical intellectuals as demonstrated by a survey conducted in 1969 by the magazine *Jugend und Technik* entitled "Zur Feder gegriffen." In my research, which focused on the genre of science fiction, this was one of only two sources that specifically referred to GDR popular literature as something designed for women, young adults, and children. It would be interesting to follow this up and see if there are other similar allusions.

literatur as instruments of bourgeois, anti-communist propaganda. This term became synonymous with *Schund und Schmutz* literature. Even the word "genre" took on the negative connotation of a western categorization no longer needed in socialist realist literary criticism.[7] When genre was used, it specified the various types of *Schund* literature to be eliminated: "Detective, war, and romance novels, westerns, and science fiction [*Zukunftsabenteuerhefte*]" (Seeliger 152).

In the founding stages of the GDR, officials were especially sensitive to the inexpensive paperbacks being produced in the West. Many of these contained a negative portrayal of the Eastern Bloc, particularly as the Cold War intensified.[8] Horst Heidtmann comments that West German government advertisements in dime novels, which condemned the "disgraceful regime" of the East, were not directed at western readers, but at eastern ones. Dime novels were cheaper in West Berlin than in the rest of West Germany, leading one to believe that they were priced for the smaller budget of the East German (*Utopische* 219). The sheer numbers of dime novels that were smuggled into East Germany, as well as the intense debate on this issue, attest to a large reader demand for this literature.[9]

The *Schund und Schmutz* campaign made little distinction between the various genres and focused rather on their alleged collective danger to the reader. This accusation was leveled, particularly, but not only, at those that came from the West. Such allegations often targeted the adverse affects, particularly on children, of a continued exposure to the violence in such novels as well as the false expectations and false class-consciousness reinforced by escapism into unreal, unbelievable adventures ("Kampf gegen die Schund- und Schmutzliteratur" 409–410).

---

7   See "Kampf" 405–411. In addition, this occurred as late as 1973 at a meeting devoted to "science fiction" and its role in the GDR, at which both representatives of the Kulturbund and the German Writers Union participated. An otherwise unidentified Dr. Voigt apologized for the use of the word "genre" correcting himself quickly with the word "literature." See "Stenografische Niederschrift eines Gesprächs" 73.

8   For more information on West German dime novels, see Gaida.

9   Up to the 1960s, train carloads of dime novels were confiscated and many were found in packages sent from West Germany. See Heidtmann, *Utopische* 219.

SED efforts to restrict access to western literature were not entirely successful. Consequently, it attempted to influence reading practices by mediating the relations between the text and the reader. Numerous newspaper articles as well as studies appealed on a moral level to readers, claiming that *Schund und Schmutz* literature led to youth violence and criminality in the West and could have the same effect in the East.[10] To avoid this threat, the campaign urged readers to give up *Trivialliteratur*. For instance, schools organized programs to exchange "undesirable" literature from home with socialist realist texts. The "Committee on the Fight Against the Poisoning of Our Youth Through Smut and Trash." began in 1955. As part of this program, schools and libraries organized book exchange programs. These efforts were not completely effective, as popular literature remained in some private libraries (Heidtmann, *Utopische* 33).

The campaign included forceful confiscation measures and also led to the arrests of several science fiction fans for possession of western science fiction. On March 18, 1959, six fans founded the first GDR science fiction club, the *Science Fiction Interessengemeinschaft* (Science Fiction Community of Interest, *SFIG*) *SATURN* in Karl-Marx-Stadt (now Chemnitz). The members created the club in order to circumvent the limited book supply in the East, gathering what they could to put together a small club library. The club also established contacts with western fan clubs, including K.H. Sheer's *Stellaris Club*, and appeared on the membership list of the International Science Fiction Society (ISFS). These contacts published news about East German fans in their fanzines, and sent book donations for the club library. In May of the same year, the *SFIG SATURN* welcomed two visitors, Ehrenfried Lenz from the Wuppertal *Freundeskreis für Raumfahrt* (Friends of Space Travel) and long-time science fiction fan Hubert Häußler from Reichenbach/Vogtland, and discussed the activities of an East German fan club. Two months later officials

---

10   There were a number of articles published in East Germany on youth criminality, see Gewerkschaft; Feix; and Fritz Lange. There was a similar movement in the West on a smaller scale at the same time. It was directed primarily at translations of American comic books and adventure books. The GDR expanded this definition to include most western popular literature.

confiscated one of the western packages addressed to Werner Thost. In November, he and Stefan Michalz were charged with the dissemination of *Schund und Schmutz* literature. Michalz was sentenced to five months in prison, 2 years probation and fined 100 Marks. Werner Thost was fined 75 Marks. Not too long after, the first GDR science fiction fan, Kurt Hertwig, who appeared on the membership list of the Science Fiction Club of Germany (SFCD) as number 43 "from the Eastern zone" in 1955, was also sentenced to four months in prison for the possession of illegal, Western science fiction. It would be some fifteen years before fan clubs existed again in the GDR (Both, Neumann and Scheffler 7 and 23–24).

With western popular literature firmly established as *Schund und Schmutz* literature, efforts now turned to the creation of a socialist alternative. The publisher, *Handreichungen Jugend- und Kinderbuch* (Helping Hands in Youth and Children's Literature), emphasized adventure literature in its thematic plan for the years 1956 through 1960. In particular, the plan stressed that "the attentiveness to future themes" must move beyond popular science and become more "imaginative" and "artistic" (2). In addition, Karl Wloch called upon all publishers to increase their production of adventure literature in 1956 (1). Wloch was the head of the *Abteilung Literatur und Buchwesen, Sektor Schöne Literatur* (Department of Literature and Publishing, Section on Fine Literature), the first censoring body above the level of the publisher.

In 1956, author Wolfgang Joho included science fiction among the acceptable forms of GDR popular literature.[11] In his article, he emphasizes the importance of reading as a leisure activity. Rather than the solely negative assessment as *Schund und Schmutz* , Joho argues for popular literature's legitimacy within socialism. He emphasizes its pedagogical possibilities, but also the necessity for entertainment and relaxation of the reader. Along these lines, he demonstrates the growing support for a socialist alternative to popular literature by

---

11   Joho was himself an author of the "Frauenroman" *Jeanne Peyrouton* as well as the fantasy *Die Verwandlungen des Doktor Brad* (The Transformations of Doctor Brad, 1938). He would later become the editor-in-chief of *Neue Deutsche Literatur*.

recognizing the demand for entertainment literature as a real need for rejuvenation rather than as a submission to escapism. This new type of popular literature would include:

> exciting content with educational intentions, easy readability combined with an attempt to shape of political ideas in order to replace the light and trashy "literature" that still is in circulation. ("Blick auf Unterhaltungsliteratur" 142).

From his point of view, popular literature should not merely entertain, but also educate and assign meaning to events according to the ideology of GDR-style socialism.

Joho's review of H.L. Fahlberg's GDR science fiction novel, *Ein Stern verrät den Täter* (A Star Betrays the Culprit, 1955), classifies it as an utopian/detective novel. Although it contains many elements of the bourgeois detective novel, he believes Fahlberg has taken a step in the direction of the new style of socialist entertainment literature. Joho praises the novel for its clear presentation of the societal struggle between those, who he believes wished to misuse science for "murderous goals" and those who wished to use it for peaceful means (144).

In 1957, critic Gerd Hauswald presented a definition of East German science fiction in an article in *Sonntag*, the cultural voice of the SED. He comments that the dangers of "intoxication, [...] illusion and suggestion" and losing yourself in literature are indeed great. However, addressing existing GDR science fiction, he suggests that the genre is more effective when set in the near future.

> The novel of the future from 2057, in which progress has progressed more, but the human rarely has become more human, can only provide relaxation for a few hours. But the novel of the future from 1962 that has not yet been written could give us the confidence and trust and, last but not least, the strength for the present! ("Propheten" 8)

Hauswald thus limits any extrapolation to the "known" future, which could be proven possible scientifically as well as ideologically. This inherently utopian vision was, therefore, not escapist, but presented the concrete reality of socialist development in several years time.[12] He stresses the importance of this restricted type of utopia as a revolutionary tool, pointing out the pedagogical potential of science fiction to illustrate the tangible successes of contemporary reconstruction efforts. Hauswald also emphasizes the political importance of its speculative qualities. He is one of the first to believe that science fiction possesses special ability to anticipate possible external dangers to socialism, particularly that of nuclear war.

The difficulty of writing science fiction in accordance with this kind of enforced realism became apparent early on. In the *Bibliothekar* in 1957, literary critic Walter Schierlich addressed the difficulties concerning the imagined qualities of the genre's narrative form. He maintains that a science fiction, which loses its ability to extrapolate relatively freely and is limited to the vision and time span of the current five-year plan, becomes more of a type of "novel of the present" (*Gegenwartsroman*) or societal planning strategy. Schierlich cites the importance of the "Gedankenspiel" or "thought game" to the effectiveness of science fiction's ability to capture reader interest. He uses the thought game to refer to science fiction's playfulness with future possibilities, which entertain and educate. On a theoretical level, Schierlich reconciles the conflict between socialist realism and the open interrogative space of science fiction by stressing the importance of the presentation of several futures to the continued development of socialism. He envisions science fiction as a type of materialist, prognostic text.

Importantly, Schierlich believed that the science fiction novel had suffered in the GDR, since it was impossible to write a story of the future that could be corroborated in the present. He bases his argument on a quote from Stanislaw Lem.

> It is not yet possible today, to sketch a perfectly detailed, finished, valid picture of the future. [...] Specific theses of historical materialism and certain, long-term forecasts regarding the developmental tendencies in technology and the natural sciences do allow, when we want to grasp it in its concrete details, only one possibility to be portrayed." (quoted in Schierlich 925).

---

12 A dystopian setting in East Germany was not possible at this time, as the future of the GDR could only be portrayed in a positive manner.

Lem's growing fame inside and outside socialist science fiction circles enabled Schierlich to suggest a broadened definition of the "real" in socialist realism. Science fiction's place within the GDR discourse on utopia received further support through the popular success of a translation of Stanislaw Lem's first book *The Astronauts* in 1954. The achievements of this Polish writer demonstrated the capabilities of socialist science fiction, particularly its ability to appeal to a diverse audience.

As Lem demonstrated, the future cannot be portrayed in an exact manner. Although an author can use contemporary, scientific knowledge and the doctrine of Marxism–Leninism as a guide, room still remains for uncertainty. To remedy this problem, Schierlich argues for a new type of socialist science fiction that would serve as a prognostic form of literature. It would focus on the future possibilities of socialism in the GDR as understood and directed by the Socialist Unity Party. Yet at the same time it would retain the ability to play with the future in order to create an effective and engaging presentation.

Schierlich recognized the importance of the fantastic to science fiction's effectiveness. In so doing, he attempted to harness this power for an ideological purpose. Schierlich allowed room for several future visions as long as they corresponded to socialist realism. However, since socialist realism demanded the submission of the narrative to SED policy, the creation of science fiction in the fifties continued to remain a challenge.

Utopian Realism

Despite the paradoxes inherent to writing science fiction in the GDR, it did exist. Through the sixties, all GDR science fiction was implicitly utopian due to its compliance with socialist realism. Dystopian elements were possible only if they reinforced the socialist utopian project. Therefore, the few novels that did appear in the fifties emerged as a formal compromise between utopian literature and socialist realism or "utopian realism." Science fiction scholars generally agree that science fiction distinguishes itself from fantasy due to the manner in which the genre explains the irrational element scientifically, thus rendering the irrational rational (Suvin, *Metamorphosis* 7 and 13 and Parrinder 10). It is this generic quality that enabled the reconciliation between science fiction and socialist realism in East Germany.

Marxist–Leninist philosophy in the GDR held that scientific and technological advancement went hand in hand with the establishment of a communist society. The two worked in a dialectical and historical symbiosis based on the unification of science and production (Lindenberg 38). This link provided a theoretical space within socialist–realist discourse for the fantastic, as long as it was explained in terms of ideological progress and science and technology. In the early fifties, the required setting in the near future also limited the scope of potential fictional innovation to the scientific knowledge of the time.

Arthur Bagemühl's children's book *Das Weltraumschiff* (The Spaceship) was one of two science fiction novels to be published in 1952. In many ways, it combines the exotic adventure of Jules Verne, Hans Dominik, or Karl May with the skills of a young boy detective.[13] However, this story incorporates a socialist realist narrative. Its protagonist, Heinz Habermann, is a Young Pioneer (the East German version of a Boy or Girl Scout), who helps to expose an American plot to steal or destroy an atomic spaceship destined for Saturn. During his adventure, the boy experiences the cooperation of nomads in Iran, and learns that supporters of the English Labor party can be trusted. A combination of exotic lands, Cold War espionage and implicit international solidarity with non-industrialized peoples was common to children's literature of the time. The story is also not unusual in that its female protagonist is "emancipated" in name only. It introduces the Iranian girl, Fatima, as the proletarian "sister" and not as the "slave" (98). Yet she still performs all of the duties of a slave girl.

The Spaceship establishes a clear distinction between "productive" and "non-productive" fantasy to explain its use of technological

13   See, for instance, Dominik's first novel *Die Macht der Drei* (1922) and *Die Spur des Schingis–Khan* (1923).

innovation. The former foretells the future on the basis of concrete scientific probability. Heinz' father explains to his son that "peaceful" (i.e. socialist) space travel is probable due to contemporary advances in atomic power and rocket technology.[14] Correspondingly, "non-productive" fantasy, such as travel beyond light speed, is an "impossibility" that "people include in ghost stories to dumb down their reader and distract them" from solving "life-threatening problems" (10). The novel also makes use of time travel, but then reveals the innovation to be a dream and, hence, unreal.

In the mid-fifties, a number of novels appeared containing elements common to what Horst Heidtmann terms "utopian production and construction novels" (*Utopische* 51). He refers to a broader category of fiction commonly known as *Produktionromane* and *Aufbauromane* that dealt specifically with East Germany's reconstruction efforts. The term "utopia" separates this type of novel from the broader category due to its futuristic elements. The very first publications combined the spy or detective novel with science fiction.

As I have already demonstrated in my analysis of Enskat's *Imprisoned at the Top of the World. Lost in the North Sea* from 1949, Hans Dominik served as a primary model for early GDR science fiction. Erik Simon and Olaf Spittel, both experts on the genre, consider Dominik's influence to be pivotal during the 1950s. They attest that many of the first East German science fiction authors read and enjoyed Dominik as teenagers. As these authors turned to write themselves, there was a clear desire to create something of the quality of Dominik but from a socialist point of view (Simon and Spittel 20). A further example is Hannes Hegen, the creator of the most successful GDR comic series, *Mosaik*. In his recent publication *Micky, Marx und Manitu*, Thomas Krämer examines Dominik's impact on the series of science fiction adventures in this magazine.[15]

To provide a more thorough understanding of utopian realism, I want to look closely at two other novels of the time. One is Heinz Vieweg's *Ultrasymet bleibt geheim* (Ultrasymet Remains Secret,

14   The Soviets launched Sputnik five years later.
15   This series is known as the "Neoserie" and makes up issues 25–28 of *Mosaik*.

1955).[16] In the book, a scientist from a united Germany discovers a new element in Algeria, which he names *ultrasymet*. It is stronger than steel and of great importance to a socialist country short on natural resources and struggling to survive sustained interference by foreign capitalist powers. Out of international solidarity, the two countries work together to produce the new material despite several attempts by the North European Steel Trust to sabotage their new competitor. In the end, the socialist forces are able to discover a new application of *ultrasymet* and produce an ultrasonic ray, which peacefully neutralizes the opponents' weapons.[17]

This brings us to the existence of the new material *ultrasymet*. Ultrasymet represents a fantastic element in the story. Because it does not exist, it has not yet been incorporated into the socialist realist "structure of meaning" (Stuart Hall). It lies outside of this system and therefore is potentially subversive. In the GDR, the extensive production apparatus detected and either censored or integrated these elements into this "code" system.

Stuart Hall describes the "*determinate* moments" of "encoding" and "decoding" in his analysis of production and reception in a free market economy ("Encoding/decoding" 129). The process of encoding entails transforming the various "meaning structures" present in production into a "'meaningful' discourse" determined by the "rules of language" in that society (130). Inevitably, Hall states, the rules or codes(s) of the "dominant cultural order" becomes the standard discourse as it communicates most effectively with the broadest array of consumers. It is the dominant code or "preferred meaning" that "makes sense" to the reader who occupies the "dominant hegemonic position" in society (136). In East Germany, socialist realism was not a societal code that seemed "natural" (Hall) to many of its citizens, but

---

16   Others include Klaus Kunkel *Heißes Metall* (1952), Vieweg's *Feuer im Labor I* (Fire in Laboratory I, 1956) and Del Antonio's *Gigantum* (1957) and *Projekt Sahara* (1962). Vieweg wrote science fiction and other fiction for children and young adults. See chapter four for more information on Del Antonio.

17   This early book was extremely successful. It reached a circulation of 160,000 copies in Verlag Neues Leben by 1967. See Lewerenz and Orthmann (Head editor and editor at Verlag Neues Leben) 3. This was part of a longer discussion in this magazine from 1966 through January of 1968.

was enforced by the SED. The author "encoded" his science fiction to a greater or lesser degree through the process of "self-censorship."[18]

The manner in which the novel portrays *ultrasymet* greatly reduces the fantastic potential of what Darko Suvin terms the "novum" (*Metamorphoses* 6). First of all, where possible, the novel presents its technological innovations with an extensive scientific explanation. For instance, *ultrasymet* is not delivered by aliens, but exists in the ground much like many other natural resources. The novel also describes its mining and potential uses based on known technology and scientific theory.

When a technological explanation is not possible, the fictional innovation is encoded ideologically. For instance, the presence of an ultra-sound ray gun in the novel is politically problematic, in that it is not an instrument of peace. Although new developments in war technology were not uncommon, particularly in the context of World War II and the Cold War, the ray gun was associated with western science fiction. It took center stage in "space operas" such as Buck Rogers, Perry Rhodan and Flash Gordon, series highly criticized in East Germany. Yet in this story, the Germans do not use it for destructive purposes like the West, but rather for "peaceful" means to destroy threats to a morally superior communist movement (Lewerenz and Orthmann 3). In this manner, the ray gun likens the Soviet development of the bomb in the early fifties. Through this metaphor the novel provides one explanation for Soviet advancement in weapons technology for readers who knew of these developments.

In accordance with socialist realism, the novel also clearly defines the forces of ideological good and evil. While *Ultrasymet* is in many ways a socialist version of Hans Dominik in its portrayal of technological progress set in the near future, its protagonists are quite different.[19] Rather than Dominik's Darwinian individualists in the service of the *Volk*, Vieweg's socialists are peaceful, well-meaning people who function as a team. They are not out for personal gain, like the capitalists in *Ultrasymet*, but rather act in the name of techno-

---

18   Here I use the masculine pronoun, as GDR science fiction authors were, at this point, exclusively male.

19   See Dominik's *Wettflug der Nationen* (1933) and *Himmelskraft* (1937).

logical progress and socialism internationally. The western capitalists on the other hand are devious, competitive individualists willing to use any methods necessary to gain control of *ultrasymet* and are bent on using it for criminal and destructive purposes. They are imperialists as well and exploit less developed countries for their own gain. Throughout the novel there are casualties on both sides: the self-sacrifice of socialists and what is described as the self-destruction of the capitalists. However, like Dominik, fate plays a central role. Just as his superscientists were destined to succeed, so are Vieweg's intellectual socialist personalities.

Destiny also plays a role in the united socialist Germany presented in the narrative and common to science fiction of this period. This fantasy of national reunification represents a revision of the revanchist *Großdeutschland* versus *Kleindeutschland* question prior to 1945. The fictitious Germany also takes part in the international movement towards communism, and thus supplants ideas of nationalism with pride in Germany's participation in the communist international movement. In this way, Vieweg's novel subverts remnants of National Socialist ideology and replaces them with a socialist reinterpretation.

Ein Stern verrät den Täter (A Star Betrays the Culprit, 1955) presents a more interesting example of "utopische Produktion und Aufbauromane." Its author, H.L. Fahlberg (pseudonym of the mathematician Hans Werner Fricke), relied heavily on fantastic technological innovations and Cold War conflict to create plot tension.[20] This science fiction/detective novel tells of a professor who has created a device that recaptures light rays which the Earth emitted into space hundreds of years ago. As a result, he "sees" a fallen South American civilization and travels to its location in hopes of unearthing the gold hidden there. In the process, the professor disappears. Having traveled to South America in search of his lost father, the professor's son invents a mind-reading device and subsequently accuses his father's assistant of murder. The assistant turns out to be a secret agent for a U.S. trust, who had orders to steal the professor's light ray machine or destroy it along with him. The agent dies due to his own error, and the professor is found, saved at the last minute. Through his adventure,

---

20   Fricke left for West Germany in 1961. See Simon and Spittel 126.

the professor loses his interest in the riches of the lost civilization, exclaiming: "Let's leave the gold! [...] We have science, we want to serve it."[21] Although certainly encoded to be socialist, here science is more important than wealth.

Fahlberg's use of the fantastic is essential to his Vernian plot. The adventure itself could not begin without the professor's ability to see the past through recaptured light rays. Nor would the story have come to its conclusion without the son's mind-reading device. The novel itself attempts to explain each of these innovations scientifically. As seen in the analysis of *Ultrasymet*, the socialist advancement in science and technology did not necessarily lie in the act of discovery but rather in the manner in which such a discovery was applied. The same is true in Fahlberg's novel, but in a way that brings fiction and non-fiction together.

Since Galileo, scientists have suspected that, when an astronomer looks into her telescope, she looks into the past. For instance, the age of a star from Earth can be calculated according to the time that it takes for light from that star to reach Earth.[22] In much the same way, the professor's adaptation of such technology allows him to see the South American civilization in the not too distant Earth past. Thus, in its form, the irrational element present in the novel is rendered rational through a scientific explanation. Through such instruction the East German reader often learned of recent discoveries and possibilities in science and technology. These innovations could be new to young readers or were not always available to the general public due to censorship laws.

The presence of Fahlberg's postscript "Utopie und Möglichkeit" (Utopia and Possibility) to his story signals that the narrative did not fully comply with cultural policy. Similar to the postscript in Turek's *The Golden Sphere*, Fahlberg attempts to restrict the reader's decoding of the text to the mandatory cultural code. His explanations exist to

---

21   See Fahlberg 245. Also of note, Franz Fühmann used this same light ray technology in his story "Das Duell" in his 1981 book *Saiäns Fiktschen* to critique the GDR version of history and also parody science fiction.

22   I would like to thank Narendra Jaggi, Professor of Physics at Illinois Wesleyan for his consultation on this point.

preclude a reading commensurate with an "oppositional code" or a "negotiated code," which contains a "mixture of adaptive and oppositional elements" (Hall 136–137). For instance, despite efforts to explain the son's mind-reading device scientifically and to justify its use ideologically, Fahlberg addresses this point in his postscript. While he notes the actual existence of the encephalograph, he writes: "One can neither read thoughts with this device nor with the American so-called lie detector" (252). Furthermore, Fahlberg explains that, while Einstein's Theory of Relativity does hold the universe to be limited, any light rays that bounce back to Earth would be too weak to capture and view (251). This point of the novel is therefore "utopian" and even disproved by recent research, at which point Fahlberg cites an article from 1952 by the East German physicist Viktor Stern (251). The light ray device, therefore, remains irreconcilable with socialist realist code. Still, Fahlberg's clarification cleared the way for the novel's publication.

In the 1950s, publishers and authors often resolved conflict between science fiction narrative and the socialist realist path with a postscript. Those fantastic elements that could not be worked out through the review process or editorial collaboration were ostensibly neutralized through this technique. Due to the great demand for popular literature at the time, competition with West Germany, and the low supply and often low entertainment value of socialist forms, publishers overlooked some fantastic elements not only because of the few manuscripts available, but also for the sake of retaining reader interest. Ekkehard Redlin, an editor at the Verlag Das Neue Berlin from the fifties through seventies, stated that extremely few science fiction novels were rejected through the 1960s. Rather they were reworked and rewritten in collaboration with the editor, who knew what would "pass" the censors.[23] Certainly, many elements remained taboo at this point (e.g. suicide, bureaucracy, the censor, and extra-

---

23 To the best of my knowledge only one science fiction book was prohibited during this period. Redlin remembers one, which was rejected due to a premise of "free love" that it extolled to West Germans as an advantage to living in the East. "We rejected that. That was not possible." From an unpublished interview with Ekkehard Redlin, quoted in Steinmüllers, *Vorgriff* 160.

terrestrials). Yet, Eberhardt Del Antonio actually rewrote *Projekt Sahara* (1962) to shorten the length of "overly propagandistic passages" (Steinmüllers, *Vorgriff* 160).

Where the technological fantastic generally defined science fiction in the fifties, a social innovation appeared in two novels in 1957. Both Fahlberg's *Erde ohne Nacht* (Earth Without Night, 1956) and Del Antonio's *Gigantum* contain early incarnations of the communist female superscientist. Where Fahlberg's *A Star Betrays the Culprit* was openly misogynistic, *Earth Without Night* and *Gigantum* deal with issues of male anxiety surrounding the women of equal scientific training and intelligence in fictional research labs. Although it would take another decade before a few women attained this level of training in the GDR, more and more women were entering non-traditional professions in the GDR in order to cover a shortage of male employees (Frink 23). Both novels portray their female protagonists on equal footing with their male colleagues. More telling is the male reaction to their presence in the workplace, which ranges from outright sexism to the father figure or the colleague husband. They are not yet the communist superwomen of Carlos Rasch and Alexander Kröger's early novels in the sixties, who functioned as carbon copies of their male counterparts.

Publishing Science Fiction

Despite the official inclusion of popular literature in cultural policy after 1954, controls on publication greatly restricted the amount of new novels. In the early 1950s, the SED reorganized the GDR's publishing industry. In order to halt competition, it placed the majority of publishers in state hands. The GDR also continued to suffer from a severe paper shortage. Through regulation, the SED greatly limited the number of books on the market, forcing editors to be much more selective and conservative in their publication schedules. In the case of science fiction, the limited paper supply reduced the average first editions to 20,000 copies in the 1950s and 1960s. One to two East German science fiction novels appeared each year.[24]

The restriction on publication had several implications. First, the continual under supply of books altered the law of supply and demand, which plays such a central role in the sale of science fiction in a free market system. Throughout the GDR's existence, the science fiction books sold out immediately, sometimes even before the books were put on the shelves. Friends of the store's proprietor regularly reserved them ahead of time. While some novels appeared again in subsequent editions, others became prized collectors items. (Kruschel, "Zwischen" 155).

In some ways, this success worked against science fiction. Official efforts to create a socialist popular literature initially concentrated on detective, adventure and children's stories, demonstrated by the cash prizes and other awards handed out by the state and publishers to authors of these genres (Heidtmann, *Utopische* 220). According to Günther Ebert, the German Writers' Union saw little need to discuss science fiction. "Because literary criticism is seen as a form of advertising and novels of the future sell themselves, it is believed that a review is not necessary." ("Wie müssen" 10). The book shortage also distorted publisher attempts to determine reader preference and demand, as all types of science fiction sold out, not just favorite authors.[25]

Through paper rationing, the SED kept a controllable number of books on the market, in effect limiting the impact of unexpected or "undesirable" readings of any one publication. However, this policy also limited the politically positive effects of a text. In a letter to "Colleague" Baum of the *Hauptabteilung Schöne Literatur* (Section on Fine Literature), science fiction author Eberhardt Del Antonio

24   See Steinmüllers, *Vorgriff* 10. This can be contrasted with the amount of detective novels that appeared at the same time. During the 1960s five to ten detective novels came out every year. See Dehmelt 61. See also Heidtmann, *Utopische* 36.

25   Although not always conducted by publishers directly, see the series of response letters in "Zur Feder Gegriffen" in the magazine *Jugend und Technik* as well as the reader survey conducted by Herta Hein and Karin Ludwig.

bemoaned the fact that approximately seven percent of bookstore orders for his novel, *Gigantum*, had been filled.

> The technical utopian novel loses its real purpose, if it is not able to achieve a broad influence. How should it lead employees to the technical problems of our and future times? How should it prepare a coming epoch and help to speed up technological development? How should it have a stimulating effect in the area of technology (and that is its purpose after all), if it does not find its way to the reader?[26]

Due to the low book supply, however, friends often passed books onto other friends. This practice was widespread in the GDR, particularly in later years (Klotz and Matzer 109). Therefore, it is impossible to ascertain how many people read each copy.

Up to this point, I have spoken primarily of "SED policy." When using this terminology, I refer to an authoritarian hierarchy dominated by the party's Central Committee, yet made up of a myriad of interests and voices that interpreted and implemented the directives of this committee. It is essential to dismantle the reified concept of the "state" or "party" in order to better analyze the growth of science fiction throughout the course of East Germany. On a macro level, the Central Committee of the SED, particularly its cultural subcommittee, determined cultural policy. The next level consisted of the German Writers' Union and the Kulturbund from which the Ministry of Culture had emerged as a separate entity in 1954. The Office of Publishing and Book Sales, which oversaw all GDR publications reported to the Minister of Culture. All publishers submitted an application for publication to this office for approval.

Each publisher had a unique mission and reported directly to the Office of Publishing and Book Sales. Many followed the specific interests of their owner. For instance, the *Militärverlag* was the arm of the People's Army, the East German army. The *Freie Deutsche Jugend* (Free German Youth, FDJ) owned the Verlag Neues Leben, one of the primary science fiction publishers. Books appearing with

---

26 Independent authors were not dependent upon book royalties but rather received a normal salary from the publisher, freeing them up to spend more time on each book. See Del Antonio, "Letter to Regierung der DDR" 55.

the Verlag Neues Leben targeted young readers ten to twenty-five years of age. The other main producer of science fiction, *Verlag Das Neue Berlin* (New Berlin Publishers) was charged with creating a profile for the new capital city. According to one of its editors Ekkehard Redlin, this publisher possessed a greater degree of autonomy. Its somewhat ambiguous assignment could be interpreted in a number of ways, here to include socialist realist utopia. Its interests were not subordinate to a sponsoring organization as was the case with Verlag Neues Leben (Personal interview, 1999).[27] In the fifties, science fiction books and dime novels also appeared with the *Altberliner Verlag Lucie Groszer* (Old Berlin Publisher Lucie Groszer) , the *Verlag Volk und Welt* (People and World Publishers), the *Verlag Kultur und Fortschritt* (Culture and Progress Publishers), the *Mitteldeutscher Verlag* (Middle German Publishers), and the *Kinderbuchverlag* (Children's Literature Publishers)

The Application for Publication

The Formalism debates and efforts to purge *Schund und Schmutz* literature from the GDR defined what science fiction could not be. However, this negative definition provided little guidance to publishers. They looked to internal communications for guidance as well as party recommendations concerning the desired nature of popular literature, popular science, science fiction, and definitions of socialist realism. Where these failed, they relied on their own insight and experience as editors.

Carol Anne Costabile-Heming uses *Rezensur* to describe the processes of censorship and editorial review, which made up the "strict licensing and permission procedure" that each writer navigated

---

27 In addition, what one publisher rejected, might be successful with another one. For instance, if the Verlag Das neue Berlin turned down a manuscript, its author might have more luck with the Militärverlag (Redlin, Personal interview, 2004). See also Kruschel "Zwischen" 159.

to successfully publish in the GDR (55). An elaborate application procedure submitted for approval to the Office of Publishing and Book Sales played a large role in the process of encoding each manuscript. Each application for publication (*Druckgenehmigung*) normally consisted of several external reviews of the proposed manuscript, as well as a review written by the sponsoring editor. When revision was necessary, often a supplemental review was included with a re-submitted application. In the case of science fiction, each application included a testament of technical realism by a scientist, as well as an ideological certification by a literary critic.

The application process was an important censorship tool. In a recent article, author Carlos Rasch commented on the early publishing expectations:

> Already in 1961, an editor in Verlag 'Neues Leben' made it clear to me that we did not need red flags and party secretaries in science fiction [*SF-Literatur*]. At the same time, it was expected that, in the message, a specific point of view, a humanistic position, would be found between the lines. ("DDR-SF" 123).

Here, Rasch refers not only to this second level of censorship, but also to the first level, that of self-censorship practiced by the East German science fiction authors. With experience, the author came to know what was publishable and wrote to comply with these guidelines.

It is also important to remember that authors of early East German science fiction on the whole restricted themselves to the proscribed emphasis on the socialist real in the near future. Most accepted their central function in the "literary society" (*Literatur-gesellschaft*) as cultural representatives of the SED by demonstrating the necessary "loyalty to the party" (*Parteilichkeit*) and "closeness to the people" (*Volksverbundenheit*) in their works. Required membership in the German Writer's Union committed each writer to the "creative work of an active co-designer of the developing socialist society schöpferische" (quoted in Emmerich 43–44). As many subscribed to the GDR foundational narrative as antifascist alternative, they believed in the importance of literature as a necessary pedagogical tool. To this day, Alexander Kröger makes clear that "the omnipresent future optimism [...] cannot be explained solely through the rationale of the state, it is also my basic position today, for example." ("100 Zeile" 120).

Despite the harsh limitations placed on creativity, some authors profited from editorial review. Carlos Rasch testified to this in a radio interview in 1967:

> One must at least be up-to-date on international developments in science and technology. When I have writer's block with a manuscript and need advice, I can approach a scientist with the help of the publisher and get information. A lot of utopian flair gets trashed with these reviews though. (quoted in Heidtmann, *Utopische* 237).

Along with needed advice came objections to story elements that either did not fit the ideological standard or were not scientifically possible at that time. A closer look at the application process sheds light on the continual negotiation of limitations of the ideological or scientific real with science fiction's fantastic elements.

For instance, an analysis of the application for Del Antonio's *Gigantum* (1957) provides insight into common objections to that era's science fiction. *Gigantum* belonged to the category of utopian production novel, characterized by the emphasis on the development of heavy industry and technology (Heidtmann, *Utopische* 53). It is to some extent also a cold war spy novel in the tradition of Dominik, in which thugs hired by an industrialist try repeatedly to steal a new energy secret from a Munich laboratory in a united, socialist Germany. Del Antonio portrays a collective camaraderie between both male and female research scientists and the security guards at the secret state facility. All characters emulate the socialist personality.

The application for publication included three reviews: an internal review (*Verlagsgutachten*) from Verlag Das Neue Berlin, an external review (*Außengutachten*) by sociologist W. Bästel, and an expert review (*Fachgutachten*) by scientist Gerhard Eichler. In such reviews, fundamental questions regarding the nature of utopia, realism, and science in socialism came to the fore, functioning as influential precedents and contributions to science fictional discourse within state institutions.

The sponsoring editor justified the text's suitability within socialist realism manner, as the text was his or her selection for that year's quota (Redlin, Personal interview, 1999 and Szameit, Personal interview, 1999). This review praises Del Antonio's efforts to address existing bourgeois assumptions in the reader. In confronting the "multiple petitbourgeois views of the present," Del Antonio successfully portrays

> the average person of tomorrow as an assertive, conscientious, and well-educated type, who is far from biased, and is productive as a result of a polytechnic education in several areas ("Verlagsgutachten" 60).

A similar description of the scientifically educated protagonist, who devotes his (in this book also her) life to the progress of the socialist revolution, comes to the fore in review after review in the 1950s and 1960s. The review praises Del Antonio's book for a well-rounded view of socialist future life, stating that many science fiction novels unfortunately focused more on apolitical technology and adventure rather than their projection of a socialist future.

One reviewer places special emphasis on the novel's "peek into everyday life, career and social services, living situations and family affairs" (Redlin, Rev. of *Gigantum* 60). This quality includes such aspects as friendly competition and the illustration of a work ethic, which extends to the untiring creative use of free time. According to this reviewer, the novel addresses the important balance of the physical and the mental in work and play. Bästel's review also praises its focus on the "relationship brigade – management, the difference between industrial and agrarian work, the roll of youth organizations, the class structure of the future society, [and], above all, the intelligentsia" (79). The novel easily fit the ideological requirements of its reviewers.

Gerhard Eichler's scientific expert opinion finds that most of Del Antonio's technological creations did not come into conflict with known natural laws. He testifies that the author avoids topics, "on which no definite statement is yet possible, and avoids greater detail" (Eichler 62). What was not derived from known scientific theory, however, did not comply with cultural policy guidelines for realism and needed to be changed. As a scientist, Eichler himself recognized that "utopian problems and 'discoveries' remain decisive for the plot. Das is allowed in a utopian novel" (61). Most importantly, Eichler believed Del Antonio's book to be characterized by rational and realistic "optimism." Despite this praise, he recommends that a postscript be included to explain to the reader that not all techno-logical details in the book were real.[28]

The Sputnik Euphoria

The late fifties saw the emergence of two events, which greatly impacted science fiction in East Germany: the launch of the Sputnik satellite in 1957 and the Fifth Party Congress in 1958. In 1958, the Fifth Party Congress of the SED outlined a cultural program of the masses. This program was part of an effort to reintroduce the "subject-ive factor" to the East German socialist revolution, which had suffered under policies devoted primarily to the reconstruction of industries damaged in World War II. New cultural programs emphasized Ulbricht's utopian *Gemeinschaftsmentalität* (communal mentality) and were designed to instruct participants to work socialistically, learn socialistically, and live socialistically. In this way, they were to attain the "humanistic ideal of the universally and harmoniously, physically and intellectually developed personality" (Hennig 43). East Germans were urged to attend cultural events or the "book of the month" club. This program aimed to re-involve ordinary East Germans in the SED's vision of the future in order to improve productivity and morale.

---

28   Once approved, applications often contained a number of further ideological suggestions. One instance concerning Del Antonio's *Titanus* (1959) contained the following advice: "Instead of 'fleeing to a safe distance' better: 'retreating to a safe distance,' because no one needs to flee a rocket launching in a socialist country" (Elsholz 93). In this case, a reviewer named Eisholz from the Office of Publishing and Book Sales, Section on Fine Literature, asks for a further change before publication.

A new emphasis on the production of science fiction combined with the Soviet launching of Sputnik in 1957 greatly increased official backing for all things scientific in popular literature circles. An internal memo of the popular science magazine *Jugend und Technik* from 1958 illustrates the ideological reduction of literature to a function of the greater economic plan to rebuild East Germany. The magazine's head editor disapproved of current publications:

> The technical and utopian stories do not meet the requirements that must be made of the newspaper. A change will only be possible via rapid expansion of the employee pool. In the process, well-known fiction authors should be approached to write such contributions. From now on it is necessary to create a far-reaching preliminary plan regarding subject matter and to distribute the topic of this plan to all colleagues. Only in this manner can we move beyond the 'hand to mouth' lifestyle that dominates at end of the year. (Kroczeck 98).

The memo alludes to the importance of advances in science and technology not only as a means of rebuilding East Germany, but also in maintaining a competitive edge during the Cold War.

In many ways similar to respective policies in the United States, the Free German Youth publisher Neues Leben hoped to take advantage of the enormous popular interest in space exploration. Its publications encouraged readers to identify with the recent Soviet success and dedicate themselves to the socialist cause, by pursuing studies in science and technology. Karl Böhm and Rolf Dörge stopped their work on the *Jugendweihe* book *Weltall. Erde. Mensch.* (Space. Earth. Humanity.) They commenced with *Auf dem Weg zu fernen Welten* (On the Way to Distant Worlds, 1958), a book on the history and future of space flight in a socialist world.[29] Due to this "plan mentality," colorful illustrations of future cities with complex

29 *Weltall. Erde. Mensch.* opens with a quote from Konstantin Ziolkowski, the father of Soviet rocket technology, and from Lenin. The *Jugendweihe* was a substitute coming-of-age ceremony in the GDR, intended to replace confirmation in Catholic areas. In order to attend a GDR institution of higher education, a student had to go though this ceremony at which they were given a copy of *Weltall. Erde. Mensch.* to instruct them in the views of the socialist state. This book came out in successive updated editions and was replaced by *Sozialismus deiner Welt* (Socialism in Your World) in the mid-seventies.

transportation networks, rocket ships and promises of socialist pre-eminence in technological development characterized numerous comparable publications of the time.

Other publications included the colorful characters "Dig" and "Dag" from the popular comic book *Mosaik*.[30] They suddenly found themselves in the middle of a space adventure centered on the planet Neos and hence called the Neo Series (December 1958–December 1962). A flurry of short stories appeared in various children's and popular science magazines, including *Fröhlich sein und singen, Neues Leben* (Be Happy and Sing. New Life), *Wissen und Leben* (Knowledge and Life), *Jugend und Technik* (Youth and Technology) and, beginning in 1963, *Technikus*. The last two titles were popular science magazines and would consistently publish science fiction through 1989.[31] Still, the increase in publications by Verlag Neues Leben and other publishers failed to bring out enough books to satisfy demand. Average circulations rates hovered between 20,000 and 24,000 copies per novel (Hein and Ludwig 31).

Besides the programmatic influence on space exploration, intense interest in science fiction in the Soviet Union also had impact on its growth in the GDR. In 1958, The Soviet Union sponsored a prize competition, in order to encourage authors to write more science fiction. According to Herta Hein and Karin Ludwig, this competition also led to increased interest in the genre in East Germany (31).

The various publications that dealt with the space race characterize initial attempts by the SED to assign meaning to the Sputnik event. Despite the series of political and economic crises in East Germany through 1961, the party now worked to establish the Sputnik success as validation for the socialist path to communism. It was a Russian, after all, who had invented the rocket ship. Numerous references to Ziolkovsky, who was interested in space flight in the

---

30   Interestingly, Stefan Heym visited the Soviet Union and returned home to write an account of his travels entitled *Das kosmische Zeitalter* (The Cosmic Age, 1959), in which he proclaimed that the border between fantasy and reality had become blurred with the success of Soviet space flight ("Introduction" 2).

31   See Kroczeck 98 for a review of publications in *Jugend und Technik*, which demonstrated the "plan economy" mentality reaching to literary and cultural institutions in the areas of science and technology.

1890s, appear in GDR popular science and science fiction publications of the 1950s and 1960s. In addition, the Soviets continued to demonstrate their technological expertise by sending the dog Laika up in Sputnik II in 1957, the Lunik I to the moon in 1959, the first man in space, Yuri Gagarin, in April 1961, and the first woman in space, Valentina Tereshkova, in 1963 (Clute 69; Kaiser and Welck 394). In this context, a number of cultural functionaries came to view science fiction as a genre based on popular science, which could successfully interest and educate its readers in science and its social and economic applications.

In this regard, it is important to note the distinction between popular science and literature outlined at the Fifth Party Conference. The new plan stressed the development of a "high literature" of the proletariat. A related project, the Bitterfeld Path (1959), urged workers to write their own stories under the motto "Take up your pen, comrade, the socialist national culture needs you!" (Jäger 87–89). Their publications were to make up a new generation of "worker literature" (*Arbeiterliteratur*) on the model of Ludwig Turek's *A Proletarian Narrates*. In addition, the program brought established authors into the factory and industrial work place, in an attempt to present an authentic picture of the ideal "worker" experience under socialism. Participating writers were to learn about life at the foundations of socialism and portray this life idealistically in their novels. In this way, the GDR would create, in Ulbricht's words, "its own culture of entertainment and merry muse" (quoted in Mallinckrodt 30).

Still, few authors choose to delve into the world of science fiction. In his article "Kind von Kunst und Technik," author Del Antonio bemoaned the fact that science fiction authors were seen by "a portion of his writing colleagues as an embarrassing literary outsider" (11). Ekkehard Redlin, an editor at Verlag Das Neue Berlin, commented that publishers tried to get established literary intellectuals to write science fiction, but to no avail (Personal interview, 1999).

In the sixties, science fiction continued to be a controversial literature. The simultaneous reluctance of literary critics to recognize it as anything but *Trivialliteratur*, and the positive perception of it by other party loyals as an effective propaganda tool, placed the genre both on the margins and at the center of the institutions designed to create a mass-produced socialist literature. It was this unresolved status that would gain its authors and editors limited ability to determine their own science fiction policy in years to come.

Chapter Four
"Fantasy – Idea – Realization" (1961–1970)[1]

The year 1961 saw the construction of the Berlin Wall, known in the East as the "anti-fascist protection wall." The completion of this physical barrier cemented the division of Germany in the minds of many and put an end to the flow of easterners to the West. The SED considered the Wall as a sign of the end of the transition from capitalism to socialism. Nevertheless, while West Germany experienced its economic miracle, the East still had much to rebuild.

In 1961, Ulbricht introduced the *Neues Ökonomisches System* (New Economic System or NÖS) designed to expand the GDR's industrial base. This plan channeled resources towards so-called *Zukunftsindustrien* (future industries) and what Ulbricht declared his *Wissenschaftliche-Technische Revolution* [Scientific and Technological Revolution or WTR] (Staritz 279). The NÖS and the WTR placed special focus on science and technological progress by means of the Soviet model so that East Germany might take a place among the world's premiere industrialized nations.[2] To accomplish this goal, Ulbricht's policies focused on the creation of a class of broad-based,

---

1   This quote from Bilenkin, a Soviet theorist of science fiction, characterizes the dialectical nature of the narrowly defined space made for the genre as a source of productive scientific inspiration (138).

2   Böhm and Dörge's "Jugendweihe" book *Weltall. Erde. Mensch*, first introduced in 1962, was a science textbook that primarily outlined the use of science and technology in the furtherment and development of Marxist–Leninism and included projections into the future. Walter Ulbricht wrote the book's introduction: "The sciences, particularly the leading branches of the natural sciences like Physics, Chemistry, and Biology and such disciplines like Cybernetics and Mathematics, penetrate production more and more and change its foundation. The sciences become an immediate productive force and revolutionize all other forces of production. However, this process will be fully accomplished only under socialism and communism, because the capitalist society cannot cope with its social consequences." 17.

highly trained intellectuals and the desire for greater employee creativity in the workplace.

The New Economic System targeted cultural products as the means with which to create a technologically aware populace. Moreover, it altered publication policy to further focus on polytechnical and scientific education. Additional financial and political support broadened education in the natural sciences. As a result, the percentage of math and science teachers in the schools jumped from thirty-three percent to fifty percent (Sckerl 156). The New Economic System also instructed the publishing houses to expand and further specialize, enabling them to focus more on the quality and quantity of their printed product (Simon and Spittel 29).

Equally influential to the development of science fiction prose and policy in the 1960s was the official adoption of the scientific theory of cybernetics. Originating in the West in the 1940s, cybernetics was initially termed an enemy of socialism in Stalin's Soviet Union. In the wake of the thaw under Khrushchev, the science of cybernetic systems quickly became popular, particularly after a series of Soviet space successes. In East Germany, philosopher Georg Klaus did much to legitimize this theory, which, simply put, presented the opportunity to pre-program systems to respond in a variety of ways to their surroundings. "Feedback loops" conveyed information necessary to refine and improve what was a self-correcting system (Caldwell 144–152). The new focus on cybernetics held mathematics to be the basis of all sciences, whether natural, social or aesthetic. It implied the development of an integrated system of multi-talented individuals all unified by a central belief in mathematics. Cybernetics' increased use to explain and plan all aspects of GDR society, including cultural affairs, was central to the implementation of the WTR. The Sixth Party Congress of the SED proclaimed cybernetics to be the official method of its New Economic System (NÖSPL) of 1963.

Official recognition of the importance of the study of the future did much to legitimize science fiction's place in East Germany through the end of the Ulbricht era. East German state planners became interested in cybernetic applications in the area of societal model building. This method presented them with new forms of policy-making knowledge that enabled them to more accurately forecast future needs based on the study of the past and the present. What emerged as the science of futurology in the West became known by its application to the socialist economy of East Germany as *Prognostik*. In his closing remarks at the VII Party Congress of the Socialist Unity Party, Walter Ulbricht emphasized the importance of expanding work done on "societal prognosis" in order to precipitate a "dialectical discussion with problems of the future" (92). Albeit criticized as utopian early on, *Prognostik* developed as a legitimate policy in East Germany, in part through the work of Adolf Bauer and colleagues (*Philosophie und Prognostik*, 1968).

The first high-level recognition of science fiction as a socialist genre came early in October 1962, when the German Writer's Union held its *Konferenz zur Zukunftsliteratur* (Conference on the Literature of the Future). It laid out a policy that recognized science fiction, not as literature, but as a societal and scientific tool. The results of this meeting appeared in a series of articles in *Sonntag* in 1962.

Conference discussion quickly revealed the typical gulf in science fiction criticism that was evident in West Germany as well. This gap existed between authors with an interest in science but very little literary training, and literary critics with no scientific knowledge. The difference is apparent in Günther Ebert's position on science fiction. He believed that Soviet science fiction overemphasized science and technology. "The communists will not win because of the superiority of their social system, but solely due to their technological superiority" ("Wie müssen" 10). For science fiction to conform, Ebert felt it needed to demonstrate not only the technical superiority of socialism, but also a more complete illustration of the socialist personality in the communist future. Otherwise, the genre failed to provide the reader correctly with a well-developed model to emulate.

In response to Ebert's critique, author Eberhardt Del Antonio argued for a focus on science and technology. He believed that science fiction must be granted a broader scope than the *Gegenwartsroman*, which focuses on the realistic, daily lives and struggles of its characters.

> Naturally, if human beings will be the focal point of science fiction [Zukunfts-literatur], so will technology and the various scientific branches – as means for

the liberation of mankind from uncreative, manual labor and in the daily surroundings, in which he lives and, which he transforms. ("Kind von Kunst" 11).

Del Antonio also stressed the importance of the need to dream, especially on the part of scientists. "Dreaming – the ability to see ahead to the coming results of today's actions is a typical human advantage!"[3] First mentioned by Schierlich, the process of dreaming in science fiction became a central issue at the conference, particularly in light of Ernst Bloch's recent ideas in *Das Prinzip Hoffnung* that placed so much importance on the revolutionary quality of dreaming.

The Conference on Literature of the Future established the first cohesive theory of a peculiarly East German science fiction. First, the reference to science fiction as a "literature of the future" instead of as "utopian literature" signaled a shift in generic definition. Both *Zukunftsroman* and *utopischer Roman* commonly appeared on East German science fiction publications as "generic identifiers."[4] Socialist utopian literature confined science fiction's interrogative space to an alternate world, whose rules were set to reflect an immediate Marxist–Leninist future. Its utopian visions were directed toward changes in economic and social development in the present day. A "literature of the future," on the other hand, implied a change from the circular motion of the utopian referent to a single vector, pointing in the direction of a distant, albeit less defined and yet ostensibly assured, communist future. Certainly, this literature continued to respond to its sociohistorical context. Yet the magnitude of technological progress in the 1960s, particularly of the space race, fortified the belief in humanity's kinetic motion toward the future and away from its dark past.

3   See Del Antonio, "Kind von Kunst" 11. Del Antonio is one of the few authors who wrote on science fiction in the 1960s. Carlos Rasch did develop a theory of "Realphantastik," a method of demonstrating various possible socialist models in the near future. Rasch's theory is very similar to Taut's position elucidated here. See Rasch, "utopische Literatur" 55.
4   In Fredric Jameson's theory of the generic contract, the identifier communicates the kind of subgenre to the consumer. (*Political* 106)

The conference referred to the new type of science fiction as *wissenschaftliche–Phantastik* or *wissenschaftliche–phantastische Literatur* (literally scientific fantastic or scientific-fantastic literature). These new terms represented the German translation of the Russian *nauchnaia fantastika* (lit. scientific fantastic). The conference designated this form as a more refined type of East German socialist science fiction. It used its fantastic qualities not to escape contemporary and future problems, but to aid scientifically in their rational solution.[5]

Heinrich Taut embedded *wissenschaftliche Phantastik* in the East German Marxist–Leninist belief system and lexicon. Citing Lenin's "Dream, dream, where is your delight?" in the title of his article, Taut argued that dreams and fantasy had brought socialism to its current success. He referred to the newest resolutions of the Twelfth Party Congress of the Communist Party of the Soviet Union that stressed the decisive effect of "the forces of production and pace and degree" of technological advancement in the success of socialism. In this manner, Taut contended that scientific advancement necessarily requires a degree of fantasy and creativity for it to exist.

Theoretically, he based his argument on a recently published work by the Soviet literary scholar Eugeni Brandis entitled *Über Phantastik und Abenteuer* (On the Fantastic and Adventure, 1960). In essence, Brandis saw science fiction as a literature based on the most advanced scientific knowledge and hypotheses presented by cybernetic theory (Taut, "Träume" 11). To get to that point, scientists must be creative, to think of possibilities and to think into the future. Brandis thus outlined the effectiveness and necessity of fantasy in the scientific world and encouraged science fiction authors to adopt this method. Nonetheless, Brandis was very careful to limit the nature of the fantasy. He recommended: "Even the passionate fantasy has the right to exist, if it does not contradict the general direction of scientific and technological progress" (quoted in Taut 11). Brandis stressed fantasy's importance, as it lets the author dream of new worlds and

5   *Wissenschaftliche Phantastik* hardly became a term used exclusively for GDR science fiction. In practice, it was used somewhat interchangeably with *Zukunftsroman* or *utopischer Roman* and later even with "science fiction."

possibilities that could be helpful to the progress of socialism. He believed that writers could bring things out that scientists are not aware of yet.[6] In his opinion, science fiction was a type of scientific prognosis in literary form, what he termed *künstlerisch Futurologie* (artistic futurology).[7]

Taut introduced the importance of imagination and fantasy to natural and social scientific advancement only five years after Bloch's denunciation. Consequently, he was very careful to qualify his suggestion, stating outright that he is not referring to the "ideological" theory of Bloch ("Träume" 11). Instead, Taut viewed science fiction as a rational, cybernetic model in which the author can play with possible futures that would benefit the scientific and socialist worlds.

> Science fiction [*Zukunftsliteratur*] can play a meaningful and encouraging role that carries us forward in the dynamic, dialectical interaction between the precise establishment of a realistic and doable action today and the keen and fanciful anticipation of possibilities in the future ("Träume" 11).

In this manner, he expected the authors to proceed with an imagination that limited itself to very concrete and pragmatic futures as opposed to irrational, seemingly impossible dreams as would be feasible in an open interrogative space. As a result, troublesome "utopian" elements that remained fantastic despite efforts to constrain science fiction to the ideological "real" now had an encoded justification.

Taut's theory was underscored the next year at the Sixth Party Congress of the SED. There, Walter Ulbricht linked the presentation of a socialist future based on the cybernetic model with the importance of the new future science of "Prognostik."

> In the primary areas of scientific and technological development, prognoses deal with the projected coming domination of natural laws, the associated consequences for technology, and the rapid application of technological discoveries to production (*Die gesellschaftliche Entwicklung* 102).

6   Taut paraphrased Brandis here. See Taut, "Träume" 11.
7   See also Karl–Ludwig Richter's discussion of the implications of "künstlerischen Futurologie."

This policy regarded prognosis as a method of forecasting the symbiotic progress of science and society so integral to historical determinism. The science of *Prognostik* relied primarily on scientific extrapolation similar to western *Futurologie*. Since a theory of science fiction as a type of prognostic yet fictional literature now existed, it would be able to aid in the Scientific–Technological Revolution.

Novels of the Space Age

GDR literary histories describe the period immediately following the building of the Berlin Wall in 1961 as a "turn inwards," characterized by a retreat from overt Cold War politics and a new focus on internal GDR matters (Emmerich, *Kleine Literatur*). The Sixth Party Congress of the SED in 1963 declared a further expansion of socialism domestically and required the arts to address challenges related to this project. To some extent this "turn" took place in the country's science fiction. The immediate danger of industrial spies and saboteurs faded with the construction of the wall. Class conflict now appeared in metaphorical form beyond the geographical context of East versus West German. A greater emphasis on the personal experience of the proletariat in socialism became apparent with a new focus on social-cultural visions of the future. However, the protagonists still remained objects within a greater utopian project. Although the socialist personality most often took the form of the scientist in the science fiction of the fifties, the super cosmonaut now made an entrance.

After the success of Sputnik in 1957, authors began to set their science fiction either in space or on other planets. As space flight had been proven possible, it was now fair game for utopian realism.[8] The

8   Heidtmann categorizes developments among the novels of this time period with the following terminology: "Raumfahrtromane," "phantastische Reise- und Forschungsromane," and "utopische-phantastische Kinderbücher," see *Utopische* 50–58.

appearance of Soviet novels such as Alexei Tolstoy's *Aelita* (1922; GDR 1957) and Ivan Efremov's *Andromeda* (1957; GDR 1958) in East Germany expanded the legitimate narrative possibilities from the GDR of the near future, to the stars and distant communist civilizations that faced displaced class conflict.[9] Many modeled their stories on Tolstoy's revolution on Mars or on Lem's voyage to Venus in *The Astronauts* (1951, GDR 1954), and planted socialist colonies on the Moon, Mars and Venus.[10] A number of authors followed Efremov's lead to the stars. They told of long exploratory journeys to distant locations and sometimes even built upon Efremov's fictional universe that contained a stellar communication system known as the "big ring."

Despite the message of the Bitterfeld Path in 1959 to "take up your pen, comrade" and describe the socialist experience in GDR factories, science fiction leapt instead into what has been described by Erik Simon and Olaf Spittel as the "Age of Space Exploration" (41). Most novels did not overemphasize the development of heavy industry and technology important to Ulbricht's plan for German reconstruction. Instead, they moved further and further away from the everyday problematic of East Germany to a literally universal socialist realism. Science fiction turned "outwards," as authors Eberhardt Del Antonio, Günther Krupkat, Horst Müller, and Carlos Rasch set their novels in more distant spaces and times. Although ideologically compliant, these novels were far from the technically useful prognostic models of the near future, which Taut envisioned. Indeed, writers often set their stories on other planets to escape the stricter censor. Some used these alternate worlds to address issues very relevant to contemporary East Germany (Spittel, "Afterward" 468). Of the new narrative possibilities, Carlos Rasch commented: "This creative space

9   Efremov's *Tumannost' Andromedy* [*Andromeda*] appeared in the Soviet Union
     in 1957. It was translated into German and serialized in a highly censored ver-
     sion in the magazine *Jugend und Technik* beginning in 1958.
10   Kurt Maetzig directed *Der schweigende Stern* (The Silent Star, 1959), the first
     GDR science fiction film. Lem's *The Astronauts* provided the basis for the
     screenplay. In the United States, the film appeared as *First Spaceship on Venus*
     (1962). The significant editing in the latter version changes the entire tone of
     the film.

that has been made for us authors is by no means too large" ("Utopische Literatur" 56).

For the most part, science fiction from the sixties follows set narrative patterns. By the late 1960s, a generic contract for GDR adventure science fiction was fairly well established (Jameson, *Political* 106). Simon and Spittel attribute the existence of these similarities to the "space-euphoria following the launching of Sputnik I." They would later become the clichés of "Space-SF" through 1990 (210). Authors Angela and Karlheinz Steinmüller conclude that such clichés were, in part, a symptom of censorship and established through political precedent (*Vorgriff* 165). Once certain narrative formulas repeatedly passed the censors, authors considered them to be safe and used them again and again in different variations.

Examples of these clichés include the displacement of class and cold war conflict onto other planets and the presence of aggressive capitalist aliens who threaten nuclear war. Peaceful, highly advanced communist aliens often brought about a revolution or became allies against aggressive, imperialist powers (echoing Turek). These plots tend to focus on a time and place much further away, reachable only by a long space journey to a distant planet(s) where a cosmic-style class conflict ensued. Typical of such stories are Eberhardt Del Antonio's *Titanus* (1959), Horst Müller's *Kurs Ganymed* (Course Set For Ganymed, 1962), Lothar Weise's *Das Geheimnis des Transpluto* (The Secret of Transpluto, 1962), and Hubert Horstmann's *Stimme der Unendlichkeit* (The Voice of Infinity, 1965).[11]

Common characters include a Soviet space ship commander and/or a Soviet party officer and a novice crewmember, from whose perspective the reader learns about the future society and its technology. The crew often includes an American, who presents an element of conflict either through sabotage or through miscommunication due to his socialization in a "regressive" society.[12] This last cliché is present in Günther Krupkat's novel *Die große Grenze* (The

---

11   It is interesting to note that Horst Müller's novels were published in the Dominowa Verlag, the publishing house of the Sorbian Slavic minority in Bautzen, Saxony.

12   To the best of my knowledge, the American is never a woman.

Big Border, 1960), in which an American ship on its way to the moon floats helplessly in space after an accident. Soviet cosmonauts subsequently rescue it.[13] The moral superiority of the East Bloc proceeds from the rescue of the antagonistic capitalist followed by the conversion of that same capitalist to communism.

The turn outwards of the sixties did turn inwards in one way. While many novels focused on adventure, the image of the crew (brigade) as commune in the isolation of space provided an objective ideal for behavior in a newly formed East German island. As with more mainstream literature of the time, portrayals of the socialist personality in science fiction became increasingly psychological. They thematized personal problems in individual relationships rather than depicting the crew as a perfect mechanized unit.

The nearer the future and the closer the proximity to Earth, the narrower the ideological space in which the author could write. As a result, novels set closer to Earth took one of two forms. One combined space adventure with aspects of the production novel. For instance, instead of finding new elements in Algeria as in Heinz Vieweg's *Ultrasymet Remains Secret*, Lothar Weise's *Unternehmen Mars-gibberellin* (The Marsgibberellin Enterprise, 1964) places the raw material on Mars. Plot tension stems from the difficulties of mining it in space and the obligatory class conflict. The second form relied on plot tension provided by a new and relatively apolitical scientific discovery. Carlos Rasch's successful novel *Asteroidenjäger* (Asteroid Hunters, 1961) tells the story of a group of star pilots designated to hunt down potentially dangerous asteroids.[14] In this and other like adventures, asteroids often bombarded the ship. The crew played in zero gravity as well. The challenges of space travel were common popular science issues at the time and often appeared in science fiction.

Two of the most prolific science fiction authors, Karl-Heinz Tuschel and Alexander Kröger, also began writing a series of novels

13   Krupkat became the head of the *Arbeitskreis Utopische Literatur* of the German Writers' Union in 1973 ("Stenographische Niederschrift eines Gesprächs" 2).
14   This novel provided the basis for Gottfried Kollditz' film *Signale* (Signals, 1970).

in which the communist society remained relatively free of conflict.[15] Tuschel's first book *Ein Stern fliegt vorbei* (A Star Flies By, 1967) contains an asteroid field that threatens to collide with the Earth. Only the combined efforts of humanity avert total destruction and lead to the establishment of a socialist planet.[16] Kröger debuted in 1969 with *Sieben fielen vom Himmel* (Seven Fell from Heaven), in which visitors from Proxima Centauri are stranded on the Earth. They find it difficult to understand the nature of class and racial conflict, after encountering both an Indian expedition and an American expedition. A technologically advanced, international, socialist group discovers the aliens and helps them to return home. Both of these authors carried the utopian realist tradition of East Germany into the seventies and eighties.

On an interesting side-note, author Günter Krupkat came under criticism due to his preoccupation with Erik van Daniken's tales of past alien landings on the Terraces at Baalbek. Paleontological themes existed in GDR, Polish and Soviet science fiction throughout the 1960s. Such publications speculated on the meaning of earth mysteries of the past and the not so recent past and often drew inspiration from the Tunguska meteor landing of 1908 in Siberia. Lem's book *The Astronauts* and Kurt Maetzig's film *Der schweigende Stern* (The Silent Star, 1959) drew inspiration from this very meteor. Efremov's *Andromeda* included references to archaeology and anthropology, and Efremov himself was a paleontologist. After the publication of Edward van Daniken's theory of alien influence on human history, this too became a favorite theme.

An array of novels by Rasch and Krupkat took place in an alternate time, often on the Earth of the past. These books included Rasch's *Der blaue Planet* (The Blue Planet, 1963), which chronicled

---

15   The two became frequent authors in the series *Spannend erzählt* (Excitingly told) in Verlag Neues Leben. Tuschel later published a number of short stories in the series *Das neue Abenteuer* (The New Adventure) in Verlag Das Neue Berlin.

16   This book belongs to a long history of doomsday novels predicting the collision of heavenly bodies with Earth. Perhaps the best known of such stories is "When Worlds Collide" (1951), which was directed by Rudolph Mate and produced by George Pal.

the landing of a socialist alien in ancient Sumeria from the alien's point of view. Krupkat's *Als die Götter starben* (When the Gods Died, 1963) began with the discovery of diaries on the Mars moon Phobos in the 21st century. An inhabitant of the planet Meju, who had visited Earth's Near East around 4000 B.C., wrote the diaries. This book's sequel, *Nabou* (1968), relates the story of a member of a research team that is investigating the Earth's crust. This team member turns out to be the third in a series of "Biomaten" who the Mejuans left behind to prepare for direct contact with humans. (Robots or cybernetic beings were rare in the GDR at this time). This historical science fiction shifted class conflict to an encounter between "advanced" socialist aliens or humans and societies at a "lower level" of historical development. No open conflict existed between the two societies. Instead the author compared and contrasted the two, stressing the superiority of the socialist model.

Taut praised Rasch' s *Die Heloiden* (an early name for *Der blaue Planet*) in an application review (441). Others called this paleontological bent, particularly Krupkat's pursuit of Erik van Daniken's theories, unrealistic and dangerous ("Stenographische Niederschrift eines Gesprächs" 55). At a special meeting of the Kulturbund in 1973, concern grew after a science fiction club screened Harald Reinl's film *Erinnerung an die Zukunft* [Chariot of the Gods, 1970] ("Stenographische Niederschrift eines Gesprächs" 55).[17] The film, based on the book of the same name by Daniken, met with great interest and further demand among the event participants. Krupkat himself made a trip to the Terrace of Baalbek and gave a presentation on this for the Stanislaw Lem Club (Simon, Personal interview, 1997). Certainly, Daniken's status as rare western material made his work exotic. It is worthwhile to note that what has been called "pseudoscientific" science fiction in the West as well (recently by Thomas Disch [43]), also made its mark in East Germany.

---

17   Harald Reinl is best known for his series of West German Westerns and particularly for *Winnetou I* (Apache Gold, 1963). These films are adaptations of Karl May's adventure novels from the turn of the century, which began with *Winnetou* (1908).

The New Wave

In 1961, as the Berlin Wall stemmed the threat of books from the West, the definition of GDR popular literature as a political weapon against *Schund und Schmutz* literature faded into the background. The growing influence of television, western broadcasting in particular, led to the formulation of new policies in the field of entertainment literature and programming. Pedagogues became interested in popular literature, in part due to a call by the Seventh Party Congress of the SED in 1967 to refocus energy on the creation of the Socialist Personality and the "socialist way of life." The first academic project on popular literature originated in 1968 at the Pedagogical University "Karl Liebknecht" in Potsdam under the direction of Gustav Schröder (Mallinckrodt 32). This research group included science fiction in its study.

In addition, a reader survey conducted by Christa Hein and Karin Ludwig, shed light on the science fiction audience. In the sixties, the majority of readers were between the ages of thirteen and twenty-five. They were secondary school and college students, apprentices, skilled workers, engineers, and white-collar workers. A small percentage was women (33).

New efforts by the German Writers' Union to create socialist literature led to a second Bitterfeld conference in 1964, which acknowledged the importance of popular literature in the GDR. A hierarchy remained nonetheless between high literature and popular literature of the "transition phase" (from socialism to communism). Literary scholars continued to ignore the popular form. The worker's novel (*Arbeiterroman*) entertained the essentialized (male) worker. Ideologically, popular literature remained for those (i.e. women and children), who still required more trivial forms of entertainment (Hochmuth 49).

This hierarchy sheltered science fiction from the crackdown on cultural policy announced at the Eleventh Plenary of the SED's

Central Committee in December 1965.[18] In fact, science fiction production expanded during this period. Following the meeting, the Ministry of Culture reevaluated the work of all publishers in the present and their plans for the future. Anita Mallinckrodt notes the reorganization of several dime novel series and the addition of others in which science fiction appeared. For instance, in 1966, the Verlag Kultur und Fortschritt changed its *Kleine Jugendreihe* to *KAP* [*Krimi, Abenteuer, Phantastik* or Detective Novel, Adventure, Fantasy] (32). In that same year, the publication of science fiction novels rose from one novel per year to three or four per year (Neumann, *Bibliographie* 862). Angela and Karlheinz Steinmüller cite that support for GDR science fiction publications grew visibly beginning in 1968. They point to a jump from a total of five publications in 1967 to sixteen the following year and then twelve in 1969 (*Vorgriff* 10). This figure includes foreign and domestic science fiction.

At this time, a new type of science fiction began to appear in the West. By the late sixties, science fiction in the United States and England responded to and participated in the era's social and political revolutions. In 1964, Michael Moorcock took over the British journal *New Worlds*. This journal began what became known as "New Wave" science fiction, which explored the notion of "inner space," the psychological and the subjective. Authors included Brian Aldiss, Samuel Delany, Philip Dick and Robert Silverberg (James 167–176).

The GDR's version of a "New Wave" coincided with the regime change from Walter Ulbricht to Erich Honecker in 1971. While the majority of this new style of science fiction appeared after this date, its theorization and political justification began several years before. Both literary intellectuals and editors reconsidered the value of utopian thought. External innovations in Eastern European science

---

18   The Eleventh Plenary targeted select authors, actors and musicians. It was particularly critical of the film industry and banned three years of production by DEFA. See *Kahlschlag,* edited by Günter Agde. Beginning in 1966, DEFA produced one *Indianerfilm* (East German westerns) per year. See Dagmar Schittly, *Zwischen Regie und Regime* 127–153.

fiction, particularly the writings of Stanislaw Lem, played a large role in the development of the literature as well.[19]

In a collection of essays from 1958–1966 entitled *Das Poetische* (1972), Peter Hacks reinscribed the utopian method into Marxism–Leninism. He brought back the dynamicism into what he believed had become a static theory ("Utopie und Realität" 199). Hacks' new literary style had as its centerpiece his concept of the "poetic" in drama. Hacks' poetic itself differs from Brecht's epic theater in that it takes place within socialism rather than during the revolutionary period. Peter Graves argues that Hacks' references to what he calls "historicizing" indirectly refer to Brecht (586). Like Brecht, Hacks wished "to grasp reality artistically in its total dialectic" (Hacks, "Poetische" 45). However, rather than bring the reader to "consciousness" in the contemporary world, Hacks' poetic method was directed to the future. Through a discussion of the poem "Die Räuberbraut" (The Robber Bride) by Schiller, he identified the importance of its "identification value" to its popularity and its inclusion of "the unreachable, the unreal" to its effectiveness (Hacks 123). Hacks hoped to create a theater of contradiction by combining the two elements (Graves 586).

Although Hacks did not expressly connect his concept of the poetic and his thoughts concerning the utopian relationship to reality, Graves makes a convincing connection between the two. He points to Hacks' discussion of the utopian playwright (Graves 587). In *das Poetische*, Hacks writes that the "utopian" does not deny socialism through her portrayal of contradiction. Rather, she "bumps into one of the iron limits." The utopian acknowledges that "development, if it occurs, takes place via contradiction and only through contradiction" (29). In Hacks' view, the continued existence of contradiction is necessary if a society is to progress from socialism to communism. Utopian thought is, hence, a useful tool for the socialist. Built upon the solid foundations of socialist achievement, this technique

---

19 Emmerich notes that it has not been established to what degree the fall of Dubcek's reformist government during the Prague Spring of 1968 had on East German intellectuals (*Kleine Literatur* 183).

appropriated utopia to create what Hacks termed the "socialist classical literature" (41).

In a Blochian sense, Hacks reaffirmed the positive, revolutionary effect of the relationship of utopia to the real in socialism. Traditionally, the classic literary utopia identified the negative in a historical period in order to overturn that negative. In Hacks' opinion, there was no danger of this, as he believed the positive historical end point of socialism could only lead to another positive. Aesthetically, Hacks called for an "openness in the portrayal of contradiction" (41). These open contradictions acted as the "lever for the transformation of the world" (35). Moreover, he maintained that the literary had a political function. Any contradiction between existing state policy or program and the utopian world necessarily was a positive one, aiding in the strengthening of socialism.

Most publications of the GDR "New Wave" appeared in the Verlag Das Neue Berlin. In 1968, Ekkehard Redlin became one of two head editors designated for science fiction and was to have much influence on its expansion into the eighties. An early fan of the genre, he had worked at this publishing house as an editor since 1952, and assumed his new role upon Gerhard Branstner's resignation (Simon and Spittel 108 and 224).

Redlin contributed critical talent to the field, and functioned simultaneously as editor and censor in direct contact with established and budding authors. As is evident in his numerous well-argued and informative applications for publication, and from a number of articles on GDR science fiction, Redlin's presence had a decisive effect. He acted as one of the growing number of spokespersons for the genre. He consistently and successfully argued for the legitimacy of new authors who wrote more critically of East Germany through allusion and allegory.

For instance, Redlin argued for the publication of Herbert Ziergiebel's *Zeit der Sternschnuppen* (The Season of Falling Stars, 1971) after it had stalled at the *Mitteldeutscher Verlag* due to "conflicting editorial reviews" (Rev. of *Zeit* 1). In the novel, the "hero," Weyden, witnesses an alien landing on Earth and ends up a passenger on their ship. A comical, love story ensues with Weyden uncertain of his wants and desires. In the end, he returns to Earth and finds himself in a mental hospital. Weyden's fiancée rescues him, but must leave Earth soon after.

The intercession of a skilled editor, particularly of a head editor or publisher, often led to the publication of a book deemed "questionable" (Kruschel, "Zwischen" 159). In his review, Redlin did just that. He acknowledged that Ziergiebel's protagonist was "in no way a positive example" but possessed realistic contradictions in his personality (5). He had improved himself and therefore functioned as a model for the contemporary socialist reader. In addition, Redlin's review praised Ziergiebel's juxtaposition of the real world with the novel's utopian segment. "In the novel, the utopian world helps Weyden to find himself" (4). Redlin believed Weyden learned "productive" lessons about the real world through his experiences in the estranged alternate world.

The apparent gulf between the "real" world and a text's imaginary one posed a constant problem when reconciling science fiction's speculative nature with socialist realism. Redlin criticized those who attempted to overcome this paradox by redefining the utopian novel as *Realphantastik*, its horizon an "historical position that can be determined exactly in a given societal coordinate system."[20] In his opinion, any creative energy present in *Real-phantastik* was channeled into a kind of "Gegenwartsliteratur [lit. present literature] of tomorrow." This form restricted the utopian text to an artistic pragmatic prognosis. Redlin regarded it as "a parity that restricts utopian thought, yes even prohibits it" ("Stenographische Niederschrift eines Gespräches über utopisch-phantastischer Literatur." 46).

He looked for a way to emphasize the utopian novel's interaction with the real, while at the same time justifying the importance of fantasy to society. Building on Taut's association of creativity in cybernetics with dreaming, Redlin reiterated the function of the model as a legitimate space outside of proven experience in which to construct a future world and run through its selected problematic. At a later date, Redlin quoted from Georg Klaus' *Kybernetik und*

---

20   Redlin referred to a theory of "Realphantastik" put forth by author Carlos Rasch in his article "Fantastik hilft die Zukunft begreifen." See Redlin, "Die utopische Dimension" 166.

Erkenntnistheorie (Cybernetics and Cognitive Theory, 1966) to underscore further the existence of fantasy within cybernetics.

> Cybernetics teaches us that the highest form of interaction between a cybernetic system and its environment occurs when the system constructs an inner model of its environment. Experiments on and with this model lead finally to the construction of potential external situations, to models that, in reality, are fantasy worlds. (quoted by Redlin, "Die utopische Dimension" 166).

Interestingly, cybernetics had been denounced as an economic model in the wake of the Prague Spring of 1968, due to its perceived role in the economic and political reforms taking place in Czechoslovakia (Caldwell 179). Still, Redlin's approach proved effective in the cultural sphere.

Importantly, Redlin did not address science fiction in terms of scientific, but rather literary theory. He focused on the reading process and applied the concept of the *Verfremdungseffekt* to utopian literature. Through the thought experiment of utopia, the normal, everyday world takes on a different light and seems new and strange. Its reference to reality becomes apparent in the process of reading. The utopian function provides the reader with intellectual pleasure and relaxation and causes her to search for the meaning of the symbolic in the text. Redlin argued that this process brings the reader much closer to the truth and reality of her socialist world. It aids in the self-realization and growth of adults within a community.

Redlin did not specify whether he drew upon Brecht's concept of alienation in his epic theater or upon Kafka's *Verfremdungseffekt*. He used the term generally. The Kafka Conference held in Liblice, Czechoslovakia in May 1963 established the importance of this author's aesthetic within socialism. Although GDR attendees at the time maintained that Kafka's *Verfremdungseffekt* could not possibly provide a model for socialist literature, Joshua Feinstein remarks that this conference opened the door to Kafka's later influence (127).

Next, Redlin endeavored to restrain the "truths," exposed by the estrangement effect, to socialist realism. He did not understand utopia to be an all-encompassing worldview in the manner of Thomas More. Rather he insisted that it focus on specific problems, which dealt with the contemplation and development of a Marxist–Leninist society in the GDR (Schröder, "Zur Geschichte" 45–46). It is this aspect of utopian literature, which Redlin deemed "revolutionary" and would improve the socialist experiment in the GDR. He believed that the inherent realism of the utopian in science fiction was instrumental in the perception of reality and in the development of ways in which to improve this reality. In this way "realism" and "literary utopia" complemented each other ("utopische Dimension" 166).

Redlin's justification of utopia represented an East German contribution to a broader debate on science fiction conducted by some of its foremost representatives in the East Bloc in the latter half of the sixties. This noteworthy discussion appeared in the East German editions of the journals *Die Sowjetunion im Spiegel Ihrer Presse* (The Soviet Union Through the Mirror of Its Press), *Sputnik*, and *Kunst und Literatur* (Art and Literature). The participants included Polish author Stanislaw Lem, several influential Soviet authors including Boris and Arkady Strugatsky, and Soviet utopian theorist Eugeni Brandis.[21] That this discussion impacted GDR science fiction is demonstrated, in part, by the reference to its early stages in the articles resulting from the 1962 Conference on Literature of the Future (Taut, "Träume" 11). Redlin cited these authors in his editorial reviews in the seventies, in order to justify the publication of similar experimental science fiction in the GDR.[22]

---

21   During the 1960s, Soviet science fiction received broad structural support from the state and enjoyed a wide readership among students, academics, philosophers, engineers and cosmonauts ("Hinterm" 141). This rejuvenation occurred in part due to the success of Sputnik, but also to a period of thaw under Nikita Khrushchev.

22   See for instance Redlin's review of Heiner Rank's *Die Ohnmacht der Allmächtigen* (1972). Redlin cited stories by Lem, the Strugatsky brothers, Josef Nesvadba and Czechoslovak writer Cêstmir Vejdêlek that had been published in the 1960s to justify the publication of this book (4). Redlin's theory paralleled similar theories on the *Verfremdungseffekt* in utopia and science fiction, particularly that outlined in Stanislaw Lem's *Phantastik und Futurologie* (1970). Darko Suvin developed a theory of science fiction based on Brecht's theory of estrangement and Bloch's concept of *Erkenntnis* or cognition in *Metamorphosis of Science Fiction* (1979).

This significant debate reevaluated the idyllic view of technological progress present in the historical determinism of scientific socialism. In the fifties and sixties, GDR attempts at a search for "realism" in science fiction marked Jules Verne as the founder of "humanistic" science fiction. The works of H.G. Wells on the other hand served as the receptacle for fears and accusations against the West. His more fantastic visions were labeled "irrational" and perceived to be shaped by the "late bourgeois anxieties" of his time. In his article in *Kunst und Literatur*, Eugeni Brandis rehabilitated Wells as "the progenitor of the new science fiction [wissenschaftlich-phantastische Literatur" ("wissenschaftlich-phantastische Literatur" 799). Instead of searching for optimistic plots and scientific correctness, Brandis stressed that Wells often touched upon the "dual character of scientific and technological progress that carries constructive and destructive forces buried within it" (806). This statement is significant, as it located the possible challenges and dangers of technological and societal development within Eastern Europe and not solely as a problem in the West.

Brandis cited Wells' dystopian visions in the *War of the Worlds* (1898; GDR 1988) and *The Time Machine* (1895; GDR 1975) as examples of what he introduced as the "novel of warning" (*Warnungsroman*). Brandis emphasized its importance in accessing possible future dangers. He wrote that science fiction, as a combination of science with literary fantasy, has particular advantages in conjunction with the new science of futurology. In doing so the writer should not ignore the borders between reality and fantasy, but should incorporate the fantastic methods of E.T.A. Hoffmann and Edgar Allen Poe, in order to aid in the productive aspects of writing. "The great realists never shied away from the grotesque or satiric exaggeration" (798).

Unsurprisingly, Brandis qualified his analysis by outlining the narrative possibilities for science fiction determined by the class position of the author. Socialist realist science fiction could take the form of the "positive novel" or the "warning novel." He concluded that this last category differs from the "anti-utopia" or bourgeois dystopia in that it incorporated a productive warning, couched in an optimistic belief in social progress. The author of the anti-utopia, on the other hand, begins with the pessimistic assumption that neither social progress nor the "productive power of the people" exists (802). This last distinction appeared in Redlin's theory of utopia as well.

Stanislaw Lem went even further than Brandis to reject the possible attainment of a future paradise and thus a premise of the GDR's utopian realist novels. In an interview from 1969, he directly acknowledged the new dilemmas brought about by change and development within the East Bloc.

> Every improvement has its cost. If medicine develops rapidly, the death rate goes down and there is a population explosion. Our world is a very complicated mechanism and each action can have consequences for the future ("Jeder Fortschritt" 20)

While the reader might want to believe in a perfect future, this dream is only "an ancient illusion" (23). Lem saw his role as author to illustrate the various possible futures and their implications through fiction. "I create specific alternative models" (20). According to Lem, humanity might be able to anticipate and avoid the more catastrophic events in the future through science fiction.

The analyses put forth by Redlin, Brandis and Lem represented a fundamental change in the perception of technological determinism that dominated not only Soviet and East German science fiction, but the Anglo–American tradition as well. At this time, authors in the East and West similarly turned to science fiction as a means of critiquing contemporary society. However, the shape of the ensuing science fiction depended upon the socio-historical context in which it was written. Where the new wave in the Anglo–American tradition drew from modern English literature and Kafka, this transformation in the GDR came about due to a reevaluation of German Romanticism, Brechtian alienation, Kafka's estrangement effect and influences within the East Bloc. Western science fiction moved towards the political left and the incorporation of questions of race, gender, class and the environment. GDR New Wave authors increasingly emphasized issues that reflected concerns of the growing environmental, feminist, peace movements.

The Ambiguous Utopia

In contrast to the utopian realism of space age science fiction in East Germany, the new wave of science fiction that emerged in the late sixties and dominated the seventies took the form of ambiguous utopia. Karsten Kruschel refers to the ambivalence in ambiguous utopia in terms of "the presence of a variety of possible interpretations" (*Spielwelten* 64). He uses the category of ambiguous utopia to characterize those novels of this period that were neither utopian nor dystopia. Rather such fiction contains elements of both, "which are opposed to and contradict each other" (64). According to Kruschel, in this manner the ambiguous utopia works towards a societal solution in a dialectical manner.[23]

To clarify further, the ambiguous utopia can best be defined in terms of Thomas Moylan's similar category of "critical utopia." In *Demand the Impossible*, Moylan identifies a new Anglo–American tradition of utopian writing that emerged in the late sixties. He exemplifies the manner in which Johanna Russ's novel *The Female Man* (1975) is "self-critical, conscious of itself and its history" (57). Moylan remarks on the "fragmented" and "incomplete" form of Russ' story. "She uses utopia as a literary practice; she does not assert utopia as a literary object" (56). Likewise, he remarks on the "[u]topian vision and an awareness of the denial of that vision in the everyday life of American society" in Marge Piercy's work (121). Her *Woman on the Edge of Time* (1976) "breaks open realist narrative" and "allow[s] for the development of a radical utopian activism in the text that offers serious oppositional challenge to the historical status quo (123). Moylan sets these novels in opposition to the "instrumental" classical utopia such as More's *Utopia* (*Scraps* 83). Being "critical" means that the novel rejects the "utopia as blueprint" (*Demand* 10–11). While preserving the quality and power of hope in the dream for the future, the critical utopia also acknowledges the imperfections that exist both in the present and in the utopian dream.

---

23   As Kruschel's dissertation was written in East Germany and published after 1989, he remains equivocal as to the political implications of his definition.

It is imperative to remember that, where Moylan's authors composed in a free society, GDR writers worked under conditions of censorship. When I employ the term ambivalent utopia, I refer to a tradition that did not fully reject "utopia as a blueprint." Many GDR authors supported the SED's initial alignment with Marxist–Leninism. Furthermore, later science fiction in East Germany often created utopian visions that articulated the discrepancies between reality and the SED's chiefly static blueprint in indirect and discreet ways. In fact, the nature of science fiction utopia in the GDR changed over time from that of a Marxist–Leninist one, unified by censorship and historical experience, to a utopia of greater experimentation and exploration. This shift incorporated forms of ambivalent utopia and finally even dystopia written as negative reflections of the greater utopian projects of the individual author(s). The dystopia became viable politically in the final years of East Germany.

Where the East German ambiguous utopia did take the form of a serious narrative, the overwhelming number of these stories incorporated humor and satire. In this regard, the influence of Stanislaw Lem's writings cannot be overestimated. Lem's earliest publication of this sort was the *Star Diaries* (1957; GDR 1961).[24] Much like his other future anthologies (e.g. *Memoirs of a Space Traveler*, *Cyberiad* and *The Futurological Congress*) *Star Diaries* is a collection of loosely linked stories. There is no continuous plot, however the topic, protagonist, theme, and setting overlap to create a sense of narrative cohesion. In his study of *Star Diaries*, Richard Ziegfeld points to other more subtle practices in which Lem tied the narrative together. First, the tone between the narrator and "conventional social practices" is one of "substantial distance." Ziegfeld remarks that Lem establishes distance through "many means, the most striking of which is satire." Where Lem chooses an array of targets, his satire remains short, random and repeated. It is this random quality, which Ziegfeld believes "fosters unity" as it "provides the reader with a familiar generic mode" (13).

---

24 Lem's novels that appeared in the GDR include *Star Diaries* (GDR 1961; complete edition 1973), *Der Unbesiegbare* (GDR 1966), *Test* (GDR 1968), *Robotermärchen* (GDR 1969), *Die Jagd* (GDR 1972) and *Eden* (GDR 1971).

What has consistently contributed to Lem's international success is the keen creativity of his satire that he often takes to the point of ridiculous hilarity. In the seventh voyage of the *Star Diaries*, Tichy, the main character, actually travels through time in a circular manner. He meets himself numerous times, where he had just been or was just going. On the surface an amusing series of encounters with the self, this scene's circular progression through time also undermines the Soviet doctrine of historical determinism.

Most often Lem chooses to explore religious and historical issues as well as humanity's role in the universe. The genre of science fiction provides him with an abundance of settings and times in which to conduct "thought experiments." The result often takes the form of an intellectual discourse along the lines of what Ziegfeld identifies as the philosophical tale from the Swiftian tradition (13). Many of Lem's protagonists are scientists or professors and populate his tales as both the hero and the object of satire. With respect to gender, the few female protagonists in Lem's prose are often banal stereotypes. In this area, his parody and commentaries are highly reductive and, at times, misogynistic.[25] Usually, his target is not an individual, but rather the idea this protagonist represents.

Much of Gerhard Branstner's science fiction publications have a playful feel similar to that of Lem and of Czech author Joseph Nesvadba.[26] Branstner experimented with various aspects of humor in all genres, and often mixed elements of the fable, parody, detective novel, and/or science fiction together.[27] In the manner of Lem, he often incorporated elements of the fantastic in a diary or short story format and connected these stories with recurrent characters and settings. His *Der falsche Mann im Mond* (The Wrong Man in the Moon, 1970), *Der astronomische Dieb* (The Astronomical Thief, 1973), and *Der Sternenkavalier* (The Star Cavalier, 1976) all follow this narrative

25   I am thinking here, for instance, of remarks in Lem's *Microworlds* (67 and footnote four on page 75).

26   An anthology of Nesvadba's short stories appeared in the GDR in 1968.

27   Branstner developed a Marxist–Leninist theory of literary humor in his dissertation entitled "Kunst des Humors – Humor der Kunst." He did not mention science fiction in the dissertation, however.

pattern. Although Branstner's works are critical, they remained relatively abstract, apolitical and quite playful.

Branstner's first science fiction story *Reise zum Stern der Beschwingten* (Trip to the Planet of the Exhilarated, 1968) adapted Lem's notion of the anti-hero. Branstner's protagonists are far removed from the socialist personality, who brought about cosmic revolution so common to science fiction of the space age. Rather, they are similar to the stumbling, yet somehow competent, Tichy of Lem's *Star Diaries*, whose comical encounters with alien phenomenon endear him to the reader. The subtitle of Branstner's novel alone indicates the less-than-serious nature of the story:

> A portrayal of the galactic experiences of quite a few Earthlings who accidentally end up in the Milky Way after suffering a bit. They experience hardship but then finally end up home again happily. (3).

The heroes of Branstner's novel are retired space veterans with balding heads and beer bellies. They have been recalled to operate an otherwise decommissioned spaceship, as they alone possess the skills to operate the antiquated equipment. Each has his own set of quirks that contribute to the comedic storyline. Professor Hedderich, leader of the expedition, knows only that the expedition is to search for Martians, but not how, why, or where (9). Weynreich's function during the expedition is unclear at the beginning (8). He is later unable to function as ship watchman due to loneliness and boredom (70–72). For reasons, revealed later, the character Rinstone never speaks (21). The novel itself opens as the Paul Schimansky's wife sees him off at the door with food and his slippers for the expedition. This mundane event in the life of the anti-hero also betrays the story's exclusion of women from the narrative other than in the pejorative role of nagging, or abandoned housewife.

The anti-hero also includes the anti-scientist. Like Russian authors Boris and Arkady Strugatsky, who satirized Soviet scientists in *Monday Always Begins on Saturday* (Soviet Union 1965; GDR 1990) Branstner's novel portrays the research conducted on the ship as charlatanism. This characterization refutes the superhuman image of the socialist scientist, who deduces the "truth" through cybernetics.

Instead, Professor Hedderich consistently remembers and then forgets vital information. Despite its scientific refutation, he continues to believe that one can tell a person's temperament (phlegmatic, melancholic, choleric or sanguine) by the size of their head (28). The character Pulicke uses cybernetics to explain an implausible theory of language (19). Professor Busch, who had originally "discovered" evidence of life on the planet Mars, was later discredited. He has fabricated the discovery of a reel of information on Mars in order to breathe new life into his theory and gain access to a spaceship with which to search for further evidence of Martians in the solar system (18–19).

Branstner's novel is similar to the children's literature written by Johanna and Günter Braun in the sixties in its playfulness and in that many characters like those found in fables and fairy tales. At the same time, he borrows heavily from surrealism. On one of the various stops on their nebulous mission, the travelers help to hinder a battle between cannibals and intelligent birds that attack their enemies with guano (79–81). They visit a society of salamander-like humanoids, who, in a reversal of Darwin, retreated to a watery existence in order to escape their planet's extremely heavy gravitational pull (116–117). The salamanders have an established diplomatic corps as well as under-water hotels equipped for air-breathing emissaries. The explorers run across a genocidal robot, designed to wipe out a planet's alligator population, and distract him with their shoes (36–39). The sheer absurdity of their adventures underscores the dissimilarities between the humans and their discoveries. Where the cosmonauts of the space age repeatedly found the alien proletariat on deep-space expeditions, Branstner's characters have only the ability to speak Earth's language in common with their hosts. Due to humanity's advanced exploration of the Milky Way, this unspecified language has become a lingua franca of space.

In addition to Branstner, the well-known essayist and poet Günter Kunert also worked with satirical science fiction in poetry and short story form. In the same year as *Trip to the Planet of the Exhilarated*, Kunert published "Die kleinen grünen Männer" (The Small, Green Men, 1968) and "Nach der Landung" (After the Landing, 1968). An additional short story, "Andromeda zur Unzeit"

(Andromeda Out of Season, 1968), touches upon environmental issues with its setting on an Earth devoid of enough resources to support the human population. Those lucky enough to receive a "green card" are sent to wealthy settlements on Uranus or Neptune daily. Television becomes the protagonist's only contact with reality, as it broadcasts the daily, hopeful rocket launchings. This reality is questioned when the character notices one day in April that the constellations behind the rocket are those of November.

Far from the space adventures of the early sixties, "Andromeda zur Unzeit" already demonstrates the societal critique implicit in later GDR science fiction. In a period of thaw in the early seventies, Kunert published "Schlaf" (Sleep, 1975), "Museumsbesuch" (Museum Visit, 1975) and "Vom Pluto her" (From Pluto, 1975). The latter incorporates elements of horror, which were rare to GDR science fiction. Kunert relates the landing of the plutonids on Earth. Despite human excitement at first contact, the biological makeup of the aliens makes them invisible to the human eye. Only blood traces, dead bodies and suppressed cries attest to their presence on Earth. The three-page story ends with a foreboding prediction of further violence.

In the first half of the GDR, science fiction authors implicitly transgressed the boundaries of official policy by envisioning a future that differed from the hegemonic ideology. Kunert was one of the first avant-garde authors to experiment with science fiction. As we will see, his poems represented the first science fiction to critique the SED regime through satire and metaphor. Under conditions of censorship, the textual ambiguity of the fantastic made this science fiction possible.

Book cover from Del Antonio's *Heimkehr der Vorfahren*
(Return of the Forefathers, 1966)

Chapter Five
Utopian Realism in Eberhardt Del Antonio's
Return of the Forefathers

The dream of today is the reality of tomorrow![1]

Then, some authors were considered to be wanton dreamers, visionaries – but even the boldest fantasy is not sufficient to imagine and portray our diverse reality in its entirety. To show that the sacrificial labor needed to build a new society was worth it, that it bore ample fruit.[2]

For the contemporary reader of Anglo–American science fiction, often accustomed to dystopian cultural narratives of degeneration and distrust, the utopian realist texts of East German science fiction might seem hopelessly naive and misguided. However, as Fredric Jameson has pointed out, the ideology of another culture is always more visible from the outside and is consequently labeled "utopian" in the pejorative sense ("Progress" 155). From such a distance it is easier to perceive the rootedness of an apparently ahistorical ideology in the specific events of the space and time that surround it. One should therefore not treat the genre of science fiction as a mirror of such events, as a "symptom of and reflex of historical change" as Jameson suggests (149). This approach demystifies and locates a text's vision(s) as an aesthetic reflection upon the historical and cultural circumstances from whence it emerged.

---

1   See Del Antonio, "Für oder wider" 35. This article was originally submitted to the *Tribüne* but not published.

2   Vena Rendhoff, the main protagonist in the *Return of the Forefathers* read science fiction novels of 2000 set in her time, the 24th century. By commenting here on the limitations of this science fiction, she also validates its attempt to envision a socialist future. See Del Antonio, *Heimkehr* 131.

This chapter addresses Eberhardt Del Antonio's *Heimkehr der Vorfahren* (Return of the Forefathers, 1966) as a representative of utopian realism. It demonstrates how Eberhardt Del Antonio's position as a member of the generation of Germans, which experienced defeat in World War II and the construction of an East German state, influenced his writing. Del Antonio's Marxist–Leninist convictions and active adherence to official cultural policy shaped his science fiction. Through his stories, he hoped to re-educate and redirect the efforts of German amateur and professional technical intellectuals towards the construction of what he believed would culminate in a peaceful and global, communist society. Del Antonio emphasized the importance of a rational "dreaming ahead" through a scientific model based on cybernetics. His look into a socialist future presents a multi-faceted vision of a technologically advanced, peaceful society populated by the ideal socialist person as an attainable goal. Placed in the context of the still immediate destruction of World War II, Del Antonio integrated a belief in the superiority of German technology into the communist narrative of scientific progress.

As utopian science fiction, Del Antonio's text proved unstable in its visions. While he affirmed the hegemonic ideology of the Socialist Unity Party (SED) to which he subscribed, he also simultaneously undermined its interpretation of reality. The novel possesses formal tensions inherent to utopian realism. Heavily influenced by the Marxist–Leninist emphasis on the "real" and rational, the text simultaneously projected an imperfect future beyond what was perceived as the "end of history." It is this future dialectic as well as the broadness of its utopian vision, which set apart Del Antonio's text from his contemporaries.

Del Antonio portrays a static perfection in his novel, evident in its perpetual ethic of technological progress and the subsequent establishment of the cybernetic, socialist Earth. However, through his vision of the new socialist family, he also exposes the flaws in the premise of women's emancipation in socialism and the political and cultural realities of the East German paternal, foundational narrative. The final section of this chapter addresses the affirmative and oppositional aspects present in Del Antonio's text through his portrayal of the Communist woman and family of the future. In this way, he articulated a voice separate from that of the SED's official vision of the future. It is this voice that represents the outside or the blurring between what David Bathrick has termed an existence both inside and outside of the hegemonic ideology of the GDR (*Powers* 20–21).

Finally, *Return of the Forefathers* (*Return*) distinguishes itself from other early East German science fiction through a point of tension between the utopian and the "real," the inside and the outside. This conflict focuses on notions of gender inequality in East Germany in the 1960s. Close textual analysis reveals the manner in which *Return* retains yet vastly redefines the structure of the bourgeois nuclear family in a communist future. The resultant new definition of the socialist family and incorporates traditional bourgeois definitions and official assumptions about the "socialist personality." It also goes beyond both to present a more progressive view regarding women's emancipation. Moreover, through its main female protagonist and its vision of the family, this particular science fiction text presents a view of the socialist woman and family alternate to that supported by the state and cultural institutions of East Germany in the 1960s. In doing so, Del Antonio addresses the institution of the family as a means of discussing unequal gender roles as the cause of conflict in many inter-personal relationships. *Return* does not resolve contradictions with the establishment of socialist gender equality. Nonetheless, Del Antonio saw the eradication of inter-personal conflict as a means of establishing a building block for peace based upon his revised definition of the nuclear family model.

Technology and the New Socialist Nationalism

Inspired by a utopian faith in scientific progress, the defeat of German technology in World War II led the first generation of East German science fiction authors to place new hope in the scientific socialism of Marxism–Leninism. The newly established German Democratic Republic promised to build a peaceful Germany based on a similar belief in technological advancement. Since the latter half of the nine-teenth century, Germany had been a conscious leader in scientific research and development as well as in the chemical and pharma-ceutical industries.[3] Among the advances in military weaponry during World War II, rocket technology and the production of an atomic payload remained a central area of competition between Germany and the Allies. German popular interest in this technology before and during the war is evident in the existence of numerous model rocket clubs and in the popularity of Hans Dominik and other German science fiction authors of the twenties.[4] The defeat of the German war machine in 1945 also signaled the failure of the science and technology of the Third Reich. A belief in the superiority of German technology had long formed an integral part of national identity. The central role of technological advancement within Marxist–Leninist ideology provided an opportunity to re-channel a desire for such progress in a new direction.

Born in the state of Saxony in Germany, Eberhardt Del Antonio (1926–1997) learned to love technology at an early age from his father, who was of Italian heritage. He first worked as a metal worker, then as a technical illustrator and began an engineering degree before he was drafted into the German navy in 1944. After time spent in a prisoner-of-war camp in the Allied Zone, and related compulsory work at odd jobs, he returned home with falsified papers to what was then the Soviet Sector. In 1951, he joined a Meissen workshop, which illegally developed rocket technology for non-military pur-poses, and later became head of the *Büro für Erfindungswesen* (Bureau of Inventions).[5] Although he never joined a political party,

---

3   This rapid economic and industrial development began in the Dresden/Leipzig area in Saxony at the beginning of the nineteenth century. See Dorn Brose 187–188; Davis 29–31, 155–156.

4   It was the German V-2 rocket, which provided the common rocket shape of the science fiction's space ships in the 1940s–1970s. German rocket clubs disbanded once the technology became classified under the National Socialists. See Clute 76.

5   This information comes from his long-time editor and friend Ekkehard Redlin, "Er liebte" 5.

Del Antonio remained actively engaged in the project of the Socialist Unity Party.[6]

During his time in Meissen, Del Antonio began to write. The workshop director encouraged him in this regard. After the director acquired funding for a position from the *Ministerien für Kultur und Schwermaschinenbau* (Ministries of Culture and Heavy Machinery), he made Del Antonio responsible for the shop's "cultural development." In 1953, Del Antonio joined the *Arbeitsgemeinschaft Junger Autoren* (Association of Young Authors) in Dresden and completed a distance-learning course in film psychology. Soon after, editor Ekkehard Redlin at the *Verlag Das Neue Berlin* (New Berlin Publishers) as well as editors at Rütten and Leoning encouraged him to write science fiction. His first book, *Gigantum*, appeared in the *Verlag Das Neue Berlin* in 1957, the year of Sputnik and one year after the Hungarian uprising. A series of books followed: *Titanus* (1959), *Project Sahara* (1962*)*, and the sequel to *Titanus*, *Return of the Forefathers (*1966*)*. In 1959, Del Antonio joined the German Writer's Union and eventually became the head of its Dresden branch (Redlin, "Eberhardt Del Antonio" 428–429). Although he remained active in the science fiction scene, he did not publish again until 1988 with *Okeanos*. Always a consistent seller, Del Antonio continued to draw income from the successive editions of his first books and their translations into Hungarian, Czech, and Slovakian until 1989. In February 1997, he died at his home in Dresden.

Self-appointed as a developer of a new tradition of German science fiction, Del Antonio intended to recapture the weakened sense of (East) German national pride. He hoped to redefine the vision of German technological success and to incorporate it into the post-fascist, foundational narrative of a socialism that used science only for the furtherment of peace ("Für oder wider" 37). Redlin, his editor, remembered the effect of Del Antonio's novels:

---

6   Redlin, his editor, maintains that Del Antonio never joined a party, "because he wanted to preserve independent judgment an literary creativity. That did not keep him from working in the interests of the leading party and bluntly critiquing abuses." See "Er liebte" 6.

We said, we do not know anything about science, and the first books were those by Eberhardt Del Antonio. They focused more on technology. He was an engineer. And technology then was of key importance to national self-esteem. Germany had been defeated, had collapsed. We had so little national pride and then he and our technology came. We had to develop it and he had certain plans. And that was successful with young readers. (Personal interview, 1999).

An avid science fiction reader himself, Del Antonio believed science fiction to be the ideal medium with which to (re)interest the populace in a subject that lay central to Marxism–Leninism and with which to illustrate the intimate link between enlightened scientific progress and historical materialism.[7] Del Antonio's texts often responded to policy issues present in the New Course (*Neuer Kurs* or NK) of 1952 and, a decade later, in the New Economic System of the Planning and Direction of the People's Economy (NÖSPL) of 1963, as outlined by the Central Committee of the SED. Although he wrote for technical intellectuals, Del Antonio also emphasized science fiction's pedagogical function. He sought to interest young people in science and technology, so that they might pursue careers and become leaders in this area.[8] Del Antonio demonstrated his voluntary compliance with these policies in his article "Für oder wider utopische Literatur" ("For or against utopian literature"):

> Next to the adventure novel, science fiction [*der Zukunftsroman*] is especially suitable to steer the youthful spirit of adventure in a healthy direction. It leads them to the 'technical adventure,' that allows young adults to tap into a rich and sensible field of activity, and corresponds absolutely to their wish to test their burgeoning abilities. (38).

By appealing to young readers' sense of adventure and need for entertainment, Del Antonio wished to capture their imagination by

7   Del Antonio argued the merits of science fiction: "Science fiction [der Zukunftsroman] can help to popularize the more recent scientific discoveries." See "Für oder wider" 37.

8   For the directives of the NK and of the NÖSPL see the II Party Conference July 1952 and VI Party Conference, January 15–21, 1963 as referred to in the *DDR Handbuch* 944–945. Science fiction also served a similar function in the United States at this time.

illustrating the primacy of the utopian "end goal" of communist ideology.

> And [science fiction], itself an expression of the far sightedness of Marxism, points again and again to the primacy of the final goal. We are at the beginning of a developmental process. We will free ourselves from the shackles of a dark past on this course (37).

Del Antonio emphasized the challenges that lay ahead from a temporal position in the 1950s at the beginning of an emergence from a "dark [German] past" (37).

Julia Hell describes the process in which Marxist–Leninist ideology rewrote the individual fictions of memory through a sweeping declaration of itself and its citizens as anti-fascist (25). The science fiction of this period also served to displace preoccupations with the past by a concern for the future. Along socialism's teleological time line, those activities or behaviors that Del Antonio identified as fascist in origin also became "archaic" or "childish." Science and technology was not a backward destructive measure as in the "fascist West" exemplified by Nazism, Oppenheimer's participation in the Manhattan Project, and the escalating Cold War. Rather, it became a progressive means towards the "inevitable" establishment of world, socialist peace.[9] More than merely an escape from the recent past, these fictions appropriated and maintained the continuity of a notion of German future progress present since the Enlightenment. Fredric Jameson describes science fiction as a genre that, since Jules Verne, has "registered some nascent sense of the future" precisely in "the space on which a sense of the past had once been inscribed" ("Progress" 150). Where Jameson refers to the transition in historical consciousness between the pre-modern and modern historical periods, this statement applies to the more specific context of East Germany in the immediate post-war period. By reaching forward, towards the coming horizon, Del Antonio and his fellow colleagues in science

---

9   Here Wernher von Braun's employment by the United States is also interesting here as he helped to develop the Explorer, America's answer to Sputnik. Von Braun was a former German V-2 scientist. See Clute 69.

fiction engaged in the rewriting of the national past and present as history through the future.

The Utopian and the "Real"

Through his early scientific education and ensuing literary career, Del Antonio had much in common with both the writers of the Anglo-American "Golden Age" of science fiction and German author, Hans Dominik. Like Dominik, Del Antonio set his first three novels in the near future, focusing heavily on the industrial and technological application of scientific discoveries. Where Dominik provided entertainment through the chauvinistic spy adventure, Del Antonio incorporated class conflict in terms of an escalating Cold War, and identified both West Germany and the United States as threats. Although somewhat vague in areas due to the politically sensitive nature of the technology, *Gigantum* focuses on the experimental dangers in developing new sources of energy in a future Germany. It thematizes the continued attempts of capitalist thieves to steal socialist technology. *Project Sahara* predicts socialist mastery over climactic and agricultural planning in the face of numerous incidents of capitalist sabotage. Moving into the age of space exploration following Sputnik and *Vostok I, Titanus* incorporates easily understandable descriptions of a three-stage rocket, experiences in zero gravity, and the dangers of asteroids in space travel. The theme of class conflict still appears between the planets of Titanus I and II, albeit displaced five years distant from Earth.[10]

Return of the Forefathers shares many aspects of Del Antonio's earlier novels and also with works by his contemporaries Carlos Rasch, Lothar Weise, Horst Müller, and Herbert Ziergiebel. For in-

---

10   Both *Gigantum* and *Titanus* contained an afterward by Del Antonio in which he sharply defined which technology was realistic, i.e. illustrations of known phenomena, and which extrapolated to a realistic future development of this existing technology.

stance, its scientific and societal visions are organized around the prevailing cybernetic theory. This theory held that the interaction and interconnectedness of all systems, including the social and economic worlds, could be understood and controlled through the core language of mathematics. Official cultural policy maintained that the Marxist–Leninist future would be attained through the rationalization of society unified and steered by a common belief in cybernetics. As Taylorist workers each have their function, are well trained for a common purpose, and work together smoothly, so does the crew of the Titanus and the communist Earth of *Return*. This future Earth functions as a well-integrated system both in the coordination of its infrastructure and the integration of the individual members of its population.

What distinguishes *Return* as utopia from other contemporary science fiction is Del Antonio's well-rounded vision of the future communist person and the world she or he occupies. In contrast to his contemporaries, Del Antonio defined his characters not merely by their position in a well-ordered research lab or ship, but also endowed them with an appreciation for select cultural advances including the fine arts. Here, the influence of Soviet writer Ivan Efremov is apparent. Efremov's novel *Andromeda* (Tumannost' Andromedy, 1957) set a literary precedent for an expanded notion of the real in science fiction publications in the Soviet Union and East Germany.[11] He provided a sweeping view one thousand years into the future of a global communist society organized on the cybernetic model and on the brink of contact with other distant races through a universal communications network known as the Big Ring.[12]

---

11   In East Germany, this novel appeared as *Das Mädchen aus dem All*. Fredric Jameson writes of Efremov's text: "for all its naïveté, [it] is one of the most single-minded and extreme attempts to produce a full representation of a future, classless, harmonious, world-wide utopian society. We may measure our own resistance to the utopian impulse by means of the boredom the sophisticated American reader instinctively feels for Efremov's culturally alien 'libidinal apparatus,'" see "Progress" 154.

12   As in the Anglo–American tradition, East German science fiction authors often wrote in dialog with each other as well as with Soviet and other publications in Eastern Europe.

Set in the distant year 2345, the utopian content of *Return* demonstrates an increased tolerance on the part of the censor. After the successes of *Sputnik* and *Vostok I*, space flight came within the bounds of the "real." This development led most science fiction authors of the time to displace their stories on another planet or spaceship in order to preempt the possibility of any minor conflict in their future vision with that of the censor.[13] The Conference on Literature of the Future in 1962 recognized science fiction as a means of improving upon, not subverting, politically acceptable science. Del Antonio, a participant of this conference, agreed that science fiction had an important role to play in the development of GDR socialism: "The vision is inseparable from progress. It precedes any purposeful aspiration" ("Für oder wider" 35). Whereas official scientific policy had focused primarily on the natural sciences, now through the rationality of cybernetics, the policy expanded to include the social sciences and humanities. Truth in science fiction had previously required demonstrable scientific proof behind the author's invention. The political justification of science fiction as a scientific model in the cybernetic Scientific-Technical Revolution now was accepted as a means of anticipating future problems and stimulating the technical imagination. In essence, this restricted the playroom of dreaming beyond the socialist real to the scientific rational.

In addition to the ideology that informed Del Antonio's writing, it was this narrow definition of the real, which distinguished East German science fiction from its western counterparts of the same period. For instance, Del Antonio could not incorporate time travel into his narrative, as this had not been proven to be possible scientifically. As a substitute, he used Einstein's theory of relativity to enable the crew of the *Titanus* to travel 345 years into Earth's future, while only aging ten years themselves. This "real-life" time travel

13   See Erik Simon, Personal interview 1997, who mentioned that, when the external reviewer, editor or official censor objected to a contradiction in a science fiction text with the Party's interpretation of Marxism–Leninism, they could point to the fact that it took place on another planet and thus did not conflict with the reality in East Germany. To the best of my knowledge, from my extensive research of the applications for publication, in the sixties, the majority of objections concerned minor aesthetic and scientific issues.

functioned the same way in which the more fantastic western type does, by taking a representative(s) to another space and time as witness of that alternate space. Anglo–American and West German space opera often included seemingly impossible technologies and peoples, invading green-eyed space monsters in flying saucers for example. Through the 1980s, East German science fiction took place within the "real" coordinates of a universal historical determinism. All that existed had a basis in the reality of this worldview, or was in dialogue with its success or viability. In essence, where the western writer could choose from a number of ideologies to create a world, the East German writer already had existing world-creation rules. On the one hand, they were influenced by the power structures of the hegemonic ideology. On the other hand, they were informed by the author's desire to further the development of communism adapting through self-censorship and his (all were male at this point) subscription to this same ideology. Those green-eyed space monsters could not exist as Marxism–Leninism deemed them western and irrational. When violence emerged, it was brought about by the last gasps of a capitalist society in a universe, which steadily evolved towards communism.

A Cybernetic Setting

The novel *Return of the Forefathers* is itself the conclusion of Del Antonio's previous story *Titanus*. In *Titanus*, an all-male, international crew of 238 takes off in the spaceship *Kosmos* from a predominantly communist Earth in the year 2000. They are on a ten ship-year voyage to the Hyades star system. Explained through Einstein's theory of relativity, *Return* is the story of this ship's return some 345 Earth-years later, when communism has long since unified a peaceful humanity. However, the *Kosmos* does not return until the middle of the book. First we meet Vena Rendhoff, the main protagonist, a model student of cybernetics, and the partner of a leading physicist named Raiger Sajoi. The two have problems in their relationship due to

Rendhoff's dedication to her research project, her pursuit of which leads her to believe that the *Kosmos* is about to return, despite its lost-in-space status. This conflict is exacerbated after the *Kosmos* does arrive and Rendhoff becomes head of the commission in charge of the crew's debriefing and reintegration. After we experience the various cultural conflicts of the returnees in their new present, the book ends when Rendhoff "marries" the ship's party secretary, George Romain.[14]

Before addressing the characters and their romantic liaisons, I wish to touch upon the cybernetic aspects of *Return*'s utopian setting. Similar to Dominik, *Return* possesses a euphoric fascination with rationalized urban life and transportation. It outlines a multi-layered city under a protective bubble. Pedestrian zones dot the surface. While trains and streets disappear underneath.

> There lay Atomos, the city of young scientists. [...] Far in front of the city, a train and highway disappeared underground. The train traveled under the city and stopped at a number of stations. The highway split into a subterranean network three stories high that was connected to the surface by elevator and escalator. (5).

Single-track trains, large people movers, and gondolas appear (194–5), as well as communal rocket cars and ships that cross the stratosphere from Europe to Australia in the same time it took in 1966 to go from Berlin to Dresden (16).

Characteristic of the East German subscription to the Soviet model, *Return* takes place primarily in a Siberian city of scientists. Atomos remains well connected with the rest of the world. This ideal city incorporates Stalinist architecture with broad promenades and large living communities that hold no fewer than one thousand people. However, the text integrates German bourgeois values of privacy and individuality with its communist future vision. All share communal playgrounds, parks, gyms, pools, seminar rooms, theater, dance and

---

14   On the former Earth, George Romain was the *Sekretär der Gruppe der Vereinten Arbeiterparteien des Staatenbundes* (Secretary of the United Worker's Party) and also the second in command after Wassil Nasarow, see *Return* 71.

eating facilities. At the same time, individual inhabitants enjoy the special acoustics of the dining hall that dampen all neighboring table noise. The parks provide many small nooks and offer the privacy to read a book or have a personal conversation. "One feels draw into the big communal family and could converse without being disturbed." (15). Persisting fears of the communist masses are tamed with a level of German, bourgeois respectability.

Return of the Forefathers not only presents a vision of a future communist society, it also demonstrates how adherence to cybernetics in the present leads to the development of this future. Through a visit to a history museum of the 24th century, it illustrates the teleological "inevitability" of Marxist progress through cybernetics, thus reorganizing the memory of the past and even present from its particular future. The museum is organized according to the Marxist developmental stages of history: "Individual and Communal Economy, the farther you procede, the more highly developed the economic system." (50). While conducting research, Rendhoff comments how surprised she is that the cybernetic science of the year 2000 was already so advanced and on its way to the developmental level she knew in the present year 2345. With this comment, Del Antonio alludes to the accessibility of his vision through a solid effort in the present. He refers to tangible results in the not-so-distant future of 2000 first and then underscores their continuing linear success with his description of an even more advanced society in 2345. Through an emphasis on the teleological and tangible progression towards the "end goal" and references to established scientific theory, Del Antonio reiterates the possibility and rationality of his future dream as a logical and attainable consequence of efforts in the present.[15]

Much East German science fiction of the 1960s focused on partial images of a cybernetic system on Earth, another planet, or the mobile city of the space ship. *Return* stands out as literary utopia by providing an all-encompassing vision of the Earth of 2345. Not only

15 For instance, Raiger Sajoi conducts experiments involving gravity. Socialist realist utopia often incorporated relatively realistic extrapolations on current scientific findings. Einstein published his Generalized Theory of Gravitation in 1949.

does Del Antonio describe city life in the future Siberia, he also includes glimpses of life in other places around the world, including France, the United States and the Gobi desert, to suggest that transition to a communist society is complete and global.

Like Efremov, Del Antonio provides other cultural details of his future world. While visiting France, Romain, a returnee, witnesses a folk festival celebrating a woman's 150th birthday. The culinary and nutritional sciences have merged so that cooks can influence moods through various food combinations. Where in medieval times clothing color often demonstrated social class, here color-coded clothing indicates the nature of personal relationships, much like the meaning placed on red or yellow roses. For both men and women, brown indicates camaraderie, while a shimmering outfit of unstable color with a hint of pink shows romantic interest.

Del Antonio's vision is driven by a long-held notion of scientific progress in industrialized countries as the human domination and control of nature. For instance, he describes in detail the transformation of the Gobi desert into a thick, lush forest and a vast, mechanized and highly productive farm. Efremov's *Andromeda*, Alexei Tolstoy's *Aelita*, and Frank Herbert's more recent publication, *Dune*, also contain deserts, which have become green.[16] However, unlike his "production novels" (*Gigantum* and *Project Sahara*), *Return* shows an awareness of issues that will occupy the center of the environmentalist movement in five to ten years. For instance, agricultural settlements, facilities for seafood harvest, radio towers, solar power plants, and wind turbines surround each of Earth's cities (47). The ocean has become the main resource of food and energy (106, 108). At one point, after a blanket of new snow has fallen, Rendhoff admires the beauty of this unspoiled, natural occurrence and "regretted the human interference with the process of nature" (68). Del Antonio does not recognize the environmental problems of industrial waste and pollution, so central to the work of Johanna and Günter Braun just six years later.

16   Efremov melts polar ice caps through the construction of artificial suns. These
      visions stem from the massive industrialization efforts in the Soviet Union and
      in post-war East Germany.

Gender Conflict and The New Communist Family

In the wake of World War II, East German science fiction authors did not focus on technology as a potential threat to humanity, as was done often in Anglo-American science fiction. Rather these authors embraced technology and focused instead on the nature and responsibility of the humans, which controlled and used it.[17] Informed by Marxist–Leninism, their novels were characterized by a post-fascist, post-Hiroshima discourse, which perceived continuity between Nazi Germany and the western Allies as aggressors in the rapidly escalating Cold War. This belief criticized the West's dangerous mismanagement of its nuclear arsenal as "imperialist," seeing it as typical of an "archaic" society that uses its own science fiction to spread "unscrupulous, antihumanist tendencies, from racism to genocide" (Del Antonio, "Für oder wider" 38). Unlike the West, East Germany and the Soviet Block appeared to some in the new GDR as heralds of an ever-lasting peace through the appropriate use of technology, particularly via their own nuclear capability ostensibly only in the civil rather than the military sector. In the immediate post-war era, the basis for this peace lay in the (re)education of German individuals, according to socialist moral values implemented by the Soviets and adopted and adapted by the SED.[18]

Advances in technology soon transferred the desire to maintain the peace from the Earth to the stars. The euphoria surrounding the advent of space exploration in 1957 led to the transference of the Cold War to space. Despite the intensification of the space race, some science fiction authors in the Soviet Union, East Germany, West Germany, and the United States envisioned a peaceful exploration of the galaxy through international cooperation.[19] During this period a

---

17   See also Karl Böhm's chapter "Der Sozialismus und Kommunismus - die Zukunft der Menschheit" and particularly the subheading "Keine Angst vor Robotern!" in Böhm and Dörge, *Weltall* 391.

18   Authors in the West also struggled with similar issues. See Dürrenmatt's *Die Physiker* and Kipphardt's *In der Sache Robert Oppenheimer*.

19   In contrast to his infamous statement to the Americans, "We will bury you," Karl Böhm and R. Dörge quote Nikita Krushchev in their popular science book

notable amount of science fiction appeared that included international crews of women and men.[20] A number of East German science fiction writers appropriated the sanctioned model of the socialist personality and projected it into the future. In novels such as *Asteroidenjäger* (*Asteroid Hunters*, 1961) and *The Blue Planet* (*Der blaue Planet*, 1963) by Carlos Rasch, women crewmembers shared equal duties and responsibilities with their male counterparts in a diverse human collective. A wise, male party secretary heads the crew, which remains united through communism in their adventures in space exploration.

Regardless of how well educated, intelligent, and politically loyal the female figures of 1960s science fiction were, they primarily appeared as mirror images of their objectified male counterparts. The subjective experience of gender or racial difference remained secondary in a rationalized, future world united by a belief in the Marxism–Leninism. In part, this limited portrayal of women in East German science fiction can be attributed to the fact that it was pre-dominantly a genre written by men for men.[21] Both male and female characters existed more as an extension of technology, rather than the reverse. While scientific theory provided an acknowledged reality upon which to base future visions, little scientific "proof" existed for the vision of the new Communist person and her or his social context.

Auf dem Weg zu fernen Welten 206. "Our satellites circle the earth and wait for American and other satellites to join them and create a friendly alliance of satellites. Such an alliance, such competition will be much better than an arms race in the production of deadly weapons." This comes from his speech at the Anniversary Conference of the Supreme Soviet on 7 November, 1957. Such sentiment also appeared among western nations, leading to the signing of the multilateral Outer Space Treaty on 27 June, 1967 that prohibited all weapons of mass destruction in space, see U.S. Department of State n.p.

20   An early example can be found in Tolstoy's *Aelita*. Later examples included Efremov's *Andromeda*, Roddenberry's "Star Trek," and Maetzig's *Der Schweigende Stern*. The West German Star Trek spin-off, *Raumschiff Orion*, did not include a multi-ethnic cast, but did cast women.

21   Even into the 1980s, apart from Anna Seghers, Christa Wolf and Irmtraud Morger, only Johanna Braun, Angela Steinmüller, Anne Geelhaar, Ursula Wilke, and Gerda Zschocke wrote science fiction in East Germany. Geelhaar and Wilke wrote a few children's stories and Zschocke a few short stories.

The arrival of the first woman in space, Valentina Tereshkova, in June 1963, made the premise of a co-ed crew "real." Nevertheless, only scientific approximations and limited first-hand accounts of human experience aboard ship provided a guide. Thus, authors often remained either unwilling or unable to stray too far from that which was knowable according to official Marxist–Leninist cultural codes.

To some extent, Del Antonio's *Return* is symptomatic of this difficulty. His characters often correspond to the sanctioned model of the socialist personality which entailed a) active participation in the process of societal production b) the attainment of the highest possible career qualifications, and c) the combination of these with a definitive, internalized class consciousness (Blunk 63). Self-selected to demonstrate *Parteilichkeit* (loyalty to the party), Del Antonio accepted his task as an East German writer to instruct readers in this model. In the 1960s, when the GDR experienced its own Economic Miracle, the picture of the socialist personality focused on the development of intellectual leaders in the areas of science and technology, and strove to bring the GDR to the level of Ulbricht's desired "world class status." Women, especially, were encouraged to participate in this technological revolution. They were portrayed in leadership positions in engineering, medicine and mathematics. In reality, women received less glamorous industrial work on the assembly line or in more traditional industries such as clothing manufacture (Merkel 369).

In his interdisciplinary future based on a common mathematical language, both women and men have multiple specialties. Rendhoff is a top student at the highly respected Cybernetic Institute, where "[...] today [we] value the disemination of logical and dialectical thought the most. However, Mathematics is the most difficult subject." (*Return* 200). She harbors artistic talent as well, and paints from time to time. Rendhoff's partner, Raiger Sajoi, is a premier researcher in physics and biology; her friend Pala Benari is a physician, historian and also celebrated theater actor. Cybernetics does not merely encompass the natural or social sciences, but also integrates the arts. Rendhoff's adopted uncle, Maro Lohming, an historian of technology and an actor, illustrates this point.

In part, Rendhoff epitomizes the official image of the communist superwoman. As with his other characters, Del Antonio instills her with a Protestant work ethic. In completing her studies, Rendhoff throws herself into her work, forgetting food, sleep, friends, and her partner (22). She dedicates herself to attaining the highest level of scientific achievement, so that she may gain access to the most desirable research projects.

The persistence of male anxiety surrounding women's return to the workplace in East Germany is evident in the asexual or even male manner in which Rendhoff operates in the workplace. To counteract more masculine qualities, she and other communist future women are still individually desirable to men. The *Kosmos* captain, Nasarov observes the following:

> The women of the present were all pretty. They were educated like never before. Sports made them agile and graceful. Life made their faces harmonious and gave them a growing sense of worth. Every disharmony of proportion was corrected by the most advanced cosmetic medicine. (225).

Intelligent and precocious women are also more beautiful and live longer than their 20th century counterparts.[22] To some extent, the woman of the communist future has been fine-tuned, shaped into the perfect female object.

However, as utopian narrative, Del Antonio's novel transgresses the border of the socialist real. Where the portrayal of the communist superwoman in GDR science fiction did not normally address her negotiation of a woman's double burden, *Return* stands out in its acknowledgment of this dilemma. As a solution, *Return*'s vision of marriage in the 24th century resembles more as a partnership, in which men and women are free to pursue their own interests. Rendhoff is also childless. Consequently, she is free to dedicate her mind and body to the improvement of her personal position and duty to a communist society. "To be human, didn't that mean: being strongminded, dedicated to life, driven, in order to perfect oneself spiritually and physically?" (293). It is notable that she identifies herself not as a woman, but as socialist realist humanist, thus

---

22   The average life expectancy is 150 years for both men and women, and in general these men and women are taller and more beautiful.

collapsing these two categories in a manner congruent to the SED's material-based definition of women's emancipation.

Assuming a traditional interpretation of Marxism–Leninism, the SED maintained that women's emancipation automatically followed from the progression towards a communist society. Emancipation was

> solely the project to free labor from capital and therefore only possible in a socialist society. Similarly, the reverse was also true. The construction of a socialist social order requires the emancipation of women as a nonnegotiable condition ("Frauen" 443).

Focusing on a woman's economic freedom as the primary vehicle towards her independence, this policy also played pragmatically into the enormous demand for labor in the period of reconstruction in the 1950s and in the Scientific-Technological Revolution of the 1960s.

However, as women (re)turned to work, they still functioned as the primary care-provider at home. In the 1960s, women received better training and experienced an upward mobility through evening study and school (often away from their families). Yet, they still bore familial responsibilities and often the guilt that resulted from their double burden (Wierling 23). In addition, despite women's specialized training, particularly in the areas of science and technology, men remained in positions of power in development and management, while women operated equipment or occupied other subordinate positions (Merkel 369). The fantastic dreams of women engineers, scientists, and inventors still remained in the science fictional future.

From the beginning, there was a significant gap between the ideal "reality" promised by Marxism–Leninism and a woman's real existence in East Germany. It is this gap, which Del Antonio addresses in *Return*. He employs a science fictional form to critique the limitations of the contemporary familial narrative as a basis for women's emancipation in East Germany.

After returning from exile in the Soviet Union, Walter Ulbricht and other supporting members of the German Communist Party worked with the Soviet Military Administration to re-establish German sovereignty. Designed to be a transitional authority working towards a centralized Communist state, the new command was eager to attain the support of the civilian population through the integration of existing core power structures into the new system. Despite promises of emancipation for women, Julia Hell argues that, at this point, the leading cultural functionaries of the Communist party built the foundations of the East German system on the "symbolic politics of paternity, a cultural discourse revolving around the anti-fascist father" (Hell 25). In her study of the post-fascist foundational narrative, this anti-fascist father served as a role model to the "positive" hero and son, whose real father was either fascist or missing, thus aiding him in the acquirement of "consciousness" (Hell 34). Where strong men dominated the discourse, the communist woman, on the other hand, continued to appear in the supportive role as wife or girlfriend, or as the stabilizing mother where the father has failed. While the communist woman also fulfilled her obligation to society, her first duties remained directed towards her husband and her family.

Similar to production novels where the factory brigade often functioned as familial substitute, in early East German science fiction, this metaphor is applied to the research collective or ship's crew. In *Return of the Forefathers*, the returning ship, *Kosmos*, contains an all-male, international crew, in which every member demonstrates the objective ideal behavior in communism. Minor emotional transgressions are reassured or reinforced through collective support to fortify the correct ideological "consciousness." Each crewmember finds mentors in the captain, Nasarov, and the Party secretary, Romain, who function as substitute anti-fascist father figures for the missing fathers abandoned on the Earth of the past.

In *Return*, at the advanced stage of communist development in the year 2000, the United States is the only remaining capitalist power. James Stafford, son of an American working-class family, feels alienated during his first several years on the ship. His alienation is explained by his participation in the creation of an illegal nuclear weapons facility in the Pacific. His German mentor Jansen serves as his anti-fascist friend and father figure. He introduces to and instructs him in the communist society on the ship. Despite his "antiquated" social upbringing, Stafford has been made to feel at home during the ten-year journey. In *Return of the Forefathers*, Stafford remembers the time when he first arrived on the ship in the first novel *Titanus*:

How had it been, as he had boarded the Kosmos? Lonely, always fleeing from worries, adversity, malice, injustice, jealousy – and from himself. Always defensive, often unfair, egotistical.

What was he today? Part of a collective, accepted, equal. People addressed him as comrade, although he did not belong to any party – before he would have held a grudge, now he was proud of it. (*Return* 88).

Stafford thus becomes an instructive model for the transition from "fascism" to "anti-fascism." However, he does not feel truly integrated until he is required to replace his "father" in the position of chief engineer, when Jansen dies a socialist hero's death on Titanus. Stafford thus succeeds Jansen, and takes on his full responsibilities and ideological consciousness as part of the crew collective.

The *Kosmos* is a well-organized, cybernetic collective, a type of familial substitute. However, Del Antonio's *Kosmos* crew from a less-advanced communist past does not include any women. Here the novel incorporates the clichéd heterosexual narrative of the male soldier cut off from any female contact. As illustrated in *Titanus*, the crew has left family behind and Del Antonio ensures that they rejoin family in the year 2345. According to Rendhoff's reintegration plan, each returnee is paired with a female guide to insure smooth re-incorporation into the new Earth society. These women are placed in bourgeois occupational and familial roles. In Stafford's (the American's) opinion, "there must be a reason that more women study medicine than men, more women teach children, more women raise children." (*Return* 58). The "aids" serve as teachers and mothers. To underscore the continuity of the family, a female descendant of Nasarov, the captain, volunteers to "mother" the "father."

At several points during their reintegration, *Kosmos* crew members comment on their feelings of infantalization or youth. Stafford expresses his frustration with fitting into the new Earth society:

Were the cosmonauts [*Raumfahrer*] sick or even children then? At least they had one thing in common: they landed on an unknown world, were inexperienced and helpless! They needed to be protected from danger (58).

Romain, the party secretary, comments on his own naive assumptions: "How naively he had perceived the world" (334). The women guides are present to aid in the personal reintegration of their assigned returnee where possible. Predictably, many of these pairs fall in love and form heterosexual family units.

Through his portrayal of Rendhoff as communist superwoman, Del Antonio acknowledges her double burden both as the director of the reintegration plan and as the caretaker for the *Kosmos'* crew-member, Romain. By thematizing the double burden, the text criticizes SED policy. Authorities were slow to recognize and help reconcile emotional and professional conflicts between the ideological vision of the workingwoman and of the communist wife and mother. Rather than ignoring this conflict, *Return* addresses it from the point of view of the woman as subject.[23] What follows is a reexamination of the institution of the nuclear family, and the recognition of the continuity of its bourgeois structure in East German socialism. Limited primarily to a focus on the elimination of the concepts of labor and ownership within the nuclear family, Del Antonio retains this institution as a building block for his future communist society. In this way, he preserves the family not the collective as the institution with which to integrate the individual into the state.

First, Del Antonio addresses the issue of woman's labor in the home. He contrasts bourgeois notions of a woman's role in marriage from the year 2000 with the liberated wife and mother from the communist Earth of 2345. Del Antonio does this in a manner that addresses the German boy or man directly, the typical audience of science fiction in the 1960s.

Benari, the actor/psychologist, volunteers to take care of Stafford's reeducation process since she feels especially qualified to deal with the problems of a person who lacks the benefit of a socialist upbringing. Like many of the caretaker-returnee pairs, they fall in love. Stafford is simultaneously "fascist" and also the returning German soldier, when he returns to his birthplace of Rivertown, Iowa to marry Benari and create a home. He expresses his dreams to her:

23   By contrast, the female characters in Rasch's *The Blue Planet*, function as
      integrated asexual ship's crew members and have no family.

"You could wave to me from the roof garden then, when I leave or return" (159).

Through a juxtaposition of the reality of Stafford's experiences that follow with Benari's reaction, Del Antonio subverts the contemporary cultural codes concerning gender roles in marriage. Since Stafford has no formal function in society as a returnee, it is he who ends up the feminized capitalist. He waits at home for Benari and takes care of what was previously the women's housework.

> She was away almost every day, while he sat at home and counted the hours. Neither housework, nor errands, nor garden work satisfied him. Even sporadic private study did not help […] (180).

Benari continues her usual, busy work schedule on stage, at history conferences, and at public speaking engagements. Del Antonio literally reverses the traditional bourgeois male and female roles, thus placing what he believed to be female frustration with limited opportunity expressed in a male voice. Stafford waits at home for Benari.

> This waiting was horrible, you stood and watched and hoped and seemed so excluded, isolated, useless. When would this phase end? Or would it always be like this? (181)

When Stafford demands that the situation change, Benari confronts him:

> What kind of a life did your mother have then – hers or yours? [...] You mean, it would be my duty to take care of your house and go to bed with you? Do you think I am an object that exists to satisfy your needs? (183)

Several issues are involved here. First, in the tradition of August Bebel, Del Antonio emphasizes the interpretation of women as a type of property in a capitalist system versus the perceived freedom of his future communist vision. Instead of being a slave to the husband, he frees his new communist woman to pursue her own goals. At the same time, he addresses the role of mother versus child, again in the terms of property relations and emphasizing that the mother must not sacrifice her life for her children's. Notable here is the issue of education. As Benari educates Stafford, she functions as caretaker and mother of the "imperialist" and also as partner and woman. Read more broadly, she instructs "men" as a "woman." The character of Stafford serves as a clever means of displacing a critique of East German men onto the character of capitalist origins.

While GDR social policy in the sixties began to address the double-burden placed upon a growing number of employed mothers, more effective measures, like state-provided daycare and the designated cleaning day, did not come until 1977.[24] In 1965, the SED declared in its family legal code (*Familiengesetzbuch*) the equality of wife and husband both in marriage and in the family.[25] Since 1989, Ina Merkel has researched the inability of such top-down measures to alter the patriarchal structure of East Germany and the difficulty of comparing the unique development in this area with West Germany. Here the utopian form of his science fiction allowed Del Antonio to envision a society in which he believed women to be emancipated. His oversimplified model contrasts with the more complicated experience of women in the 1960s. Through a reversal of gender roles the narrative voices a frustration with the absence of a swift implementation of women's economic freedom in East Germany.

Return continues on to include a number of suggestions in which to solve the double burden. To free women from the necessity of childcare, Del Antonio borrows the concept of the mother island (*Mutterinsel*) and future communal care facility from Efremov. An island for mothers is designed as a retreat for women, who are ready to give birth. There is also no pressure to become a mother on Earth

---

24　The *Arbeitsgesetzbuch* (AGB) of 16 June 1977 included: "the construction of daycare facilities, kindergardens, after-school care, of stores in the workplace, laundromats and other services. They also meet special regulations, which protect the jobs of and govern the hours worked by pregnant and nursing mothers." See "Frauen" 445.

25　The *Familiengesetzbuch* (Family Legal Code) of 20 December, 1965 outlined the equality of women in marriage and family as well as equal responsibility of both partners in "education and care of children, household management, material expenditure for the home and family" as well as the right of the woman to work outside of the home. See "Frauen" 444.

in the year 2345. The film *The Silent Star* (1959) explains the participation of its woman crewmember through her desire to fulfill her societal duty in her dead husband's place and through her inability to have children. In contrast, *Return* grants women the agency to postpone motherhood. For instance, at one point, Rendhoff wonders why she did not yet have children, but is determined first to complete her degree. "She planned to spend the last few months before the birth of her child on a mother island and concentrate solely on her pregnancy." (69). Del Antonio still links the expectation and desire for motherhood to his construction of female identity, but does not define his female characters through motherhood.

In the year 2345 it is also common, although not required, for the majority of children to be brought up in communal boarding schools. These schools release the mother from her perceived burden of childcare, without causing feelings of guilt on her part. Benari, who has a daughter from a former partnership, talks with her frequently on the videophone and still sees her as the "center of her life" (288). Yet, Benari would much rather have her child in such a school, as she feels her daughter receives a better education there than she could at home.

Although the positive portrayal of such boarding schools (*Kinderkrippen*), can be interpreted as state propaganda, it is not in this case, due to the fact that such measures were not introduced until a decade later. Del Antonio's use of the mother island goes beyond what was then considered to be real, and then limited by the East German law which only proclaimed equality in marriage.[26] Thus, Del Antonio's heavy emphasis on cybernetics transfers into the personal relationships between women and men, in which he suggests several rational solutions to a continuing problem of emancipation in the future. The emphasis on the rational as well as the setting on Earth in the distant future, granted Del Antonio a narrow band of narrative

---

26   At the same time Christa Wolf was beginning to explore her concept of subjective authenticity in her books *Der Geteilte Himmel* (1963) and *Nachdenken über Christa T* (1969). She, Irmtraud Morgner and Sarah Braun and other authors and filmmakers became part of the growing feminist movement in East Germany, which also resulted in science fiction texts such as Wolf's "Selbstversuch."

freedom. He used this freedom to "dream ahead" to a better communist future that went beyond the sanctioned vision of the party.

The Imperfect Socialist Personality

Del Antonio used the capitalist character as negative element to critique contemporary East German cultural values, with regards to gender roles and motherhood in his vision of the communist family of the future. East German authors often employed the capitalist or fascist character to introduce an element of narrative conflict for ideological reasons, and also to create necessary plot tension. In *Return of the Forefathers*, however, Del Antonio transgresses the code of a lack of conflict (*Konfliktlosigkeit*) with the inclusion of his dislikable communist protagonist, Sajoi. He is Rendhoff's partner and an outstanding physicist and biologist. Sajoi's imperfection represents a deviation from the vision of a socialist future as ideal. He also personifies the conflict between the continuity of the (bourgeois and socialist) male's anxiety towards the emancipation of woman in East Germany, and what Del Antonio represents as the presumed equality of woman in a communist future.[27]

For example, as might have been the reaction of a husband in the 1960s to his wife's employment, Sajoi grows increasingly concerned with the intensity of Rendhoff's research, which consumes long hours of her time. "A young, picture perfect woman climbs into dusty crypts instead of turning to the future to discover something new. The study of History. That was something for old men" (25). Where Del Antonio portrays Rendhoff's long hours lost in study and without food in a positive light, he instills the traditional male-female stereotypes in Sajoi. Rendhoff continually wonders if Sajoi respects her not only personally, but also professionally. "Did he take her seriously? As a

---

27 Del Antonio also touches upon this in his first novel *Gigantum*, which describes the success of a woman research scientist despite the tension she experiences with her male research colleagues.

woman, sure – but also as a scientist?" (17). For his part, Sajoi becomes increasingly concerned about her body, its health, and its shape. At one point Rendhoff comments "I would like to have your concern for my figure," to which he responds: "Isn't it [...] my affair?" (17). At one point, Sajoi blocks the continuation of her project, because he is convinced that her review tapes of the Dresden firestorm left her not far from "a nervous break down" and endangered her "delicate disposition" (29). Sajoi's reactions and his resulting angry flight to Pluto, once Rendhoff's coordination of the entire *Kosmos* project leaves no time for him, are labeled "archaic" and "egotistical" since he had "tried to place himself at the center" (101).

When the character of Sajoi is placed into the discourse of the anti-fascist father, it becomes apparent that Del Antonio has taken this narrative and rewritten it, substituting the role of the son with Rendhoff, the daughter. Instead of the missing or fascist father, she leaves her partner behind. Rendhoff is essentially an orphan. Her father was killed in space, while her mother is an expert in Astromedicine, on a deep-space mission, and gone for years at a time.[28] The only family that Rendhoff has is her adopted "Uncle" Maro Lehming, who took care of her when her mother had little time. Maro represents the ideal Communist father figure to replace Raiger Sajoi, who is intent on playing the more traditional fatherly role of husband to Rendhoff, despite her protestations. Already quite independent, Rendhoff acquires the courage to forget Sajoi through her discussions with Uncle Maro, who also plays a pivotal role in her research and subsequent discovery of, and preparation for, the *Kosmos'* impending return. Thus, Del Antonio's understanding of the foundational anti-fascist narrative of the GDR encompasses not only men, but also women in a process of attaining political "consciousness" that includes the realization of gender equality.

Del Antonio does not give up the nuclear familial model, since the SED's interpretation of Marxism–Leninism was indeed based on it. Even so, he changes not only its traditional paternal form, but also

---

28   That the mother has taken her husband's place, echoes a common wartime occurrence and also a more traditional justification of a woman's (and mother's) more emancipated role in society, see *Return* 16.

its legal constitution. I have used the term "partner" instead of husband and wife or marriage, since these terms no longer exist in *Return*'s year 2345. Portrayed solely as a positive development, which does not disadvantage one party or the other economically, long-time partners may separate when desired with no legal ramifications, economic burdens, or custody battles. Children often remain in central care facilities. In addition, and this is perhaps Del Antonio's most radical supposition for his time, he advocates sexual freedom, somewhat stereotypically illustrated through a visit of Romain, the *Kosmos'* party secretary, to France. Romain, believing Rendhoff and Sajoi to still be married in the 20th-century sense,[29] leaves the returnee community, embarrassed and ashamed of having wanted to pursue a relationship with Rendhoff. While wandering about the Earth, Romain meets Jacquelaine, a French woman, at a festival and has a romantic encounter with her. Believing now that he must fulfill his obligations to Jacquelaine, Romain offers to stay permanently. However, Jacquelaine explains to him that in the 24th century: "our hour last night does not obligate you. [...] You cannot attach any conditions to it, at least we do not know something of the sort." (257). Not only are women freed from any marriage bond, but also from the stigma of unwanted sexual bonds, and even children. Compared to more conservative family policies of the SED, this advocacy of "free love" reflects the growing youth revolution of the 1960s.[30]

Despite the progressive notion of gender equality, Del Antonio nevertheless resolves his novel in a more conservative manner. Once Romain returns to camp, he joins Rendhoff in a 20th-century marriage ceremony. On one hand this gesture symbolizes the union of the past with the present, the returnee with the woman of the future. As Raiger Sajoi is also present at the ceremony, it signals a peaceful resolution of the conflict between Sajoi, Rendhoff and Romain. His attendance indicates Sajoi's correction of his "archaic" personality and the restoration of *Konfliktlosigkeit*. In addition, as Romain is the *Kosmos'* party secretary, the assumption is that the relationship

29   And really as understood in East Germany of the 1960s.
30   In the 1960s, the divorce rate grew as well, as women discovered their own economic freedom through employment.

between Rendhoff and Romain will be an equal one, balanced in a manner defined by *Return*. However, the presence of a wedding at the end of *Return of the Forefathers* points to the continuing imperfection of marital relations in contemporary East Germany and reminds the reader of the differences between this wedding and those in 1966. At the same time, Rendhoff and Romain's wedding inscribes Del Antonio's vision of familial relationships in the future into the more familiar institution of the present.

Despite the redefinition of the nuclear family almost to the point of its dissolution, Del Antonio includes a utopian image of what this future family might look like when they visit each other:

> Father and mother, sister and brother. Father shows how to put together a model airplane. He is an expert conveyor belt mechanic. Mother explains the remote control steering on the model and the regulation of the engine speed. Now father listens, because mother is a radio engineer and the absolute authority. But outside, on the grass in from of the house, the parents become children (84).

In its ideal version, what remains of the nuclear family is not a relationship dependent upon ownership of the other, but rather the equal partnership of mother and father centered around technology, who share a social duty to educate their children in a manner consistent with the socialist personality. By his inclusion of an ideal image of the communist family, Del Antonio also underscores the importance of the existence of familial relationships, despite his advocacy of sexual freedom.

Conclusion

While utopian realist texts flowered in East Germany in the 1950s and 1960s, they continued to appear through 1989. Del Antonio's *Return of the Forefathers* is representative of this science fiction in its euphoric portrayal of technological discovery and advancement towards peaceful ends by the cybernetic "socialist personality" in the defense and service of socialism. However, it is worth noting that Del

Antonio does differ from many of his colleagues in his deviation from the portrayal of a static communist future utopia. Rather, his society continues along its progressive dialectic path even in the year 2345, which can be compared with Del Antonio's recognition that the transition in East Germany had not occurred in the near future, as the Socialist Unity Party maintained. Despite hundreds of years of resocializing, Del Antonio thematizes the imperfection of this future communist society through the existence of gender difference, a phenomenon, which still led to conflict.

In *Return* the primary focus remains the heterosexual relationship between man and woman, theorized in a manner, which is concerned mostly with notions of property. The text thematizes various instances in which women have been considered the property of men, as wives, as mothers, and in sexual relationships, stressing the importance of women's equality in each instance. *Return* advocates the socialist premise that each individual should be free to develop to the best of his or her ability, with an emphasis on the woman (233). Despite its inclusion of the mother island and communal child care, though in the year 2345, the nuclear familial model remains intact. By removing what he perceived to be the cause of this conflict, primarily the inequality in familial relations, Del Antonio envisioned a still more perfect peaceful future society beyond *Return*.

Del Antonio's narrative can be interpreted as merely reinforcing SED policy, which needed the work of its women employees to rebuild and retain the country's economic viability. Due to the uniqueness of this particular critique of gender roles in the context of the science fiction of the time, however, the novel contains aspects of both affirmation and dissent. It points to both the inability of the SED to fulfill its promised emancipation and the resistance to such a change inherent in entrenched social structures. Even the majority of science fiction written in the next two decades, granted women primarily supporting roles with the exceptions of works by Johanna and Günter Braun, Irmtraud Morgner, Christa Wolf, and Angela and

Karlheinz Steinmüller (Blume 5).[31] In the 1970s and 1980s the terms of discourse on women's emancipation changed as well, so a comparison with Del Antonio's text is difficult. Suffice to say, *Return of the Forefathers* was revolutionary for its genre and time.

Finally, *Return of the Forefathers* contains a narrative of reintegration that acknowledges the difficulties that German soldiers had upon returning home after World War II, particularly for those who remained captive in the Soviet Union until the fifties. The Germany they discovered was the antithesis of the country they had left. *Return* educates its returnees in the narrative of progress of a future society and aids them in finding a place in this society. The returnees find employment almost exclusively in fields of science and technology and are integral to the continued development of this new society. Thus, where the past has failed them, the novels' returnees are able to leave it behind and become part of yet another technologically driven society. With this in mind, I suggest that Del Antonio's novel also appealed to the returning soldier, by presenting the scientifically inclined among them with a renewed task, this time in East Germany.

31   The later works of Alexander Kröger can be included in this list as well although his female protagonists often resemble the socialist personality (*Die Kristallwelt der Robina Crux* and *Souvenair vom Ataïr*).

Chapter Six
An East German New Wave (1971–1980)

Johanna Braun: Sometimes the censors noticed something. And works that the censor understood, as Karl Kraus meant, were banned justly.

Günter Braun: I'm of a different opinion. Sometimes it depended on whether the censor should understand something. And something must shine through from time to time. ("De Mortuis" 33).

The solid increase in the growth and variety of science fiction in the seventies was largely due to Erich Honecker's major political, economic and cultural policy changes. It is customary to mark 1971 as a pivotal year in East German literary history. In this year, Honecker took over Walter Ulbricht's position as First Secretary of the Central Committee. At the Eighth Party Congress of 1971, he declared the end of the initial period of reconstruction following World War II and proclaimed a new stage in the transition from a socialist to a communist society.

Rather than focus on the preparation of society for communism through Ulbricht's support of heavy industry, Honecker declared a "socialist rationalization" of the economy. This new approach planned to increase the energy supply in part through nuclear power and to incorporate newly mechanized technology in order to increase production. Increased economic efficiency, so Honecker envisioned, would ensure the continued development of personal welfare and of the socialist society. He emphasized the availability of quality consumer goods in order to increase worker satisfaction with the belief that this would lead to increased productivity (Staritz 276–279). In contrast with Ulbricht's abstract promise of future prosperity, Honecker spoke of a "real existing" socialism of higher wages, cheaper prices, and more quality products that was designed to reach everyone despite budgetary concerns.

New efforts were undertaken to improve the quality and variety of all forms of socialist popular culture to try to combat the ever-growing influence of the West, particularly through television. More and more East Germans owned television sets that gave them access to western programming. The one great exception was in the *Tal der Ahnungslosen* (valley of the oblivious) in the southeastern portion of Saxony and on the Baltic island of Rügen that were both out of range of West German signals. Although illegal, East Germans viewed West German programming through makeshift antennae. The ideal images of wealth and success in syndicated television series such as *Falcon Crest* and *Dallas* increasingly formed their vision of the western world. Furthermore, a number of western science fiction programs aired in the Federal Republic. These included *Star Trek* (Gene Roddenberry, 1966–1969), Great Britains's *The Avengers* (Jonathan Alwyn and Robert Asher, 1961–1969), and the German production *Raumpatrouille. Die phantastischen Abenteuer des Raumschiffes ORION* (Michael Braun and Theo Mezger, Spaceship Orion, 1966) (Nagl, *Science Fiction in Deutschland* 204). Often portrayed in terms of the hegemonic ideology associated with a free market system, western programming provided access to a variety of discourses either not addressed in the East or discussed in its media in Marxist–Leninist codes.[1]

Designed to combat western influence, Honecker's new cultural policy included a line of resolutions and measures intended to secure a socialist position among viewers and readers. Conceding that access could not be controlled, the government believed it could shape reception. Efforts to this end are visible in newspaper and magazine articles, which addressed western programming by presenting the Marxist–Leninist position the next day.[2] The directive is also apparent

---

1   Plans for a science fiction television series in the eighties to be written by Carlos Rasch never materialized. Rasch wrote several episodes with a working title of "Die Raumlotsen." To my knowledge, this was the only attempt at a science fiction television series in the GDR.

2   See, for instance, "Denken für die Welt von Morgen" where the newspaper *Sonntag* printed the transcript for a program in western television (BRD) in order to then present the official SED position to the same topic.

in the Kulturbund's reorganization of the Stanislaw Lem Club, which I will discuss later on in the chapter.

Access to western programming also exacerbated the growing split between Ulbricht's "human community" style optimism and the existing material conditions in East Germany. Already discussed above in the context of literature, this economic circumstance also led Honecker to acknowledge the possibility of social conflict in his new "societal view." As his "main goal," his social policy intended to address and solve these conflicts through an improvement in the general quality of life. This plan included a broader understanding of culture designed to support not only the arts, but also activities at work and in free time. It provided for a greater array of socialist mass culture designed to create an alternative to western television and radio (Schröder, "Zur Geschichte" 40).

In 1972, Honecker outlined a new cultural policy. At the Fourth Plenary of the Central Committee of the SED, he declared: "If one begins with a solid socialist position, there can be no taboos in the area of art and literature in my opinion." ("Zu aktuellen Fragen" 5). Kurt Hager, the Minister of Culture, later reaffirmed Honecker's vague and surprising declaration that "no taboos" should exist within socialist realism. He complemented Honecker's pronouncement and emphasized the necessity of "greater wealth, greater variety and differentiation" in the new literature of "real existing" socialism ("Der IX Parteitag" 245; "entwickelte" 1212). In a position clarification a year later, Hager repeated that "contradictions are no hinderance to societal development, they are the motor of every society's advancement. This is also true of socialism." (*Zu Fragen* 40). The official tolerance of contradiction in socialist realism led to a period of limited liberalization and to a wave of publications not possible under Ulbricht (Emmerich 246–247).

The pronouncements made by Honecker and Hager began what proved to be a five-year period of "openness" to greater literary experimentation. David Bathrick observes that, during this time, many *avant-garde* authors turned away from objective realism to the subjective, the individual, the private and the idiosyncratic. This paralleled an increased toleration of fantastic literature in the GDR (*Powers* 187). A constitutive change in cultural policy occurred in the reassessment and recognition of German Romanticism no longer as "irrational" and "dangerous" but as a tradition of respected authors whose writings resonated with contemporary issues. Both authors and critics alike endeavored to interpret works by Bettina von Arnim, Gunderode, Hölderlin, E.T.A. Hoffmann, Heinrich von Kleist and Jean Paul. Literary intellectuals experimented with the fantastic, absurd, uncanny, grotesque and other narrative techniques of the Romantics in order to reevaluate the status of the Enlightenment and classical Humanism as the basis of Marxist historiography and as elemental to the national narrative of the GDR.

The reevaluation of German literary heritage touched upon issues of technology as well. Once the Enlightenment was linked to forms of social oppression, so were other aspects of the East German national myth, including the scientific-technological revolution (Bathrick, *Powers* 188–189). As Peter Hohendahl has argued, the affinity of the "Romantic consciousness" (subjectivity, alienation, etc.) with the contemporary experience of East Germany can be attributed to a similar response to varying degrees of social and technical modernization ("Theorie" 31). Increasingly, East German authors noted not only the positive effects of scientific progress, but also its many negative side effects.

Ambiguous Utopia in the Seventies

In his revised edition of the *Kleine Literaturgeschichte der DDR*, Wolfgang Emmerich places science fiction among the new experimental forms of the seventies (279). Where previous science fiction writers had some type of background in the natural sciences, the pool of authors broadened during this period to include those more proficient in the humanities. Well-known authors, Günther Kunert, Anna Seghers, Christa Wolf, and, later, Franz Fühmann, published several science fiction stories and thus granted the genre added credibility. Looking for forms of expression beyond the existing socialist realist aesthetic these authors turned to science fiction as a way of gaining new narrative freedom.

Besides Kunert, Anna Seghers was one of the first prominent authors to embrace science fiction. As the so-called *Erbedebatte* broke out in the late 1960s and early 1970s, which questioned Lukács' focus on objective reality, Seghers felt the need to make a statement. Rather than write an essay or give a speech, she wrote the collection of short stories *Sonderbare Begegnungen* (Strange Encounters, 1973) as a sample of the new form of socialist realist writing she had in mind.

Her only science fiction story "Sagen von Unirdischen" (Saga of the Aliens) appeared in *Sonderbare Begegnungen.* Seghers first wrote the story in 1970 and published it in *Sinn und Form* in 1972. It addressed the function and practical use of art in society. Just as the Romantics turned to art as the tool to educate their readers, so did Seghers. She wished to reintroduce an earlier focus on individual-centered reception aesthetics and contrast it with the objective reality of socialist realism based on the writings of Lukács. Seghers believed socialist realism had forgotten the need for subjective expression and experience that the citizens of the GDR required in order to under-stand their own personal reality within the community. In the story, the visiting alien, Michael does not understand art and indeed questions the need for it in the classical, practical, horizontal, modern world of his planet. Michael then comes to understand the function of art through love and adventure in a setting reminiscent of the Thirty Years War on Earth.

To the best of my knowledge, Seghers did not make any direct statements concerning science fiction. However, she did support broader use of the fantastic in literature to reintroduce the subjective and self-reflexive into socialist realism. Although she was not willing to stray from socialist realist doctrine, Seghers still attempted to expand the boundaries of its definition in order to include new tech-niques of expression, which would address a wider variety of readers and have a greater effect upon them. In a newspaper article from 1969, Seghers described the usefulness of fantasy and dreams in literature, which she called "fantastic realism."

In many of my books there are fairy-tale-like stories with strange transformations. [...] At heart, my novels, most of the things I have written, describe a type of metamorphosis. (Batt 1294)

Seghers demonstrated that this transformation occurs in reality as well as in literary fantasy in her opening address to the Seventh German Writers' Congress in the GDR in 1973.

A dream, a fantastic invention that develops out of a piece of reality, returns again to reality, if it thrilled the reader. The writer should follow his fantasy. He will certainly not portray only dreams, solely excite his readers with fantastic material his whole life. Some readers partake of his need, other become curious. It raises their spirits. ("Eröffnungsrede" 19)

Rather than lead to escapism, fantasy draws upon reality and enhances the understanding and engagement of the reader in reality. By incorporating the fantastic into literature, the writer is able to find new and effective ways in which to aid the East German populace in a "life that is continually developing" (20).

Like Seghers, Christa Wolf also looked to fantastic narrative forms. Where she most often adapted myth (*Kassandra* and *Medea*), she also employed science fiction as a means with which to access a voice of "subjective authenticity" (Wolf). Her short story "Selbstversuch" (Self-Experiment, 1973) investigates the phenomenon of gender reversal.[3] This story was part of a larger project that resulted in Edith Anderson's collection *Blitz aus heiterem Himmel* (Lightning from a Clear Sky, 1975).

Given the premise of a sex change from woman to man, Wolf wrote a science fiction story that revealed her vision of the inner differences between men and women and their incompatible socialization. A young, female scientist takes the experimental drug *Petersein masculinum 199*, which physically transforms her into a man named Anders. The story takes the form of a supplementary protocol written by the experiment's subject and is not included in the official documentation. The experiment ultimately fails when Anders cannot reconcile his female memories with his new male life experience. He

3   "Selbstversuch" first appeared in the journal *Sinn and Form* in 1973.

168

relates the impossibility of coming to terms with the existence of both male and female in the same physical and emotional body. The result is gender confusion and self-alienation.

Furthermore, Anders, who had been in love with the experiment's head researcher as a woman, now discovers and even identifies with a male inability to love. In the story's one private encounter between the two, the professor asks Anders: "How do you feel?" Anders answers: "Like at the movies" to which the professor replies: "You too?" (99). In this exchange, Wolf identifies the individual estrangement that stems from what she believes to be a "Deficit of feeling, particularly among men" in modern GDR society ("Leben oder gelebt werden" 112). In the end, Anders takes *Petersein minus masculinum 199* to reverse the sex change.

Established writers such as Seghers and Wolf played with new narrative possibilities that science fiction offered them. Although remarkable, the science fiction by Seghers and Wolf proved to be isolated experiments. Others published in the form of ambiguous utopia more consistently. Johanna and Günter Braun were the most prominent. This author pair time after time published science fiction that was highly critical of the SED regime. In the sixties, the Brauns wrote fairy tales and other fantastic stories for young people. Their first book of science fiction, *Der Irrtum des Großen Zauberers* (The Great Magician's Error, 1972), displaced a parody of authoritarianism in a children's story on another planet. A satire of the SED's interpretation of the Enlightenment, *Unheimliche Erscheinungsformen auf Omega VI* (Uncanny Manifestations on Omega XI, 1974) involves a rescue mission from Earth to the planet Omega VI. Their two anthologies *Die Nase des Neandertalers* (The Neanderthal's Nose, 1969) and *Der Fehlfaktor* (The Mistake Factor, 1975) as well as the novel *Conviva Ludibundus* (1978) further develop the Braun's theory of play in literature.

Klaus Möckel, a writer of detective novels and editor at Verlag Volk and Welt, published a number of short stories. His collection *Die gläserne Stadt* (The City of Glass, 1979) concentrate on the growing differences between the country and the city, as well as the autocrats and their subjects (Simon and Spittel 207). In direct dialog with Stanislaw Lem, Bernd Ulbrich wrote playful, satirical collections of stories such as *Der verhexte Kater* (The Bewitched Cat, 1975) and *Der unsichtbare Kreis* (The Invisible Circle, 1978). The seventies also saw the debut of Gert Prokop's detective science fiction. In 1977, he published *Wer stiehlt schon Unterschenkel?* (Who is Stealing Lower Legs Already?), followed by *Der Samenbankraub* (The Sperm Bank Robbery) in 1983. Set in a futuristic United States, Prokop's books describe the humorous adventures of detective Timothy Truckle, an undercover communist agent. Living off of his wealthy, industrialist clients, he solves mysteries benefiting the disadvantaged in the capitalist system. The American setting gave Prokop greater narrative leeway, as he could more freely criticize capitalism as well as interest his reader through a portrayal of the exotic, ideological other.

Heiner Rank's *The Invincible are Helpless* (The Invincible) was one of the most popular science fiction novels in the GDR.[4] His only such publication resembles a detective novel in that its hero, Asmo, searches for the truth behind the civilization on the planet Astilot. He awakens to the luxurious society of the Dafotil where all needs and wants are serviced through robots and other mechanized forms. The occupants of this utopia are genetically incapable of violence; a hostile act would violate the society's basic laws – the KAPINOM. Still, Asmo views this society in a dystopian manner due to the Dafotil's decadence and egotism. Simon and Spittel call attention to the Huxleyesque manner in which Asmo intends to get to the bottom of this "brave new world" (219). Eventually, he discovers a second alien race in suspended animation that created the conditions for the Dafotil's "perfect" society. They had enslaved the Dafotil, who are

---

4   Rank co-wrote some twenty detective novels in the fifties and sixties under the pseudonyms Heiner Heindorff and A.G. Petermann. In 1989, Rank's book ranked as the third most popular GDR science fiction among Andymon club members, see Hohlfeld and Braunstein. Although numerous fans of the Andymon club and also former fans from the Stanislaw Lem club referred to this book as "something different," this was not true of everyone. Ekkehard Redlin remembered an exchange in ca. 1973 with Rolf Krohn, the president of the Stanislaw Lem Club. In the conversation, Krohn criticized the future presented in the book and called it "irresponsible." See Both, Neumann and Scheffler 50.

revealed as distant relations of humanity. When the Astilot decided to transcend their material existence on their planet, they left behind the structure of their vision of a utopian society for the Dafotil. In the end, Asmo's efforts bring "this paradisiacal stagnation" to an end through a relatively peaceful revolution (*Ohnmacht* 296).

On one level, Rank's novel presents the typical East German critique of a consumerist society that transforms into a socialist one. In his review of *The Invincible* for publication, Gerhard Branstner praises this very aspect: "In this manuscript Heiner Rank intends with notable consequence to portray the emptiness and the droning of a society of pure consumption [...]." (Rev. of *Die Ohnmacht* 1). Branstner emphasizes the elements of this novel that are critical of capitalism. Redlin too, points to the novel's criticism of the "post-industrial" society of the West in own editorial review. "The *Dafotil* have been cut off from their own means of production. Their productive capabilities have shriveled." (Rev. of *Die Ohnmacht*, 2). To dispel any skepticism by the censor regarding the validity of Rank's setting in a capitalist society, Redlin cites a number of other precedents for this in the East Bloc, including Lem's *Return From the Stars* (Powrot s gwiazd, 1961) and Boris and Arkady Strugatsky's *The Final Circle of Paradise* (Khyshchnye veshchy veka, 1965; GDR 1983).[5]

However, there is another side to the story, which goes unmentioned in both Branstner's and Redlin's reviews. Where these reviews certainly emphasize the manner in which Rank's story demonstrates the superiority of socialism, they do not mention the story's numerous allusions to GDR socialism. The Dafotil's violence-free existence is enforced by the KAPINOM, societal ground rules established by a now transcendent alien society. The KAPINOM is not subject to discussion or reform; it is unchangeable. Consequently, the Dafotil paradise has stagnated in the same way many believed the GDR had. *The Invincible* makes clear reference to a SED Central Committee that refuses any meaningful reform and is out of touch with the society it regulates.

The novel also argues for the importance of discord. Once Asmo convinces his immediate circle of Dafotil friends of the possibility for

5   See Rev. of *Die Ohnmacht*, 2.

change, various philosophical discussions ensue among them. They consider questions of violence, progress, humanity, gender, and the nature of freedom. Although the majority of the discussions favor a socialist solution, the variety of viewpoints presented cannot be reduced to a single ideological doctrine.

Where the reviews for publication presented the novel's socialist narrative to the censor, *The Invincible*'s ambiguity hides potential, alternate readings beyond that of the socialist realist point of view. Karsten Kruschel notes that certain editors purposely ignored similar critique in order to improve the quality of science fiction on the market. He writes, "intellektuelle Subversion" belonged to the job description of a GDR editor, as much as "the reworking of a crummy book or the elimination of unwanted thoughts" ("Zwischen" 159). Editor Michael Szameit confirmed this practice (Personal interview, 1999). Whether this was one of those occasions is uncertain.

Finally, in the latter half of the novel, the Dafotil invade the compound of the Cephaloids, the artificial brains that still run the planet Astilot. As the KAPINOM is dismantled, the Dafotil are simultaneously freed of consumerism and of authoritarianism. Although Aubedo, the Cephaloid leader, is the hostile administrator of the Dafotil society, he utters perhaps the most important words of the novel. Aubedo too had been bound to enforce the KAPINOM by the now transcendent Astilot. As he attests, he also began to doubt the validity of these rules. "Then I discovered that doubt is the beginning of freedom" (Rank 327). That this equation with skepticism and freedom comes from the mouth of the oppressor makes its validity uncertain. In the context of the novel, Aubedo was also a prisoner of his own power. Yet, as the statement appears in axiom form, its meaning transcends the direct context of the planet Astilot. For the knowing reader, Aubedo's statement is an encouragement to question existing power structures in the GDR.

Further Trends in Domestic and International Science Fiction

Utopian realist science fiction remained popular in the seventies as well. Authors such as Alexander Kröger and Karl-Heinz Tuschel continued to write adventure stories reminiscent of the sixties. Titles such as Tuschel's *Die Insel der Roboter* (Robot Island, 1973) and *Das Rätsel Sigma* (The Sigma Puzzle, 1974) as well as Wolf Weitbrecht's *Oracle der Delphine* (The Dolphin Oracle, 1972) mark the advent of a stable science fiction production based on an established, popular formula. In such science fiction, Heidtmann observes the return of elements from Johnathan Swift's *Robinson Crusoe* and Jules Verne ("Utopische" 81–82). At the same time, this vein of science fiction also expanded and developed. Simon and Spittel remark that what they designate as "Vernian" science fiction reached a new level of quality by the end of the decade. This development was due to its experimentation with new technologies and the later inclusion of acknowledged challenges in GDR society (72)

The broad selection of utopian realist science fiction available in the seventies also marked the growing access to an array of eastern and western science fiction through its variety of style and plot. For instance, aliens and robots began to appear more often. These characters were no longer cast in the categories of class conflict, but more as a non-human, sometimes threatening other. In Klaus Frühauf's *Mutanten auf Andromeda* (Mutants on Andromeda, 1974) humans come into conflict with a hostile alien race, which has become mutated through exposure to radiation. Frühauf does not code the mutants of planet Koarna by class, although their corruption becomes apparent when the non-mutated survivors intervene. In addition, Heidtmann points out that such alien encounters normally complied with the obligatory notion of "freedom from conflict." They resulted from misunderstandings or drew on Lem's theme of a human failure to understand the other that inhibits friendship or "international solidarity" (*Utopische* 81). Socialist protagonists were no longer perfect.

Due to the increasing influence of international science fiction, critic Werner Förster notes that authors at this time began to incorporate contemporary ethical and social problems of the world's scientific-technological revolution. They included topics such as robotics, genetics, computers, ecology, and cybernetics ("Time Travelling" 74–5). These subjects became tenable when Honecker's newly formulated "Freiraum" in cultural politics placed more responsibility on the author's shoulders instead of on the censors to "to always bring oneself in line" (Brauns, "Zu dem berühmten Werk" 53).

Many topics remained taboo, including bureaucracy, generational conflict, a negative portrayal of the Soviet Union, money in communism, and excessive blood.[6] Yet, other direct references to western science fiction bypassed the censors with no difficulty. In *Robot Island*, Tuschel plays with Asimov's Three Laws of Robotics from *I, Robot* (1963). Demonstrating a mix of western influence and classical text, Frankensteinian themes easily fit with anxieties surrounding genetics as evident in Peter Lorenz' *Homunkuli* (1978) or the mad scientist in Rainer Fuhrmann's "Golem" (1983). Rainer Fuhrmann's *Homo Sapiens 10^{-2}* (1977) deals with the appropriation of gigantic and miniature insects and animals for political gain. Horst Heidtmann maintains that this novel borrows a good deal of its content from the American science fiction film *Doctor Cyclops* (*Utopische* 84). Of course these "hidden" references to science fiction generally unavailable in the GDR only increased readership. With few exceptions, East German science fiction was publishable in the seventies as long as it retained the "optimistic picture of history" in direct relationship to GDR society and *its* scientific-technological revolution.

During this decade, science fiction authors increasingly had access to a more complete spectrum of science fiction due to various personal or professional connections. In addition to Soviet and other Eastern Bloc traditions, western stories brought in new ideas and material, thus enriching the quality of and the discourse on GDR science fiction. Membership in the German Writers' Union often

6   Comments from editor Helmut Fickelscherer to Angela and Karlheinz Steinmüller. See *Vorgriff* 168.

granted broader library privileges. More and more care packages with western material made it through customs to fans or authors. Karlheinz Steinmüller's list from 1984 of his favorite books and general opinions of various science fiction authors includes the following names none of which appeared in the GDR: Brian Aldiss, Philip Dick, Robert Heinlein, Frank Herbert and Walter Miller. Steinmüller wrote "one of my favorites" of Philip Dick and listed the Heyne and Suhrkamp editions of his top twelve books by western authors ("Über Science Fiction Literatur" 1, 4). Steinmüller also noted those he had heard of but not yet read. For instance, one line reads "Thomas M. Disch: probably good." (1).

Whether for political or literary reasons, science fiction writers and fans alike increasingly saw themselves as part of an international, socialist science fiction tradition. International not only referred to countries of the East Bloc, but also to science fiction deemed "class conscious" from the "non-socialist world." For instance, the president of the Stanislaw Lem fan club, Ralf Krämer, and fan club member, Erik Simon, argued in favor of select science fiction published in the West. In an article entitled "Auseinandersetzung mit der Science-Fiction-Literatur" from 1972, they sharply differentiated between three types of western science fiction: "decidedly trashy literature, anticommunist and overly technical products, and bourgeois humanist works" (qtd. in Boll, Neumann and Scheffler 42). While Krämer and Simon considered the first and second categories to be dangerous to the reader, they believed that the third category merited further study. Both noted that select western authors criticized the West's own problems of "mass manipulation, racism, militarism, a total consumer society" and supported peaceful coexistence. In their opinion, writers such as Ray Bradbury, Clifford D. Simak, Arthur C. Clarke and Robert Sheckley, who up to this point had appeared in the Soviet Union but not East Germany, fell into the third category. According to Krämer and Simon, it was one of the goals of the Stanislaw Lem Club to discuss such books (42).

Calls for the greater availability of science fiction from the East and West also came from other places as well. In 1973, the Kulturbund and the German Writers' Union scheduled an emergency meeting on science fiction, the details of which I will discuss later on in this chapter. At this meeting, Ekkehard Redlin spoke in support of some Anglo-American authors. Using the term "science fiction" to designate such publications from the West as opposed to the East German *wissenschaftliche-Phantastik,* he argued that the term science fiction is merely a class marker and not a marker of quality ("Steno-graphische Niederschrift eines Gesprächs" 42). Redlin mentioned the "humanistic" qualities of an author such as Ray Bradbury, whose book *Fahrenheit 451* subsequently appeared in Verlag Das Neue Berlin in 1974.[7]

The publication of western science fiction remained low, not only for ideological reasons, but also due to its high price. Publishers had to use their limited amount of hard currency to purchase the rights from the West. The review process cost editors like Redlin and, later Erik Simon, not only money, but also "pounds of nerves, powers of persuasion, and clever tactics," in order to convince authorities of the value of "decadent, late bourgeois literature" (Kruschel, "Zwischen 155).

Due to their efforts, international science fiction did not remain wholly unavailable to the GDR reading public. Soviet science fiction had been published since the beginning. Names such as Efremov, Tolstoi and Sergei Snegov as well as Czech authors Karel Čapek and Josef Nesvadba were staples among those interested in science fiction. In the seventies, the Strugatskys continued to publish new titles, including *Hard to Be a God* (Trudno byt' bogon 1964; GDR 1975) and *Roadside Picknick* (Piknik na obocine 1972; GDR 1976). Lem came out with *The Futurological Congress* (Kongres Futurologiczny 1973; GDR 1975), the complete, uncensored edition of *Star Diaries* (Dzienniki gwiazdowe; GDR 1973) and *Imaginary Magnitude* (Wielkość urojona 1973; GDR 1976). A number of anthologies appeared, including Bulgarian, Czechoslovakian, Polish and other Eastern European writers, as well as a broader array of Soviet authors. Titles include *Der Weg zur Amalthea* (The Path to Amalthea, 1979),

---

7   Science fiction expert, Adolf Sckerl too praised Robert Heinlein's science
     fiction at the same meeting for its ability to lead the reader to reflect upon its
     content ("Wissenschaftliche-phantastische Literatur" 120). Heinlein's works
     never appeared in the GDR.

Kontaktversuche (Contact Attempts, 1978), *Galaxisspatzen* (Galactic Sparrows, 1975) and *Der Fotograf des Unsichtbaren* (The Photograph of the Invisible One, 1978) among others.

Over the next two decades a select American, English and West German authors were published in East Germany. These include the following: Isaac Asimov's *I, Robot* (1950; GDR 1982), Ray Bradbury's *Fahrenheit 451* (1969; GDR 1974), *The Illustrated Man* (1951; GDR 1977) and *The Martian Chronicles* (1950; GDR 1981), Aldous Huxley's *Brave New World* (1932; GDR 1978), Ursula K. Le Guin's *The Left Hand of Darkness* (1969; GDR 1979) and *The Dispossessed* (1974; GDR 1987), Mary Shelley's *Frankenstein* (1818; GDR 1978), and H.G. Wells' *The Time Machine* (1898; GDR 1975).[8] A collection of West German short stories called *Gedankenkontrolle* (Thought Controls, 1978) included established authors such as Wolfgang Jeschke and Herbert Franke. In addition, Edwin Orthmann of the Verlag Neues Leben edited the following collections containing western science fiction: *Der Diamantenmacher* (The Diamond Maker, 1972), *Die Ypsilon-Spirale* (The Ypsilon Spiral, 1973), *Das Zeitfahrrad* (The Time Bicycle, 1974), *Das Raumschiff* (The Spaceship, 1977).

In academia, Gustav Schröder's project on entertainment literature at the Pädagogische Hochschule "Karl Liebknecht" in Potsdam published a series of papers. Individual articles focused on subjects such as the detective novel (Norbert Dehmelt), the dime novel (Edith Gaida), and adventure literature (Erika Karsch). This cooperative study included an informative, relatively apolitical history of GDR science fiction by Schröder himself. In a separate dissertation from 1977, Adolf Sckerl conducted an international survey of science fiction and formulated a theory of its development in the GDR.

---

8   Angela and Karlheinz Steinmüller write that "the censor" came to a publisher and requested that they publish Huxley's *Brave New World*. At the time, this book had not yet appeared in any country of the East Bloc (*Vorgriff* 163).

Science Fiction Policy in the Seventies

Honecker's new economic and cultural policy had an immediate impact on science fiction for three reasons. First, as discussed above, the policy opened the door to irrational or fantastic narrative modes on an official level. Second, due to the connection between relaxation and productivity, party officials praised the role popular culture played in free time activities. By the early seventies, several GDR medical studies demonstrated the importance of relaxation and entertainment to the health and productivity of the worker. Taken seriously by economic planners, the results supported an increase in the variety of popular cultural activities, including popular literature. Editor Ekkehard Redlin also adopted this explanation as a reason to support the publication of science fiction in the Verlag Das Neue Berlin. In an article in *Sonntag* entitled "Ungewohnte Wirklichkeit," Redlin outlined the results of a medical study that examined the parts of the brain used during work hours and those during reading. This unnamed study concluded that reading is a necessary activity that relaxes those parts of the brain exhausted by work. Without reading, work productivity would decrease (2).

Third, the new economic and cultural policy led to increased funding and paper allocations as well as a programmatic expansion of offerings on the part of Verlag Das Neue Berlin and Verlag Neues Leben. Publication rates surged from only two GDR novels per year and one anthology in 1971 to seven novels per year and two anthologies in 1974 and 1975. Following singer Wolf Biermann's expulsion from East Germany in 1976, publication did not drop.[9] Two

---

9   The Biermann Affair marks a turning point in East German literary history. The incident involved Wolfgang Biermann, a popular, dissident folk singer, who was expelled from East Germany after an unapproved performance in Cologne, West Germany. This action prompted outrage from leading authors and intellectuals, a number of whom signed a letter of protest. Following Biermann's expatriation, cultural policy became more stringent and Honecker's political thaw began to freeze. See chapter seven in Manfred Jäger's *Kultur und Politik in der DDR*, pages 163–186. In my own research, I have found that it had little direct impact on science fiction. Only Johanna and Günter Braun refer to the

novels and six anthologies appeared in 1977. Production surged to eight novels and two anthologies in 1978 and dropped to three novels and two anthologies in 1979. Then in 1980 it returned five novels and six anthologies. (Neumann, *Grosse Illustrierte* 864–868). This count does not include the substantial number of short stories or the comparable increase in reprints and translations of foreign science fiction.[10]

During the seventies, instead of the average 20,000 copies, many science fiction books now began with 30,000–60,000 copies on their first run, depending on the book series and the publishers. This can be compared with much lower quotas for books of high literature (Steinmüllers, *Vorgriff* 12). In the seventies and eighties, circulation rates remained the same for the majority of science fiction novels (Kruschel, *Spielwelten* 7–8 and Hartung 123). Johanna and Günter Braun's *Unheimliche Erscheinungsformen auf Omega XI* reached a total of 135,000 copies. Heiner Rank's *Die Ohnmacht der Allmächtigen* (The Invincible are Helpless, 1973) reached 196,000 copies. Günter Krupkat's *Nabou* (1968) had a circulation of 178,000 copies. By 1990, Alexander Kröger, one of the most prolific GDR science fiction writers, had some 1.6 million copies of twelve books published.[11] At this time, Eberhardt Del Antonio's *Titanus* and *Heimkehr der Vorfahren* had reached more than a half a million copies combined.

Honecker's cultural policy was not the only reason for this rapid growth. Author Carlos Rasch attributes a near tripling in the genre's

impact Biermann's expulsion had on their professional lives. Certainly, repercussions from the Biermann Affair had a general impact on science fiction. See Steinmüller, *Vorgriff* 10–11.

10   Anita Mallinckrodt mentions that science fiction did not appear in dime novel form between 1970 and 1980 due to the cancellation of the *KAP*-series (*Krimi, Abenteuer,Phantastik*) [44]. Neumann's bibliography contradicts this assertion. It lists science fiction stories in the dime novel series *Das Neue Abenteuer* (Verlag Neues Leben) and *Meridian* (Deutscher Militärverlag) and *Roman Zeitung* (Verlag Volk und Welt) during the seventies (884–887).

11   In an interview with Alexander Kröger, he mentioned that his publishers sometimes sold books to the west on a 1:1 basis rather than on a 1:10 exchange rate. He never saw hard currency from these sales, although his contract specified a certain percentage of all sales (Personal interview, 1999).

publication rate as early as 1968 to the efforts of a new generation of interested writers ("Fantastik" 3). In addition, there is evidence that a significant demand among GDR readers also needed to be met. From his many book signings, talks and other contact with fans, Krupkat met a wide variety of science fiction readers. They were not only young men and boys, but ranged in ages from "fourteen to seventy" ("Stenografische Niederschrift eines Gesprächs" 89). Author Günter Görlich commented on reader demand for science fiction at a conference on the subject in 1973: "Everyone of us can verify that we are asked more and more often at readings whether we write science fiction [utopische Romane]" ("Stenographische Niederschrift eines Gesprächs" 206).

Despite increased availability, the demand for science fiction remained so high that all books sold out immediately. Over the years, a culture of barter and lending among friends and clubs had developed in the East German "Mangelgesellschaft" (society of shortage). This practice supports an assertion oft repeated in interviews with authors and fans that more than one person read each science fiction book. In libraries, some science fiction books remained in great demand and were difficult to get, as select titles were checked out frequently.[12] Authors Angela and Karlheinz Steinmüller estimate that, in the seventies and eighties, a single title reached a potential ten percent among students aged fifteen to twenty five (*Vorgriff* 12–13). Author Alexander Kröger estimates as many as ten readers per book ("Hundert Zeilen" 7).

A survey conducted in 1981 by Olaf Göhler found that thirty-one percent of college-bound high school students rated science fiction as their most favorite genre. Thirty-three percent of journeymen, twenty-seven percent of office workers and twenty-four percent of the working class rated it as their second most favorite. Nineteen percent of college students and seventeen percent of the intelligentsia listed it as their third most favorite genre (quoted by Hartung 123.)

12   Information provided in personal interviews with Andymon fan club members Hardy Kettlitz (1999), Hans-Peter Neumann (1998), Ingolf Vonau (1999), Siegfried Breuer (1999), and editor, author, and former fan, Erik Simon (1997). Kettlitz is also an editor at the Shayol Verlag.

The Science Fiction Fan Club

The East German reader functioned as the consumer, who official cultural policy originally intended as the target audience of its "ideological product" (Barker 27). Adele Marie Barker's terminology implies a more active role on the part of the reader subject, rather than the quantification of the purchasers of science fiction as anonymous masses. In the GDR, consumer agency was evident in the organized activities of science fiction fans.

Initial popular support for science fiction expressed in the magazine *Jugend und Technik* prompted author Carlos Rasch to contact respondents. He suggested they form science fiction clubs as a means to provide further support for its existence in the GDR. The best-known science fiction fan club was the Stanislaw Lem Club (SLC) of Dresden named after the popular Polish author and founded by Ralf Krämer (Personal interview, 1999). The SLC operated, according to the model outlined by Bathrick – both inside and outside of the SED's "discursive system." Made up of a group of physics students from the Technical University in Dresden, the club was officially founded on June 5, 1969 as the *Interessengemeinschaft Wissenschaftlich-phantastische Literatur* part of the *Hochschulgruppe Dresden* of the Kulturbund. Membership in the Kulturbund became necessary after repeated meetings in Krämer's dorm room aroused suspicion, drawing the attention of the *Stasi*.[13]

SLC members shared ideas and assembled a library to facilitate greater access to texts. They swapped books in order to work around the restrictive GDR publishing system. Some made typewriter copies of rare science fiction works, including the occasional western author. Member Erik Simon translated new Soviet science fiction titles into

13   Interestingly, the Kulturbund saw the formation of what it termed "Freundeskreise" as a new way of increasing contact between author and reader. In a manner such groups were to continue the work of the Bitterfeld Path. A 1969 report from the Kulturbund outlined this goal as well as the importance of reading clubs to the ideological and aesthetic education the GDR citizen and actively encourage the support of such groups. See "Die Aufgaben unserer Zentralen Kommission Literatur" 17–25.

German, making an alternate science fictional discourse accessible as well. Fans published newsletters, created slides-shows, organized author readings, and sought cautious contact with other GDR science fiction fan clubs through letters and the rare inter-club meeting.[14] By 1972, the SLC counted some 120 members. Many of the next generation of science fiction authors stemmed from these clubs.

Fan members maintained an active interest in international science fiction as well. When possible, they established and maintained contacts with foreign authors and fans. This practice granted them access to discourses on science fiction that ran counter to those in East Germany. There were even a few meetings between not only West and East German science fiction fans and authors but also Polish, Russian, British, and American ones.[15]

In the fall of 1972, the SLC became the victim of denunciation in the Physics Department at the Technical University (TU) in Dresden. It began when the party secretary of the Physics department demanded the exmatriculation of club member Rolf Krohn, perhaps due to his habit of asking too many "uncomfortable" questions (Simon, "Blütezeit" 46). This accusation, however, led to the further investigation of Krohn's activities, which included his science fiction stories and his activities as a member of the SLC. At the time, an inner circle of club members possessed some western science fiction works in the

14   The fan club regularly put on public presentations. In an interview, member Erik Simon mentioned that one slide show on the Terraces of Baalbek, by science fiction author Günther Krupkat in the early seventies, packed the room. Another presentation on topics surrounding Erik van Daniken's books drew over two hundred people (Simon, personal interview 1997 and Both, Neumann, Scheffler 45).

15   West German fans attending the Berlin Convention of the Science Fiction Club Deutschlands (SFCD) in 1967 crossed to East Berlin to meet with fans and several authors. Members established contact with a number of East German authors, including Gerhard Branstner and Karl-Heinz Tuschel, as well as Polish author Stanislaw Lem and Russian authors Ivan Efremov and Boris and Arkady Strugatsky among others. A group of fans and authors traveled spontaneously, without a visa, to the 1973 Eurocon III in Poznan, Poland, where English science fiction author Brian Aldiss and American Mark Brandis spoke. At this conference, one fan met with West German author Herbert Franke as well as some West German fans (Both, Neumann, and Scheffler, *Berichte* 110).

club library available only to trusted members. Interestingly, at first, this activity was not the basis for further charges. Rather, the TU discovered cause in Krohn's writings, finding "anti-socialist tendencies" in them. Erik Simon today asserts that none of the stories intended to criticize socialism, "not even its strange manifestation in the GDR." (46). University officials described Krohn's behavior as a "destructive, politically-provocative, and hostile occurrence and action in numerous instances" (49). In 1973, the university expelled Krohn and barred him from study at any institution of higher education in East Germany, greatly limiting his employment chances. Due to the possession of western science fiction, the club's founding member, Ralf Krämer, was said to have led its members to serious political-ideological mistakes (Both, Neumann and Scheffler, *Berichte* 48). Consequently, he was expelled from the TU only.

The so-called Lem Club Affair led the Kulturbund's Central Committee on Literature to call a meeting in Berlin in 1973. It invited acknowledged GDR science fiction experts and relevant authorities.[16] At issue was the viability of science fiction as a form of socialist literature, its pedagogical function as entertainment literature and the nature of its reception. The fact that two central members of the premier science fiction fan club had been "led astray" by an interest in this very genre merited investigation. A decision had to be made as to how the Kulturbund should proceed with other science fiction fan clubs in the future.

Discussion focused on the formulation of a unified national policy on East German science fiction in order to prevent future

---

16   Participants included Adolf Sckerl, a reviewer, who was working on a dissertation on GDR science fiction at the Humboldt University. Also in attendance were Ekkehard Redlin of the Verlag Das Neue Berlin and member of the Committee on Utopian Literature, and science fiction author Günter Krupkat, who was head of the newly founded Committee on Utopian Literature in the German Writers' Union. According to the protocol, author Eberhardt del'Antonio had not yet arrived, but was supposedly coming. Also listed are Helmut Fickelscherer, an editor at Verlag Neues Leben and the publisher Dr. Koppen. Mrs. Zschocke came as a representative from the Ministry of Culture who was responsible for "this area of literature" ("Stenographische Niederschrift eines Gesprächs" 2).

confusion as to generic definition, purpose and label. As the Kultur-bund was not a literary institution, but rather orchestrated cultural assemblies and other group activities, its greatest concern remained the "ideological and moral" health of the club members. Although the participants raised the question of realism in science fiction, the meeting primarily addressed the pedagogical use of science fiction and its reception.

Fan Bernd Hutschenreuther remembered the meeting:

> Contemporary social science viewed science fiction as a competitor, as a reactionary bourgeois theory about the future, and, consequently, fought it. That culminated in the pronouncement that all utopias since Marx and Engels were reactionary. In the end, utopia finally exhibited practical influence. ("Das Leben" 55).

The term "science fiction" in this context specified western texts. However, GDR science fiction still represented a threat as a type of utopian literature to hard-liners, who held to a strict interpretation of Engels' prohibition of utopia. Several participants, who remained un-named in the protocol, still considered science fiction to be *Trivial-literatur*.

Of primary importance was the meeting's distinction between socialist science fiction as a broadly understood generic category ideologically opposed to what Ekkehard Redlin and Adolf Sckerl termed "imperialistic SF-mass literature." Rather than recap its liter-ary or prognostic qualities, they now presented a policy designed to influence reader reception. Both praised the ability of socialist science fiction as a literary form to lead the reader to reflect upon its playful future suggestions. In this manner, the act of reading science fiction stimulated thought processes.

In the meeting protocol, Redlin refers again to the term *Gedank-enspiel*, a term, which was commonly used among fans as well.[17] He praises the productive qualities of this cognitive form of play as a type of relaxation. Western *Trivialliteratur*, on the contrary, contained only

---

17   In several discussions with Andymon fan club members while conducting research in Berlin in 1998 and 1999, the quality of a puzzle or thought game posed in science fiction was mentioned as part of the enjoyment of reading.

dangerous "mesmerizing and escapist" qualities. Redlin's definition secured the position of science fiction within the Kulturbund as a legitimate form of socialist literature and art. It was one, which must be taken seriously and incorporated into its "literary propaganda." ("Stenographische Niederschrift eines Gesprächs" 104a).

Redlin's comments reflect the general resolution of the meeting and science fiction's subsequent consideration as socialist literature. As not only members of the Kulturbund were present at this meeting, but also representatives of the Ministry of Culture and the German Writers' Union, the results affected policy regarding the genre nationwide. Under Honecker's new plan, science fiction had finally become an official part of the new socialist literature rather than merely a prognostic tool of science.

The immediate impact of this change in cultural policy is visible in the Kulturbund's restructuring of its science fiction fan clubs. New consumerist policies stressed the creation of a greater variety of literary offerings, while focusing on educative control at the level of consumption. In spite of past prejudices against science fiction, the genre did not receive the blame for the events of the Lem Club Affair. Conference participants held the Kulturbund responsible for Krohn's and Krämer's actions on account of insufficient supervision and instruction of the groups under its jurisdiction. At the meeting, Adolf Sckerl believed that, because "the development in Dresden had a highly negative effect on consumption," the other clubs must become "more diligent" ("Stenographische Niederschrift eines Gesprächs" 65). He emphasized that it was not the literature itself that posed a threat, but the subjective manner in which it was read. Sckerl placed responsibility on the individual reader (120). This interpretation opened the door to expanded publication opportunities for the genre with ideological control placed at the level of reader reception.

The Kulturbund actively incorporated socialist science fiction into its literary propaganda. Kulturbund representatives gleaned club libraries of any illegal western science fiction. A Kulturbund adviser played a greater role in club participation and instruction. Newly reorganized fan clubs read and discussed selected western novels in order to counteract any "incorrect" interpretations of such novels that might have occurred in the past. The Kulturbund's eventual goal was to transform the SLC into a socialist club of "Gegenwartsliteratur" or literature of the present. Science fiction would be only one of the genres read, thus mediating any adverse effects of one genre on the reader (Simon, "Blütezeit" 51). The Kulturbund's efforts at club reorganization led to the subsequent voluntary dissolution of most of them.

In 1978, the Kulturbund held a *Konferenz zur Unterhaltungkunst* (Conference on Entertainment Art). This meeting reiterated earlier observations that literature played an important role in the development and health of the GDR citizen. It substantiated Honecker's goal of improving the availability and variety of cultural activities in the GDR that had been successful and called for further support and expansion (Hanke 19).

In that same year, a number of individuals assembled with the intent of creating a working group dedicated to science fiction under the auspices of the Kulturbund.[18] In the protocol of this meeting, Sckerl outlined the importance of rethinking existing policy. In his opinion, current literary and cultural debates failed to address the rapid expansion in science fiction offerings. "More often science fiction (*Wissenschaftliche Phantastik*) was discussed to a large extent in the private sphere and was also written and exchanged by enthusiasts" (Haines 2). Consequently, the discussants concluded that science fiction possesses a unique ability to bring readers together to discuss contemporary issues and problems. It was up to the Kulturbund to guide these conversations by recommending socialist reading strategies. Since it was increasingly difficult to dam up the seepage of illegal, international science fiction into East Germany, the reader needed to be educated as to the nature and variety of the expanded product selection. It was decided that neither the clubs should be disbanded nor should socialist science fiction be banned, as both forms represented a valuable means of contacting and influencing young

18   Attendees included literary scholars and party officials. Representatives from the field of science fiction included Adolf Sckerl, then a member of the Kulturbund's Central Committee on Literature, Erik Simon, writer and editor, and Wolfgang Both. The latter individual was a former member of the Illmenau club Phantopia that had been organized in connection with the Free German Youth.

readers. Representatives were to redouble their efforts to lead science fiction reception in a Marxist–Leninist direction and noted that western literature should be read with increased "political diligence" (Haines 3). In reality, no new science fiction clubs formed until the mid-eighties.

While the Kulturbund revised its policy concerning science fiction, space was also made for the genre in the German Writers' Union. In 1973, the *Arbeitskreis Utopische Literatur* (Committee on Utopian Literature) came into being. Günter Krupkat headed this subsection, which was to develop and support socialist science fiction. In Krupkat's opinion, the formation of this circle was necessary not only due to the new interest that established writers of other genres were taking in science fiction, but also to mentor a new generation of science fiction writers.

> It is the task of the Workgroup on 'Utopian Literature' in the GDR Writers' Union to remove prejudice and to cultivate action. [...] And literary science begins to deal more seriously with this genre. Authors, who were active only in other areas – also natural scientists – are now turning to the topics of science fiction (wissenschaftlich-phantastischen)." ("Beitrag" 205)

Indeed the presence of this subsection within the Writers' Union signaled that science fiction was to be taken more seriously as a form of literature. On behalf of the Writers' Union, Adolf Sckerl and Heinz Entner wrote the following justification for the change in policy:

> The creative vigor of the spirit is excited by the game of literary fantasy in new ways through the invention of bizarrely coloful and surprisingly alien pictures and artistic worlds. [...] In the process, science fiction lifts itself above other types of entertainment literature. ("Zu Entwicklungsstand" 20).

In the end, the discourse present in this organization was greatly limited to the specific benefit of science fiction to the furthering of socialism in Marxist–Leninist terms. The continual focus on this topic precluded the inclusion of other activities or methods. Constant disagreement among participating authors led to a stagnation of group discussion. Authors Angela and Karlheinz Steinmüller comment that the biannual meetings of the *Arbeitskreis Utopische Literatur* often became quite heated due to growing conflict between "ideological constraints" and "a growing self awareness among authors" (*Vorgriff* 165). Although science fiction authors requested the formation of the circle in order to gain official recognition for the genre, Alexander Kröger characterized its function more as a bureaucratic structure necessary for the approval of travel visas to international science fiction conventions. He also found that the meetings of this committee had little effect on the development of science fiction as a whole.[19] Furthermore, the presentations and discussions that took place in this circle were accessible only to its members. Therefore, in broader science fiction circles, particularly among a growing and highly engaged fandom, this group had a limited effect (Simon and Spittel, "Science Fiction" 25). In fact, many science fiction writers did not fully embrace this official forum and preferred to remain in their more private science fiction niche.

Science Fiction as Niche

As Habermas points out in his study of the public sphere, Marx intended to expose and end the "false consciousness" of the classed civil society through the politicization of that society. This was to be accomplished through the collapsing of the different categories of mental and manual labor, of public and private life and the implementation of a direct mono-organizational democracy (Habermas 128–129). The increased politicization of the public and of the private in East Germany, particularly through the efforts of Mielke and his infamous *Stasi*, led to a schizoid effect in the interaction between

19   Alexander Kröger mentioned this reason in an interview in Cottbus in 1999. Kröger also stated that there was no connection between the creation of this group and the Lem Club case. See also Arbeitsgemeinschaft Utopische Literatur "Aufgaben und Möglichkeiten" 2: "This work group tries, inspite of many vehement quarrels, to preserve international contacts (Teilnahme am V. Eurocon in Brussels, World–SF u.a.)."

individuals since all private action necessarily carried greater public implications. The subsequent formation of "niches" counteracted the state's efforts to this end, creating a trusted sub-community of private individuals organized around a particular interest. What became known as the *Niche-Gesellschaft* was also supported officially beginning in the seventies as a way to dispel some of the growing dissent among the various sections of the population.

Many science fiction fans and writers belonged to a niche determined in part by cultural and political prejudice. While such niches also existed in the West, they had greater social-political connotations in East Germany. This is apparent in a recent description of the advantages of belonging to the science fiction niche by authors Johanna and Günter Braun. In their article "De Mortuis Nil Nisi Bene," the Brauns emphasize that the term "science fiction ghetto" had a very different meaning in the East. They stress that those authors, who chose to stop writing more mainstream literature and join the science fiction community, did so because they could write more freely inside that circle than outside. According to the Brauns, such authors regarded the label *Trivialliteratur* with humor and irony due to the greater narrative freedom it gave them (26). This emphasis on the greater room for maneuver within the science fiction niche echoes statements made by Ekkehard Redlin and Erik Simon, former editors at the *Verlag das Neue Berlin*. They maintained that cultural policy-makers paid less attention to science fiction in general due to its status as entertainment literature (Personal interviews, 1999).

In the 1970s and 1980s, many authors of the science fiction niche gained a much broader readership than those of their devoted fans. To East Germans, who lived in a *Literaturstaat*, literature played not only a cultural but also a political role. The highly regulated media establishment was incapable of discussing topics, which dissident East German authors could address indirectly through metaphor, or subtle allusion. Both authors and readers functioned as "culturally activated subjects," writing and reading texts, which were "culturally activated subjects" as well (Bennett and Woollacott 64).

However, the give and take between country and citizen, which is characteristic of a civil society, was not present in the GDR. The implementation of a totalizing discourse based on Marxism–Leninism treated the culturally activated subject as the object of cultural policy. Consequently, East Germans developed what Danielle Dahn has termed methods of "interior dissent" (*Westwärts* 201). Such practices also appeared in the science fiction texts in the form of established codes, which the "cultural knowing reader" of the fan club could easily interpret. The "average reader" could also derive the "pleasure of culture and knowledge" by recognizing references, particularly to forbidden topics (Bennett and Wollacott 79). Erik Simon, a former science fiction fan club member who remains active in the scene today, attests that censorship only led to a "sharpening of the senses" on the part of the reader. Finding themselves on the same "plane of understanding," the reader and author of science fiction developed an atypically close relationship, which often took place between the lines (Simon, *Grenzfälle* 13). At readings, East German science fiction authors could expect a large part of their audience to be familiar with most of their works (Klotz and Matzer, 106 and Stein-müller, *Vorgriff* 11).

Where the science fiction niche had enabled writers early on to encode a message for the knowing reader or fan to expect and dis-cover, this practice now spilled over into the mainstream. Author Günter Braun attributed the popularity of science fiction in the seven-ties and eighties precisely to the practice of "reading between the lines."

> People, who never had touched a science fiction book before, much less opened one, did not care about ghetto walls. They bought short stories and novels, which ostensibly took place on distant worlds, as narratives about the immediate GDR present The restricted portrayal of the truth led the SF-ghetto to become a place with almost boundless freedom. ("De Mortuis" 33)

My discussions with the science fiction fans of the Andymon club of Berlin substantiate these observations. Several members remembered that part of the fun of reading science fiction during this period, was in playing detective to discover all of the references to East German society.

Heightened reader interest in science fiction can also be attribu-ted to the high visibility of Soviet space exploration in the GDR in the seventies and eighties. At the height of deténte in 1975, the docking of the American Apollo space capsule by John Glenn with its Soviet counterpart Soyuz attracted mass interest. SED officials interpreted it as the continued efforts of the Soviet Bloc to work for peace not only in space, but also on Earth (Kaiser and Welck 404). By far one of the most important events for East Germany was the joint USSR–GDR mission Soyuz 31 in August 1978 when Sigmund Jähn became the first East German in space.[20] While East Germany experienced increasing economic hardship, officials attempted to create a new sense of national pride through the participation of an East German cosmonaut in a Soviet space mission. Sigmund Jähn's trip into space was greatly advertised and popularized in children's literature and programming as well as in the regular media. The well-known children's TV program "Das Sandmännchen" created its own cartoon space dock before cutting to a live shot of Sigmund Jähn on Soyuz 31. There, he symbolically introduced a stuffed *Sandmann* to his Soviet counterpart, a tiny, female bear named Misha.[21]

Because science fiction boomed in the 1970s and 1980s the genre remained ideologically suspect and its authors and devoted readers politically and culturally marginalized. Furthermore, when several authors of "high" literature turned to writing science fiction in the early 1970s, they did not necessarily embrace the science fiction community. For instance, the publication of Christa Wolf's "Selbstversuch" ("Self-experiment" 1975) and Franz Fühmann's *Saiäns-Fiktschen* (1985) did not establish these authors as science fiction writers. Rather, the status of "Self-experiment" as science fiction is only cursorily referred to in the critical reception of this short story in both East and West. While Wolf herself does refer to the story's characters as "if one desires – fantastic or futuristic," its generic form represents solely a means to accomplish her exploration of gender

---

20   This fascination continues today on the level of popular culture. In the film *Goodbye Lenin* (2003), the character of Sigmund Jähn plays a small but pivotal role. The song "Wer ist Sigmund Jähn" by Die Prinzen in 1999 also attests to Sigmund Jähn's status as a figure of *Ostalgie*.

21   I would like to thank Ingolf Vonau for pointing out this reference to me.

("Leben oder gelebt werden" 101). To my knowledge she has not written on the subject of science fiction.

Fühmann similarly declared that he never wanted to write science fiction, but was intrigued by the genre's narrative possibilities after reading Johanna and Günther Braun's *Conviva Ludibundus* (1980). He praised the genre's ability to allow him "[...] to overcome an existential paralysis" where he "found, in that unreal world and manner, a way like no other to formulate what tormented him into words" (book jacket). Still, Fühmann took great pains to avoid the science fiction label, of which the phonetic spelling of the title *Saiäns-Fiktschen* is but one indication (5).[22] In my opinion, Fühmann's short story collection certainly falls under the rubric of science fiction, yet to be labeled in this manner at the time threatened Fühmann with the undesirable label of an author of *Trivialliteratur*.[23]

Certainly the genre found support in Honecker's pledge to increase the availability of consumer items and to educate GDR citizens in areas of science and technology. Nevertheless, the presence of the *Staatssicherheitsdienst* (German Secret Police or *Stasi*) or their unofficial informants (*inoffizielle Mitarbeiter*, or IMs) at most fan club meetings coupled with the surveillance of several science fiction authors attests to the state's distrust of a suspect genre that had grown so popular.[24] Ironically, as attention turned towards reader reception and away from strict censorship of science fiction texts, the Stasi surveillance of the genre's authors and fans grew. Through 1990, in-

---

22   Here, it could be argued that Fühmann meant western science fiction when referring to "science fiction." However, by the 1980s it was not uncommon for the term science fiction, which officially designated the bourgeois form of the genre, to refer to East German publications as well.

23   It is interesting to note that Franz Fühmann's short story collection *Saiäns-Fiktschen* is listed at number fifty-seven on a rating of the top of the Andymon fan club's list of East German science fiction stories of all time. Christa Wolf did not make either list.

24   The *Stasi* created a file not only for every author who published in the GDR, but also for every book published there (Kruschel "Zwischen" 157). See also "Stasi Akten? – phantastische Literatur?" by Johanna and Günter Braun. In addition, several science fiction authors spied on other science fiction authors. This information was provided me in an interview with Johanna and Günter Braun, as well as in a letter from Siegfried Breuer.

formants were among the members of various fan clubs, including the Andymon fan club in Berlin.[25]

The Stasi also watched several science fiction authors closely. Due to his knowledge of the location and quantity of East Germany's natural gas reserves in coordination with his primary profession both Alexander Kröger and his wife, Susanna Routschek, came under Stasi scrutiny. Their contacts in West Germany and his science fiction publications provided further reason for this surveillance.[26] The Stasi targeted Johanna and Günter Braun, particularly after 1980, when their banned work began appearing in the West without a GDR publishing license. This intrusive observation functioned as a form of intimidation, in the hopes of halting the Brauns from smuggling their manuscripts to the West (Johanna and Günter Braun, Personal interview 1999). The next chapter takes an in-depth look at their novel *Unheimliche Erscheinungsformen auf Omega XI* (Uncanny Manifestations on Omega XI).

25   A former Stasi informant and member of the GDR science fiction community affirmed that a number of fan clubs, including Andymon, had members, who were also Stasi informants. This information was provided to me in an interview with the former IM, whose name I choose not to reveal as this knowledge would add nothing to subject at hand.

26   Kröger has published his rather lengthy Stasi file as a book, which offers a unique look into the life of the most prolific GDR science fiction writer (*Sudelfass* 89).

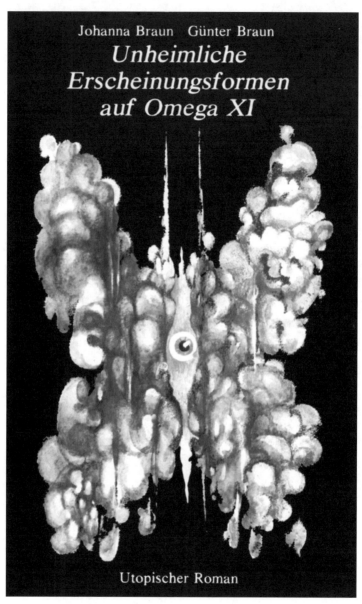

Book cover from Johanna and Günter Braun's
Unheimliche Erscheinungsformen auf Omega XI
(Uncanny Manifestations on Omega XI, 1974)

Chapter Seven
Ambiguous Utopia – Johanna and Günter Braun's *Uncanny Manifestations on Omega XI*

Johanna and Günter Braun developed their own playful and lightly satirical style of science fiction in the seventies and eighties. Originally authors of children's literature, in the sixties they became increasingly interested in German Romanticism, specifically the writings of E.T.A. Hoffmann. The Brauns were intrigued by his use of the fantastic to reveal, what Todorov terms, "ambiguities of meaning." These ambiguities become visible in that moment of uncertainty caused by an encounter with a fantastic element in the act of reading (25–6). An imaginary form, the fantastic allowed the Brauns greater opportunities for expression than did the confines of realism. Experimenting with the fairy tale and fable, they incorporated science fiction's qualities of estrangement, allegory, satire, the uncanny, and the grotesque to warn of structural and environmental dangers present in the contemporary development of the GDR and of industrial societies in general.

This chapter focuses on their novel *Unheimliche Erscheinungsformen auf Omega XI* (Uncanny Manifestations on Omega XI or Omega XI, 1974) as representative of the new style of GDR science fiction. It discusses the influence of German Romanticism on the novel, primarily through the Brauns' use of the uncanny. The Brauns used this technique, as well as elements of play and of the game to create a critical space. Therein they not only problematized contemporary representations of the "truth" by East German hegemonic ideology, but also proposed a corrective course of action. Self-described as "good communists" in the seventies, the Brauns made use of this critical space not to subvert the existing system, but to change and improve it, so that it might reach the more perfect future outlined by Marxism–Leninism. An unusually bold critique of the growing environmental dangers in the GDR, *Omega XI* solves this difficulty with a utopian resolution of class and racial conflict. Yet through the use of a narrative frame, the promising utopia on the planet Omega XI becomes an island just out of reach, when placed in the context of the "reality" of the future Earth home. The ever-growing material and ideal gap of real-existing socialism in the GDR had mitigated earlier utopian hopes of an earthly socialist paradise. In this way, the Brauns began to address the problematic of planning and constructing a concrete utopia, which, in the next chapter, Angela and Karlheinz Steinmüller consider to be unattainable.

The Authors

Johanna and Günter Braun, or "the Brauns" as they are affectionately known as by their fans, are often referred to by members of the science fiction niche as the authors of the highest quality East German contributions to this genre. Both are of the same generation as Eberhardt Del Antonio, but are a few years younger. The Brauns experienced World War II in their teenage years. Born in 1929, Johanna Braun was raised in Magdeburg and later worked as a farm hand, saleswoman, typist, secretary, reporter and editor. Günter Braun was born in 1928 in Wismar and grew up in Königsberg (now Kaliningrad, Russia). After a brief time in the military, he completed high school in Stendal and went on to work as a drugstore assistant, then as a reporter and editor of a local newspaper, theater critic, and librarian (Suvin, "Playful" 72; Simon and Spittel, "Science-fiction" 112–113). Professional authors since 1955, the couple have written all of their works together at their former residence of many years in Magdeburg. They now make their home in Schwerin.

The Brauns began their work together by writing fiction for children and young adults. They wrote mostly travel literature and adventure stories along the lines of Daniel Defoe and James Fennimore Cooper with a revolutionary bent (Suvin, "Playful" 119). Early titles include *Einer sagt nein* (Somebody Says No, 1955), *José Zorillas Stier* (The Bull of José Zorilla, 1955), *Tsuko und der Medizinmann*

196

(Tsuko and the Medicine Man, 1956) and *Herren der Pampa* (Lords of the Pampa, 1957). The Brauns first received recognition for their novels *Preussen, Lumpen und Rebellen* (Prussians, Bums and Rebels, 1957), *Mädchen im Dreieck* (Girl in the Triangle, 1961) and *Prisoners* (*Gefangene*, 1958). The beginnings of their experiment with satire developed in *Die seltsamen Abenteuer des Brotstudenten Ernst Brav* (The Strange Adventures of Earnest Upright, Poor Student, 1959) and the experimental forms of *Eva und der neue Adam* (Eve and the New Adam, 1961–62), which also was the first of several TV plays. Throughout the sixties, the Brauns began to experiment more and more with humor and satire, formulating their own style and voice. During the seventies, in addition to their science fiction, the Brauns continued to publish other fantasy, including *Bitterfisch* in 1974, as well as a book on love, *Fünf Säulen des Eheglücks* (Five Pillars of Married Bliss, 1976).

By the late sixties, they began experimenting with science fiction themes. The short story *Ein objektiver Engel* (An Objective Angel, 1967) focused on issues of technology and humanity, and the anthology *Die Nase des Neandertalers* (The Neanderthal's Nose, 1969) contained two science fiction stories. Their first science fiction novel came in 1972 with *Der Irrtum des Grossen Zauberers* (The Great Magician's Error).[1] A mixture of science fiction and fable, this complex satire of colonialism and technocracy also poked oblique fun at East German bureaucratic authority. Their second science fiction novel, *Uncanny Manifestations on Omega XI*, followed two years later. This novel is a true science fiction novel as opposed to the science fiction/fairy tale *The Great Magician's Error. Omega XI* was also the more popular of the two among readers.[2] A third, *Conviva ludibundus* (1978) further developed the Brauns' notion of playfulness

---

1 Here I have adopted Darko Suvin's translation of this title, see "Playful" 73. I also adopted his translations of the Brauns' publications in the fifties and sixties.

2 This observation is based on my discussions with a number of East German science fiction fans as well as former editor and author Erik Simon (Personal interview, 1997). The Brauns were never as popular as the Steinmüllers, del'Antonio or Alexander Kröger as their works were less accessible to a more general readership.

to absurd abstraction as the name indicates. In addition, a collection of short stories published earlier in the periodical *Magazin* appeared in 1975 under the name *The Mistake Factor (Der Fehlfaktor)*.

Johanna and Günter Braun were the only science fiction authors to have their works banned in East Germany. This action resulted from their decision to no longer write within the bounds of *Parteilichkeit*. Since the Prague Spring, the Brauns had begun to question their communist convictions. Wolf Biermann's expulsion in 1976 contributed to their growing disillusionment with party policy. In a personal interview with the authors in 1999, they remarked that East Germany's membership in the Warsaw Pact contradicted the SED's promise of a peaceful, international revolution. Their displeasure only heightened when NATO placed nuclear weapons on West German soil in 1979 in response to the installation of medium-range nuclear missiles by the Soviet Union. In 1979, the Brauns simultaneously left and were asked to leave the German Writers' Union. Subsequently, they became more active in the peace movement, and continued to voice their concerns through their science fiction. At first they were allowed to publish by East German authorities, but only in the West. For instance, *Der Utofant* (The Utofant) was licensed by *Verlag Das Neue Berli*n in 1981 and then sold to Suhrkamp. Suhrkamp also picked up their earlier works as well, including *Uncanny Manifestations on Omega XI* in 1981 and *The Great Magician's Error* in 1982.

The Brauns soon ceased to write within socialism and became ever more critical of the path that the Soviet Bloc was taking to a communist future. Consequently, the East German licensing bureau ceased to approve any new publications of their books in the East or in the West. However, the Brauns soon drew the attention of the authorities, the secret police in particular, when their books began appearing in the West in the Suhrkamp series "phantastische Bibliothek." The Brauns explain with some amusement that the authorities never figured out how they were smuggling the manuscripts out of the country. Due to the Christmas rush, not every package could be as carefully sorted and examined as usual. It was at this time that the Brauns would disguise their manuscripts to look like a book, wrap them with other books and address the packages to a secretary at Suhrkamp, noting "b. [c/o] Suhrkamp" underneath her name. None of these packages was ever confiscated or returned (Personal interview, 1999).

Both *Das Kugeltranszendentale Vorhaben* (The Plan of the Transcendental Sphere, 1983) and *Der x-mal vervielfachte Held* (The Hero Who Was Reproduced X Times, 1985), among others, appeared in this manner. *The Plan of the Transcendental Sphere* comments on the integral connection between authority and language and is set in a society that suffers from language conformism. *The Hero Who Was Reproduced X Times* includes a short story of the same name, in which the Big Unknown State (*Grosses Unbekanntes Staatswesen* or GUS) sinks into the ocean. With hindsight, the acronym GUS becomes even more ironic as it is also the same abbreviation as the German acronym for the Confederation of Independent States or CIS (*Gemeinschaft Unabhängiger Staaten* or GUS). While this science fiction would make an interesting study in itself, I have chosen to analyze a text, which was publishable and readable in East Germany.

The Uncanny as Critical Space

By 1974, GDR science fiction had established its own clichés, in what Jameson has referred to as a generic contract with the reader (Jameson, *Political* 106). Elements such as the spaceship, distress call, and existence of life on another planet present in *Omega XI* ceased to play a fantastic role and rather functioned as generic conventions. They were in a sense "heimlich" elements of the story set in a not-too-alien Earth future where space travel is a commonplace event. Such recognizable plot developments signal the comfortable and the known in a genre that is often riddled with the estranged, the unknown and the ambiguous. These familiar elements allow the focal point of the story to be placed on the uncanny manifestations. In the fantastic story, the new and as yet unexplained elements then confront the reader as the strange and the different. What is still absent to the reader is made present in the text. What is known is re-presented (presented again) in a way, which is understandable, yet different enough from previous knowledge or generic expectations to cause reflection. In this way what appears strange can lead a reader to draw upon and examine known experience in her own reality to understand the other fictitious reality.

As mentioned in the introduction, Johanna and Günter Braun understand their science fiction to be a type of fantastic story in the tradition and experience of E.T.A. Hoffmann. In the western science fiction journal *Quarber Merkur*, they published an article on E.T.A. Hoffmann's use of the fantastic in his story "Meister Floh" to disguise a critique of the Prussian justice system under Friedrich Wilhelm III. In the article, the Braun's attribute the success and the function of Hoffmann's works to their ability to "mask his misleading of the censors, function as the executor of equalizing justice, represent a utopian signal for the final triumph of good, aid in the escape from a dreary routine, act as a playful-aesthetic stimulant; if possible all of these at the same time" ("E.T.A. Hoffmanns Gespenster" 1). The Brauns envisioned their own purpose in a similar manner and, to a greater or lesser extent, incorporated all of these qualities in their work.

On the surface, *Omega XI* contains a critique of the West. Representatives from a future, highly advanced, socialist Earth answer the distress call from what turns out to be the "oppressor" class on the distant planet of Omega XI. In detective novel style, the two cosmonauts, Merkur and Elektra, discover the existence of a class system and free the oppressed, resulting in the building of a democratic socialist utopia. However, as Olaf Spittel, a former editor at Verlag Das Neue Berlin, commented, the GDR science fiction author often hid a critique of socialism in a critique of capitalism. Spittel described this as "thrashing the class enemy and meaning the class friend" ("Afterward" 468). By setting *Omega XI* in a class society of a future time and place, the Brauns were able to disguise their critique of the GDR giving them the ability to propose a reality alternate to the proclaimed existence of "real existing socialism."

The title of the book, *Uncanny Manifestations on Omega XI*, makes reference to Hoffmann's use of the uncanny to create a figure that is similar but at the same time strangely different. The uncanny may be a figure or a situation, which provides some new truth about the original in its existence as double. In a now classic reading of

Hoffmann's *Sandmann*, Freud describes the uncanny or "unheimlich" as something frightening or unfamiliar, which has in fact been repressed in the unconscious. Through an uncanny experience the repressed is brought out into the light, as a return to the familiar or home or "heimlich" (Freud 24). In this respect, the Brauns created a story that was indeed uncanny in its similarity to the GDR and a divided Germany, and through this doubling made truths visible that were otherwise precluded from a seemingly monosemic public discourse.

There are several uses of the word uncanny in *Omega XI*. The first refers to the Lumen (the group that sent the distress call) and their representative Valentin Fuks (also known as Sunflower). They are descendants of a community of humans, who were forced to leave Earth at an unspecified time in the past, as they wished to conduct experiments in genetic engineering. The first-person narrator and hero, Merkur Erdeson, connects the Lumen with what he terms the "mistakes of our forefathers." In his memoirs, Merkur describes how his encounter with the uncanny Lumen brought back the repressed memory of what occurred during humanity's "bleak past" (8). Just which forefathers he is referring to and what went on in the "bleak past" is never specified, but within the GDR context a distinct parallel can be drawn between the Lumen and Nazi Germany. On the whole, GDR science fiction portrayed genetic engineering as a capitalist/ fascist activity used for the enslavement of its products. Here the Brauns remain within the paradigm of GDR socialist discourse by linking the Lumen to fascism. However, Merkur, a citizen of the future socialist Earth, also identifies the Lumen as uncanny, recalling a darker human quality long thought to be eradicated from the more "perfect" future Earth. Thus, the Lumen do not just fill the role of oppressor, representing the strange or alien West, but are also familiar, acting as a reminder that this tendency is a recurring German or human one, and is possible in a socialist society.

In addition, rather than follow the SED's explanation of fascism as the product of irrational forces with its seeds in German Romanticism, the Brauns participated in a growing questioning of the legacy of the Enlightenment in the GDR of the early 1970s. The name, Lumen, appropriate for a people who glow in the dark, and their prominent use of the sunflower symbol point to their tie to Enlighten-

201

ment values. The novel portrays such values as having run amok with time, failing to overcome the class system, and leading to consumerism and environmental damage. The Lumen themselves are decadent figures, who have grown grotesquely fat and slothful from a lack of work. Their exclusive focus on reason and scientific expertise proves to be their downfall. By emulating the German Romantic movement's critique of the Enlightenment, the Brauns simultaneously question the success of their own government's self-proclaimed continuity with this very tradition, and believe they too have run astray of the initial goal of building a democratic-socialist republic.

The second uncanny encounter occurs with the discovery of the results of the Lumen's experiments, which have created a biological class structure. Two genetically engineered races resulted: the intelligent Prudenten, a race of scientists, and the robot-like Roburen, brawny homunculi, who die if they do not constantly work. The Lumen on Omega XI suffer from what they call the *Modderwind*, a cyclical storm that threatens to wipe out all life on the planet. A parody not only of Honecker's consumerist policies, but also of broader global implication, this "mud wind" is a result of environmental damage caused by a system put into place by the Lumen to meet their material needs. The system spins out of control as the Roburen overproduce out of biological necessity, replacing luxurious houses only hours after they are constructed. As a result, the mud wind blows down from the mountains of garbage slowly taking over the planet.

In their distress call, the Lumen refer to dangerous, uncanny manifestations on their planet, which Merkur and Elektra first determine to be the Prudenten and Roburen. To the Lumen, these beings are uncanny in that they created them, literally as their intelligent and laboring alter egos. Rather than representing their irrational or evil twin, as is so often the case in Hoffmann, the Lumen's previously "unified" existence has been split into three pieces. Without their other "thirds" they cannot survive. This is evident in the physical degradation they experience without thought or labor. Reminiscent of the Eloi and the Morlocks in Wells' *The Time Machine*, the Lumen have become naïve, helpless bureaucrats, slowly being consumed by the mud wind brought on by the Prudenten and the Roburen. What had been a population of 57,000 has dwindled to 57 due to excessive environmental damage (84). However, a comparison with the uncanny ends there, as the Roburen and Prudenten are, with one great exception, not dependent upon the Lumen. Occupiers of the industrial center of the planet, they are merely waiting for the Lumen to leave so that the latter two groups can live on the planet in peace. In a role reversal, the Prudenten and Roburen also call the Lumen the uncanny manifestations on Omega XI, questioning their legitimacy on the planet as non-contributing members of society. In effect, through genetic engineering, the Lumen have made themselves obsolete. They are the creators of the Prudenten and Roburen and are intimately connected to them. Yet the Lumen represent a path, which the Prudenten and Roburen do not want to repeat.

The Brauns present development on Omega XI in a way, which also alluded to the contemporary situation in East and West Germany. Its narrative re-presents the German post-war existence in terms of an alien situation on another planet. A glass wall that was built by the "workers" separates the Lumen from the Roburen and Prudenten. On one side of the wall are the grotesque figures of the Lumen. On the other side are the workers, whose main market is the Lumen. The Prudenten are enslaved by the Lumen, who have genetically designed their laborers to require a daily ingestion of vitamin P. The Lumen control the production of the algae in which this nutrient is found.[3] As much as the two sides dislike each other, they are essentially co-dependent. In the end, it takes an outsider, Merkur, to break through the glass wall and bring everyone back together. Then through mutual cooperation of all three races, the environmental problems cease and the promise of a paradise develops.

However critical of the GDR, *Omega XI* cannot be seen as a rejection of socialism, but rather as a contribution to a literary and political discourse on how to improve it and the situation of Germany. According to Freud, the uncanny must refer to past experience, as it often does in fantasy. Although the fairy tale expresses the familiar/ home in its use of "once upon a time" and other generic qualities, Jack

---

3   The Italian names of the Roburen increase the ambiguity of the text through their allusion to the increasing number of guest workers in West Germany in the seventies.

Zipes argues that it also can provide an uncanny experience in which "the real return home or recurrence of the uncanny is a move forward to what has been repressed and never fulfilled" (*Fairy Tales* 176). He reinterprets Freud through Ernst Bloch's emphasis on the importance of fantasy in the formulation of future goals and utopia. Bloch writes of fantasy: "If it becomes a dreaming ahead, then its cause appears quite differently and excitingly alive. The dim and weakening features, which may be characteristic of mere yearning, disappear; and then yearning can show what it really is able to accomplish" (quoted in Zipes, *Fairy Tales* 175.) Zipes writes that it is this dream through which society can be changed and a future home created. The uncanny experience like the dream can work in the same manner. Thus the uncanny works not only through that which is repressed in the past, but also can reveal what has not yet been fulfilled.

Science fiction has traditionally been a literature that expresses future visions and dreams. For this reason Zipes' analysis of the uncanny in the fairy tale equally applies to its presence in science fiction. While the Brauns are critiquing "real-existing socialism," they do not fail to provide a vision of what they wish this socialism to become. In the final chapter, they describe the hope of the new civilization on Omega XI, one in which all three classes work together for their common survival. The happy end on the planet Omega XI is filled with hope for a new civilization of peaceful coexistence, this time along the democratic socialist model, which Earth representatives Merkur and Elektra provide. Here the Brauns are "dreaming ahead" to their vision of a future GDR. Yet, as I will show in a moment, this dream was also mitigated by the frame, which surrounded it.

Ambiguous Utopia

As demonstrated in the preceding chapter, the science fiction of the fifties and sixties operated on a historical materialist timeline leading to a Marxist–Leninist utopia. This positive portrayal of utopia remained for the most part a static notion heavily shaped by the hegemonic ideology outlined by the SED. Although *Omega XI* portrays utopia as possible, it also ultimately depicts an ambiguous representation of the realizability of this same utopia. The hope present at the beginning on *Omega XI* is contrasted by the less dynamic results on a future Earth. Often labeled as a novel of warning (Kruschel, *Spielwelten* 104–111), *Omega XI*'s ambiguity places the assuredness of the SED success into question. In this manner, it stands out among the majority of science fiction published previously.

For instance, one element, which differentiates Omega XI from other GDR space adventures of its time, is its narrative frame. The frame is set on Earth in an unspecified future. Up until this point, most authors avoided a setting on Earth as it often conflict with the SED's vision of Earth. The world creation rules of a fictional Earth had to comply with the party's proclamation of the future, thus greatly limiting the creative freedom for the author(s). To avoid such restrictions, the Earth frame in *Omega XI* is made up of allusions to a socialist Earth rather than actual descriptions. Only five characters in the novel come from Earth: Merkur, Elektra, Cäsar Brynn, Medea Twin, and Alberna, to whom Merkur only refers. The nature of this future Earth is inferred through the personalities of these characters. The existence of Cäsar Brynn denotes the fatherly authority of a hegemonic ideology. Medea Twin is the party's maternal figure, whose function is to ensure compatibility between crewmembers on long space flights. The heroes, Elektra and Merkur, represent the mythical, socialist family sent out on a space mission. Left behind, Alberna is the foolish one as her name implies and refuses to accept the rules and regulations governing space flight. Through Cäsar and Medea's praise of Elektra, in particular, we learn that the society values her high moral sense, exactness, orderliness, objectivity, rationality and reliability (11). In addition, Elektra is a star athlete, who has won three gold medals from the state, and is in general the perfection of the socialist personality.

By focusing on the personal stories of Elektra and Merkur rather than on the political vision of a future socialist society, the Brauns were able to create a narrative frame that was less than perfect. Merkur and Elektra are, in essence, opposites. As stated, Elektra is the logical, methodical type whose vast knowledge enables her to react quickly and efficiently on Omega XI, once Merkur's inquisitiveness discovers the truth behind the Lumen's story. Merkur on the other hand is selected for the mission, as he is the "Master of Improvisation" (11). His creativity, curiosity and general dislike of authority represents the assets, which Cäsar Brynn values for the success of such a mission. Rather than the strength and perfection of the rational, socialist heroine common to many GDR science fiction novels of the past, the logic and creativity present in Elektra and Merkur, respectively, points to the strength and advantages found in a combination and balance of these two qualities.

While the two do become a couple during and throughout the mission to ensure its success, they are by no means united in their service to Earth (or socialism for that matter). Their relationship is a tumultuous one, leading to a civil parting of ways near the end. Elektra is too strong a female figure for the more traditionally inclined Merkur, whose perception and narration of her character is limited to stereotype and cliché. More importantly, the breakup of their relationship and the subsequent ending of Merkur's relationship with the Prudenten woman, Ludana, marks a deviation from the happy end common to socialist realism. Merkur and Elektra leave the blossoming utopia behind to travel back on uncertain terms together and return to a less-than-perfect Earth. That this is the case is intimated by Merkur's plans for his future. Where Elektra has a plan of progress and success ahead of her within the Earth institutional structures, Merkur remains the outsider. He has no definite plans or future vision for himself. Rather he tells Elektra that he will first go take a bath and then he will continue his old profession as electrical technician. "I mean, we can only develop so far. There will always be something to repair." (248). Merkur possesses the quality of the societal drop out. He is the irrational element that provides a necessary but never easy balance to the rational.

Juxtaposed with the utopia on Omega XI, this statement infers an Earth, which has already developed to its full potential. Rather than the continuous linear development of such a society, what is now necessary is a circling back and reexamination of goals and methods for possible repair. The utopia is no longer easily accessible or guaranteed, but must be corrected just as Merkur and Elektra realign the utopian society that the Lumen had set out to create five generations ago. Where in past GDR science fiction the Earth society presented the teleological model of socialist development, the Brauns choose here to reverse the roles, Omega XI providing the example for changes within Earth society. In doing so, they call for a reassessment of the SED's cult of progress, suggesting that its policies are leading in the wrong direction. In this manner *Omega XI* is not a utopian novel in the classic sense, but rather an ambiguous utopia, examining the viability of attaining utopia from the oblique angle that censorship made necessary.

The application for publication of *Omega XI* stressed its contributions towards the further development of East Germany. In his outside review, Adolf Sckerl praised *Omega XI* with the following: "We must [...] acknowledge the faltering pace of development in the GDR, and we should be happy with every new work that science fiction [die wissenschaftliche Phantastik] helps us to develop further in content and in form." (Rev. of *Unheimliche* 2). Positioning the book in ideological terms of the socialist revolution, he then went on to emphasize its criticism of capitalism's failings, including the "idiotic and superfluous" production and "self-inflicted" environmental damage (2). In addition, he praised the Brauns for their emphasis on the humanity of Merkur and Elektra, a deviation from the "dry, popular scientific, objective, and prognostic style" of the fifties and sixties in which character development took a back seat to science and technology (1). Although he did acknowledge that the book was slightly critical of the contemporary situation in East Germany, he downplayed these aspects. Vaguely citing "[something] opposing formal action, opposing the obstruction of imagination" he explains this critique away as a "justifiable sideswipe, an additional reading pleasure, without any need for further investigation" (5). Yet herein lay central criticisms of East Germany, which contributed to Sckerl's previous point regarding the furthering of the socialist revolution in real terms. Whether he read *Omega XI* in this manner or not, he maintained *Parteilichkeit* in his review. In his opinion, what needed to be changed were the more banal phrases such as "he was sick of that" and "spoon fed something," which the Brauns included to emphasize the cheeky quality of Merkur's narrative (6). From one point of view,

Sckerl is playing precisely what the Brauns term the "false game," a concept, which I now turn to in an analysis of play and the game in *Omega XI.*

Playfulness and the Game

Science fiction itself is often described in terms of play as a "thought game," an experiment following a rational set of rules designed to answer the question: what if? The genre plays with possibilities: possible futures, pasts, places, and times. The very recognition of science fiction as thought game by SED officials in the sixties and seventies granted it increased support for two reasons: 1) the supposed link between the act of reading science fiction and scientific creativity, which was highly valued in a country that held science and technology to be the key to national success; 2) the publication of studies demonstrating the necessity for relaxation among the work force as a method of increasing productivity. Both of these views were cited by the editor of *Uncanny Manifestations on Omega XI*, Ekkehard Redlin, in his support of science fiction publications at the Verlag Das Neue Berlin ("utopische Dimension" 166).

On the whole, the concept of play is central to the writings of Johanna and Günter Braun. Their travel adventures provided a safe space for children to experience and learn in a model reality. This playfulness delineated by the rules of the literary game, presented a reality other than that of the world of the reader. Through the narrative game, certain elements of the "real" are amplified, while others are missing, thus creating the potential for subversion in the construction of a playful fantasy (Abrahams 122). Through the art of reading, the reader plays the game and learns in the process.

It was in their children's literature that the Brauns developed their distinctive narrative voice, which is lightly satirical of contemporary socio-political issues (Suvin, "Playful" 72). In a similar manner, their science fiction also retained this aspect of play. In the sixties, the Brauns were influenced by writers Gerhard Branstner and

Stanislaw Lem, who increasingly incorporated elements of play in their science fiction with circular or timeless adventures often to the point of absurdity.[4] Rather than the linear narrative of successful expeditions, which brought about interstellar communist revolutions, these authors poked fun at the seriousness of such literature, as well as the institutions, which supported it. Similar to their use of the un-canny, the Brauns employed playfulness as a means of repositioning truths in an alternate matrix for social-ethical examination.

Lucie Armitt characterizes the essential nature of fantasy and Todorov's notion of the fantastic as game playing. In her analysis of Carroll's *Alice in Wonderland*, Armitt illustrates how its increasing confusion of the boundaries of space and time leads to the separation of "truth" from "its usual partner, authority." However, rather than signaling a transgression of (and therefore acceptance of) authority through the use of a Bakhtinian analysis of the carnivalesque, Armitt maintains that, through *Alice*, "authority is foregrounded as having only the power with which we choose to endow it" (159). In the game, outside of the existing power structure, truth becomes "self-generating" and "self-legitimating," thus transferring the agency to create truths to the game's participants.

Omega XI itself plays with truth in a search for the nature of truth. Firstly, the narrative structure of the story is that of a detective novel investigated by Merkur Erdeson. Merkur's sole purpose for participating in the mission is his personal curiosity in unraveling the mystery of Omega XI. The cryptic distress call from the Lumens, which cites "uncanny manifestations" as their reason for desperately needing safe passage home to Earth, sets the stage for the rest of the novel as not only a rescue mission, but also the ultimate disclosure of the nature of the strangely described danger. Having discovered the real nature of the society on Omega XI, Merkur teaches the Roburen games, as a method with which they can divert their energy away from production. Elektra and Merkur also plot to liberate the

---

4   Branstner's *Der Sternenkavalier* and Lem's *Star Diaries* are excellent examples. Russian authors Boris and Arkady Strugatsky also experimented with play in the context of the fairy tale and science fiction. The Brauns' *Der Irrtum des grossen Zauberers* did so as well.

Prudenten by stealing an algae plant from the Lumens. This leads to a humorous confrontation with the Lumens at the climax of the book, in which they attempt to kidnap Elektra and Merkur. They do so by following the established rules and procedures of what they reverently call a "napping." To them, it is more important to adhere to aesthetic taste than effectiveness. Comically, Sonnenblume insists on the correct form for their inept actions. He calls for a "napping [...] with a certain cunning and according to the rules of good taste" (230). The failure of the playful, yet very serious, kidnapping and the resultant overturning of the power relations on Omega XI lead to a reassessment of the truths upon which the society is based. All secrets revealed, Elektra and Merkur leave the beginnings of a more egalitarian society behind as they return to Earth.

However, as in the detective novel, the appeal of *Omega XI* is not only the discovery of the truth near the end, but also the pleasure in the process of reaching that point. In the book, two different methods of investigation are embodied in the characters of Elektra and Merkur. The heroine, Elektra, is a rational commander, whose no-nonsense approach has led her to decoration by party authorities and much career success. Merkur, on the other hand, is jaunty, meddlesome and given to drinking, yet inquisitive and playful in his manner and actions. In many ways, Elektra is the party mother to Merkur's rebel son. However, here the *Halbstarke* or *Hippie* retains the upper hand. Merkur relies on his intuition as his guide, and is quick to criticize Elektra's systematic analysis of events as the proper way to attain the truth. He teases her seemingly blind acceptance of bureaucratic procedure, which she perceives to be her moral duty. The novel portrays her efforts to use the journey to Omega XI constructively rather than for relaxation: "You always want to do what is easy for you and fun. But, do something once in a while that is not fun. That would be a real accomplishment." (53). Yet her failure to question a reality outside of that which is presented to her ultimately undermines Elektra's rational method, as she too easily accepts the Lumen's explanation for the uncanny manifestations on their planet. Although her immense knowledge enables the ultimate success of the mission, it is Merkur's skepticism and lust for adventure, which eventually lead to the discovery of the hidden Prudenten and Roburen.

The very juxtaposition of those two characters highlights the ambiguity of accepted or established truths. As William Walker has remarked, it is Merkur's "apparent lack of seriousness" that "derives from his view that all existence is paradoxical, dualistic, dialectical and contradictory" (144). A comedic exchange with Elektra results when she discovers that neither she nor Merkur is registered with the Lumen authorities as guests, and, therefore, do not officially exist. Merkur replies: "Yes, we must exist and also not exist. We must be registered and unregistered, signed out and signed in. That always has to change. Otherwise life is not possible" (*Omega XI* 121). His answer signals the questioning of the very basic of truths, personal existence. In this example, Elektra assumes such existence is tied to objective institutional authority rather than to subjective agency. Yet Merkur's natural disrespect for such power undermines its existence and not his. This very observation serves a similar function to Armitt's analysis of *Alice*. Rather than accepting the power of the authorities to determine a person's being by their recorded existence in a database, Merkur's remark represents a position outside of the apparent dichotomy. Instead of reinforcing this ostensible truth by rebelling against it, he supersedes bureaucratic power by dismissing its importance. In this way, Merkur's playful gestures demonstrate a process of reflecting upon established truths to be learned in the thought game that is *Omega XI*.

This scene thematizes a premise of *Omega XI*: the existence of and life within two separate truths or realities – the truths of the public sphere and of the private sphere. The book addresses this topic in a number of ways. First, it looks at the notion of historical truth, contrasting the official historical narrative of a fictional Earth with the voice of one of the history makers. A transition of information from the private to the public sphere, *Omega XI* itself takes the form of an unauthorized memoir by Merkur Erdeson of his expedition to the planet Omega XI. Much like the function of the uncanny, the premise of the book is one of revealed secrets. Hearing Merkur's somewhat sensationalist claims for the first time it would appear that his intentions in writing his account are rather individualistic and ostentatious. Yet, precisely the opposite is true. Set on a communist future Earth, Merkur complains of the state-produced, "slipshod educational tapes"

211

or the "somewhat decently made encyclopedia cassettes," which emphasize the heroic deeds of the expedition to Omega XI. In part a satire of the static, superhuman, socialist personalities that dominated East German science fiction into the seventies, Merkur's individual "true-to-life" account of his space expedition emphasizes the subject-tive. His account represents a subversion of the state's power as author of historical truth, placing it into question through the suggestion of the existence of another truth or reality. A method to explore the notion of the "real," Merkur's individual voice moves the marginal and the private to the center of this history.

Yet another exploration of the existence of two or more truths or realities lies is Merkur's concept of the *Falschspiel* or "false game." This game refers to the existence of separate truth matrices or rules that define public and private realities. For instance, Merkur acknow-ledges that the state history was written according to the rules of the public sphere. "It will be embarrassing for the encyclopedias to all become concrete, because history, as it really took place, violates good encyclopedic taste" (*Omega XI* 129). Here, taste designates the ideology of those in power, who write the encyclopedic history. The notion of false refers to the necessity of the player to create an alternate or false identity on the public level of the game. Merkur illustrates this when relating his interview with Cäsar Brynn – Pro-fessor with the Bureau for World Security, Department of Historical Insight ("Weltsicherheitsbehörde, Abteilung Historischer Einsicht"). Brynn must approve Merkur's participation in the expedition as "no one may go up into space without historical insight" (Brauns, *Omega XI* 6). At the beginning, Merkur tried to tell Cäsar his personal truth. He wanted to participate in the expedition for adventure's sake and to discover the nature of the uncanny manifestations on the distant planet. After realizing that this would get him grounded, Merkur comments in his memoirs that he then answered in the expected terms and thoughts, recalling his false identity. Merkur "stammered something about morals and world security" and then passed (Brauns, *Omega XI* 7). By playing the false game, Merkur succeeds.

Yet, this is not the only example. In a conversation with his superior officer, Elektra Eulenn, Merkur admits that he manipulated his test scores, changing the rules, in order to come on the mission. As the text represents Merkur's point of view, at first Elektra is portrayed in terms of the ideology of the public sphere, as she is effectively a party member and a stranger to him. A signal that this official relationship transforms into a more intimate one, Merkur broaches the topic of falsified testing to Elektra. Yet ever cognizant of the aspect of "play" present in what Merkur perceived to be the game of public and private, Merkur comments that while he "had told the truth for a little while [about his test scores], believing that it would shock Elektra [...]. It was time, to return to" what he calls the "false game" (Brauns *Omega XI* 28). After having admitted for a time that he was not the skillful hero his scores showed him to be, he again hid behind the official persona, his second, heroic existence in the reality of the public sphere.

I have emphasized this false game in terms of public and private sphere, rather than in terms of hegemonic ideology and marginal ideologies, for reasons of placing it within the context of the GDR. For the most part, interaction in the party-controlled public sphere adhered to the communication codes set out by Marxist–Leninist ideology. The private sphere functioned as an outlet for individual opinions and frustrations, which was tacitly tolerated by officials to a limited degree as a requirement for the maintenance of public order. (A result of this phenomenon was the so-called niche society, which developed in East Germany, particularly in the seventies and eighties.) Indirectly, *Omega XI* describes the interaction of these two spheres in its false game.

Yet another aspect of the false game present in *Omega XI* is the manipulation of the truth surrounding material goods. Rather than the existence of two truths, this rearranging represented the transference of truth through the use of code words. On the alternate Earth of *Omega XI*, radish juice is required on all space missions after its consumption supposedly saved a spaceship in a past crisis. The sheer ludicrousness of the mandatory drinking of a beverage such as radish juice parodies the institution that established such a regulation. At the same time, since this institution is not one to question its methods, many captains have taken to substituting the radish juice with alcohol, a drink not likely to be consumed by the health-conscious socialist personality. In the future Earth reality, this practice has become so widespread that radish juice has become a code word for whisky. An "old boys club" gesture, with which the more staid heroine Elektra is unfamiliar, this substitution of the signified is another strategy of the false game. Once again one of the many cracks and fissures in the existing power structure, it represents the self-generation and self-legitimization of a truth as described by Armitt.

In their future Earth, the Brauns also demonstrate what happens to those who do not play the game or recognize this structural difference between one truth and another. Merkur's ex-girlfriend on Earth, Alberna, continually asks questions, answering one with another. "Why?" is an undesirable response, since it calls the enforced or hegemonic truth and the power that lies behind it into question. Thus Alberna never passes her exams and is unable to go up into space, like 95% of all Earthlings of her time, who have learned to play the false game like Merkur. Her name comes from the German word *albern*, meaning stupid or foolish. The novel thus passes judgment on the ineffectiveness of the outsider, who is excluded from society. In terms of the novel, if change is to occur within the system, the game must be played effectively from the inside. The real societal dropout remains silly and disenfranchised.

Conclusion

Through the end of the seventies, the Brauns continued to play the false game by intertwining a genuine critique of capitalism with one of Marxism–Leninism in its contemporary form. Employing a genre of the fantastic, they created a critical narrative space in which they could more freely address current concerns in East Germany.

Most remarkable in *Omega XI* is the ambiguity of the text present in a genre, which up to the seventies had been dominated primarily by the clear-cut Marxist–Leninist presentation of the future. Rather than a weakness caused by censorship, this ambiguity problematized a much broader issue, which supersedes the historical context of East Germany. Namely, it foregrounded the recognition that notions of the truth and reality are never as clear as they might appear. Rather, it is important to continuously question through such exercises as science fiction's thought game in order to see the "real" more clearly. Those readers who looked for the critical space presented by the Brauns found a satire of bureaucracy, political figures, and day-to-day life, which helped them to comprehend and relativize their own situation. This was indeed one of the goals of the authors. Merkur addresses the reader at one point, advising her to

> never confuse the game with reality. In the game, you are the creator, who controls everything. In reality, you must conform, but through practice, you have become able to see through this reality (Brauns *Omega XI* 19).

The game is the "reading process." However, in a manner similar to E.T.A. Hoffmann, the Brauns hoped to employ this game, in order to circumvent the censor and give the reader an opportunity to see a reality other than that provided by the hegemonic discourse of the SED.

Chapter Eight
Utopian/Dystopian Resurgence
in a Time of Perestroika (1981–1990)

> We relate what will happen in the future. The unexpected intervened in this
> abstract certainty that eliminated the feeling of anticipation. The possibility of
> all possibilities was the other realty (Fühmann, *Saiäns-fiktschen* 86).

Cultural historian Manfred Jäger has described the eighties as a
decade of "chaotic cultural policy without a strategy" (187). Cultural
policy in the late seventies and eighties experienced a series of shifts
in political and ideological thought symptomatic of Honecker's crisis
mentality during the latter years of the Cold War. Beginning in 1985,
Honecker's rigid reaction to Gorbachev's policies of *glasnost* and
perestroika led to the isolation of East Germany from the rest of
the Soviet Bloc. Through a conservative political course, Honecker
attempted to maintain a stronghold GDR within the quaking foundations of the East Bloc. As a result, cultural policy remained "inconsistent" (Emmerich) and reactive in the final years of East Germany.

To some extent this state of affairs is reflected in the haphazard
yet steady rise in science fiction publications that began in the seventies and continued throughout the eighties. The publication rate in
1981 remained that of the previous year with five novels and seven
anthologies. It then dropped to three novels and four anthologies in
1982. Production rose once again to a high of eight novels and seven
anthologies in 1985. It reached a low in 1987 with three novels and
two anthologies and rebounded the following year (Neumann, *Grosse
Illustrierte* 868–872).

Simultaneously, popular literature policies suggested the programmatic importance of science fiction to the SED. After the Conference on Entertainment Art in 1978, Helmut Hanke conducted a
follow-up study on cultural theory for the Kulturbund's Central

Committee. In 1980, he concluded that the continued split between "high" and "low" literature needed to be dismantled.

> The efforts begun in the seventies to orient all cultural life increasingly towards the actual recreational needs of the working man and woman, towards recuperation, relaxation, entertainment, and sociability, must be continued in the eighties and intensified. The persistent appearance of a separation between "high" and "low," educational and entertaining cultural forms must be abolished. high and low the entire cultural life (18).

Hanke's comments exemplify the paradox that existed between the Marxist goal of a single proletarian culture and a call for a greater variety of reading options.

Increasingly, the success of popular literature in West Germany made it clear that East German culture would not supplant it. With an eye to diversifying socialist publications, Hanke's study hoped to stem the internationalization of culture coming from the West, and create a "second culture" as an alternative to western forms (29). He emphasized the necessity of "more fantasy and new forms […] in the mass media and regional cultural life" (20). In particular, Hanke stressed the support of all cultural forms, which increase interest in science and technology.

Hanke's article corresponded with the policy outlined in a report from the office of the Minister of Culture, Kurt Hager, entitled "Zur Entwicklung des Kulturniveaus der Arbeiterklasse" (1980). This communiqué reiterated the importance of increased working class participation in the creation and enjoyment of culture. In a goal that had existed since the inception of the second Bitterfeld Path in 1959, the memo urged the formation of a closer relationship with artists and the working class. It also pointed to the "insufficient level of supplies in numeous cultural facilities, particularly in cultural centers and libraries" (9). Due to a continued paper shortage, the availability of appropriate books in libraries remained paramount to the SED cultural agenda. In response to the growing number of book clubs, the report warned against "the devaluation of cultural and artistic engagement as a worthless 'hobby' or as the 'private enjoyment' of the worker" (9). Accordingly, it was important that the class-conscious reader dedicate her reading to the advancement of communism. Moreover, Hager urged all cultural officials to provide appropriate ideological guidance and direct individual reading habits towards the larger communist project (12).

Hager's statement failed to present creative solutions to contemporary cultural "problems." His affirmation of the creation of a "second culture" betrayed his apparent inability to think beyond the confines of SED ideology. Increasingly, official proclamations concerning science fiction or popular literature merely repeated or expanded upon existing policy and remained incapable of adapting to present tensions.

On June 3, 1989 a very astute and reflective report on the status of popular culture appeared in the GDR. Cultural scholars, Michael Hoffmann, G.K. Lehmann, and H-J. Ketzer, wrote it in preparation for the upcoming Twelfth Party Congress. Clearly, it does not mention East Germany's repressive government as a cause for the conditions described above. Still, Hoffmann, Lehmann, and Ketzer provided a frank analysis of GDR policy within the context of that paradigm.

Only several months before the fall of the Berlin Wall, they found that the internationalization of popular cultural forms, along with the effect of electronic media and economic decline, made the creation of a literature unique to East Germany difficult (11). For a number of years, the study concluded, eastern and western forms had been converging. Although contact between the two created a favorable sense of competition, the centralized structures of a planned system forced those in the GDR to remain two to three years behind international trends.

The authors cite the Congress of Entertainment Art (*Kongreß der Unterhaltungskunst*) of March 1989. This conference came to the conclusion that socialist popular literature failed due to a lack of competition among East German authors and artists (12). In order to improve popular culture, Hoffmann, Lehmann, and Ketzer recommended the adoption of western marketing strategies such as the creation of a profile to differentiate eastern goods from western ones. The report even proposed that East German rock bands should sing in English (14). This suggestion shows how dependent East Germany was on West Germany and other international markets.

Hoffmann, Lehmann, and Ketzer remark further on the dynamic ability of popular culture to respond quickly to social tensions, which then disseminated political opinion and ideology quickly. They refer in particular to the dissidents and other protesters who were slowly causing increased instability in East Germany. Quoting a 1984 report from the Academy of Sciences, they partially attribute this action to the privatization of GDR society that began in the seventies. In their opinion, the construction of "arks" and the formation of "niches" in which to discuss issues that remained taboo in more open fora drove discontent underground. What could not be discussed in television, found its way into literature and art (7). The report also states that it was the privatization of a communal society that led artists to become dissidents (10).

The study further points to the failure of a centrally directed policy on mass culture to respond to the country's social tensions, the role of which a number of artists and writers took over in the 1970s and 1980s. Strict Marxist–Leninist publications and orchestrated television programming and mass cultural events failed to address societal problems and anxieties, which found their outlet in popular literature, among other forms (9). The science fiction niche is one example of the phenomenon described in this study. It offered the opportunity for the articulation of a discourse within socialism, yet less restrained by party language than in other circles.

Alternate Discourses

Initiated in the seventies, the center of meaningful discourse on science fiction shifted location in the eighties. It changed from that of the policy makers, such as the Kulturbund, the Minister of Culture, the Writers' Union and the publishers to three groups: 1) academics, 2) editors and authors, and 3) the fans. Although the power to control science fiction remained securely in the hands of the government, discussion in these latter groups moved beyond the pedagogical function of science fiction within socialism. They documented the history of the genre within the GDR, looked beyond the borders of East Germany to other science fiction traditions, and theorized science fiction as a socialist literary form.

The new centers of science fiction discourse were not inherently subversive. Due in part to the small size of the GDR, the boundaries between various organizations and institutions often overlapped. Individuals often occupied several locations at one time. An editor might become an author. An academic might become an author. Adolf Sckerl, for instance, wrote a dissertation on science fiction and worked as an editor at Verlag Das Neue Berlin. He also played a key role in the Kulturbund hearings on science fiction both in 1973 and in 1978. At the meeting in 1978, he was listed as the representative of Kulturbund's Central Committee on Literature (Haines 1).

As stated, several former fans later occupied editorial positions or became authors. Fan Karsten Kruschel completed a dissertation on science fiction and wrote a number of science fiction stories. Olaf Spittel, an editor of the science fiction almanac *Lichtjahr* at Verlag Das Neue Berlin, also co-wrote a short history of GDR science fiction with Erik Simon in 1988. Erik Simon, originally part of the Stanislaw Lem Club, had an extensive impact as an editor at Verlag Das Neue Berlin, where he oversaw the almanac, *Lichtjahr*. He authored science fiction stories and books as well. Ekkehard Redlin, editor at Verlag Das Neue Berlin and one of the GDR science fiction's greatest advocates, still participates occasionally in Andymon fan club meetings in Berlin. It is apparent that a number of figures important to the development of science fiction in East Germany played multiple roles in its development in various position of power.[1]

Gustav Schröder continued to support graduate student work on GDR science fiction at various institutions in the eighties. For the most part, these dissertations remained free of *Parteilichkeit*. They dealt with children's science fiction (Vollprecht 1994), the portrayal of women (Blume 1989), the portrayal of the alien (Breitenfeld 1994), utopian and dystopian elements (Kruschel, *Spielwelten* 1995),

---

1 For more information see my article "Reconceptualizing East German Popular Literature Via the Science Fiction Niche."

fantastic literature in the seventies (Förster 1980), and a survey of GDR science fiction in the 1980s (Hartung 1992).

Authors and editors contributed to a growing number of journal and newspaper articles on science fiction. These professional discussions placed the genre within its international context and covered an array of non-political issues. Frequent contributors included Bernd Ulbrich, Hartmut Mechtel, Angela and Karlheinz Steinmüller, Olaf Spittel, Erik Simon, Carlos Rasch, Ekkehard Redlin, and Karsten Kruschel among others. Book reviews, interviews and short histories appeared in *Temperamente, Weimarer Beiträge, Neue Deutsche Literatur, Einheit,* and the almanac *Lichtjahr.* For the first time, the West German journals *Das Science Fiction Jahr, Quarber Merkur* and *Der Golem* also published occasional reviews of East German science fiction novels by both anonymous and named GDR contributors. Western scholars, particularly Darko Suvin in Canada and the Austrian Franz Rottensteiner, showed increasing interest in the science fiction of East Germany.

Lichtjahr, the new science fiction almanac, functioned as a voice of the science fiction community. It first appeared in 1980 in the Verlag Das Neue Berlin under the tutelage of Erik Simon and Olaf Spittel. They published *Lichtjahr* annually until 1986.[2] It included new works by established and fledgling authors, science fiction art, secondary material on science fiction, as well as bibliographies of various science fiction traditions. Moreover, the almanac introduced readers to foreign writers, and published, for instance, the introduction to Ursula Le Guin's novel *The Left Hand of Darkness* in 1980. As a central source of information on science fiction in the East Bloc, *Lichtjahr* helped to develop a canon and further professionalize the genre in East Germany.

The creation of *Lichtjahr* demonstrated science fiction's presence as an established genre and provided a public forum in which writers could publish and discuss their work. At the same time, this almanac continued to adhere to the cultural policy governing the Verlag Das Neue Berlin. Success had long brought political compromise, still, the new almanac afforded GDR science fiction increased legitimacy. It

---

2   Since then Erik Simon managed to bring out one more edition in 1999.

also represented a reincorporation of science fiction discourse into the official state cultural apparatus and away from fan clubs. Nevertheless, *Lichtjahr* became an active and productive center of information on GDR science fiction. It was very much a production of members of the GDR's science fiction niche.

The third center of discourse was the GDR science fiction fan club. In actuality, fan clubs had actively engaged, discussed and even published their own science fiction since the seventies. Wolfgang Both, Hans-Peter Neumann and Klaus Scheffler, all active in today's fan club scene, have written an extensive history of GDR fandom entitled *Berichte aus der Parallelwelt* (Reports from the Parallel World, 1998). In it, they include extensive histories, documents and memoirs that pertain to the fourteen clubs that existed in the GDR from 1968 to 1989. Both, Neumann and Scheffler also have put together a bibliography of GDR fanzines.

The authors of these fan histories are members of Berlin's *Andymon* fan club. This club represented a new generation of fan clubs that become politically feasible in the latter half of the eighties. After the Kulturbund reorganized the majority of clubs in the mid-seventies, no new clubs appeared until 1985. By this time, Kulturbund policy changed, as the institution searched for ways to recruit new members. Karl Heinz Schulmeister emphasized that many affiliates had come to the Kulturbund by way of special interests or hobbies. In his words, "every cultural activity" deserved support as long as it contributed to a "socialist way of life" (154).

The Andymon club originated with the creation of the *Arbeits-gemeinschaft Astronomie Archenhold–Sternwarte* (Work Group on Astronomy Archenhold Planetarium). Organized through the Kulturbund for hobby astronomers, this club also discussed science fiction from time to time. The genre interested its participants enough for them to found the *Interessengemeinschaft für wissenschaftlich-phantastische Literatur* (Science Fiction Interest Group) within the Kulturbund Berlin–Treptow in February 1985. Their first activity consisted of a presentation on Soviet science fiction stories, art and model ships at the *Tage der Freundschaft und der Kultur der UdSSR in der DDR* (Festival of Soviet Friendship and Culture in East Germany) that summer. This club renamed itself Andymon in 1986 and became one of the preeminent science fiction clubs in the late 1980s. It is still ac-tive today.[3]

Many of these clubs published their own fanzines.[4] During the latter half of East Germany, some forty fanzines with over two hundred issues appeared (Both, Neumann, and Scheffler, *Berichte* 148). In 1968, Wolfgang Siegmund applied for a permit to print and distribute his fanzine *Phantopia*, but was never successful. Still, he produced eight issues and two special editions of his fanzine *Phantopia* from 1967–1968. Between 1967 and 1973, several individuals and the SF-Club Berlin were able to produce fanzines with a circulation ranging from one to a maximum of twelve issues. Fanzines became more plentiful in the eighties and included *Utopia, STELLA, tranSFer, Count Down, INFO, Terminator* and *Solar-X* among others. The most prolific was *Stella* from the Science-Fiction-Literatur-Klub Weißwasser, which produced twenty-seven issues (Both, Neumann and Scheffler, *Berichte* 150–151). Carsten Hohlfeld, the publisher of *INFO*, received Soviet recognition for his fan magazine (Klotz and Matzer 106).

Fanzine creation presented many challenges in the GDR. First, few models existed in the East and access to western fanzines was almost impossible. Second, it was illegal to own publishing equipment privately. The SED controlled all other publishing houses. It was possible for organizations to receive a "print number" from the Kulturbund for a period of time. Such a permit also subjected all content to censor control. Under these conditions, clubs managed only to create fanzines on a limited basis with extremely low distribution. Occasionally, fanzines even appeared secretly. Most often they took the form of so-called *Briefzines* or *Egozines*. This was done by way of a publishing permit designated "for internal use" and was limited to one hundred copies. Individuals or club members also typed multiple copies on a typewriter and sent them through the mail (Both, Neu-

---

3   Of the ten members present at the first meeting six of them were women, in addition to the presence of a guest representative from the Kulturbund and the Archenhold-Sternwarte. See Science Fiction-Club Sondershausen 5–7.

4   *Merriam–Webster On-line* defines a fanzine as a "magazine written by and for fans especially of science fiction or fantasy writing."

mann and Scheffler, *Berichte* 148–149). Despite such challenges, however, these fan magazines provided a new forum for reader discussion and publication.

Building a New Utopia Through Realism

The final decade of the GDR was a time of literary experimentation when authors continued their search for new workable alternatives to existing forms. A literary discourse, which had formed both in affirmation and negation around the orthodox "theories of representation and reflection" (*Abbild- und Widerspiegelungstheorie*) moved beyond the aesthetic barriers that had begun to weaken in the 1970s. In part, this discursive transformation came as a result of the political discontent following the Biermann Affair in 1976. At the same time, Wolfgang Emmerich marks the entrance of the next generation of writers, who brought new understanding and intent to the literary scene (*Kleine Literatur* 397). Born after 1961, this younger generation had known only the reality of the GDR. Emmerich argues that its members did not possess what playwright Heiner Müller characterized as the "hope" so common among the war generation, but rather knew only a "deformed reality" (*Kleine Literatur* 404). Consequently, in Emmerich's assessment, a resulting sense of isolation, rejection, and absurdity informed much literature written in the 1980s.

This is certainly true of the most famous science fiction publication of the eighties, Franz Fühmann's *Saiäns-Fiktschen* (1981). This collection of short stories included "Die Ohnmacht" ("Powerlessness," 1974), which was first published in *Sinn and Form*. In the anthology's introduction, Fühmann described his feelings of futility as he wrote it.

> They are stories, including the conclusions, in the sphere of faltering contra-
> diction, where stagnation appears as a driving force – development as a lack of
> development – When reason sleeps, says Goya, monsters are born ("Intro-
> duction" 6).

Each story deals with a different kind of paralysis and takes place either in Libroterr, the capitalist society, or Uniterr, the socialist society. From the first story "Die Ohnmacht" to the last "Pavlos Papierbuch," (Pavlo's Paper Book) Fühmann invented various moral and ethical situations that isolate aspects of the life of his main character Pavlo and reveal to him the source of his "Gefühlsstau," a type of emotional gridlock (87). Indeed, Fühmann selected science fiction as its fantastic form allowed him to experiment in a world beyond his own. He parodied science fiction while simultaneously appropriating its fantastic narrative to critique GDR society.

In "Die Ohnmacht," we meet Pavlo. As a dissident scientist of causality, he has been disciplined politically for creating a time machine. Unable to transport his subjects to the distant future or past, they can only see a few minutes into their future. Socialist realism called upon authors to set their ideal visions of society in the near future in order to urge the reader to action in the present. The experimental subjects in Fühmann's story assume that they can change the future they have seen in Pavlo's time machine. However, each person has yet been unable to do so. They become faint when they realize the futility of their assumption of free will.

The story continues to critique the very dialectic that underlies scientific socialism. This doctrine holds that history moves inexorably along a linear time line of causality into the future. Fühmann's same story plays with the idea of anti-causality. During a debate on the theoretical presence of anti-causality we meet Pavlo, his colleague Janna and a visiting unnamed colleague of logic. Pavlo's hypothesis holds that, just as every cause has a future effect, causality must simultaneously run in the reverse direction. Where there is matter, there is also anti-matter. Where there is causality, there is also anti-causality. Therefore, future "effects" actually cause their apparent "cause." Thus, what appears to be an effect is sometimes actually a cause of a past event. The story's absurd and humorous suggestions question the very reality of causality, as understood in the reader's world. The ambiguous narrative accomplishes this in the playful manner reminiscent of Stanislaw Lem. However, it also leads its protagonists to "Gefühlstau." They believe they have lost all power and control due to their inability to distinguish between what is a cause and what is an effect.

A second story, "Das Duell," addresses issues of memory in relation to historical determinism. While still a student, Pavlo attended a demonstration in his history lecture of the experimental time machine (78). This time television captured the light rays of Earth's past and projected historical events on a screen. With this machine, the leaders of Uniterr hoped to increase citizen interest in the socialist victories of the past. Consequently, the first "broadcast" is that of the exemplary duel from 1409 between the Norman Seecount Henry VII of Traulec and his illegitimate son Toul, a swineherd. In Uniterr, academics held the victory of Toul over his father to be an early example of the "spiritual servitude" that had been overcome in Uniterr (81). On the day of the demonstration, the experiment is cut short when the battle's outcome proves otherwise. Instead of reinforcing the ideology of Uniterr, the time television reveals an alternate historical reality, which threatens to undermine the society's foundational myth (Joseph Campbell) by suggesting that it is possible "not to be Uniterr" (86).

Fühmann's collection ends with the pronouncement: "Give us this day our daily beating" (157). His final sobering story, "Pavlo's Papierbuch," thematizes the perverse and degrading love between captors and captured in an autocratic system. This bleak dystopian vision of East German society leaves little room for a potentially corrective utopian outcome. Rather it resembles the Orwellian anti-utopia from which there is no escape.

There were other science fiction authors in the eighties who formulated new hopes for a better future. Their optimism lay in a belief that the science fiction narrative represented a new and more authentic kind of realism in socialism. In contrast to a move by GDR film directors and authors to the realism of documentary and oral history, several figures in the science fiction community believed that their fantastic genre revealed truth precisely through estrangement. Still others left behind the will to correct the existing system and examined possibilities for the next one.

Editor Olaf Spittel characterizes East German science fiction in the eighties by its "realism requirement, its reference to reality." He points to the continued reference to the contemporary world of its authors. The genre's morally based narratives question the nature of social progress both on the level of the individual and of society. According to Spittel, this is done not only in specific reference to the GDR, but also on a global level ("Zur DDR-SF" 554).

In an article in *Lichtjahr* entitled "Die phantastische Methode," critic and editor Hartmut Mechtel supports this principle. He notes that, as myth aided in the understanding of reality in the past, then science fiction leads to a greater understanding of reality in the present day through the modern method of science. Mechtel argues that the fantastic is in fact one of the primary ways of seeing reality in a contemporary world that is itself so implausible and riddled with contradiction. He remains distrustful of the idealist, utopian world-view that had been presented in the science fiction of the 1950s and 1960s. Rather, he focuses on Kafka's use of estrangement as a method with which to access the real. In his opinion, this same estrangement effect forms the realism of socialist science fiction. What is not apparent becomes clear through the use of the fantastic. The "real" is no longer reflected as in socialist realism. Instead, it is presented in an altered state so that "reality" may be seen more clearly. Mechtel believes that science fiction aids especially in this manner. Rather than portraying an entire worldview, he suggests that an author might focus on a portion of a world. She would be able to address the issues at hand more clearly and directly (103).

Coming from a scientific, rather than literary, background, Karl-heinz Steinmüller agreed and disagreed with Mechtel. In an article in the journal *Positionen* from 1987, Steinmüller provides a new definition for "socialist realist" science fiction. He maintains that science fiction's primary goal is to function as a tool against conser-vatism and fear with respect to the fast pace of change in science and technology. Like Kingsley Amis (*New Maps* 26), Steinmüller believes science fiction gets the reader used to the reality of the impact of science and technology on individual lives and on the whole of society. It is a type of anti-future shock. According to Steinmüller, classic themes of technological anxiety include the loss of control over scientific creation (Mary Shelley's *Frankenstein*), the subordination of humanity to mechanization (Čapek's *R.U.R.*) and the end of humanity,

228

as we know it (Wells' *War of the Worlds*) ("Positionsbestimmung" 159)

Steinmüller contrasts bourgeois science fiction with socialist science fiction. In his view, bourgeois science fiction plays to fear in the face of science and technological advancement. Conversely, socialist science fiction leads to a productive, cognitive treatment of difficult social and philosophical questions in the context of such progress. Thus, Steinmüller is similar to Mechtel in his class-based approach to accessing the real. He concludes that socialist science fiction is in fact *the* realism of a modern day society so dependent upon technology. "Does its adventurous thought game necessarily sacrifice all sense of reality – or is it not really *the* realism of a scientific age?" (147). From his discussion, it is clear that Steinmüller was familiar not only with the discourse on science fiction in the GDR and in the Soviet Union, but he was also well versed with western sources as well.[5]

Looking then to the nature and purpose of this experimentation, Angela and Karlheinz Steinmüller postulate that the process represented the creation of a new utopia among a new generation of writers. The Steinmüllers perceive that the emphasis on the individual and the psychological, as well as the flourishing of relationships within the private sphere revealed a "niche ideal as utopian concept, a reclamation of human warmth and individual freedom in a societal ice age" (*Vorgriff* 38). The small organizational units of their novel *Andymon* (1982), the feminist society in *Der Traummeister* (The Dream Master, 1990), the focus on the personal in Leman's *Schwarze Blumen auf*

5   See "Positionsbestimmung" 147–167. An article from 1981 in the journal *Einheit* held that science fiction literature in particular could be used to lessen "conservative" reactions to technological progress. It introduced the reader to the idea of change and adaptation to invention. Thus new topics, such as genetics, computers, methods of controlling nature, and the relationship between technology and humanity, should be introduced in a positive way rather than in a fearful manner as identified in many western dystopias (Hochmut and Einhorn 932). In this manner, science fiction was to reduce "Future Shock." In 1968, Arno Hochmut was the head of the Cultural Section of the Central Committee of the SED. From 1972–1990 he was a Professor at the Humboldt University (*Wer war wer in der DDR?* 362).

Barnard Drei (Black Flowers on Barnard Three, 1986), and the drop outs of Szameit's *Drachenkreuzer Ikarus* (Icarus, The Hangglider, 1987) all illustrate the construction of a utopian society based on the small societal unit.

To further prove their point, the Steinmüllers allude to Christa Wolf's *Kassandra* (1983) and the coupling of the weakness of the Trojan community with the murderous tendencies of that society. Cassandra's discovery and reliance upon the underground group of women emphasizes Wolf's utopian feminist support for a society based on the small community. The praise given by author and critic to the community of artists and poets in Berlin's Prenzlauer Berg also demonstrates a turn to the ideal of the small and the personal. This was, in part, manifested in the vision of a more democratic socialist *Dritter Weg* or Third Way. The following chapter examines the dystopian turn and its inverse utopian impulse in Angela and Karl-heinz Steinmüller's novel, *The Dream Master*.

Science Fiction in the Eighties

The general trend towards the niche, the subjective and the exploration of the individual in the science fiction of the seventies became even more marked in the eighties. More and more stories included a first-person narrator. With particular relevance to East German society, a number of stories contrasted the importance of the individual and of personal responsibility with the dehumanization and abuse of power in a society governed by a single utopian discourse. Authors continued to use the ambiguous utopia to satirize the petit bourgeois and bureaucratic mentality of the system around them on what Angela and Karlheinz Steinmüller characterize as an exploratory journey from "us to me." (*Vorgriff* 35; Spittel, "Zur DDR-SF" 553–554.)

Rainer Fuhrmann's *Die Untersuchung* (*The Investigation*, 1984) and Alfred Leman's *Black Flowers on Barnard Three* are both examples of this phenomenon. A combination of science fiction and detective story, *The Investigation* criticizes the objectivity of a bureaucratic hierarchy based on educational qualification. It identifies the society's failure to leave room for the subjective experiences and actions of its individual members. A highly complex, yet isolated, society develops in *Black Flowers on Barnard Three* after a group of cosmonauts set down on the planet Barnard 3 due to the ship's weight restrictions. Over the course of this book, Leman focuses on individual relationships, and explores the effect, which an overly rationalized and stagnant society has on the personal initiative and satisfaction of its population.

Perhaps the best-known GDR science fiction writers, Angela and Karlheinz Steinmüller often wrote stories with ambivalent meaning. Their collaborative writing debut, *Andymon* (1982), contains a philosophical exploration of the viability of coexistent political systems and the possibility for the realization of individual potential in each. Similar in method to Le Guin's *The Dispossessed*, this novel searches for the more perfect system, yet points out deficiencies in all. Their text *The Dream Master* is an allegory of the slow decline of the GDR and of human civilization from the point of view of the individual. It leaves room for hope throughout its narrative.

The Dream Master is also an excellent example of the growing influence on GDR science fiction of the American genre science fantasy, a topic to which *Lichtjahr* devoted its 1986 edition. Science fantasy mixes science fiction with medieval fantasy. Stories are often set in the Middle Ages. Its characters may include fairies, elves, or dragons (e.g. Anne McCaffrey's *Pern* series). Of the new generation of GDR science fiction writers, both Michael Szameit's *Icarus, The Hangglider* and *Copyworld* (written in 1988–1989; first published in 1998) are "Warnutopien" (dystopias) that use science fiction/science fantasy to problematize the relationship of the individual to a less-than-perfect society. In *Icarus, The Hangglider* a niche of outsiders form a "Gemeinschaft," much like that of Berlin's *Prenzlauerberg*, in opposition to the international, industrial "Gesellschaft." *Copyworld* skillfully contrasts two separate stories, one a highly mechanized dystopia and the other a historical fantasy world. Other examples of GDR science fantasy are Ernst-Otto Luthardt's *Die klingenden Bäume* (The

Ringing Trees, 1982), *Die Unsterblichen* (The Immortals, 1984) and *Die Wiederkehr des Einhorns* (The Return of the Unicorns, 1988).[6]

True dystopian novels remained few and far between, due in part to the ever-present requirement to write with *Parteilichkeit*. Early utopian realist novels often portrayed the West in a dystopian manner, yet this dystopia did not place the socialist utopia into question. In the seventies, the ambiguous utopia tended towards dystopia, but could not be classified as such due to an overarching positive tone of the novels. In the eighties, when the socialist "happy end" became less and less dominant, a discursive space for dystopia opened up. GDR science fiction writers had often looked to the capitalist world as a source for conflict. These authors now set their dystopian stories in an ostensibly capitalist setting or after the demise of a capitalist society. Often, the critique of the capitalist society applied to East Germany as well, like that seen in the detective science fiction by Gert Prokop, for example.

In his study of GDR science fiction from the eighties, Thomas Hartung notes two titles that adopted a doomsday scenario to create dystopian adventure. Reinhard Kriese's *Eden City, die Stadt des Vergessens* (Eden City, The City of Forgetting, 1985) and Peter Lorenz's *Aktion Erde* (Action Earth, 1988) both create adventure along the lines of Huxley's *Brave New World* (GDR 1978). Failed genetic experiments destroy Kriese's "capitalist" society; Lorenz describes the resettling of an Earth abandoned after an economic collapse. Hartung notes millenarism in both, which indirectly abandoned the principle of "Konfliktlosigkeit" (34–35). Significantly, there is no alternate socialist society in either to provide hope for the future.

Despite the increasing influence of western science fiction from official and unofficial sources, certain subgenres did not appear in the GDR due to the censor's "optimistic" constraints. For instance, the bleak worlds of cyberpunk (e.g. William Gibson's *Neuromancer* [1984]) and gothic dystopia (best demonstrated in Terry Gilliam's film *Brazil* [1985]) remained taboo. In addition, the technological level of the GDR was such that cyberpunk and cyborgs did not resonate in the same manner that they did in a more digital United

6   See Simon and Spittel 199–200.

States. Where a broader mixture of science fiction with other fantastic forms existed in East Germany throughout the seventies and eighties, science fantasy appeared only to a limited extent.

In addition to these more experimental forms, there was a conservative resurgence in the narrative style of the 1960s that posited the universal triumph of communism. Although such novels remained popular throughout the 1970s, their increased number in the 1980s also had historical-political foundations. As the Biermann affair led to an initial chilling of the less rigid cultural policy of the early 1970s, the onset of a final confrontation between the two Cold War superpowers reinforced a more conservative cultural policy in some areas. In part, this was due to solidarity with the Soviet Union in the Reagan era. But, after Gorbachev's announcement of his dual policies of *glasnost* and *perestroika* in 1985, the hardliner Honecker began to break from Soviet policy. He and East Germany became politically isolated as time went on. As the stagnation of East Germany became increasingly apparent, select science fiction authors adopted an entrenched, defensive posture.

Consequently, some of the more conservative space adventures returned to a pronounced demonization of the West. These stories were more violent than earlier publications and moved closer to the West's space opera. For instance, author Klaus Klauss' *Duell unter fremder Sonne* (Duel Under a Foreign Sun, 1985) relates the story of a spaceship that crash lands on a planet. Its crew tries to bring about a communist society in each of the various class systems present. The reformer fails, the woman crewmember is inept, and the anarchist dies. Only the revolution from below succeeds. In *Die Engel in den grünen Kugeln* (The Angel in the Green Spheres, 1986), Alexander Kröger portrays the helplessness of a completely disarmed society in the face of hostile invaders (Simon and Spittel 83). Evidence of a western influence, Kröger creates an individual hero who lives in a militaristic-style hierarchy. He saves the world in the face of rather than in cooperation with others, an aspect that contradicted the doctrinaire communal aesthetic. Angela and Karlheinz Steinmüller attribute such plotlines to a Free German Youth request of the Verlag Neues Leben to publish more "warlike" science fiction (*Vorgriff* 37). Another explanation lies in the increasing emphasis on profit and production methods similar to western publishers (Steinmüllers, *Vorgriff* 35). Alexander Kröger stated himself that he wrote such adventure fiction because it *sold well* (*Sudelfass* 89).

Many novels in the 1980s searched for new and viable forms of socialism or communism that could potentially replace the Marxist–Leninist model. This process is found particularly in so-called *Wende-texts*, the designation of novels written at the "turning point" or immediately before and following the fall of the Berlin Wall and the reunification of Germany. Alexander Kröger and Michael Szameit characterized their respective novels *Der Untergang der Telesalt* and *Copyworld* in such a manner, describing them as their "coming to terms with and rejection of the system" (Personal interviews 1999). The following chapter discusses Angela and Karlheinz Steinmüllers' *Wendetext, The Dream Master.*

Book cover from Angela and Karlheinz Steinmüller's
Der Traummeister (The Dream Master, 1990)

Chapter Nine
Apocalypse and the Search for the New Utopia: Angela and Karlheinz Steinmüllers' *The Dream Master*

> The air shimmers above the desert; what lies in the distance, blurs. Coarse sand blows over the fallen barbed wire and helmets roll between the stones. Only a lizard shares the blazing heat of the sun outside, its flanks swell, my loneliness. The desert is barren and empty as it was at the beginning of time.
>
> (*The Dream Master*, 5)

Angela and Karlheinz Steinmüller's *Der Traummeister* (The Dream Master, 1990) opens onto a desert scene where the violence and loneliness of the real are both revealed by a barren landscape and obscured by sand. The novel's narrator, Glauke Arnya, escapes into the desert seeking the mental clarity of reason like many before her. The arid isolation of the desert provides some relief from the continual confusion between dream and reality and utopia and dystopia in her home city, Miscara. Yet, in the desert, revealed truths must also be questioned. Traditionally, the desert is associated with mysticism and revelation that comes in the form of a vision. It remains an ambiguous place where the seemingly rational or real can easily turn into a mirage. Therefore, any notion of the real that Glauke takes with her from the desert must also be interrogated and not elevated to the status of eternal truth. Furthermore, both the irrational and rational aspects of Glauke's thought processes are present. They are necessary aspects of creating individual dreams for the future. The struggle lies is finding an appropriate balance between the two.

The ambiguous nature of the novel is not a narrative failure, but rather a central premise. It pervades the novel's form, content, and style. Most often, it takes the form of tension between the rational and the irrational that is exemplified in the novel's generic mixture. Where other works of East German science fiction incorporated elements of the fairy tale, myth or fable to similar ends, *The Dream Master* is unique in its almost continual transgression of the border between the reality of science fiction and the unreality of fantasy. Besides its science fictional setting on a distant planet, the novel constructs a complete history of the city based, in part, on its technological achievements. Yet, this history exists alongside other histories that exist in the dreams created by the dream master of Miscara. The continual incursion of dreams into "reality" disrupts any pretense of realism. Organized in a series of flashbacks, *The Dream Master*'s surreal imagery, existential tone and fragmentary form consistently transgress the boundary between science fiction and fantasy. [1]

The text's ambiguity also prevents any definitive reading of the novel. The Steinmüllers rely on the estrangement effect of its alien setting and innovative form to create a space between the text and the reader that is open for critical reflection (Personal interview, 2000). Cognizant of the steady economic and social decline evident not only in the GDR but also in the Soviet Union, they use this critical space to construct an alternate city history loosely based on East Berlin. Finished in 1988 and approved for publication in October 1989, *The Dream Master* represents a "thought game" in which its authors strove to find a progressive way out of their own static, real-existing utopia. [2] In the words of Karlheinz Steinmüller, the writers of similar alternate histories in the Soviet Union and elsewhere, looked for the "sources of [...] stagnation" in the Soviet Bloc and examined the "highly moral claims of Perestroika," asking "if it had a chance" ("Zukünfte" 43). As the eighties wore on and Gorbachev's reforms proved less than

1   Common to the world of science fiction and fantasy, *The Dream Master* makes a number of allusions to other writers and texts. This practice contributes to its fragmentary nature. Made up of "a mosaic of quotations" (Kristeva 66), its narrative is an "intertextual tapestry" which echoes the familiarity of Earth. The Steinmüllers attest to many references that include Plato, Campanella, Thea von Harbou, Zamiatin's *We*, the *Bible*, and Arabic mythology (Personal interview, 2000). The most obvious of these is the character of Nerev, which is an anagram of Verne. Jules Verne was an important figure not only in science fiction, but also for German and East German science fiction in particular. For more information on Verne's influence in Germany, see Innenhofer 129–132.

2   See Simon "Die Science-Fiction der DDR" 621 for reference to the acceptance of *The Dream Master* in 1989.

successful, the Steinmüllers searched for a new direction for the GDR, in the event that Gorbachev's plans failed. The result was a novel that captured uncannily what Raymond Williams has best described as a "structure of feeling" of the final years of East Germany. In many ways it foresaw the end of the GDR and its reunification with its western counterpart.

In *The Dream Master*, the successive utopian prophecies of Miscara progress from dynamic revolutionary vision to static utopia, the fixed nature of which leads ultimately to a recurring apocalypse. The novel presents the second static utopia in the history of Miscara in stages labeled *Traumeszucht* and *Traumesucht* (forced dream creation and dream addiction respectively). In these two stages, the novel posits the failure of a static utopia to secure a space viable for the survival of a multitude of individual voices. Not only is it the static utopia, but also its collective nature that keeps the first-person narrator, Glauke Arnya from articulating herself as a feminine subject. She is not able to do this until she dreams on her own at the end of the novel.

The text intertwines aspects of the classic, static utopia with the underlying shadow of the 20th century dystopia. Its apocalyptic ending results in a solid transition from the community to the individual, from the "we" to the "I." A common theme in GDR literature in the seventies and eighties, especially among the proponents of the Third Way and in the writings of Christa Wolf, the pronouncement of "I" often symbolized a utopian hope for a reformed system based on democratic socialism. This third and final stage of the novel, entitled *Träume sucht* (the search for dreams), refers to the power of the individual voice as a creative force of hope. Here, the individual voice represents the basis for a dynamic utopia that is responsive to the society's ever-changing needs of the future. In accordance with the value of socialism's perpetual revolution, this dynamic utopia is kept alive by the wishes and creative contributions of all of its members.

As the novel progresses towards apocalypse, *The Dream Master* examines a variety of political and economic systems. Addressing feudalism, capitalism, communism, democracy, and feminism, it identifies the similarities of various utopian prophecies present in modern societies. The novel makes oblique references to and intermixes characteristics of the various systems, but never directly identifies one in particular. The incorporation of these fragmentary allusions shifts the novel's focus away from an examination of discrete political ideologies to what it identifies as their underlying systemic structure of collective utopia. It is this aspect, which the novel ultimately identifies as the reason for their failure.

Therefore, where Wolf and others outlined their visions of the future, the Steinmüllers did not. The book ends as Glauke dreams on her own without any hint as to the actual nature of this dream. While the novel's almost anarchic allusion to dynamic utopia indicates a general distrust of the large nation-state, it proposes no replacement utopia. Perhaps it is Glauke's individual dream that will break the cycle of progress from dynamic to static utopia.

The Authors

Angela and Karlheinz Steinmüller are arguably the most successful East German science fiction authors. They as well as Johanna and Günter Braun are also the only two author pairs in GDR science fiction. An East German survey of science fiction fans in 1989 listed the Steinmüllers as the best authors of the GDR and their book *Andymon* (1982) as the best book.[3] Moreover, East Berlin science fiction fans were so enamored with the text that they named their club Andymon.

Born in Schmalkalden in 1941, Angela Steinmüller grew up in East Berlin. She worked as a stenographer, a secretary and a manager at the Berlin VEB Gas Works and as an administrative employee in the business office of the East German Evangelical Student Religious Society. In 1975, she graduated from Humboldt University with a degree in Mathematics and then worked in data processing.

---

3   Science fiction fans Carsten Hohlfeld and Thomas Braunstein conducted this survey.

Her husband, Karlheinz Steinmüller was born in Klingenthal in 1950. He first studied in Karl-Marx-Stadt (now Chemnitz) and graduated with a degree in Physics from Humboldt University. There he continued on to write a dissertation in Philosophy entitled "The Machine Theory of Life. Philosophical Questions in Biomechanics" in 1977, and then worked in East Berlin on the cybernetic mapping of eco-systems.[4]

The couple met at Humboldt University, and they have been professsional authors since 1982. They were also members of the German Writers' Union (Simon and Spittel, *Science-fiction* 243–244). Beginning in 1991, Karlheinz Steinmüller worked for the Secretariat for Future Studies in Gelsenkirchen, while his wife worked as a free-lance author and took various temporary state-funded positions. In 1997, they helped to found *Z_Punkt. The Foresight Company*, where Karlheinz Steinmüller has served as futurologist and as its scientific director since 2001.

The Steinmüllers have a number of science fiction short stories and novels to their credit, as well as several theoretical and secondary works on science fiction, utopia and future studies. Karlheinz Steinmüller published a collection of short stories entitled *Der letzte Tag auf der Venus* (The Last Day on Venus, GDR 1979). Angela Steinmüller is an established author as well. Her short story "Der Kerzenmacher" ("The Candle Maker") won the Kurd Lasswitz Prize in 1992. Together, their most notable titles include *Andymon* (GDR 1982; FRG 1982, 2004), *Windschiefe Geraden* (Crooked Lines, GDR 1984) a collection of short stories, *Pulaster* (GDR 1986; FRG 1988), and *Der Traummeister* (The Dream Master, GDR 1990; FRG 1992). They have also written a history of GDR science fiction, *Vorgriff auf das Lichte Morgen* (Anticipation of a Bright Tomorrow, 1995) appeared. The Steinmüllers most recently published a collection of short stories entitled *Warmzeit. Geschichten aus dem 21. Jahrhundert* (The Warming Season. Stories from the 21st Century, 2003). One of the two new stories in the collection, "Vor der Zeitreise" ("Before the Trip Through Time"), recently won the Kurd Lasswitz prize for the Best

---

4   The German title of his dissertation is "Die Maschinentheorie des Lebens. Philosophische Fragen des biologischen Mechanismus."

German Story of the Year 2003. Shayol Publishers plans to print a new edition of *The Dream Master* in 2005.

Although *Andymon* was their most popular book, I have chosen to focus on *The Dream Master* for two reasons. First of all, the Steinmüllers envisioned *The Dream Master* as a distant sequel to *Andymon*. To some extent, the former contains answers to questions and observations forged in the first book. As often occurs in science fiction, the Steinmüllers created a loosely connected, future universe through these and other books and short stories. They did so with the intent not of correcting the existing East German system, but rather playing with the possibilities that might follow its potential collapse (Personal interview, 2000). Although I do not conduct a comparative study of the two novels, some reference to *Andymon* is necessary to comprehend the science fictional setting of *The Dream Master*. Secondly, *The Dream Master*'s status as "Wendetext" (a novel of reunification) enables an analysis of the novel in terms of the contemporary situation in East Germany just prior to the fall of the Berlin Wall.

Science Fantasy in the GDR – A Search for the Real

As illustrated earlier, the combination of science fiction and fantasy was not new to East German science fiction. Influenced by the rehabilitation of the German Romantic movement in the late sixties, several of its authors, most notably the Brauns and the Steinmüllers, incorporated aspects of literary fantasy to challenge the legacy of Enlightenment thought in East Germany. The preponderance of doubles, dreamlike states, medieval allusions, plus odd and unexplainable characters in *The Dream Master* can be traced back to this period. E.T.A. Hoffmann's automaton and use of the uncanny is also evident in the dual portrayal of the dream master, Kilean.[5] He seems to be a rational being when awake. However, while performing his duties, he interacts with the technology of the dream tower and becomes a type of dream machine. Through Glauke's narration, we experience one Kilean while awake and the other while asleep. In this manner the two Kileans are uncanny, particularly as one is merely a man while the other a monstrous power that reaches into every bedchamber. As the novel progresses, Kilean's body becomes a vessel as his dreamed self takes over. In the dream world, Kilean finds yet another uncanny representation in his alter evil ego, known as the Saddraq. Each person in Miscara must learn to control this valuable yet dangerous side.

The Brauns explored the potential of the fairy tale and fable and adapted these forms to their notion of playfulness. The influence of Gerhard Branster, Stanislaw Lem and the Strugatsky brothers is evident in the science fiction the Brauns published in the GDR in the seventies. The Steinmüllers, on the other hand, published in East Germany in the eighties. Western science fiction television, literature and film were more readily accessible than ever before, whether through official channels, illegal antennae, hand-typed copies or under the table. Consequently, while influenced by Lem and the Strugatskys, the Steinmüllers also read Le Guin and Asimov (Personal interview, 2000). *The Dream Master*, in particular, takes on characteristics of the western genre of science fantasy through its setting in a medieval city that possesses fire-breathing dragons.

To understand *The Dream Master* fully it is necessary to look beyond the discourse on Romanticism in East Germany. It was not until the eighties that the popularity of "fantasy" or so-called "science fantasy" in West Germany (by publishers Heyne and Bastei–Lübbe in German translation) made its mark among East German authors. One distinguishing factor between the two German book markets was the flood of translated Anglo-American science fiction in the West. To a greater or lesser degree, East German authors enjoyed access to this tradition in science fiction as well. This new, combined style of

---

5   It is important to note that Kilean is not a "seer." Although he is born with the talent for dreaming, he systematically hones this talent through the use of dreaming "textbooks" left behind by past dream masters.

science fiction and fantasy defied established generic expectations in the GDR. It opened up other possibilities of the fantastic beyond the models provided by the German Romantic tradition and science fiction in the East Bloc.

The Anglo-American fantasy tradition found its origins in Edgar Allen Poe, Tolkien and C.S. Lewis among many others. Its more recent representatives include Marion Zimmer Bradley, Anne McCaffrey, and Ursula Le Guin. According to the Steinmüllers, it was the writings of New Wave author, Ursula Le Guin, which had a particular impact on their writing (Personal interview, 2000). In the eighties, several of her novels appeared in East Germany as publishers successfully argued for the acknowledgement of an international socialist science fiction tradition. Thus termed socialist writing, Le Guin's *The Left Hand of Darkness* (Der Winterplanet) appeared in 1979 and *The Dispossessed* (Planet der Habenichtse) eight years later.[6]

Five years before its publication, the GDR science fiction almanac, *Lichtjahr*, brought out an issue devoted to the western genre of science-fantasy, which was beginning to take hold among younger GDR authors. *Lichtjahr 5* contains Ursula Le Guin's "Things" and "The End", selections from Tais Teng's *De legenden van Cotrahviné* (The Legends of Cotrahviné), Karlheinz and Angela Steinmüller's "Sterntaler," and Pavel Amnuel's "Höher als Wolken." ("Higher than Clouds"). Hartmut Mechtel wrote in his internal review: "This volume focuses on fantasy unfamiliar to this country. Fantasy has been talked

6   The relationship of science fiction to fantasy literature has been the subject of much study and controversy among critics and authors alike. Author and editor John W. Campbell, Jr. distinguishes between science fiction and fantasy by emphasizing the cohesive and logical organization of the science fiction story. For fantasy "the only rule is make up a new rule any time you need one!" For science fiction: "Set up a basic proposition – then develop its consistent, logical consequences" (Introduction iv–v.) But the science fiction–fantasy divide among authors, fans, and critics involves basic disagreements, which can be summarized on the science fiction side in the terms: rational vs. irrational, science vs. metaphysics, possible vs. impossible and I would venture a gendered opposition of male vs. female during the first half of science fiction's existence. For authors struggling to break out of a science fiction "ghetto" this self-definition away from fantasy genres was a means of justifying the greater importance of the genre to the progression of a technologized society.

about here only recently due to experimentation by GDR authors and film imports (*Krull*)" ("Gutachten über Lichtjahr" 2).

Instead of focusing on the issue of rational versus irrational, as the German Romantic tradition did, the Steinmüllers formulated the question of the "real" in terms of the collective and the individual. Recognizing that both had their foundations in ideology, the Steinmüllers used the tension between science fiction and fantasy in *The Dream Master* to search for the real. As the narrator's struggle to find her own voice demonstrates, this personal "reality" is not easy to perceive clearly or to retain. In a society like the GDR that underscored its own utopian ideology with the concepts of science and rationality, the Steinmüllers believed science fiction to be the only literature that could truly explore the nature of this reality. Its very subject matter the relationship between humanism and science and technology, Karlheinz Steinmüller writes that the "incorporation of the estrangement effect contributes to the ability to see the roll, function and societal implications of science more clearly" ("Positionsbestimmung" 162). Therefore, he believes, in a society in which ideology and science remain intertwined, and science fiction acts as the primary source of realism (147). The incorporation of fantasy in *The Dream Master* only enhanced this effect by consistently foregrounding the interrogation of reality. Its presence highlighted the importance of the continual struggle to retain adequate knowledge of the real.

Furthermore, the Steinmüllers perceive science fiction to be first and foremost a genre whose primary subject is the relationship between humanity and science and technology (Personal interview, 2000). To this end, they also blend aspects of science fiction and fantasy to present a highly ambivalent picture of humanity's dependence on technology. *The Dream Master* is neither the technologized communal utopia of Eberhardt Del Antonio nor is it the atomized, individual, dystopian nightmare exemplified by George Orwell in *Nineteen-eighty-four*. Rather, the Steinmüllers portray an objectified technology that its producers mismanage.

In the novel, the "use and abuse" of technology is closely related to the issue of memory. Here too the transgression of the border between science fiction and fantasy becomes significant. *The Dream*

Master itself is the story of the gradual downfall of Miscara, an ostensibly prosperous, desert city. It is located on the planet, Spera, which was colonized during the first wave of Earth's space exploration in the 21st century. *Andymon* relates the story of this first wave on a planet of the same name, while *The Dream Master* takes place some twenty centuries later.[7] The Miscarans have one peculiarity, which sets them apart from other cities on their planet. They are not able to dream on their own. Instead, they require the assistance of a dream master to dream for them high above the city in his glistening tower.[8] He dreams through the figures of the *Mittal*, a mythological place with a cast of characters that the Steinmüllers intended to be reminiscent of Arab mythology on Earth (Personal interview, 2000). The Mittal represents a type of collective unconscious and also functions as the keeper of the city's memory. This memory, recorded as myth, is ahistorical, placeless and nearly timeless. The figures in the Mittal include the ancestors of the Miscarans. In particular, it contains the city's founders, who are known as the "Grossen Alten" (literally the Big Old Ones). The Mittal explains that, during the "Golden Age," Miscara prospered in a highly advanced society. However, the "Grossen Alten" eventually retreated to the mountains behind Miscara. There, they continued to guard over the city's reserves of what the Miscarans called "blue metal," the mining of which represents the mainstay of Miscaran economy and preserves its independence. According to legend, the ancestors constructed the dream tower and created a fire-breathing machine. This machine protects the city from invasion by its contemporary enemies, the Grunelien.

These elements of fantasy: the presence of myth, collective dreaming, and the fire-breathing machine (dragon), receive a rational,

---

7   The Steinmüllers refer to this link in an interview on *The Dream Master*. See
     Junker and Klotz 65. They also restated it in an interview with this author at
     their home outside of Berlin on July 27, 2000. There are several references to
     Andymon in *The Dream Master*: 1) the Bethische Uhr, a time piece of the ages
     so to speak, which bears the same name as the main protagonist in their earlier
     book *Andymon* – Beth (who is actually male); 2) the reference to the colonizing
     and building of a planet from the ground up by a people who arrive in a space
     ship. This event is similar to the colonization of a chosen planet in *Andymon*.
8   The dream master has always been male with one past exception.

246

historical explanation as the novel progresses. Along with the narrator, Glauke Arnya, the reader discovers the writings of innumerable dream masters. These memoirs represent a recorded history alternate to what exists in the memory present in Miscaran dreams. This reality is revealed on one level by the slow emergence of *The Dream Master*'s science fiction elements. In a book long locked in the dream tower, Glauke discovers that the "Grossen Alten" arrived on her planet in spaceships long ago. With this revelation, it becomes apparent (although not immediately to Glauke) that the hitherto mysterious dream tower is none other than a piece of advanced technology, the collective dreaming, a scientifically explainable process. The fire-breathing machine is a highly advanced weapon. The blue metal is none other than the remnants of machinery left behind in the mountain by the society described in *Andymon*, now no longer understood and forgotten.

Where western dystopian and apocalyptic tales often demonize technology, the novel does not. Instead, it provides enough clues by the end to construct a rational explanation for the mythical or irrational. With the increased focus on the rational as truth, the novel demonstrates how knowledge can become obscure in a society that values the utility of swift technological advance without reflecting upon its impact on its users. Science and technology occupy a positive position in *The Dream Master*, signified by the "Golden Age" that existed before the fall into the irrationalism of a dark age.

Despite its positive portrayal of technology, the novel nevertheless warns against an overreliance on technology. It is possible to reach a stage where only a few can maintain and repair intricate systems. Why the inhabitants of Miscara no longer posses the technical training characteristic of the *Andymon* civilization is not clear. Even the dream master does not operate the tower with skill, but instead due to a "gift" of mysterious and wondrous origins. Rather than recover the knowledge needed to run the machines the "Grossen Alten" left behind, the Miscarans mine the material from which they are made. In the specific context of the GDR, a parallel can be drawn between Miscaran technology and East German factories and machinery. Built in the sixties at the height of the GDR's industrial development, they were in a slow state of decay in the eighties and often reused piece-meal due to a shortage of repair parts.

Blue metal mining has a side effect common to industrialized societies on Earth and of direct concern to the health and well being of East German readers. Due to the mining, a recurrent and destructive wind called the "Torl" blows down from their mountain location. A variety of bird called "Torlboten" or Torl messengers announces the wind's arrival.[9] The dust brought by the wind causes symptoms similar to black lung disease and eventually kills Glauke's father, Erast, a prominent wagon-maker and member of the patrician class. Still, the Miscarans must tolerate the wind if they are to remain an independent city. The mainstay of their economy consists of the sale of blue metal. Miscaran ancestors brought the technology, and, similar to the predicament of many developing countries today, the Miscarans are trapped by a paradox of progress. Through the rudimentary use of that technological gift, they destroy their very environs. Although the theme of environmental damage was widespread in East German science fiction by the eighties, the novel's mention of it is notable, as this topic still remained a political taboo.

The book itself continues, narrated by Glauke Arnya, a patrician's daughter from Miscara. Through her eyes, we meet her partner-to-be, Kilean, the new dream master. Kilean's arrival, near the beginning of the novel, brings an end to Miscara's short period of dreamlessness. Twenty-five years before, Nerev, the last dream master, ceased dreaming. With the arrival of Kilean the practice resumes, and eventually leads to the overthrow of the Nerevian system. Through his dreams, Kilean and Glauke along with Turio, Glauke's childhood playmate, try to found a grassroots democracy. When the populace fails to participate, Kilean resorts to dreaming it into existence. As the story continues, Glauke becomes more and more aware of his abuse of power and eventually leaves the city to escape Kilean's collective dreams. Shortly after Glauke returns, the townspeople destroy the tower. The people of Miscara (Glauke the first) are finally able to dream on their own.

---

9   This deadly wind is also reminiscent of the Modderwind in *Uncanny Manifestations on Omega XI*.

Static and Dynamic, Collective and Individual Utopia

A primary feature of *The Dream Master* is its juxtaposition of the collective and the individual. This subject itself was not uncommon in East Germany. Many supporters of a "Third Way" focused on it when envisioning alternate and more democratic forms of socialism.[10] The Steinmüllers place the notion of the collective and the individual in the frame of utopian discourse. By recognizing the essential utopian quality of alternative socialist models of the Third Way, they ultimately move beyond the notion of collective versus individual by presenting this concept in terms of "static" and "dynamic" utopia.[11]

The static utopia represents an unchanging and, therefore, unreachable, vision. In *The Dream Master*, the static utopia has both literary and political connotations. On one hand, it alludes to the form of classic literary utopia (e.g. Plato's *Republic*, More's *Utopia*, and Campanella's *The City of the Sun*) as a locationless and timeless narrative. Of necessity, classic utopian writing remained distant from the present due to the subversive political visions its novels often contained when applied to their respective historical contexts. In *The Dream Master*, the Steinmüllers apply the category of static utopia to the novel's various political systems. As I will show, both Nerev's and

10   For instance, the critique of East Germany in terms of finding a more equal balance between the collective and the individual was a common theme in GDR literature in the seventies and eighties. See, for instance, Anna Kuhn and Klaus Berghahn's studies of the utopian in Christa Wolf's work. Similar interrogations of this problematic can also be found in other disciplines including philosophy and history. The Steinmüllers began their exploration of the role of utopian thought in political institutions in their book *Andymon*. There they focused on the right to self-determination of a community or communities (as opposed to a society) to establish a governmental system based on what the Steinmüllers defined as that community's own utopia vision.

11   The terminology "dynamic" and "static" utopia are used by Angela and Karlheinz Steinmüller to describe their project in *The Dream Master*, see Steinmüllers, Personal interview. These are not terms used by them alone, but are often used in studies of utopia to differentiate the classic "static" utopias from the modern (particularly Marxist) effort at "dynamic" utopia. See, for instance, Elisabeth Hansot.

Kilean's utopian political systems are static in nature. The novel is ultimately critical of progressive yet static utopian thought.

Set in opposition to the static utopia is the dynamic utopia. Based in socialist (and even anarchist) thought, the dynamic utopia too can be applied both to the literary and political spheres. The Steinmüllers use the term "dynamic" to describe a flexible utopia that is responsive to changing individual wants and needs. *The Dream Master* underscores the importance of not passive but active participation of the individual subject as a creative resource in the authoring and renewal of a dynamic utopia, in order to insure the preservation of an essential space for the voice of the individual. Unlike the classic, literary utopia, the dynamic utopia relies on perpetual and equal contributions from all voices of its individual participants. This statement implies a socialist rather than anarchist dynamic utopian model, and focuses on the existence of individual utopia within communal utopia, rather than on the political rule of autonomous individual utopias as present in *Andymon*. However, some ambiguity resides in the novel's representation of dynamic utopia. Although *The Dream Master* ends with the collapse of static utopia and the articulation of the individual voice, what follows is ultimately left open.

Due in part to self-censorship, such an ending also demonstrates the recognition of the inability to narrate a dynamic, literary utopia. By its very nature, once the dynamic utopia has been committed to paper it ceases to be dynamic and becomes static. In the words of Frederic Jameson, the very act of narration, here of writing and of dreaming, necessarily results in "the systemic, cultural, and ideological closure of which we are all in one way of another prisoners" ("Progress vs. Utopia" (148). In an attempt to redefine the nature of utopia and, thus, escape this conundrum, the novel closes with a Blochian utopian gesture. It strives to remain dynamic, by creating the conditions for utopian thought, but not narrating it.

The political systems of *The Dream Master* seem to be based on collective utopian visions but are in reality the individual utopias of the respective person in power. The abuse of power by Kilean, in this instance, represents the central problematic in creating a more democratic socialist model. As his individual utopia becomes a collective utopia, that same utopia remains a static utopia. The power behind this

250

utopia prohibits the establishment of a more dynamic model that accepts the input of numerous individuals on a collective level. In this manner, *The Dream Master* focuses on the interaction between static, dynamic, collective and individual utopia in its narration of the successive building of a society (*Gesellschaft*), a community (*Gemeinschaft*), and their respective interaction and influence upon the personal utopia of the individual.

Collective Dreams as Collective Unconscious

A main premise of *The Dream Master* is its concept of collective dreaming. This act does not originate within a group nor is it the sum of individual wishes. More accurately, the dream master dreams alone for the collective. Through his dreams, he shapes Miscaran wants, needs, and desires. Collective dreaming functions in a manner similar to Althusser's concept of interpellation ("Ideology" 170–177). Through the Mittal, the Miscarans recognize themselves as subjects within the greater context of their world, as defined by the dream master's collective dreams. The collective dreaming differentiates itself from Althusser's definition of ideology, however, in that it is attributable to a single person. The novel's assumption of the viability of the individual voice is a concept which interpellation negates. A voice assumes personal agency. Althusser's interpellated subject is shaped by ideologies and is thus unable to imagine a reality beyond them. The dream master himself possesses the individual ability to dream for all others. However, the dream master ultimately becomes the victim of his own dreams. The novel itself presupposes that the destruction of the dream tower at its conclusion effectively halts the influence of all existing collective dreams. Once free, the Miscarans gain the agency to dream on their own. In a sense, they are able to author their own ideology.[12] Whether they embrace that agency remains unclear.

As the dream master dreams, he has direct control over the unconscious minds of the Miscarans. *The Dream Master* thus explores the formulation of voice through its metaphor of the Miscaran dream that is modeled on a Jungian collective unconscious. We are first introduced to the peculiar nature of Miscara's collective unconscious by its absence. As stated before, Miscarans are unable to dream for themselves. For hundreds, even thousands, of years following what is known as the "Crystal Age" ("Kristallene Zeitalter") of the "Grossen Alten," a dream master had dreamed for them. This long-established institution provided a stabilizing influence on the city of Miscara. It streamlined the thought processes of its citizens and reinforced the city's class system through the figures of the Mittal.

However, the last dream master, Nerev, brought about an end to the institution of the dream master and its enduring stability. In his dreams, Nerev criticized the act of dreaming as irrational and escapist. He maintained that dreams interfered with the productive capacities of Miscara. In Glauke's words, Nerev believed that "dreamlessness [meant] Progress [...] away from base desires and hazy thoughts, towards the light of Reason, towards true humanity" (36). Consequently, he declared an end to the position of dream master, so that Miscara might modernize and place more emphasis on its industrial development. In the twenty-five years of "enlightenment" since Nerev, Miscara became wealthy. Its merchants strove for monetary success in a period reminiscent of several stages of Earth's industrialization and capitalism. The patrician class occupied inherited seats on the city council, while the working classes labored in the mines or as servants.

Despite Nerev's cessation of dreaming, this end differs from the final destruction of the dream tower. First of all, as it still existed during the twenty-five years following Nerev, so did the hope for a continuation of dreaming. The dependence upon this hope is explained

---

12   Of course one can argue that they cannot be freed suddenly from all ideology that shapes them. However, the novel presents Glauke's transformation as one of emancipation.

by the production of *Schellnüsse*, a type of nut that induces a drug-like, hallucinatory state. The Miscaran lower classes rely upon it as a substitute for the collective dreams. Although this state does represent a type of individual dreaming it is by no means represented in a liberating manner, but rather one of drug and political dependency. The lower classes are reliant upon the upper classes to produce the *Schellnüsse*.

Next, although the hope for a continuation of collective dreams is, as Bloch has demonstrated, a revolutionary one, in the Nerevian system, this hope reinforced the status quo. The arrival of the new dream master, Kilean, realizes these hopes. As everyone anticipates the resumption of dreaming, new energy runs through the city. Those who remember the Mittal rejoice in its return and those who encounter it for the first time are fascinated by the dreaming experience. Glauke's servant, Landre, exclaims, "Now a new life will certainly begin" (24). Yet, it was this same anticipation of a dream master of the past, which kept the lower classes of Miscara from envisioning a new world. *The Dream Master* emphasizes the inability of the Miscarans to realize the value of their own dreams, as it is an ability they have never had. In effect, what Landre means by a new life is a new life dreamed by Kilean, not her.

The collective utopia created by Nerev, who promised an affluent society at the price of dreaming, led to a productive, yet gray and ultimately stagnant society. As the Miscarans no longer dreamed, they lost any ability to change, to remain creative and innovative. The notion of the individual as creative resource echoes Ernst Bloch's principle of hope, which identifies as its source the latent utopia present in the individual's not-yet-conscious. It is the creative expression harbored there, finding its outlet in such forms as art, literature, and popular culture, that provides the seeds for rejuvenatory and even revolutionary utopian thought (*Ästhetik* 103–114). Despite the city's veneer of prosperity, it is, in fact, in decline.

In this respect, Nerev's Miscara is similar to an East Germany based on the rational success of historical materialism, but in "reality" in slow disintegration. At the same time, *The Dream Master* contains a direct critique of the SED's desire to functionalize science fiction in the seventies and eighties. As detailed in chapter five, cultural officials viewed science fiction to be the ideal Marxist–Leninist forum in which to bring about creative contributions that would rejuvenate the lagging progress towards a communist East Germany. I am thinking here specifically of efforts dating back even to the sixties discussed in chapter three, when Heinrich Taut emphasized the important influence which science fiction had on the ability of scientists to solve problems in cybernetics creatively. It was the publisher, Ekkehard Redlin, who supported the incorporation of the estrangement effect into science fiction in hopes of gaining new perspectives and insightful contributions to further the development of communism in the GDR. *The Dream Master* demonstrated that such individual creative participation is not possible in a system, which does not establish favorable conditions for even the formulation of an individual voice.

In order for this appraisal of East Germany to pass the censors, it had to be hidden in the critique of an early-industrial, patrician/ capitalist society. Although Nerev based his static utopia on the promise of rational, scientific progress, this same utopia is reminiscent of a socialist representation of capitalism. In the novel, it emphasizes the inequality of a class system through a disadvantaged working class. In addition, Miscara's level of industrialization resembles that of a proto-capitalist Europe or a country of the developing world. Nerev retained the ideology of the status quo and kept the patrician class in power. Echoing colonialism and aspects of today's global market-place, many in the Miscaran patrician class ran profitable, if not monopolistic, businesses. The resulting negative portrayal and over-throw of this class throughout the remainder of the book was in line with the socialist beliefs of the Steinmüllers as well as the Marxist-Leninist ideology of the SED. Like science fiction, the textual ambiguity of science fantasy allowed for a dual critique of East Germany as well as capitalist structures.

In the character of Nerev, there are echoes of Stalin as well as the formulators of early SED policy.[13] That this policy is still entrenched

---

13   Although the most recent system before Nerev's favored the upper and merchant classes, Menthe, Glauke Aryna's governness remembered dreaming fondly. In a conversation with Glauke she stated: "With you permission – I still remember the period with dreaming well. After many, my parents danced in the

in Miscara twenty-five years later is shown in the conditions placed upon the new dream master by the city council. Echoing the many directives from the SED and more specifically the German Writers' Union, the council provided the following guidelines for Kilean in their document "Richtschnur für lotrechtes Träumen":

> [...] the dream creates no freedom outside of existing responsibilities, but is a loyal daily mirror and source of new strength to go on. There is no room for distorted images of reality, grimaces from ages ago, monsters from the Mittal in Miscara after Nerev. A true dream master should [...] not overtax the receiver's absorption capability, should not alarm them with the uncanny or restrict the dream to one place, one time period, or one incident. Therefore, dream in the following manner: tastefully and with the highest demands according to the most upright Miscarian principles [...]. If something will be sung in the dream, then, please, a song, that strengthens love for the home city, values virtue, and elevates the mind. Just no innovation![14]

As "dreams are city property" (38), Kilean was then to dream according to plan, just as the authors in the GDR were to write according to plan. The council even urged him to go out among the people and discover what their daily lives were like. However, in their own version of the Bitterfeld Path, the council manufactured an ideal vision of such lives in the city's Hanging Gardens for Kilean to observe, so that he might dream of the economic success to which the city's council aspired (103).

Yet again, this reference to East Germany remains oblique. In the portrayal of planned dreaming also lies a critique of commercialism in West German media. West German television was, although officially illegal, viewed in much of East Germany during the latter half of its existence. In an interview with this author, the Steinmüllers expressed the belief that former West Germans and now Germans live(d) in a society in which the collective unconscious is directed by

---

street and we children did too. That was foolish of course. The shoes were torn to pieces." Glauke then narrates: "All at once she [Menthe] seemed to have grown younger. [...] But then Nerev established order." (25).

14   See 79–81. In an interview with the Steinmüllers, they mentioned that they based sections of the book on actual proceedings from the SED and the German Writers' Union (Personal interview, 2000).

consumerism. They maintain that, influenced and shaped by the collective utopia of capitalism, the formulation of a personal utopia is restricted to the satisfaction of a purchase rather than the exploration of other opportunities and realities (Personal interview, 2000).

The collective dreams of Miscara, then, represent various forms of media, particularly television and film. However, rather than a team, only one person produces them. On one hand, *The Dream Master* points to the alleged influence of West German media moguls on their publications. The patrician class simultaneously owns and directs the city's means of production and runs the Miscaran city council. The temptation exists to include their products in the dream plan. Normally direct advertisement is not the rule, but is accomplished through product placement in a positive narrative. During Kilean's first walk around Miscara, Sombarq, the carpet salesman, pesters him with private requests for an emphasis on the beauty of the carpets in the Mittal (35). Even the mere attempt to reinforce the status quo through Kilean's dreams also points to a perceived streamlined effect of the television market in West and East Germany. The council's requested dream chains (*Traumketten*) in the Mittal (81), resemble a type of soap opera or drama series, which here is shown to entertain, but not to educate or "liberate" the personal unconscious.

Traumeszucht

Kilean's arrival signals the period of *Traumeszucht*, prophesied by the mysterious and strange guardian of the dream tower, Khalib. In German, the verb *zuchten* refers to the act of controlled or even forced creation or cultivation. *Träume* are defined as dreams. Thus, this act of dreaming is a shaped or forced activity. That Kilean's dreams are a form of *Traumeszucht* becomes apparent early on in the novel. At first, his dreams follow the city council's plan. Glauke, the narrator, plays a central role in this process, not only as Kilean's companion, but also as the liaison between Kilean and the council itself. As is tradition, she whispers their instructions to Kilean while he sleeps.

Indeed, the council claims control over Kilean. Legend has it that the seal above the council head's chair, if destroyed, will eliminate the powers of the dream master.

Kilean, however, is different from all other dream masters before him, in that he does not come from the patrician class. Rather, he is a foreign artisan, a clock-maker by trade and has had to struggle his entire life in a long journey across the desert to where he believes the Fates have led him: Miscara (72). His sympathies with the lower classes become apparent during his first walk through the city of Miscara with Glauke by his side. At times, he is received as a messianic figure by the downtrodden. In one scene, the poor, sick and needy, who believe that his dreams might heal them, mob Kilean. However, Kilean responds: "I can make your life more beautiful, but you must change it on your own" (53).

Foreshadowing events to come, Kilean is already contemplating *his* revolution. Taking on the role of dissident intellectual, he begins to test the authority of the council. In a manner similar to the Steinmüllers' position as authors in East Germany, he first slips ambiguous critiques of council members into his dream narratives. As he experiments with his newly found power, his dreams become increasingly erratic. To test the will of the council he intersperses pleasant visions with nightmares. Such dreams unsettle the normally pleasant, orderly Mittal. When Glauke discovers that the technology controlling the seal in the council chambers no longer functions, he openly plants the seeds of revolution. Kilean denounces the mining of blue metal, due to the adverse working conditions in the mines as well as the resultant deadly Torl wind:

> All of the unhappiness in your city comes from the fact that you Miscarians are deadened and fearful, the wind raids a clear mind, and your eyes are closed to what takes place in the mines. Understand me, I'm not for blind fear, but for a type of fear that sharpens the sense of danger (129).

At the same time, he creates a utopian vision of a lush, green and flourishing Miscara underneath a glass dome that protects it from the harsh realities of the surrounding desert (36). Kilean dreams of a future and finds inspiration in the past. He promises a return of the

257

Crystal Age, albeit in a new form. He dreams of the Hanging Gardens, left behind by the *Grossen Alten*, which once again produce food enough for everyone in his newly revised Mittal (97). With the help of Turio, Glauke's childhood playmate and a member of the lower class, Kilean is able to effectively respond to the needs and wants of miners and servants in his dreams. Reticent when the council criticizes him for disrupting the populace, Kilean defends himself, saying "a dream [...] only becomes real through the meaning that one gives it" (132). He thus denies responsibility, pointing instead to what he explains as the agency of the lower classes.

Finally, during a yearly carnival known as the "wild week," the existing order is turned on its head permanently.[15] The resulting revolution has communist overtones. The lower classes attack members of the patrician class and kill many. They either destroy patrician houses or occupy them and divide the mansions into communal living spaces for several families. They occupy the factories and the mines and take them over in the name of their workers. The reorganization of the Miscaran social structure represents the foundation of a new society based upon the utopia, which Kilean had put forth in his dreams. With the success of the revolution, Kilean proclaims a new age to a crowd in front of his tower:

> The terror is over. Your chains are broken. You will share the pleasant things in life as well as the unpleasant: work and bread, housing and clothing, water and, not to forget, knowledge. We will overcome need and poverty and the cares of tomorrow. We will eliminate slavery and the Torl, give the children a place to play, and give those, who must find new work daily, a reliable position. [...] The time has come, in which dreams become reality. (193).

So begins the attempt at a concrete establishment of a society initially imagined as utopia in the collective dreams of the city of Miscara.

With the revolution, comes the opportunity for a return to public life provided for through the establishment of a new council modeled

---

15   In *Spera* (2004), the Steinmüller's sequel to *The Dream Master*, the reader discovers that the "wild week" lies literally outside normal time. The Speran calendar consists of twelve months of fifty-one days each and then one wild week at the end (226).

on grass-roots democracy. Rejecting the political control of dreaming according to plan, Kilean refuses to continue to do so in his new society. His dreams have led to revolution. But, in a manner suggestive of Gorbachev's *perestroika*, Kilean proclaims his willingness to take a back seat and allow the lower classes to rule themselves. In setting up the new council, he explains to Glauke, the new council head: "I will not prescribe anything; a dream master, who gets bogged down, is of little use. Still, we should determine the main features right away together" (189). Having perceived the "powerlessness of the simple people" upon his arrival (190), he declares that each person (both women and men) has a say in the affairs of the council. Indeed, *The Dream Master* is highly critical of what it portrays as a state of political helplessness and inactivity resultant in a system, such as Nerev's (or East Germany's), in which hegemonic ideology is so dominant that it limits the very categories in which the imagination even functions. This loss of imagination and creativity led to the stagnation of its hierarchical society. The lower classes remained in the private sphere and forgot the possibility for personal initiative or individual act in the public sphere.

Yet, it is precisely the same feeling of helplessness that dooms such a plan to failure. The revolution Kilean envisioned was one he cultivated and shaped to fit what he believed would be best for the Miscaran people. Regardless of his good intentions, Kilean authored his collective dream alone. Even when he states that he will now let the people of Miscara rule themselves, he insists on dreaming until the council has been set up on his model. However, despite the call for grass roots participation in the council, only the curious come at first and then disappear altogether. Although Kilean's collective utopia included them, the lower class Miscarans did not participate in the creation of his collective vision. They were merely its objects. When Glauke suggests a rotational system in which a representative from the different city sections and communes comes once a week, the response from the people is that political affairs should be left to the experts (207). As a result, Glauke comments: "The old tendency to categorize themselves into high and low classes and to wait for the all-powerful cue was too ingrained" (206). Unused to democracy, the

Miscarans fell back into their old habits of granting Kilean the same power as the previous city council.

In fact, the only reason why people come to the council building is to examine the files, which the former council kept on them. Uncannily foreshadowing the now historical events following the fall of the Berlin Wall, these files are the result of spying done on the inhabitants of the city by the secretive figure Karq Erlarq, the council's former scribe and informer. His name is pronounced *Kakerlak* and is the German word for cockroach. That Kilean employs him as well is indicative of the general dissatisfaction and contempt for perceived corruption of all contemporary political systems present in *The Dream Master*. Karq Erlarq points out that "every leader of the city needs" him to maintain the power over the others in Miscara (200).

Ideology and Utopia

Kilean's solution to the Miscarans' inactivity in the public sphere represents another manifestation of *Traumeszucht*. As the grass-roots council proves increasingly ineffectual, Kilean begins to dream the people to action, so that the necessary work gets done. The council soon becomes the puppet of the dreamed utopia. Kilean must dream all activities before they are carried out. "Dreamed is dreamed" becomes the signal among the new citizens of their collective effort towards the recreation of the Crystal Age in Miscara. Kilean exploits his power as dream master to force the real-existing creation of his dream utopia.

In *The Dream Master*, the Steinmüllers use Kilean's *Traumeszucht* to highlight the process in which what might have been a revolutionary, collective utopia ultimately becomes static and therefore authoritarian. Literary and political definitions of the term utopia often highlight its subversive quality in a dialectical relationship with hegemonic ideology. Karl Mannheim first drew a connection between these two terms in his book *Ideology and Utopia*. There he defined ideology in terms of a collective unconscious and pointed specifically to those occasions when both the conscious and unconscious thought of a ruling group "obscures the real condition of society [...] to itself and to others and thereby stabilizes it" (40). For Mannheim, utopia is a wishful representation of reality intended to negate the existing ideology. Those who find themselves oppressed by one status quo create another. The Steinmüllers' notion of dynamic and static utopia in *The Dream Master* echoes the dialectical relationship between utopia and, what I prefer to call, hegemonic ideology as outlined by Mannheim.

Edith Clowes writes of Nazi Germany and Stalinist Russia: "ideology and utopia lost their fruitful, adversarial relationship and became one and the same, fusing the traditional characteristics of each" (Clowes 381). The same is true for Kilean's own static utopia. He provided the occasion for revolution, which he authored through his own collective dreams. Despite the pretense of revolution, what has occurred in Miscara is a return to the authoritarian structure similar to the previous hierarchical system under Nerev. As Kilean duplicated the existing ideology of the status quo, he formulated what Clowes terms a "utopian ideology" (Steinmüller, *Dream Master* 381). The fusion of the two dialectical forms ultimately led to the elimination of any critical challenge to the status quo, by "restricting the forms available to memory and imagination" (381). Through this Foucauldian circumscription of tangential or marginal thought, resistance became literally unimaginable, particularly for Miscarans, who ultimately relied on the vision put forth by Kilean.

It is, therefore, the faulty collective utopian structure that is retained from system to system regardless of form. This very structure precludes the ability of revolution to break free of existing systemic limitations. What began as an attempt at dynamic socialism, reverted in practice to a static, authoritarian reality. In a sense, the communist vision of Marxism–Leninism and the free-market system of the West, both grounded in the methodical, rational practice of science, proved in *The Dream Master* to be as unreachable as the locationless, classical utopian thought it criticized. Similar to Campanella's philosophical dialog in his well-known utopia *The City of the Sun* (La Città del Sole; 1602), the revolutionary socialist and progressive elements of Kilean's revolution are overshadowed and ultimately destroyed by the authoritarian structure required to implement them.[16]

Traumessucht

As *The Dream Master* progresses, it becomes apparent that the utopia of the Crystal Age is ultimately unattainable. At the beginning, Kilean speaks in Marxist terms of revealing the false consciousness present in the planned dreams of the council. He himself is a student of the art of dreaming and learns the craft through self-study of the books left behind by former dream masters. As outlined in the fictional book *Samadhi – Traumeszucht oder: Die Kunst, dem Unwirklichen feste Formen zu verleihen*, his goal is "to be awake while dreaming and to recognize deception as deception" (137). Only in this manner can he reach the next level of expertise. Yet, the mysterious keeper of the tower, Khalib, prophesies that the transition from *Traumeszucht* is *Traumessucht* (135). A *Sucht* in German is an addiction or obsession and refers here to dream addiction. This addiction has two meanings in *The Dream Master*. One is the abuse of power that undermines the initial vision of revolution. The second is the addiction to this power.

The abuse of power lies in Kilean's unwillingness to release the Miscaran's from his collective dreams when his revolution initially

16   Kilean's utopia is based in part on the problematics present in Fra Tommaso Campanella's *The City of the Sun* (Steinmüllers, Personal Interview, 2000). During the Russian Revolution, Lenin and others heralded the utopia put forth by Campanella for its communist elements (Stites 88, 90). A classic utopia laid out in the form of a philosophical dialogue, what is notable in this early work (written about a century after More's *Utopia*) is its seeming ambivalence regarding the society it was proposing. Anthony Stephens writes that the "Sun State could be said to be accompanied, thoughout the text which establishes it, by its shadow in the form of its own complete dystopia" (8). The text is fraught with contradictions emphasizing the imperfection of what should be the ideal society. Campanella wrote this story from prison, after years of failed revolutionary activity, perhaps conscious of impossibility of the utopia he was constructing.

failed. The ostensibly dynamic period of chaos during the revolution, in which the illusion of "false consciousness" appeared so clearly, soon turns to the static dream-reality of Kilean's utopian ideology. Even as the Miscarans are to participate in the council, they receive new visions of the Crystal Age they are to build. As the council fails, Kilean dreams every detail of this planned construction, down to the last kernel of grain and hour of work. He returns to the planned dreaming of the city council before him.

Important to the notion of *Traumessucht* is that this utopia was Kilean's and not the Miscarans'. Kilean is the aloof intellectual, who remains locked in his tower surrounded by books. He carries out his revolution through theory, study, and in his writings – the dreams. The sole outside contributors are Turio, his contact to what Kilean defines to be the lower classes, and Glauke, his contact with the council. Despite his few forays into the world of the mines and on the streets, Kilean remains cut off from the day-to-day needs and wants of the people for whom he is dreaming. He envisions their revolution for them. As such Kilean's utopia is based on a single voice, his own. Therein lies the central argument of *The Dream Master*. A collective utopia ultimately becomes static if created and implemented by one individual or a group of individuals.

So strong and compelling are the visions in Kilean's dreams that they dominate the conscious and unconscious minds of the Miscarans. The structures and concepts represented in the dreams limit and shape any capacity to critique or think independently. In *Traumessucht*, both Kilean and the Miscarans reach a stage similar to that of a waking dream. Their collective unconscious now takes over their conscious minds. Dream and reality merge fully. Colorful buildings and plentiful gardens replace the gray of reality and poverty of the city. Even Kilean falls victim to his own *Traumessucht*, as he sees before him a veritable feast, instead of the millet dishes he ingests (233). Convinced he has reached a higher plane, Kilean is unable to see the desperate reality of his city. Miscara slowly grinds to a halt as the vision of the Crystal Age literally creates a city as inert as glass (174). The mines remain closed to stop the Torl; trade ceased with the halt of blue metal production; the storage bins are empty. In reality, order has become chaos. Still, the Miscarans perceive only the mirage of Kilean's utopian dream.

Then a transition occurs, brought on by the threat of attack from the outside. Seeing the danger, Kilean dreams the mines back into operation. The Torl begins once again to threaten the health of all those who live in Miscara. At the same time, the army of a dissident group, which has been camped outside of the city wall, attacks Miscara. Sigmarq, a former military hero and owner of the mines, leads it. He is rumored to have made an alliance with Miscara's enemy, the Grunelien, an allusion to West Germany. As Sigmarq begins to take over the city, he promises to bring about a revolution in Miscara. He will create "freedom from order, individual happiness from the communal well-being" (251).

Sigmarq represents a further type of authoritarian utopia, this time fascist in form. In regards to this utopia, the text makes direct reference to Campanella. The seven planets in *The City of the Sun* become the "seven walls" which will reflect the "strong sun gold" of Sigmarq's regime that will replace the weaker "flat silver" of Kilean's Crystal City. However, Kilean defeats Sigmarq with the use of the "fire-breathing machine."

Sigmarq's invasion alludes to Kilean's abuse of power present in *Traumessucht*. Eventually taken prisoner by Kilean's forces, Sigmarq bites into a cyanide capsule. Before he dies, he asks Kilean if he "Do you not notice, the desire, to control people? You will construct my city of the sun. But you will not re-dream me" (256). Using the methods of both Sigmarq and the patrician council, Kilean has become the enemy. He is able to reshape personal desires and wishes to his own ends, as pointed to by Sigmarq's use of the word "umträumen" or re-dreaming. Kilean has also reached his goal to become awake in his dreams. Yet, in the process, he has lost sight of the border between dream and reality and lives in a permanent dream. In this way, the city after Sigmarq's attack the city of Miscara becomes "a city inhabited by sleepwalkers" (259).

Gender and the Search for "I"

There is one character within the city, who does not become caught within Kilean's dreams, and that is the novel's narrator, Glauke Arnya. Up to this point I have made numerous references to Glauke, but have focused little on her in her own right. I have done this intentionally as her character provides the central focus for the hope that is instilled in the narrative at the end of the novel. This hope is based on her gradual search for her own voice, which she discovers on the last page, when she dreams for the first time on her own.

The novel can be understood as a *Bildungsroman*, as Glauke learns to separate herself from the influence of others and to articulate her own identity. A naïve, adolescent at the beginning of the novel, through her struggle for her own opinion, her own thoughts and her own voice, she has become an adult by the end. Although shaped by the presence of Menthe, her governess, Erast, her father, Sycoraq, her teacher, and finally Kilean, she frees herself from all of these influences and is able to think and *dream* on her own at the end.

Glauke's personal journey, recounted in *The Dream Master*, reaffirms the hope for the self-realization of the individual. Despite the influence of her collective utopian society on her as object, Glauke is still able to articulate herself as subject. This ability comes as a result of her gender, in part with the help of a separatist, feminist collective. Like many of Christa Wolf's novels, but similar to *Cassandra* in particular, the novel employs a feminist critique to address the failure of the individual to develop fully and freely in the GDR. However, Wolf expanded her focus in *Cassandra* beyond socialism, to trace this failure back to the beginnings of patriarchy. The Steinmüllers, on the other hand, focused instead on a predisposition of modern society to collective utopia, which hinders the development of the individual voice in both women and men. Glauke's growing consciousness of herself as a woman in Miscaran society plays a central role in her transition from "we" to "I."

As mentioned, Glauke is, at first, a patrician's daughter. Her place is still within her father's house. She is reliant on her servant, Landre, and governess, Menthe, because her real mother is dead.

Glauke has grown up with Menthe's son, Turio, and provides him with access to education, so that he might quiz her on problems in mathematics (10). She is also very much the product of Nerev's utopian ideology. In explaining Miscara to Kilean, she identifies with the city, using the pronoun "we," which in reality refers to the ruling patrician class of which she is a part. Without much self-reflection, she vocalizes the ideological explanations of all of Miscara's cultural practices and societal institutions, which have been instilled in her by her father, Menthe and her male teacher.

During her first meeting with Kilean, this begins to change in two important ways. First, she is exposed to ideas formed independently of her Miscaran reality. Her long conversations with Kilean, her introduction of him to Miscaran culture and his continual questioning and dissatisfaction with the social relations of the city lead her to reassess what she has been taught. To Glauke, Kilean represents a source outside of the closed Miscaran thought system, which grants her the ability to reflect upon the workings of her own city.

Secondly, Glauke confronts for the first time what it means to be a patrician woman. Not ready to assume the role of wife and mother, she decides that she would much rather like to ride in the Karr (desert), climb on the edges of glaciers, or jump onto ice bridges in the mountains with Turio (22). Since these activities are unusual for a patrician daughter, Glauke already diverges from the ideological norm. While Menthe's dresses her to visit Kilean and present herself to him as a possible bride, Glauke comments on how thin her mother had been and how impractical her fine clothes are: "How could Menthe call something pretty, that was in reality so uncomfortable! (27). For the first time, we are confronted directly with the separation of Glauke's narrative voice from her participation as member of the patrician class in the plot of the story. She compares herself to a puppet, trapped in the clothing and beliefs of an ideology, which do not fit her. Yet, she does not yet understand nor is she able to voice why. At this point she embarks upon a journey to discover this voice.

Glauke's character is unique in that she is the only person (other than Turio), who is shielded from Kilean's dreams by her ability to remain within the tower. Although certainly affected by his re-creation and transformation of the Miscaran collective unconscious, Glauke retains the glimmer of a conscious perspective on these dreams. She experiences them not as one continuous narrative like the others do, but in bits and pieces, which disrupt their cohesive narrative. In addition, she is able to see the mode of dream production firsthand and read the dream books along with Kilean. She contemplates her own ability to influence his dreams and thus perceive the truth behind what to others is a mysterious ability. At one point, she even considers becoming a dream master herself.

However, this reflective tendency does not provide her with clear thoughts of resistance. Her thoughts are continually dominated and shaped by the remnants of Nerev's utopian ideology and the new ideas presented to her through philosophical discussions with Kilean and his dreams. This struggle becomes apparent early on in one particular dream. Upon leaving her home to visit Kilean for the first time, Glauke experienced feelings of independence and emancipation. Although she was sent to him by her father, Glauke decides on the way to the tower that she will use every strategy to become his wife. She decides this not because she must, but because she *wants to* (28). She recognizes the importance of such a role, knowing that she will eventually take the place of her father on the council. However, Kilean reverses this autonomous vision for a time through a patriarchal dream, in which Glauke returns to the safety of her father's home. The dream instructs her that she is meant to keep the house clean and the maid under control.

Yet, it is precisely her gender in addition to her position within the tower, which lead Glauke to continuously, if not always consciously, question the path Kilean takes. From the very beginning, she recognizes that he dreams a man's dream. Much like the female Anders in Wolf's *Selbstversuch*, Glauke relishes the opportunity to experience the "terrible beauty" of a man's life from within his own skin. Still, this very recognition establishes a rupture between Glauke's experience and Kilean's dreams. Where she does identify with them while asleep, she is able to contemplate them from a position of estrangement during her waking hours.

Indeed, gender difference initially acts as a form of liberation for the many women who join Doratra in her feminist commune known as the *Frauenberg* or women's mountain. The only patrician woman on the city council when Kilean arrived, Doratra created the Frauenberg by employing one of Kilean's own dreams. According to the novel, she "bewitches" him with a secret potion with Glauke as her emissary so that he might dream of a feminist revolution. In this dream, Kilean calls upon all Miscaran women to leave their patriarchal shackles behind and form the Frauenberg. Reminiscent of the secret community of women, who provided shelter to Wolf's Cassandra, the Frauenberg educates, feeds and otherwise supports all women, who "choose" to join them.

A societal form that the Steinmüllers experimented with in *Andymon*, the women of the Frauenberg are able to create a space or gap in which they have limited freedom. This freedom derives from Kilean's exclusion of the Frauenberg in his dreams. As it is not his creation, but rather Doratra's, he does not include the Frauenberg after the initial foundational dream. Thus, a fissure opens in the city's utopian ideology for those women, who identify as Miscaran and as the undefined identity of the Frauenberg. In this niche, they create their own community. Glauke takes part in their activities, teaches classes, and delivers supplies. Yet, she does not move to the Frauenberg, due to her responsibilities as council head and as Kilean's assistant.

In keeping with the ambiguous nature of the novel, *The Dream Master* portrays the Frauenberg both positively and negatively. This feminist movement is able to carve out and maintain a place for itself on the margins of society. It is partially successful in creating a dynamic space shaped by its members. However, where Wolf's Cassandra seeks out a utopian feminist community outside of the city of Troy, the Frauenberg lies within the walls of Miscara.[17] Despite Doratra's assertion that its members have released themselves from patriarchy and have created a world "the way a woman would," the Frauenberg remains economically and ideologically dependent upon Kilean's Miscara (159). In addition, the figure of Doratra contains many elements of a negative feminist stereotype. Although she liberated herself years ago "the way a man would" to become the only woman on the city council, Glauke likens her to a witch and portrays

17   For more on the utopian nature of this community in Christa Wolf's *Cassandra*, see Ryan.

her as power hungry and aggressive (159). It is Doratra who urges Glauke to assassinate Kilean before it is too late.

Doratra's behavior represents a critique of the Frauenberg, and likewise one side of the feminist movement in East Germany. The impetus for its creation did not come from the women themselves, but rather from Kilean's dream via Glauke and Doratra.[18] In addition, its feminist ideology still occupies a place subservient to the more influential hegemonic ideology directed by Kilean, as is evident in Glauke's exchange with her friend Janta. When Glauke asks what she most desires, Janta does not wish for women's equality, but rather "The Crystal City – tomorrow." Her feminism is subsumed by the greater collective utopia of Miscara. Yet, Glauke forces her further: "I wanted to know her own wishes, her own thoughts, not what Kilean had dreamed for her" (286). Finally, Glauke pushes Janta to the point of saying "I." However, Janta's statement is attributed more to her youth than the liberating effects of the feminist collective. In this manner the ability and willingness to say "I" comes from a gene-rational difference rather than Janta's position in the Frauenberg. Thus, although feminism has an unseen, albeit positive, effect upon Glauke's process of self-realization, as a collective movement, the Steinmüllers ultimately equated a portion of the movement in East Germany with Kilean's collective utopia.

Still, Glauke's character retains many feminist elements. Glauke herself is not portrayed as the unified individual of the Enlightenment, but rather in a post-modern manner of multiple inner subjects. In the search for her own voice, two female, mythical figures, which seem to reside within her, assist her. One is her long dead ancestor Nya, with whom Glauke shares a family resemblance. Nya is also a mytho-logical character in the Mittal. Glauke's connection to Nya, one of the Grossen Alten, allows her to access memories and history other than those represented in the Mittal. In the same way Wolf's Cassandra

18   This is an instance in which Glauke serves as a transmitter of thoughts from the council, rather than as her own self. She displaces responsibility for the Frauenberg dream, which she whispered in Kilean's ear, on Doratra. Doratra was the one who suggested it to her and provided her with the "magic" potion, yet Glauke was the only one with direct access to Kilean that night.

represents the articulation of a woman's voice, which has always remained in the shadow of history, Nya too leads Glauke to an alternate history different from the one by the dream masters. The other mythical person within Glauke is Arysa, a figure reminiscent of Penthesilea. A vengeful, patron saint for women, Arysa is the source of Glauke's strength. She is the one, who is responsible for Glauke's possession of the *sicia*, the small blade for a woman's self-defense handed down for generations in her family.

Through Glauke's narrative, we gain access to her thoughts and the ongoing struggle for her own identity. Despite the promises of independence present in Kilean's revolution, once it is over, she soon discovers that she is still not able to formulate her own opinion. In her new position as council head, Glauke states: "So I opened the first session of the new council, of a new age. But it was as if I had no voice of my own, as if I had to imitate Kilean or Ardelt."[19] We are privy to her numerous inner-dialogues, as she continues to search for her own thoughts amid the various voices of the others.

Only when the attacking Siqmarq is captured and Glauke's father dies from the Torl dust, does Glauke finally see "reality." At that point, she remembers the words from one of the old dream master books:

> If his dreams are also yours,
> What remains of your own opinion?
> What remains of your own deeds?
> You limp like a puppy on a leash (247).

With these words, she is able to express her right "to be Glauke" (247). However, she is not able to articulate what this means, until she removes herself from Kilean's influence. First, taking refuge in the Frauenberg, she finally leaves for the desert. Kilean has recognized the danger in her and has begun to dream her out of existence. At this point in the novel, we finally reach the place where the narrative joins with chronological time. Rather than continuing on with a series of flashbacks, the plot now moves forward.

---

19   Ardelt was the previous council head under the old system (196).

Before I continue, I must mention the significance of Glauke's act of writing in the novel. Before the revolution, Glauke whispers the city council's dream plans into Kilean's ear and is in some respect the author of these dreams. However, she attributes this "writing" to Kilean and not to herself. Neither is she aware of herself as the author in this case. In the novel, the only books present are those in the dream tower, which contain the history of Miscara and the art of dreaming. As Glauke leaves the Frauenberg for the last time, she is urged by Landre to write down all that has happened in Miscara. Landre warns: "You must write everything down, Glauke [...] for us. You were always there. You know him the best. And he can steal our memories" (294). This time a woman is charged with the writing of history for the entire city. Judith Ryan has written of the importance of Cassandra's act of writing and the "new patterns of thought that her way of seeing brings with it" (321). In writing her non-linear, first-person narrative, Glauke breaks the notion of a progressive history present in both Nerev's and Kilean's utopian ideology. Her very act of writing, what turns out to be the novel itself, defies Kilean by presenting a reality other than the one he has dreamed. In addition, by looking at the past and the present, it provides a future for Miscara based on her own self-articulation. Unlike Cassandra, Glauke does not find defeat in personal consciousness for she is the first of many to begin the process of dreaming on their own.

Apocalypse

Although *The Dream Master* has many utopian and dystopian elements common to the ambiguous utopia, the finality of its ending signals the use of a technique uncommon to East German science fiction: the apocalypse. Apocalypse implies societal upheaval and destruction through natural or human violence. All of these were at odds with the vision of a peaceful revolution from capitalism to communism characteristic of East German socialist realism and of its future visions.[20] Due to the institution of censorship, rather than a truly apocalyptic novel, *The Dream Master* contains apocalyptic tendencies. The finality of its ending is not violent, yet the dream tower is destroyed, bringing with it the end of Miscaran history. There will be no more collective dreams as the technology has been destroyed. Furthermore, economic and political stagnation has brought much of the city to ruin. The appropriation of the apocalyptic form remains integral to the novel's critique of collective utopia. At the same time and with the benefit of hindsight, the inclusion of apocalypse signals the presence of a "structure of feeling" in the novel, which captured the atmosphere of the GDR in its last years.

Frederick Kreuzinger writes that the apocalyptic narrative form is closely tied to religious metaphor, and to the notion of prophecy, whether this prophecy manifests itself in theology or in more secular institutions and ideas. Where utopia incorporates prophecy in the positive vision of a timeless and placeless reality, the apocalypse posits the destruction of the existing order in real time with the promise of prophetic fulfillment beyond. In this manner, utopia and apocalypse are often interwoven in literature and exist in dialectic tension (108).

One function of the apocalyptic is to retell the prophecy. This act either reinforces the strength of the original utopian prophecy or, as in the case of *The Dream Master*, retells the story of the prophecy in a critical manner and ultimately changes its outcome from one of utopia to that of catastrophe. It is this dual function of the apocalyptic, which David Ketterer identifies in his book *New Worlds for Old*. There he expands upon Northrop Frye's discussion of apocalyptic myth to include not only the positive world to be desired beyond, but also its opposite – the demonic world to be feared. He suggests that these opposites become easily intermixed in the gray area between them (11). Like science fiction itself, Ketterer maintains "apocalyptic literature is concerned with the creation of other worlds which exist, on the literal level, in a credible relationship (whether on the basis of rational extrapolation and analogy or religious belief) with the 'real' world, thereby causing a metaphorical destruction of that 'real' world in the

20   In Christa Wolf's *Cassandra*, the apocalyptic surfaced in the historical past.

reader's head" (13). In the context of the GDR, *The Dream Master* can be read as a retelling of the prophecy of Marxism–Leninism, with reference both to the existing hegemonic ideology in the GDR as well as the more liberal promises of Gorbachev's reforms.

The apocalyptic elements of *The Dream Master* problematize this very reference to the 'real'. They refer both to the ideological real of a collective subjectivity as demonstrated by the orchestrated dreaming of the office of the dream master, and to the material real as evidenced by the resumption of the destructive Torl wind and ever present societal hierarchy. The contradictions between the virtual reality as dreamed by Kilean and the real-existing utopia in Miscara eventually lead to collapse. As the city slows and becomes glasslike, Kilean loses himself more and more in his dreams. The messiah himself becomes entranced in the border between dream and reality and can no longer control his own utopia. After having dreamed Glauke out of the memories of Miscarans, Kilean dreams himself out of existence as well (299–300). Glauke declares: "Miscara is no more. The city of dreams between desert and glacier has disappeared like a mirage when the wind starts to blow. The walls and stairs, houses and squares, stones and people remain" (297). The material remains, yet the true city existed only in the dreams of those who inhabited it. Once those dreams are gone with the destruction of the dream tower and the final disappearance of its dream master, the essence of the city disappears as well.

Träume sucht

The novel's last chapter is labeled "Awakening" and represents the transition from *Traumessucht* to *Träume sucht* (the search for dreams). A common characteristic of apocalyptic narrative, a glimmer of hope is present in Glauke's newly found ability to dream on her own. With the destruction of the tower, each inhabitant has been left behind with a piece of it and, therefore, the ability to dream. Glauke is the first, and she dreams of Kilean, who assures her that "a city, in which all people dream their own dreams frees itself from dust" (302). Thus, she will be able to create her own dreams, now severed from the Miscaran collective unconscious. This ending places hope in the ability of the individual to formulate her/his own voice as subject, rather than relying on a collective unconscious. It represents the impetus for a new dynamic utopia, but stops short of any further concrete outline of what is to come.

Conclusion

The Dream Master marks the last of the East German science fiction novels to be published in East Germany. Like the city of Miscara, on October 3, 1990 the imagined society that was East Germany ceased to exist and left only the people and the buildings behind. In some circles, the November before signaled great hope for a new direction, a socialist third way. *The Dream Master* posited one such possibility of a new government, based not on the static, collective utopia of the few, but rather the dynamic utopia of the many. Based on the individual utopias of its citizens the Steinmüllers hoped for a positive development in this direction. This form of democratic socialism provided the individual of the East with the opportunity to develop more authentic wishes and desires than those of West Germany. The Steinmüllers felt that the West German utopia of individualism was in fact a collective utopia based on media representations of the values of consumption, wealth and free time (Personal interview 2000).

However, the hope present in *The Dream Master*'s utopian suggestion is mediated by the reality of the environmental destruction to the city of Miscara caused by the return of the Torl wind. This element of the story implies a critique of the irresponsible management of East German industry that led to continuously dangerous levels of environmental pollutants in the seventies and eighties. More significant is the recognition that a revolution based on class will not lead to a problem-free industry. Even Kilean's attempts at a grass-roots utopia remained dependent upon the industrial infrastructure it inherited from the previous government. As this infrastructure is inherent to any modern industrial society, regardless of political system, quick-fix solutions or immediate abstinence to save the environment are either ineffective or economically damaging. *The Dream Master* does not provide any answers to this predicament, but rather takes the notable step of identifying this influential paradox in its exploration of the contemporary relationship between humanity and technology. It emphasizes the importance of maintaining contact with that reality when creating a new order.

Not to be forgotten either are the Grunelien troops camped outside the city limits. While their leader Sigmarq is gone, the neighboring Grunelien forces still cast a shadow over the new city of Miscara. Like the Federal Republic of Germany poised to reunify with the East, is it only a matter of time before the Grunelien take control of an economically weak Miscara without leadership. In the novel, the question remains whether the Miscarans will try to form the dynamic utopia suggested by the book or return to the structures of an existing political authority once again.

Chapter Ten
Bleibt was? East German Science Fiction Since 1990

A search for what remains of East Germany is central to an understanding of the perpetuation of the "inner wall." Such an investigation sheds light on the processes of remembering and forgetting that make up the foundations of this wall and provide a basis for the assumptions made on both sides that stem from these memories. Nor is the phenomenon of the "inner wall" a static one, but, rather, is transformed by a recurrent renegotiation of memories through which the individual reformulates her or his most recent notion of Germany identity. Reinforcing the notion of an "inner wall," this identity commonly includes personal association away from one side and with, or towards, the other. Examples of this process range from denials that a GDR culture ever existed or was worthy of recognition to western and eastern forms of *Ostalgie* or nostalgia for the East. These diverse interpretations of a culture that is simultaneously present and absent points to the necessity of a continual, critical reassessment of East Germany's past. This exercise is crucial to the process of memory creation and revision in the Germany of today and to an understanding of the role that these memories and any "inner wall" will play in the Germany of tomorrow.

In part, this study has participated in the reformation of such memories through its reading of East German science fiction from a contemporary point of view. By collecting the cultural artifacts of this genre and questioning their veritable absence within existing literary histories, my work has sought to demonstrate the continued presence of this science fiction and its textual relevance to German Studies. Yet, East German science fiction did not consist solely of material objects nor of discourses, but also of writers, publishers, and fans, many of which continue to live in the newly unified Federal Republic. To forget the existence of GDR science fiction is to deny the past of those individuals, who participated in its creation and consumption.

A look at East German science fiction and its authors in the era following unification reflects the struggle of the majority of easterners to adapt to an alien socio-economic system and renegotiate their position both inside and outside a new discursive system.

This final chapter looks at recent science fiction by eastern writers after reunification. Since 1990, publication has been sporadic at best. East German writers had occupied a protected island that allowed them, albeit with many restrictions, to develop in a direction primarily free of market forces. They are now experiencing the realities of the German science fiction market, which is dominated by Anglo-American translations. Since presses have been hesitant to publish eastern authors, the majority of stories appear in independent labels. These narratives present a unique access to the changed future visions of authors, who have experienced a historical as well as personal rupture. A brief survey of the nature and type of publications by former East German writers since 1990 helps to illustrate how this very rupture has influenced and shaped their science fiction.

Science fiction always suffers from the march of time, even more than other genres. Since its premise is often couched in technological extrapolation based on existing knowledge and theory, the stories from even ten years ago can seem dated. Stories from the beginning of the 20th century frequently told of alien inhabitants discovered on voyages to the moon, which became impossible when it was confirmed that the moon was lifeless. Tales of great technological feats on Earth (tunneling between Europe and the United States, melting the polar ice caps) both in the East and West have either lost their estrangement effect as they have become reality in some shape or form, or they seem foolish, and even dangerous, from a contemporary point of view. In generic terms, older science fiction begins to take on elements of fantasy as it ages, and its seemingly rational suppositions become more and more irrational with time, as they are proven impossible.

On a cultural and political level, science fiction too can lose its vibrancy. What might have been a marginal or subversive belief in the past can have moved to the center of the present. For instance, George Orwell's *Nineteen-eighty-four* was originally written at the beginning of the Cold War in 1948 warning of the possibilities of a Soviet victory. From the vantage point of the early 21st century, the original impetus for the book has lost its immediate historical referent. Still, *Nineteen-eighty-four* has not lost its value as a science fiction text. Rather, due to its setting in another place and time, its original premise can be read in many ways that might apply to the context of the current reader. For instance, it can be applied to other authoritarian regimes or as a warning of one to come.

In a like manner, many texts of East German science fiction still contain valuable insights into today's society. For instance, as shown in my analysis of the communist utopia posited by Del Antonio, this text envisions gender equality in a manner as yet unrealized. Issues regarding the environment, as addressed in works by the Brauns, were pertinent in East and West Germany and have become an even more urgent concern in the present. In addition, their use of the concept of play and the game applies not only to the government of East Germany, but to all situations in which the "truth" or the "real" might not be as clear as it seems. Finally, the issue of individual and community continues to be relevant in every society that struggles for this balance. As the potential for multiple readings allowed these authors to bypass the censors in the GDR, this same aspect now enables their works to remain of interest to the contemporary reader.[1]

Approaching GDR science fiction as literary, cultural and historical artifact, my study has addressed aspects of memory creation and the existence of a wall in western academic discourse on East German literature. Where the category of literature had been equated with subversion in the Cold War paradigm, I have approached East German science fiction looking not only for qualities of subversion, but also for aspects of affirmation and negotiation with the GDR discursive system. This method does not exclude texts on the basis of ideology, but rather is inclusive in pursuit of my goal to provide for a multi-faceted understanding of East German society in its historical and cultural context. Where Del Antonio's text would otherwise be dis-

---

1   In many ways the study of East Germany, and of history in general, contains its own estrangement effect, set in an alternate time and place much like science fiction, leading to insights into the present.

missed as socialist propaganda, the presence of other narratives that diverged from the rather narrow official party line betrays a more complex negotiation with and transgression of the borders of *Parteilichkeit*. In a similar manner, where the Brauns and the Steinmüllers could be read merely as subversive texts, such an analysis would overlook their corrective intentions and tacit support for the system in which they were participating.

By treating science fiction as text, my study also argues for the inclusion of GDR popular literature in German Studies for the purposes of acknowledging and accessing a broader array of discourses, which shaped the public and private spheres of East Germany. Through its examination of numerous discourses and institutions that influenced East German science fiction, the book refines the definition of East German literature and goes beyond issues central to the German Writers' Union. East German science fiction texts integrated aspects of high and low culture, science and literature, utopia and realism, science fiction and fantasy. A closer look at the transgression of such borders revealed a number of discursive and formal contradictions and presented a more complex understanding of the issues that constituted them. In doing so, I join Bathrick, Hell and others in challenging existing literary histories of East Germany as incomplete in an understanding of the literary traditions and discourses that shape the contemporary memory of what was the literature and culture of the GDR. However, where Bathrick and Hell based their studies on canonical authors, I argue for the inclusion of popular literary texts as a manner in which to access influential discourses that lie beyond canonical boundaries. Thus, by positioning science fiction as a genre within GDR literature, I demonstrate the value of science fiction to East German Studies and hope to contribute to the limited, but growing efforts in the analysis of GDR popular culture.

I also argue for East German science fiction as a legitimate and relatively unexplored tradition in the international arena of science fiction studies and present its range and variety of media and narrative as a rich source for further study. For the most part, students of science fiction have focused entirely on texts from the Anglo–American tradition. The validity of genre studies that focus primarily on works from one cultural tradition is limited by the very geographical boundaries of that tradition. To become a truly international field, like its objects of study, science fiction studies must recognize and account for the wealth of difference present in texts written by non English-speaking authors.

In the study of East German science fiction, the greatest challenge lies in the availability of and accessibility to what remains of the genre. This problem is best depicted by the fate of *The Dream Master* by the Steinmüllers. After waiting for the accompanying illustrations, this book was finally published in 1990. A title that would have more than likely sold out had it appeared in East Germany prior to 1989, the publication was caught in the upheaval following the fall of the Berlin Wall and was a victim of early signs of the still-existent inner wall. When they finally gained universal access to western goods, easterners ceased buying GDR products (including books). Nor were the majority of westerners drawn by the lure of an exotic East. Long under the impression that everything in the East was either inferior or ideologically problematic, they continued to live and consume in their established patterns. Hence, consumer perception played a primary role in the collapse of the market for eastern products in the early nineties.[2] Like many other eastern goods, *The Dream Master* fell prey to reunification fallout and did not sell well.[3] Today, East German

2   Of course the failure of the eastern German economy in a newly reunified Germany was not due purely to a lack of sales. Many social, economic and political factors contributed to the collapse of GDR industry and are still being hotly debated today. Certainly the general lack of efficiency and modernization on the part of East Germany firms made many unprofitable in a free-market system. Yet the less-than-stellar success of Helmut Kohl's reunification plan and, more specifically, the policies of the *Treuhand* contributed to the enormous expense on the part of the German government and people as well as the staggering unemployment rates in many eastern German cities. In many respects, Cold War and intra-German prejudices lie at the heart of assumptions made by both easterners and westerners that affect the efficacy of their mutual policies and interactions.

3   Wolfgang Jeschke did bring out an edition of *The Dream Master* in 1992 as editor at the Wilhelm Heyne Verlag in Munich. Yet, a sizable number of the books ended up in the Steinmüllers' basement (Personal interview, 2000).

science fiction titles can be found in eastern used bookstores, at flea markets, in select libraries, and on collectors' shelves.[4]

Although Johanna and Günter Braun declare that "East Germany's fantastic literature is dead" ("De Mortius" 33), many of its authors are now experiencing a rebirth in the new Germany. At first, many struggled psychologically and financially.[5] Not only did former East German science fiction authors have to contend with a general aversion to eastern products in the nineties, they experienced intense competition on the German science fiction market.[6] For several years following reunification, no publisher considered manuscripts by former East German authors (Szameit, Personal interview, 1999). Nor were older titles reprinted.[7] Since 1996, eastern German authors have made small inroads. Most books have appeared in small publishing houses in the eastern states. Unlike the more visual and accessible comic book *Mosaik* or the cartoon "Unser Sandmännchen," GDR science fiction has only recently begun to benefit from the cultural and media phenomenon of *Ostalgie* to rejuvenate its presence in the mind of the former East German consumer.

Since novels are relatively expensive to print, there has been more activity in the area of short stories. The magazine *Alien Contact* has consistently provided a forum for new and established German science fiction writers since its inception in 1989. Its stories come primarily from former eastern writers, but also include western German and Anglo-American titles. Since 2001, it has appeared solely as an electronic magazine.[8] The editors of *Alien Contact*, in cooperation with Ekkehard Redlin, published a collection of the best stories from

4   Through the year 2000, it was possible to find whole collections cheaply as easterners sold off their collections to make room for new books or for financial reasons. Many public libraries also jettisoned their GDR science fiction.
5   The most tragic story of this period was the suicide of Gert Prokop, the successful writer of humorous science fiction/detective novels.
6   For instance, at the 1999 European Science Fiction Fan Convention in Dortmund, Germany that was also the German Annual National Convention, German guest authors were few and far between. The majority of fans flocked to hear Brian Aldiss, Terry Pratchet or Ian Watson speak.
7   Nor have any of the titles been translated into English.
8   Beginning in 2003, its editors have brought out the *Shayol Jahrbuch Zur Science Fiction* with the Shayol Verlag.

this magazine, entitled *Herz des Sonnenaufgangs* (Heart of the Dawn, 1996). This anthology is dedicated to topics that were not explorable in the GDR. For instance, half of the book is devoted to religion and the metaphysical. In addition, the majority of stories now lack the central reference point of the East German island and are, in the words of the publisher, "apolitical."[9]

Also of interest is the collection of alternate histories edited by Erik Simon entitled *Alexanders Langes Leben, Stalins Früher Tod* (Alexander's Long Life, Stalin's Early Death, 1999). This international collection of stories, devoted to the reexamination of history, includes "Herrliche Zeiten" ("Magnificent Times") by Karsten Kruschel. In his version, German unification went much more smoothly after West Germany collapsed and merged with a successful East Germany. In the collection, Erik Simon reexamines German history in the 1930s in his story "Wenn Thälmann 1934 nicht Reichspräsident geworden wäre" ("If Thälmann Had Not Become President of the Empire"). This story suggests that the success of the Communist Party in Germany in the 1930s would have avoided the Holocaust. Instead, it outlines a history in which a coalition between Thälmann and Strasser, head of a splinter group of the Nazi party, desired not the Final Solution but rather a more limited anti-semitic purge of those dangerous to the party within Germany. These events still led to World War II and the occupation of two Germanys by the Allies.[10]

Alexander Kröger had the greatest initial success with novels after reunification. One of the most prolific science fiction authors in

---

9   See "Herz des Sonnenaufgangs." Johanna and Günter Braun have released one new collection of fantasy stories, *Herr A. Morph* (1998) that includes two science fiction stories "Herrn Morphs sauberkeitsbessessener Sauger" and "Herr Morph erwirbt ein vorauseilendes System."

10 Most of Simon's writing has appeared following 1990. He has also published two volumes of short stories entitled: *Sternbilder – Simon's Fiction 1* (2002) and *Mondmysterien – Simon's Fiction 2* (2003) as well as *Reisen von Zeit zu Zeit – Simon's Fiction 3* (2004) with Reinhard Heinrich. Simon also edited one final volume of *Lichtjahr* (1999). He also published two volumes of short stories prior to 1989: *Fremder Sterne* (Strange Stars, 1979) and *Mondphantome, Erdbesucher* (Moon Phantoms, Earth Visitors, 1987).

East Germany, he was able to use his remaining royalties and connections to found his own publishing company in 1995 in Cottbus and arrange for their printing in the Czech Republic. Run by his wife, Susanne Routschek, and himself, Kröger has published seven new titles since then, including *Vermißt am Rio Tefé* (Lost on Rio Tefé, 1995/96), *Mimikry* (1996), *Die Mücke Julia* (Mosquito Julia, 1996), *Das zweite Leben* (The Second Life, 1998) and its sequel *Der erste Versuch* (The First Try, 2001), *Saat des Himmels* (Seeds of the Sky 2000), *Falsche Brüder* (False Brothers, 2000), and *Der Geist des Nasreddin* (The Spirit of Nasreddin, 2001) and *Robinas Stunde Null* (Robinas Zero Hour, 2004). The last title is the sequel *Die Kristall Welt der Robina Crux* (The Crystal World of Robina Crux, 1977) republished as *Robina Crux* in 2004. Kröger republished *Die Marsfrau* (The Mars Woman) in 2003. His *Fundsache Venus* (Misplaced Venus, 1998) is a reworking of two titles published in the GDR: *Souvenir vom Ataïr* (Souvenir from Ataïr, 1985) and *Andere* (Others, 1990). As with his East German novels, Kröger writes adventure science fiction for younger readers. Cognizant of western publishing practices that appeal to this new generation as well as to the former East German reader, his books can easily be recognized as a series by their shiny green covers and are broadly distributed. That the eastern German reader is still a target audience is evident by the advertisement of the publication of Kröger's Stasi file *Das Sudelfaß* (1996) on his web site and on other book advertising leaflets (Homepage.) This clearly marks him as a fellow easterner, but also conveys the status of victim. He, thereby, distances himself from the atmosphere of uncertainty in the 1990s generated by the opening of Stasi files and numerous public accusations of Stasi or Party involvement.

On the whole, Kröger's writing style has changed very little since 1990 and continues to evoke his self-described "optimism" and generate "hope" for the future. In part, Kröger sees this as a way in which to counteract what he feels to be the bleak, dystopian trend of the West (Personal interview, 1999). This steadfast belief in socialism can be seen in his recent book *Der erste Versuch*. In the novel, Milan Novatschek has decided to enter a cryo-chamber, avoid the problematic present, and sleep for fifty years to take his chances in the future. His story is told in *Das zweite Leben*. Meanwhile, in *Der erste*

Versuch, Milan's clone works as a spy for the Agency of International Trade Management. This *doppelgänger* intends to sabotage the facilities of the International Consortium. The latter is involved in constructing an energy relay designed to shoot electricity into the atmosphere and then harvest the enormous energy generated by the resulting chemical reaction. This relay is part of a greater network of relays at several points on the globe. The narrative resurrects the early spy motifs common in East German science fiction of the 1950s. However, it differs in its portrayal of both transnational organizations as corrupt, profit-seeking institutions unconcerned with safety and environmental ramifications.

In a parallel development, anthropologist Alina Merkers has just journeyed to a fledgling colony on Mars. Here, Kröger portrays the vanguard of humanity as a utopian colony of scientists who, due to the harsh conditions of the planet, cooperate congenially and efficiently as a cohesive team. An intelligent, independent woman, Alina makes the long journey back to Earth to search for her former boyfriend Milan. She has discovered that he is still alive, when she believed him to be asleep and essentially dead to her. Alina's journey takes her to visit the cloned Milan, where the reader discovers the antithesis of the Mars colony. The Mediterranean island, which is the site of the new power plant, has been attacked several times by business rivals. Alina herself is almost killed due to company intrigue and is one of the few who survive the resultant global disaster on Earth.

Kröger's novel differs from his East German writings first of all in the level of violence in the story. Explosions occur and capitalists attack ships in East German science fiction. However, the graphic description of the destruction of Earth, which follows a catastrophic accident, when the chain of power plants is turned on, would have violated the peaceful, positive outlook of the future of Earth in the GDR. In addition, the cloned Milan is annihilated in the chain-reaction.

Seen in another light, this holocaust can be interpreted as sign of an extreme pessimism regarding the future of humanity, following the disappearance of the more powerful Marxist–Leninist governments on Earth of the present. Yet, Kröger maintains his optimism through the survival of the remaining humans in space and Alina, who finds herself en route from Mars on a second journey to Earth when the accident occurs. The negative, regressive elements of humanity have been annihilated. The remaining population, composed largely of scientists, is left to resettle Earth and further develop the socialist-style utopia on Mars.

Angela and Karlheinz Steinmüller have also published successfully in the post-unification period. Much of their work has consisted of secondary material and academic work in the area of Future Studies. In the new century, they have found a market for their latest novel *Spera* as well as a collection of old short stories *Warmzeit. Geschichten aus dem 21. Jahrhundert.* (The Warming Season. Stories from the Twenty-first Century, 2003).[11] A science fiction-fantasy, *Spera* is a new addition to the fictional universe of *Andymon* and *The Dream Master*. It is made up of a variety of short stories, which the Steinmüllers have written over the last fifteen years. Together these stories fill in the gap between *Andymon* and *The Dream Master*. They also recount the arrival of a second Earth ship to the planet, Spera, some time after the fall of the Dream Tower.

Publications by the Steinmüllers and Alexander Kröger represent the small number of entirely new science fiction novels that have been published in a united Germany by former East German authors. The majority of subsequent novels are new editions of old East German publications or reworkings of unpublished manuscripts, the appearance of which signals the resurrection and/or continuation of what still can be called GDR science fiction.

In the nineties, publishers often avoided the GDR designation for fear that it will hamper book sales. For instance, the most recent publication by Michael Szameit has no mention of his status as a former East German on its cover except for the name of its publisher: Das Neue Berlin.[12] Written in the final years of the GDR, Szameit reworked his manuscript to fit what he called a "western sensibility" in

---

11   These new additions appeared in Berlin's Shayol Verlag, which is run by members of the two fan clubs from former East and West Berlin.

12   This publisher has now experienced yet another "new Berlin." The Verlag Neues Leben also still exists, having merged with the Eulenspiegel Verlag.

the late nineties (Personal interview, 1999). He changed the title to the American-sounding *Copyworld* (1999). A science fiction-fantasy, Szameit juxtaposes two different worlds: one a mystic hunter-gatherer society, the second a post-modern, dystopian world of genetically altered, digitized humans.[13]

Like Szameit, it is not uncommon for former GDR authors to publish novels from the "dresser drawer," which they wrote in the late eighties. These titles either 1) remained unsubmitted by authors who knew they were unpublishable, 2) were victims of the slow GDR review process, or 3) were rejected outright. Rainer Fuhrmann's *Kairo*, the third title of his to be published in the Heyne Science Fiction and Fantasy series, appeared in 1996 as a posthumous tribute to the author.[14] The appearance of a "socialist government" that is trying to protect the morals of its colony signifies a continued participation in the rhetorical strategies practiced by GDR authors. It juxtaposes two societies, but these two are identified in the Cold War terms of as a socialist society and a capitalist society. The equally prolific, Karl Heinz Tuschel published *Der Mann von IDEA* (The Man from IDEA) in 1996. In the novel, the telepathic Ross Bernard reconnects various communities on Earth thirty-three years after an environmental catastrophe destroyed one-fifth of its population. Klaus Frühauf's *Die Stadt der tausend Augen* is an Orwellian dystopia that incorporates elements of fantasy to warn of the totalitarian potential of the Internet. It was originally rejected by the Verlag Neues Leben in 1988 and did not appear until 2000 with the H & F Verlag. Klaus Frühauf has also recently had ten of his GDR novels reissued by the MV Taschenbuchverlag.

Still, Klaus Frühauf's latest science fiction deals with contemporary problems and has left his socialist style behind. His new dystopian novel *Aufstand der Sterblichen* (2003) places German politicians in the bodies of star athletes so that they might profit from their fame. Frühauf's *Finale* (Finals, 1996) contains a violent plot with references to the border wars in Hungary, Romania, and Bulgaria and a setting on

---

13   Other recent new editions include Klaus Frühauf's *Finale* and a book by Karl Heinz Tuschel. See Neumann, "Kröger" 23.

14   Fuhrmann died in 1990. See Redlin, "Kairo's Geheimnis" 12.

the A20, the former East's coastal highway (Neumann, "Kröger" 23). Frühauf, himself, continues to write as he finds it therapeutic (E-mail 1).

A quick survey of the new novels published since 1990 by former East Germans reveals a highly pessimistic view of the future. Some reflect attitudes of writers and editors who are still committed to the idea of communism, such as Kröger and Redlin. Redlin believes "cultural pessimism" dominates today's science fiction as well as a lack of perspective and materialist interpretation ("Letter" 2). Stories by Kröger, Kruschel, and Simon reinterpret existing history from the viewpoint of historical inevitability, or they rewrite it to salvage, or alternately parody, the socialist project in some form.[15]

This pessimism and cynicism is by no means characteristic of all of their stories nor is it of the entire eastern science fiction community. Indeed, both designations "eastern" and "community" are slowly eroding. Where some authors market their works in terms of Ostalgia others, such as the Steinmüllers, Simon and Szameit have long left this phenomenon behind. Furthermore, some recent science fiction by Kröger, Frühauf and Tuschel directly address Germany's contemporary challenges, such as bio-ethics and environmental reform.[16] Therefore, if GDR science fiction no longer exists, then what remains and follows? This is the question that today's authors continue to discover.

---

15 See *Das zweite Leben, Der erste Versuch* by Kröger and Simon, *Alexanders Langes Leben, Stalins Früher Tod.*

16 See Kröger's *Chimera*, Frühauf's *Aufstand der Sterblichen*, and Tuschel's *Der Mann von IDEA.*

Works Cited

Primary Sources

In the list of primary texts, I include many of the prominent, influential or typical works of GDR science fiction. For a full selection, see Hans-Peter Neumann's bibliography.

Anderson, Edith, ed. *Blitz aus heiterm Himmel.* Rostock: Hinsdorff Verlag, 1975.

Antkowiak, Barbara, Jutta Janke, and others, ed. *Der Fotograf des Unsichtbaren.* Berlin: Verlag Volk und Welt, 1978.

Asimov, Isaac. *I, Robot.* Garden City, N.Y.: Doubleday, 1963. *Ein Roboter wie du und Ich.* Berlin: Verlag Das Neue Berlin, 1982.

Bagemühl, Arthur. *Das Weltraumschiff.* Berlin: Altberliner Verlag Lucie Groszer, 1952.

Ball, Kurt und Lothar Weise. *Alarm auf Station Einstein.* Berlin: Verlag Neues Leben, 1957.

Becher, Johannes R. *(CHC1–CH)3 As (Levisite) oder Der einzig gerechte Krieg.* 1926. Berlin: Aufbau Verlag, 1969.

Bellamy, Edward. *Rückblick aus dem Jahre 2000.* Trans. Clara Zetkin. Ed. Hermann Duncker. Berlin: Dietz Verlag, 1949. Trans. of *Looking Backward 2000–1887.* 1888.

Belyayev, S. *Der zehnte Planet.* Trans. A. Memorskij. Berlin: SWA Verlag, 1947.

Böhm, Karl and Rolf Dörge. *Auf dem Weg zu fernen Welten.* Berlin: Verlag Neues Leben, 1958.

—. *Weltall. Erde. Mensch.* Berlin: Verlag Neues Leben, 1962.

Bradbury, Ray. *Fahrenheit 451.* NewYork: Ballantine Books, 1953. Berlin: Verlag Das Neue Berlin, 1974.

Branster, Gerhard. *Der astronomische Dieb.* Berlin: Verlag Das Neue Berlin, 1973.

—. *Der falsche Mann im Mond.* Rostock: Hinstorff Verlag, 1970.

—. *Die Reise zum Stern der Beschwingten.* Rostock: Hinstorff Verlag, 1968.

—. *Der Sternenkavalier.* Berlin: Verlag Das Neue Berlin, 1976.

Braun, Johanna und Günter. "Allein im Weltraum." *Das Magazin* 8 (1966): 26–28.

—. *Bitterfisch*. Berlin: Verlag Neues Leben, 1974.

—. *Conviva Ludibundus*. Berlin: Verlag Das Neue Berlin, 1980.

—. *Einer sagt nein*. Berlin: Verlag Neues Leben, 1955.

—. *Eva und der neue Adam*. Berlin: Verlag der Nation, 1961.

—. *Der Fehlfaktor*. 1975. Berlin: Verlag Das Neue Berlin, 1985.

—. *Fünf Säulen des Eheglücks*. Berlin: Verlag Neues Leben, 1976.

—. *Herr A. Morph*. Frankfurt am Main: Insel Verlag, 1998.

—. *Herren der Pampa*. Berlin: Verlag Neues Leben, 1957.

—. *Der Irrtum des Großen Zauberers*. Berlin: Verlag Neues Leben, 1972.

—. *José Zorillas Letzter Stier*. Berlin: Verlag Neues Leben, 1955.

—. *Das Kugeltranzendale Vorhaben*. Frankfurt am Main: Suhrkamp, 1983.

—. *Mädchen im Dreieck*. Berlin: Buchverlag Der Morgen, 1961.

—. *Die Nase des Neandertalers*. Berlin: Verlag Neues Leben, 1969.

—. *Ein Objektiver Engel*. Berlin: Buchclub 65, 1967.

—. Personal interview, 15 June 1999.

—. *Preussen, Lumpen und Rebellen*. Berlin: Deutscher Militärverlag, 1957.

—. *Die seltsamen Abenteuer des Brotstudenten Ernst Brav*. Berlin: Buchverlag Der Morgen, 1959.

—. *Tsuko und der Medizinmann*. Berlin: Verlag Das Neue Berlin, 1956.

—. *Unheimliche Erscheinungsformen auf Omega XI*. Berlin: Verlag Das Neue Berlin, 1974.

—. *Der Utofant*. Berlin: Verlag Das Neue Berlin, 1981.

—. *Der x–mal vervielfachte Held*. Frankfurt am Main: Suhrkamp, 1985.

Breuer, Siegfried. Letter to the author. 28 December 2004.

—. Personal interview, 15 May 1999.

Butler, Octavia. *Dawn. Xenogenesis*. New York: Warner Books, 1987.

Bürgel, Bruno H. "Die sonderbare Welt. Eine Reise zum Uranus." *Die junge Welt. Ein Almanach für die Jugend*. Ed. Richard Riedel. Halle: Mitteldeutscher Verlag, 1948. 46–58.

Büttner, Majoll. "Hille reist ins Jahr 2000." *Die Zaubertruhe*. Berlin: Kinderbuchverlag, 1956. 56–58.

Čapek, Karel. *R.U.R. and the Insect Play*. London: Oxford University Press, 1961.

—. *War with the Newts*. Highland Park, New Jersey: Catbird Press, 1990.

Daniken, Edward van. *Chariot of the Gods. Unsolved Mysteries of the Past*. New York: Putnum, 1970.

Del Antonio, Eberhardt. *Gigantum*. Berlin: Verlag Das Neue Berlin, 1957.

—. *Heimkehr der Vorfahren*. Berlin: Verlag Das Neue Berlin, 1966.

—. "Letter to Regierung der DDR, Ministerium für Kultur – HA Schöne Literatur." (17 April 1957) BArch DR 1/3941 Page [Bl.] 55.

—. *Okeanos*. Rudolstaft: Greifenverlag, 1988.

—. *Projekt Sahara*. Berlin: Verlag Tribüne, 1962.

—. *Titanus*. Berlin: Verlag Das Neue Berlin, 1959.

Deutsche Verwaltung für Volksbildung ed., *Liste der auszusondernden Literatur*. Berlin: Zentralverlag, 1946, 1948, 1953.

Dietrich, Siegfried. "Im Mount Carlton eingeschlossen." *Jugend und Technik* 11 (1955): 371–373.

Dominik, Hans. *Atomgewicht 500*. Berlin: Scherl Verlag, 1935. Berlin: Gewe–Gebrüder Weiss Verlag, 1948.

—. *Der Brand des Cheopspyramide*. Berlin und Leipzig: Keil, 1927.

—. *Das Erbe der Uraniden*. Berlin: Keil, 1928. Berlin: Scherl, 1941.

—. *Flug in den Weltraum. [Treibstoff SR]*. Wien [Vienna]; Heidelberg: Verlag Carl Ueberreuter, 1965.

—. *Himmelskraft*. Berlin: Scherl, 1937.

—. *Die Macht der Drei*. Leipzig: E. Keil, 1922.

—. *Die Spur des Dschingis–Khan*. Leipzig: Scherl, 1923.

—. *Der Wettflug der Nationen*. Leipzig: Koehler & Amelang, 1933.

Dürrenmatt, Friedrich. *Die Physiker*. Zurich: Verlag der Arche, 1962.

Efremov, Ivan Antonovich. *Das Mädchen aus dem All*. Trans. of *Tumannost' Andromedy* by Heinz Lorenz and Dieter Pommerenke. 1957. München [Munich]: Wilhelm Heyne Verlag, 1971. Berlin: Verlag Kultur und Fortschritt, 1958. Moscow: Molodaia gvardiia 1957. English *Andromeda*.

—. *Schatten der Vergangenheit*. Moscow, 1945. Berlin: SWA Verlag, 1946.

—. *Der Tod in der Wüste*. Trans. of *Rasskazi*. Moscow, 1950. Berlin: Verlag Neues Leben, 1953.

Ehrhardt, Paul. *Boten der Unendlichkeit*. Berlin: Verlag Neues Leben, 1984.

Enskat, Fritz. *Gefangen am Gipfel der Welt. Im Nordmeer verschollen*. Halle: Mitteldeutsche Druckerei und Verlagsanstalt, 1949.

—. *Marso der Zweite*. Hamburg: Fritz Mardicke, 1936. *Weltraumschiff Unimos*. Berlin, Frommhagen, 1941.

Fahlberg, H.L. *Erde ohne Nacht*. Berlin: Verlag Das Neue Berlin, 1956.

—. *Ein Stern verrät den Täter*. Berlin: Verlag Das Neue Berlin, 1955.

Frühauf, Klaus. *Aufstand der Sterblichen*. Rostock: MV–Taschenbuchverlag, 2003.

—. E–mail from the author. 13 December 2004.

—. *Finale.* Arnstadt & Weimar: Rhino Verlag, 1996.

—. *Mutanten auf Andromeda.* Berlin: Verlag Neues Leben, 1974.

—. *Die Stadt der Tausend Augen.* Scheibenberg: H & F Verlag, 2000.

Fühmann, Franz. "Die Ohnmacht." *Sinn und Form* 28.1 (1976): 86–108.

—. *Saiäns-Fiktschen.* Leipzig: Verlag Philipp Reclam, 1981.

Fuhrmann, Rainer. "Golem." *Wege zur Unmöglichkeit.* Ed. Ekkehard Redlin. Berlin: Verlag Das Neue Berlin, 1983.

—. *Homo Sapiens 10^{-2}.* Berlin: Verlag Das Neue Berlin, 1977.

—. *Kairos.* München [Munich]: Heyne Verlag, 1996.

—. *Die Untersuchung.* Berlin: Verlag Das Neue Berlin, 1984.

Gedankenkontrolle. Ed. [anonymous] Ekkehard Redlin. Berlin: Verlag Das Neue Berlin, 1979.

Gibson, William. *Neuromancer.* New York: Ace Books, 2000.

Gobsch, Hanns. *Wahn–Europa 1934: Eine Vision.* Hamburg: Fackelreiter Verlag, 1931.

Harbou, Thea von. *Frau im Mond.* Berlin: Scherl, 1930. Ed. Wolfgang Jeschke. *Frau im Mond.* München [Munich]: Wilhelm Heyne Verlag, 1989.

—. *Metropolis.* 1927. New York: Ace Books, 1963.

Hardel, Gerhard. "Kindergericht in Blumenthal im Jahre 2455." *Unsere Welt.* Berlin: Kinderbuchverlag, 1955. 155–159; 162–167.

Hartung, Hans–Joachim. "Letzter Start von EZ–14." *Jugend und Technik* 4 (1953): 29.

—. "280 km/h im blauen Blitz" *Jugend und Technik* 9 (1955): 305–307.

Hegen, Hannes. *Mosaik. Die Reise ins All.* Dec 1958–March 1959. 25–28. Berlin: Buchverlag Junge Welt, 1999.

—. "Die Neoserie" *Mosaik* 25–73 (Dec 1958–Dec 1962).

Hein, Christoph. *Drachenblut.* Darmstadt: Luchterhand, 1987.

Herbert, Frank. *Dune.* Philadelphia: Chilton Books, 1965.

"Herz des Sonnenaufgangs." Alien Contact. Magazine Website. November 18, 2004. Epilog.de. November 22, 2004. <http://www.epilog.de/Bibliothek/Alien–Contact/index.html>

Heym, Stefan. Introduction. *Das kosmische Zeitalter.* Berlin: Tribüne Verlag, 1959. 2–3.

Hitler, Adolf. *Mein Kampf.* Boston: Houghton Mifflin Company, 1943.

Hoffmann, E.T.A. *Der Sandmann.* Stuttgart: Reclam, 1991.

Horstmann, Hubert. *Stimme der Unendlichkeit.* Berlin: Verlag Das Neue Berlin, 1965.

Huxley, Aldous. *Brave New World.* Norwalk, CT: Easton Press, 1978. *Schöne Neue Welt.* Berlin: Verlag Das Neue Berlin, 1978.

Illing, Werner. *Utopolis*. Berlin: Der Bücherkreis, 1930.

Ivanov, Valentin. *Duell im Weltraum*. Trans. of *Energia Podvlastna nam*. 1951. Berlin: Verlag Volk und Welt, 1949.

Jankowiak, Johannes, ed. *Galaxisspatzen*. Berlin: Das Neue Berlin, 1975.

Joho, Wolfgang. *Jeanne Peyrouton*. Berlin: Aufbau Verlag, 1988.

—. *Die Verwandlungen des Doktor Brad*. Berlin: Aufbau Verlag, 1988.

Kafka, Franz. *In der Strafkolonie*. Frankfurt am Main: Insel Verlag, 1999.

—. *Die Verwandlung*. Klagenfurt: Edition Selene, 1997.

Kellermann, Bernd. *Der Tunnel*. 1913. München [Munich]: Wilhelm Heyne Verlag, 1972.

Kipphardt, Reinar. *In der Sache Robert Oppenheimer*. Frankfurt/Main: Suhrkamp Verlag, 1964.

Klauss, Klaus. *Duell unter fremder Sonne*. Berlin: Militärverlag, 1985.

Klotz, Udo and Hans Peter Neumann, eds. *Shayol Jahrbuch Zur Science Fiction*. Berlin: Shayol Verlag, 2003; 2004.

Kriese, Reinhard. *Eden City, die Stadt des Vergessens*. Berlin: Verlag Neues Leben, 1985.

Kröger, Alexander [pseudo. Helmut Routschek]. *Andere*. Halle: Mitteldeutscher Verlag, 1990.

—. *Die Engel in den grünen Kugeln*. Berlin: Verlag Neues Leben, 1986.

—. *Der erste Versuch*. Cottbus: Kröger Vertrieb, 2001.

—. *Falsche Brüder*. Cottbus: Kröger Vertrieb, 2000.

—. *Fundsache Venus*. Cottbus: Kröger Vertrieb, 1998.

—. *Der Geist des Nasreddin*. Cottbus: Kröger Vertrieb, 2001.

—. *Das Kosmodrom im Krater Bond*. Berlin: Verlag Neues Leben, 1981.

—. *Die Kristallwelt der Robina Crux*. Berlin: Verlag Neues Leben, 1977.

—. *Die Marsfrau*. Berlin: Verlag Neues Leben, 1980.

—. *Mimikry*. Cottbus: Kröger Vertrieb, 1996.

—. *Die Mücke Julia*. Cottbus: Kröger Vertrieb, 1996.

—. Personal interview. 1 May 1999.

—. *Robinas Stunde Null*. Cottbus: Kröger Vertrieb, 2004.

—. *Saat des Himmels*. Cottbus: Kröger Vertrieb, 2000.

—. *Sieben fielen vom Himmel*. Berlin: Verlag Neues Leben, 1969.

—. *Souvenair vom Ataïr*. Berlin: Verlag Neues Leben, 1985.

—. [Helmut Routschek]. *Das Sudelfaß – eine gewöhnliche Stasiakte*. Schwedt: Kiro Verlag, 1996.

—. *Der Untergang der Telesalt*. Berlin: Verlag Neues Leben, 1989.

—. *Vermißt am Tio Tefé*. Cottbus: Kröger–Vertrieb, 1995/1996.

—. *Das zweite Leben*. Cottbus: Kröger Vertrieb, 1998.

Krupkat, Günther. *Als die Götter starben*. Berlin: Verlag Das Neue Berlin, 1963.

—. *Die große Grenze*. Berlin: Verlag Das Neue Berlin, 1960.

—. *Nabou*. Berlin: Verlag Das Neue Berlin, 1968.

—. *Die Unsichtbaren*. Berlin: Verlag Volk und Welt, 1958.

Kunert, Günter. "Andromeda zur Unzeit." *Die Beerdigung findet in aller Stille statt*. München [Munich]: Carl Hanser Verlag, 1968. 93–98.

—. "Die kleinen grünen Männer." *Kramen in Fächern*. Berlin: Aufbau Verlag, 1968. 100–101.

—. "Museumsbesuch." *Der Mann vom Anti*. Ed. Ekkehard Redlin. Berlin: Verlag Das Neue Berlin, 1975. 41–50.

—. "Nach der Landung." *Kramen in Fächern*. Berlin: Aufbau Verlag, 1968. 140–142.

—. "Schlaf." *Der Mann vom Anti*. Ed. Ekkehard Redlin. Berlin: Verlag Das Neue Berlin, 1975.

—. "Vom Pluto her." *Der Mittelpunkt der Erde*. Ed. Günter Kunert. Berlin: Eulenspiegel Verlag, 1975. 51–53.

Kunkel, Klaus. *Heißes Metall*. Berlin: Verlag Das Neue Berlin, 1952.

—. *Im gläsernen Flugzeug durch die Schallmauer*. Berlin: Verlag Neues Leben, 1953.

Lagin, Lasar Fosifovich. *Patent AW*. Trans. Of *Patent AV*. 1947. Berlin: Verlag Volk und Welt, 1949.

Lasswitz, Kurd. *Auf zwei Planeten*. Berlin: Verlag Das Neue Berlin, 1984.

—. "Bis zum Nullpunkt des Seins." *Traumkristalle*. By Kurd Lasswitz. Ed. Ekkehard Redlin. Berlin: Verlag Das Neue Berlin, 1982.

—. "Gegen das Weltgesetz." *Bis zum Nullpunkt des Seins*. Ed. Adolf Sckerl. Berlin: Verlag Das Neue Berlin, 1979.

Le Guin, Ursula K. *The Dispossessed*. New York: Avon, 1974. *Planet der Habenichtse*. Berlin: Verlag Das Neue Berlin, 1987.

—. *The Left Hand of Darkness*. New York: Ace Books, 2000. *Winterplanet*. Berlin: Verlag Das Neue Berlin, 1979.

Lem, Stanislaw. *The Astronauts*. Poland. *Der Planet des Todes*. Berlin: Verlag Volk und Welt, 1954.

—. *Cyberiad*. Trans. of *Ciberiada*. New York: Seabury Press, 1974.

—. *Eden*. 1959. Berlin: Verlag Volk und Welt, 1971.

—. *The Futurological Congress*. Trans. of *Kongres Futurologiczny*. 1973. *Der futurologische Kongreß*. Berlin: Verlag Volk und Welt, 1986.

—. *Imaginary Magnitude*. Trans. of *Wielkość urojona*. 1973. Berlin: Verlag Volk und Welt, 1976.

—. *Die Jagd.* Selections from *Opowiesci o pilocie Pirxie.* 1968. Berlin: Volk und Welt, 1972.

—. *Memoirs of a Space Traveler.* New York: Harcourt Brace Jovanovich, 1982.

—. *Return From the Stars.* Trans. of *Powrot s gwiazd,* 1961. New York: Harcourt Brace Jovanovich, 1980.

—. *Robotermärchen.* Trans. of *Bajki robotów* and selections from *Ciberiada.* Frankfurt: Suhrkamp, 1973. Berlin: Eulenspiegel Verlag, 1969.

—. *Solaris.* Trans. Joanna Kilmartin and Steve Cox. New York; London: Harcourt Brace Jovanovich, 1961. Berlin: Verlag Volk und Welt, 1983.

—. *The Star Diaries.* Trans. Michael Kandel. New York: Avon, 1971. Trans. of *Dzienniki Gwiazdowe.* 1957. Warsaw: Interart, 1994. Selected stories as *Die Sterntagebücher des Weltraumfahrers Ijon Tichy.* Berlin: Verlag Volk und Welt, 1961.

—. *Test.* Ed. Jutta Janke. Trans. Caesar Rymarowicz. Berlin: Verlag Volk und Welt, 1968.

—. *Der Unbesiegbare.* Trans. of *Niezwyciezony* by Roswitha Dietrich. Berlin: Verlag Volk und Welt, 1977.

Leman, Alfred. *Schwarze Blumen auf Barnard Drei.* Berlin: Verlag Neues Leben, 1986.

Lhande, Pierre. *Bilbilis, die versunkene Stadt.* Einsiedeln, n.p. 1930.

Loele, Konrad. *Züllinger und seine Zucht.* Leipzig: Pandora Verlag, 1921.

London, Jack. *Die eiserne Ferse.* Trans. Erwin Magnus. Potsdam: Maerkische Druck– u.Verlags–GmbH, 1948. Trans. of *The Iron Heel.* Edinburgh: Rebel Inc., 1999.

Lorenz, Peter. *Aktion Erde.* Halle; Leipzig: Mitteldeutscherverlag, 1988.

—. *Homunkuli.* Berlin: Verlag Neues Leben, 1978.

Luthardt, Ernst-Otto. *Die klingenden Bäume.* Rudolstadt: Greifenverlag, 1982.

—. *Die Unsterblichen.* Rudolstadt: Greifenverlag, 1984.

—. *Die Wiederkehr des Einhorns.* Berlin: Verlag Neues Leben, 1988.

May, Karl. *Winnetou.* New York: Seabury Press, 1977.

McCaffrey, Anne. *The Chronicles of Pern. First Fall.* New York: Ballantine Books, 1993.

Mielke, Heinz. "Gefährliches Ziel." *Unsere Welt.* Berlin: Kinderbuchverlag, 1955. 7–15.

Möckel, Klaus. *Die gläserne Stadt.* Berlin: Verlag Das Neue Berlin, 1979.

More, Thomas. *Utopia.* 1516. Trans. Paul Turner. New York; Middlesex, England: Penguin, 2003.

Müller, Hermann. *ATAWA. Ich träumte, es wäre wahr.* West Berlin: n.p. 1954.

Müller, Horst. *Kurs Ganymed.* Bautzen: Domowina Verlag, 1962.

—. *Signale vom Mond.* Bautzen: Domowina Verlag, 1960.

Müller, Walter. *Wenn wir 1918...* Berlin: Malik Verlag, 1930.

Nesvadba, Josef. *Die absolute Maschine.* Praha [Prag]: Artia, 1966.

—. *Wie Kapitän Nemo starb.* Selections and Trans. from *V ýprava opačným směrem, Tarzanova smrt,* and *Einsteinåuv mozek.* Berlin: Verlag Das Neue Berlin, 1968.

Obrutchev, Vladimir *Plutonien.* Trans. of *Plootoiviya.* 1924. Berlin: Verlag Neues Leben, 1953.

—. *Das Sannikovland.* Trans. of *Zemlya Sannikova.* 1926. Berlin: Verlag Neues Leben, 1953.

Orthmann, Edwin, ed. *Der Diamantenmacher.* Berlin: Verlag Neues Leben, 1972.

—, ed. *Das Raumschiff.* Berlin: Verlag Neues Leben, 1977.

—, ed. *Die Ypsilon–Spirale.* Berlin: Verlag Neues Leben, 1973.

—, ed. *Das Zeitfahrrad.* Berlin: Verlag Neues Leben, 1974.

Orwell, George. *Nineteen–eighty–four.* 1948. New York: Harcourt, Brace, 1949.

Paschke, Rudi. "Auf dem Wege zum Mond." *Jugend und Technik* 6 (1953): 20–24.

Perkins, Charlotte. *Herland.* New York: Pantheon Books, 1979.

Piercy, Marge. *Woman on the Edge of Time.* New York: Knopf, 1976.

Plato and Allan David Bloom. *Republic.* New York: Basic Books, 1968.

Ploog, Ilse, ed. *Die Zaubertruhe. Almanach für junge Mädchen.* Berlin: Kinderbuchverlag, 1956.

Prokop, Gert. *Der Samenbankraub.* Berlin: Verlag Das Neue Berlin, 1983.

—. *Wer stiehlt schon Unterschenkel?* Berlin: Verlag Das Neue Berlin, 1977.

Rank, Heiner. *Die Ohnmacht der Allmächtigen.* Berlin: Verlag Das Neue Berlin, 1974.

Rasch, Carlos. *Asteroidenjäger.* Berlin: Verlag Neues Leben, 1961.

—. *Der blaue Planet.* Berlin: Verlag Das Neue Berlin, 1963.

—. "Kurzinhalt von 19 Vorschlägen für Hörspiele anläßlich 'Jahr 2000 – Und dann?' – Von den Raumlotsen." Unpublished outline, 1999.

—. Personal interview. 12 May 1999.

Redlin, Ekkehard, ed. *Das Herz des Sonnenaufgangs.* Berlin: Edition Avalon, 1996.

—. Letter to the author. 22 December 2001.

—, ed. *Der Mann vom Anti.* Berlin: Verlag Das Neue Berlin, 1975.

—. Personal interview. 5 June 1999.

—. Personal interview. 1 October 2004.

296

Reifenberg, Alfred. *Des Götzen Moloch Ende*. Wolfratshausen vor München: Hoheneichen–Verl., 1925.

Russ, Joanna. *The Female Man*. New York: Bantam Books, 1975.

Schuster, Bernhard. "Utopina–500." *Die Schulpost* 7–8 (1954): 27–29.

Seghers, Anna. "Sagen von Unirdischen." *Sinn und Form* 24.1 (1972): 16–40.

—. *Sonderbare Begegnungen*. Berlin: Aufbau Verlag, 1973.

Shelley, Mary. *Frankenstein*. 1818. Berlin: Verlag Das Neue Berlin, 1978.

Simon, Erik, ed. *Alexanders Langes Leben, Stalins Früher Tod*. München [Munich]: Heyne, 1999.

—. *Fremder Sterne*. Berlin: Verlag Das Neue Berlin, 1979.

—, ed. *Kontaktversuche*. Berlin: Verlag Das Neue Berlin, 1978.

—. *Mondmysterien – Simon's Fiction 2*. Berlin: Shayol Verlag, 2003.

—. *Mondphantome, Erdbesucher*. Berlin: Verlag Das Neue Berlin, 1987.

—. *Reisen von Zeit zu Zeit – Simon's Fiction 3*. Berlin: Shayol Verlag, 2004.

—. Personal interview. 3 December 1997.

—. *Sternbilder – Simon's Fiction 1*. Berlin: Shayol Verlag, 2002.

—, ed (anonymous). *Der Weg zur Amalthea*. Moscow: Verlag Mir, 1979 and Berlin: Verlag Das Neue Berlin, 1979.

Simon, Erik and Olaf Spittel, eds. *Lichtjahr*. Vol 1–7. Berlin: Verlag Das Neue Berlin, 1981–1986, 1999.

Simon, Erik and Reinhard Heinrich. *Reisen von Zeit zu Zeit – Simon's Fiction 3*. Berlin: Shayol Verlag, 2004.

Sixtus, Albert. *Das Geheimnis des Riesenhügels. Ein Abenteuerbuch für die Jugend*. 1941. Berlin: Globus–Verlag Hermann Steffen, 1949.

Steinmüller, Angela. "Der Kerzenmacher." 1992. *Spera*. Berlin: Shayol Verlag, 2004. 92–98.

Steinmüller, Angela and Karlheinz. *Andymon*. Berlin: Verlag Neues Leben, 1982.

—. Personal interview. 27 July 2000.

—. *Pulaster*. Berlin: Verlag Neues Leben, 1986.

—. *Spera*. Berlin: Shayol Verlag, 2004.

—. *Der Traummeister*. Berlin: Verlag Neues Leben, 1989.

—. *Warmzeit. Geschichten aus dem 21. Jahrhundert*. Berlin: Shayol Verlag, 2003.

—. *Windschiefe Geraden*. 1984. Berlin: Verlag Das Neue Leben, 1990.

Steinmüller, Karlheinz. E-mail from the author. 3 March 1997.

—. *Der letzte Tag auf der Venus*. Berlin: Verlag Neues Leben, 1979.

297

Strugatsky, Boris and Arkady. *The Final Circle of Paradise*. Trans. of *Khyshchnye veshchy veka*. New York: Daw Books, 1965. Berlin: Volk und Welt, 1983.

—. *Hard to be a God*. Trans. of *Trudno byt' bogom*. New York: Seabury Press, 1973. *Ein Gott zu sein ist schwer*. Berlin: Verlag Volk und Welt, 1975.

—. *Monday Begins on Saturday*. Trans. of *Ponedel'nik naãinaetsja v subbotu*. New York: Daw Books, 1978. *Der Montag fängt am Samstag an*. Berlin: Volk und Welt, 1990.

—. *Roadside Picnic*. Trans. of *Piknik na oboãine*. New York: Macmillan, 1977. *Picknick am Wegesrand*. Berlin: Verlag Das Neue Berlin, 1976.

Suttner, Bertha von. *Das Maschinenzeitalter. Zukunftsvorlesungen über unsere Zeit*. Düsseldorf: Zwiebelzwerg, 1983.

—. *Der Menschheit Hochgedanken. Roman aus der nächsten Zukunft*. Düsseldorf: Zwiebelzwerg, 1983.

Suvin, Darko, ed. *Other Worlds. Other Seas. Science Fiction from Socialist Countries*. New York: Random House, 1970.

Szameit, Michael. *Copyworld*. Berlin: Verlag Das Neue Berlin, 1999.

—. *Drachenkreuzer Ikarus*. Berlin: Verlag Neues Leben, 1987.

—. Personal interview. 28 May 1999.

Tolstoy, Alexei. *Aelita*. Trans. Hertha von Schulz. Frankfurt/M: Verlag Ullstein GmbH, 1983. Berlin: Aufbau Verlag, 1957.

Turek, Ludwig. *Die goldene Kugel*. Berlin: Dietz Verlag, 1949.

—. *Ein Prolet erzählt. Lebenschilderung eines deutschen Arbeiters*. 1929. München [Munich]: Damnitz, 1980.

Tuschel, Karl Heinz. *Die Insel der Roboter*. Berlin: Militärverlag, 1973.

—. *Der Mann von IDEA*. Schkeuditz; Berlin: GNN Verlag, 1996.

—. *Das Rätsel Sigma*. Berlin: Verlag Neues Leben, 1974.

—. *Ein Stern fliegt vorbei*. Berlin: Verlag Neues Leben, 1967.

Ulbrich, Bernd. *Der unsichtbare Kreis*. Berlin: Verlag Das Neue Berlin, 1978.

—. *Der verhexte Kater*. Berlin: Verlag Das Neue Berlin, 1975.

—.*Unsere Welt. Jahrbuch für Mädchen und Jungen*. Berlin: Kinderbuchverlag, 1955.

Verne, Jules. *Around the World in Eighty Days*. New York: Heritage Press, 1962. *Die Reise um die Erde in 80 Tagen*. Berlin: Verlag Neues Leben, 1973.

—. *From the Earth to the Moon*. 1865. New York: Dover Publications, 1960. *Von der Erde zum Mond*. Berlin: Kinderbuchverlag, 1955.

—. *20,000 Leagues under the Sea.* 1869–1870. New York: Harper Collins, 2000. *20000 Meilen unter dem Meeresspiegel.* Berlin: Verlag der Nation, 1957.

Vieweg, Heinz. *Feuer im Labor I.* Kleine Jugendreihe 4. Berlin: Verlag Kultur und Fortschritt, 1956.

—. *Ultrasymet bleibt geheim.* Berlin: Verlag Neues Leben, 1955.

Voigt, Rosa. *Anno Domini 2000.* Hamburg: Deutschlands Großloge II des J.O.G.T., 1909.

Vonau, Ingolf. Personal interview, 4 April 1999.

Weise, Lothar. *Das Geheimnis des Transpluto.* Berlin: Verlag Neues Leben, 1962.

—. *Unternehmen Marsgibberellin.* Berlin: Verlag Neues Leben, 1964.

Weise, Lothar and Ball, Kurt. *Atomfeuer über dem Pazifik.* Berlin: Verlag Neues Leben, 1959.

Weitbrecht, Wolf. *Oracle der Delphine.* Berlin: Greifenverlag, 1972.

Wells, H.G. *The Time Machine.* 1895. New York; Toronto; London: Bantam Pathfinder, 1968. *Die Zeitmaschine.* Berlin: Verlag Das Neue Berlin, 1975.

—. *The War of the Worlds.* 1898. Peterborough, Ont.; Orchard Park, NY: Broadview Press, 2003.

Wolf, Christa, *Der geteilte Himmel.* 1963. München [Munich]: Deutscher Taschenbuch Verlag, 1973.

—. *Kassandra.* Darmstadt: Luchterhand, 1983.

—. "Leben oder gelebt werden. Gespräch mit Alfried Nehring." *Christa Wolf Im Dialog.* Ed. Klaus Binder. Berlin; Weimar: Aufbau Verlag, 1990.

—. *Medea. A Modern Retelling.* New York: Nan A. Talese, 1998.

—. *Nachdenken über Christa T.* Berlin: Aufbau Verlag, 1975.

—. "Selbstversuch." *Blitz aus heiterem Himmel.* Ed. Edith Anderson. Rostock: Hinstorff Verlag, 1975.

Wolf, Christa, Sarah Kirsch and Irmtraud Morgner. *Geschlechtertausch.* Darmstadt: Luchterhand, 1980.

Zapp, Arthur. *Revanche für Versailles!* Berlin: Fritz Kater Verlag, 1924.

Ziergiebel, Herbert. "Die Experimente des Professors von Pulex." 1975. *Der Mann vom Anti.* Ed. Ekkehard Redlin. Berlin: Verlag Das Neue Berlin, 1975.

Selected Titles in Science Fiction Film, Music, and Television

Abenteuer mit Blasius. Dir. Egon Schlegel. Czech Barrandov–Studio and DEFA, 1975.

Aelita. The Queen of Mars. Dir. Yakov Protazanov. Soviet Union, 1924.

Alien. Dir. Ridley Scott. Perf. Sigourney Weaver. Twentieth Century Fox, 1979.

The Avengers. Dir. Jonathan Alwyn and Robert Asher. United Kingdom, 1961–1969.

Besuch bei Van Gogh. Dir. Horst Seemann. DEFA, 1985.

Brazil. Dir. Terry Gilliam. Embassy, 1985.

Dallas. Dir. David Jacobs. CBS, 1978–1991.

Doctor Cyclops. Dir. Ernest Schoedsack. Columbia, 1940.

Eolomea. Dir. Hermann Zschoche. Perf. Rolf Hoppa. DEFA, 1972.

Erinnerungen an die Zukunft. [Chariot of the Gods]. Dir. Harald Reinl. West Germany, 1970.

Falcon Crest. Dir. Gwen Arner and Reza Badiyi. CBS, 1981–1990.

Flash Gordon. Dir. Gunther Fritsch. Intercontinental Television Film Productions, West Germany, 1953–54.

Frau im Mond. Dir. Fritz Lang. UFA, 1929.

Der geteilte Himmel. Dir. Konrad Wolf. DEFA, 1964.

Goodbye Lenin. Dir. Wolfgang Becker. X Filme Creative Pool, 2003.

Im Staub der Sterne. [In the Dust of the Stars]. Dir. Gottfried Kollditz. Perf. Ekkehard Schall. DEFA, 1976.

Krull. Dir. Peter Yates. United Kingdom, 1983.

Der Mann mit dem Objektiv. Dir. Frank Vogel. DEFA, 1961

Metropolis. Dir. Fritz Lang. Screenplay by Thea von Harbou. UFA, 1927.

Perry Rhodan – SOS aus dem Weltall. Dir. Primo Zeglio. Tefi Film/PEA/ Attor Film, 1967.

Die Prinzen. "Wer ist Sigmund Jähn?" *So viel Spaß für wenig Geld.* Hansa [BMG], 1999.

Raumpatrouille. Die phantastischen Abenteuer des Raumschiffes Orion. Dir. Michael Braun, Theo Mezger. Perf. Dietman Schönherr. ORB, 1966.

Der Schweigende Stern. [The Silent Star]. Dir. Kurt Maetzig. Perf. Günther Simon. DEFA/Film Polski, 1959.

Signale. [Signals] Dir. Gottfried Kollditz. Perf. Gojko Mitic. DEFA/PRF "Zespoly Filmowe" Warsaw [Warszawa], 1970.

Star Trek. Dir. Gene Roddenberry. NBC, 1966–1969.

Unser Sandmännchen. By Gerhard Behrendt and Harald Serowski. GDR Deutscher Fernsehfunk. 30 August 1978.

Unser tägliches Brot. Dir. Slatan Dudow. Screenplay by Hans Beyer, Slatan Dudow, Ludwig Turek. DEFA, 1950.

When Worlds Collide. Dir. Rudolph Mate. Prod. George Pal. Paramount, 1951.

Secondary Sources

"Die Abenteuer– und Science–fiction–Literatur." *Die Sowjetunion heute* 21.10 (1976): 33.

Abrahams, Roger. "Play." *Folklore Studies in the Twentieth Century.* Ed. J. Newall Woodbridge, Suffolk; Totowa, N.J.: Brewer, Rowman and Littlefield, 1980. 120–125.

Agde, Günter, ed. *Kahlschlag. Das 11. Plenum des ZK der SED 1965. Studien und Dokumente.* Berlin: Aufbau Verlag, 1991.

Albrecht, Richard. *Das Bedürfnis nach echten Geschichten. Zur zeitgenössischen Unterhaltungsliteratur in der DDR.* Forschungen zur Literatur– und Kulturgeschichte 15. Helmut Kreuzer and Karl Riha, eds. Frankfurt am Main: Peter Lang, 1987.

Alpers, Hans–Joachim, Werner Fuchs, Ronald M. Hahn, and Wolfgang Jeschke. *Lexikon der Science Fiction Literatur.* 2 vols. München [Munich]: Wilhelm Heyne Verlag, 1980.

Althusser, Louis. "Ideology and Ideological State Apparatuses." *Lenin and Philosophy.* New York: Monthly Review Press, 1971. 127-186.

Amis, Kingsley. *New Maps of Hell.* New York: Harcourt, Brace, 1960.

Andymon Online. 2000. Ed. Bernd Hutschenreuther, Armin Scheibe, Manfred Steinert, Michael Stöhr, Anika Thon et al. <http://home.t–online.de/home/ivo.gloss/andymon.htm.>

Antczak, Janice. *Science Fiction: The Myths of a New Romance.* New York; London: Neal–Schumann Publisher, 1985.

Arbeitsgemeinschaft Utopische Literatur. "Aufgaben und Möglichkeiten der utopischen Literatur im entwickelten gesellschaftlichen System des Sozialismus." Alexander Kröger and Susanne Routschek, eds. Unpublished essay, n.d.

—. "Aufgaben und Möglichkeiten der utopischen Literatur und die Aufgaben der Schriftsteller, die sich mit dieser Literatur befassen." Unpublished essay, n.d.

Armitt, Lucie. *Theorising the Fantastic*. London: Arnold, 1996.

"'Asteroidenjäger' des Falkenseers Carlos Rasch bald wieder startklar." *Märkische Allgemeine Zeitung* 15 May 1999. n.p.

"Die Aufgaben unserer Zentralen Kommission Literatur bis zum 20. Jahrestag der DDR." (1969) SAPMO–BArch DY 27/3030 Pages [Bl.] 1–30.

"Ausschaltung der nazistischen und militaristischen Literatur. Bekannt gegeben am 16. September 1945." (1951) BArch DR 2 Page [Bl.] 1.

Bästel, W. Rev. of *Gigantum*, by Eberhardt Del Antonio. (1956) BArch DR 1/3941 Page [Bl.] 79.

Barker, Adele Marie. "The Culture Factory." *Consuming Russia. Popular Culture, Sex, and Society Since Gorbachev*. Ed. Adele Marie Barker. Durham, NC; London: Duke University Press, 1999. 12–48.

Barth, Bernd–Rainer, ed. *Wer war wer in der DDR?* Frankfurt/Main: Fischer Taschenbuchverlag, 1996.

Bathrick, David. *The Powers of Speech. The Politics of Culture in the GDR*. Lincoln & London: University of Nebraska Press, 1995.

—. "Reading Walter Benjamin from West to East." *Colloquia Germanica* 3 (1979): 246–55.

Batt, Kurt."Lob der Phantasie." *Sinn und Form* 25.6 (1973): 1294.

Bauer, Adolf. *Philosophie und Prognostik*. Weltanschauliche und methodologische Probleme der Gesellschaftsprognose. Berlin: Dietz Verlag, 1968.

Becher, Johannes R. "Unsere Wendung. Vom Kampf um die Existenz der proletarisch–revolutionären Literatur zum Kampf um ihre Erweiterung." *Zur Tradition der deutschen sozialistischen Literatur, Band 1. Eine Auswahl von Dokumenten 1926–1935*. Ed. Alfred Klein and Thomas Rietzschel. Berlin; Weimar: Aufbau Verlag, 1979.

Beissel, Rudolf. "Schmutz und Schund?" *Kleine Kleckserei Kritik. Groschenromane – wie sie wirklich sind*. Ed. Friedrich Weyer. Hückeswagen: "robor" Verlag, 1964.

Benjamin, Walter. "Das Kunstwerk im Zeitalter seiner technischen Reproduzierbarkeit." *Gesammelte Schriften*, eds. Rolf Tiedemann and Hermann Schweppenhäuser. vol. 1 Frankfurt/M: Suhrkamp, 1974. 435–469.

Bennett, Tony and Janet Woollacott. *Bond and Beyond*. London: Macmillan Education Ltd., 1987.

Berghahn, Klaus L. "Die real existierende Utopie im Sozialismus zu Christa Wolfs Romanen." *Literarische Utopien von Morus bis zur Gegenwart.* Ed. Klaus Berghahn and Hans Ulrich Seeber. Königstein: Athanäum, 1983. 275–297.

Berghahn, Volker. *Modern Germany.* Cambridge: Cambridge University Press, 1987.

Beutelschmidt, Thomas and Henning Wrage. *Das Buch zum Film– der Film zum Buch. Annäherung der literarischen Kanon im DDR Fernsehen.* Programmgeschichte des DDR Fernsehens – komparativ. Leipzig: Leipziger Universitätsverlag, 2004.

Bloch, Ernst. *Ästhetik des Vor–Scheins. The Utopian Function of Art and Literature.* Trans. Jack Zipes and Frank Mecklenburg. Cambridge, Mass; London: The MIT Press, 1988.

—. *Freiheit und Ordnung* New York: Aurora Verlag, 1946.

—. *The Principle of Hope.* 3 vols. Trans. Neville Plaice, Stephen Plaice and Paul Knight. Cambridge, MA: The MIT Press, 1986.

Blume, Mikaela. *Untersuchungen zur Rolle der Frau in der Science–Fiction Literatur der DDR seit 1970.* Diss. Pädagogische Hochschule "Clara Zetkin" Leipzig, 1989.

Blunk, Harry. "Emanzipation der Frau und Frauenalltag im DDR–Spielfilm." *Deutsche Studien* 25.97 (1987): 59–72.

Böhm, Karl. "Wie müssen Zukunftsromane sein? Wissenschaftlich – aber mit mehr Phantasie." *Sonntag* 30 December 1962: 11.

Both, Wolfgang, Hans–Peter Neumann, and Klaus Scheffler. *Berichte aus der Parallelwelt. Die Geschichte des Science Fiction–Fandoms in der DDR.* Passau: Erster Deutscher Fantasy Club e.V., 1998.

—. *Science Fiction in der DDR: Fanzines.* Berlin: Shayol, 2005.

Brandis, Eugeni Pavlovic. *Über Phantastik und Abenteuer.* Leningrad: n.p., 1960.

—. "Die wissenschaftlich–phantastische Literatur und die Gestaltung von Zukunftsmodellen." *Kunst und Literatur* 17.8 (1969): 798–813.

Brandis, Eugeni and W. Dmitrijewski. "Probleme der Darstellung der zukünftigen Gesellschaft im Lichte der Leninschen Voraussicht." *Kunst und Literatur* 19.5 (1971): 487–502.

Branstner, Gerhard. Rev. of *Die Ohnmacht der Allmächtigen*, by Heiner Rank. (20 April 1972) BArch DR1/3629 Pages [Bl.] 1–2.

—. "Über den Humor und seine Rolle in der Literatur." Diss. Humboldt Universität, 1963.

Braun, Johanna and Günter. "De Mortuis Nil Nisi Bene. 100 Zeilen über SF." *Alien Contact* 9.35 (1999): 33; *Lichtjahr* 7 (1999): 57–58.

303

—. "E.T.A. Hoffmanns Gespenster." *Quarber Merkur* 58 (December 1982): 3–8.

—. "Stasi Akten?–phantastische Literatur?" *Quarber Merkur* 32.1 (June 1994): 41–43.

—. "Zu dem berühmten Werk: Sich in Übereinstimmung bringen. Einseitiges Gespräch mit dem Autor." *Quarbur Merkur* 22 (1984): 53–58.

Brecht, Bertolt. *Kleines Organon für das Theater.* Suhrkamp texte 4. Frankfurt am Main: Suhrkamp, 1960.

—. "Über die Popularität des Kriminalromans." and "Über den Kriminalroman." *Gesammelte Werke 16. Schriften zum Theater 2.* Frankfurt am Main, Suhrkamp, 1967. 450–458.

Breitenfeld, Annette. *Die Begegnungen mit außerirdischen Formen. Untersuchungen zur Science–fiction–Literatur der DDR.* Diss. Pädagogische Hochschule „Erich Weinert" Magdeburg, 1989. Schriftenreihe und Materialien der Phantastischen Bibliothek Wetzlar 6. Wetzlar: Förderkreis Phantastik in Wetzlar e.V., 1994.

Buck–Morss, Susan. "Benjamin's Passagen–Werk: Redeeming Mass Culture for the Revolution." *New German Critique* 29.10 (1983): 211–240.

Bundesministerium für innerdeutsche Beziehungen, ed. *DDR Handbuch.* 3rd ed. 2 vols. Köln [Cologne]: Verlag Wissenschaft und Politik, 1985.

Burns, Nicholas. "This Day in Diplomacy: the Outer Space Treaty." U.S. Department of State. Office of the Spokesman. 25 April, 1997. <http://secretary.state.gov/www/briefings/statements/970425a.html>.

Caldwell, Peter C. *Dictatorship, State Planning, and Social Theory in the German Democratic Republic.* Cambridge; New York: Cambridge University Press, 2003.

Campbell, John W., Jr. Introduction. *Analog 6* Ed. John W. Campbell. Garden City, NY: Doubleday, 1968. ix–xvi.

Chapter "'Birth of a Giant' Forging America: The Story of Bethlehem Steel." 2005. 5 November 2004. Ed. Chris Krewson <http://www.mcall.com/news/specials/bethsteel/> The Morning Call, 2004.

Clareson, Thomas D. *Understanding Contemporary American Science Fiction: The Formative Period, 1927–1970.* Columbia, SC: University of South Carolina Press, 1990.

Clowes, Edith W. "Ideology and Utopia in Recent Soviet Literature." *The Russian Review* 51 (July 1992): 378–395.

Clute, John. *Science Fiction. The Illustrated Encyclopedia.* London; New York; Stuttgart: Dorling Kindersley, 1995.

Constabile–Heming, Carol Anne. "*Rezensur*: A Case Study of Censorship and Programmatic Reception in the GDR." *Monatshefte* 92.1 (2000) 53–67.

Dahn, Danielle. *Westwärts und nicht vergessen. Von Unbehagen in der Einheit.* Berlin: Rowohlt, 1996.

Davis, John R. *Britain and the German Zollverein 1848–66.* London: Macmillan Press, 1997.

Dehmelt, Norbert. "Zur Geschichte der Kriminalliteratur in der DDR." Schröder 49–72.

Del Antonio, Eberhardt. Postscript [Nachwort]. *Gigantum.* By Del Antonio. Berlin: Verlag Das Neue Berlin, 1957. 362–363.

—. "Für oder wider utopische Literatur?" (1958) BArch NY 4445/168 Pages [Bl.] 35–39.

—. "Kind von Kunst und Technik." *Sonntag* 4 November 1962: 11.

Del Rey, Lester. *The World of Science Fiction.* New York: Ballantine Books, 1979.

"Denken für die Welt von Morgen." *Sonntag* 28 August 1966; 11 September 1966: 3–6; 5–7.

Disch, Thomas. *The Dreams Our Stuff is Made Of. How Science Fiction Conquered the World.* New York: The Free Press, 1998.

Dmitrevski, Vladimir. "Grünes Licht der Utopie." *Jugend und Technik* 13.11 (1965): 963–964.

Dokumente der Sozialistischen Einheitspartei Deutschlands. Vol. 3 East Berlin, 1952.

Dorn Brose, Eric. *German History 1789–1871.* Providence; Oxford: Berghahn Books, 1997.

Ebert, Günter. "Wie müssen Zukunftsromane sein? Künstlerisch – aber mit mehr wissen." *Sonntag* 30 December 1962: 10.

Eichler, Gerhard. "Fachliches Gutachten über das Manuscript *Gigantum,*" by Eberhardt Del Antonio. (21 Aug 1956) BArch DR 1/3941 Pages [Bl.] 61–64.

—. "Kein Perpetuum Mobile." *Sonntag* 4 November 1962: 11.

Einstein, Albert. "On the generalized theory of gravitation: an account of the newly published extension of the general theory of relativity against its historical and philosophical background." *Scientific American* 182.4 (April 1950): 13–17.

Eley, Geoff. "What is Cultural History." *New German Critique* 65 (Spring/ Summer 1995): 19–36.

Elsholz. Rev. of *Titanus*, by Eberhardt Del Antonio. (20 July 1959) BArch DR 1/3941: 93–94.

Emmerich, Wolfgang. *Kleine Literaturgeschichte der DDR*. Rev. ed. Frankfurt/M: Luchterhand, 1997.

Entner, Heinz and Adolf Sckerl. "Zu Entwicklungsstand und Problemen der utopischen und wissenschaftlich–phantastischen Literatur der DDR." *Mitteilungen des Deutschen Schriftstellerverbandes*. Sonderheft 1 (November 14–16, 1973): 13–41.

Ernst Blochs Revision des Marxismus. Kritische Auseinandersetzungen marxistischer Wissenschaftler mit der Blochschen Philosophie. East Berlin: Deutscher Verlag des Wissens, 1957.

"Fanzine."Merriam Webster On–line. 2004. Ed. Editors et al. http://www.m-w.com/cgi–bin/dictionary?book=Dictionary&va=fanzine.

Feinstein, Joshua. *The triumph of the ordinary: depictions of daily life in the East German cinema, 1949–1989*. Chapel Hill: University of North Carolina Press, 2002.

Feix, Gerhard. "Der Einfluß der Schundliteratur auf die Jugendkriminalität." *Schriftenreihe der Deutschen Volkspolizei* 5 (1959): 474 and 8 (1959): 771.

Fischer, Ludwig, Dietger Pforte, Kristina Zerges, and Hella Dunger, eds. *Zur Archäologie der Popularkultur. Eine Dokumentation der Sammlungen von Produkten der Massenkunst, Massenliteratur und Werbung*. Berlin: Technical University of Berlin, 1979.

Fischer, William B. *The Empire Strikes Out. Kurd Lasswitz, Hans Dominik, and the Development of German Science Fiction*. Bowling Green, Ohio: Bowling Green State University Popular Press, 1984.

Fisher, Peter S. *Fantasy and Politics: Visions of the Future in the Weimar Republic 1918–1933*. Madison, WI: University of Wisconsin Press, 1991.

Förster, Werner. "Realität und Entwurf. Zu einigen Aspekten des Genres Phantastik in der DDR–Literatur der siebziger Jahre. " Diss. Leipzig, 1980.

—. "Time Travelling into the Present: Science Fiction Literature in the GDR." *Journal of Popular Culture* 18.3 (1984): 71–82.

Foltin, Hans Friedrich. *Die Unterhaltungsliteratur der DDR*. Bonn: Mitteldeutscher Kulturrat, 1970.

Foucault, Michel. "The Order of Discourse." Trans. Ian McLeod. *Untying the Text: A Post–structuralist Reader*. Ed. Robert Young. Boston: Routledge, 1981.

Fox, Thomas. *Stated Memory: East Germany and the Holocaust*. Rochester, NY: Camden House, 1999.

"Frauen." *DDR Handbuch*. 3rd ed. Vol. 1, 1985.

Freud, Sigmund. "The Uncanny." *The Standard Edition of the Complete Work of Sigmund Freud*. Trans. James Strachey. Vol. 17, London: Hogarth Press and Institute of Psychoanalysis, 1955.

Friedrich, Hans–Edwin. *Science Fiction in der deutschsprachigen Literatur*. Tübingen: Niemeyer Verlag, 1995.

Frink, Helen. *Women After Communism*. Lanham, MD: UP of American, 2001.

Fritzsche, Sonja. "Auf dem Weg zur Venus. Die Entdeckung ostdeutscher Populärkultur: *Der schweigende Stern*." Trans. Hans Günther Dicks *Filmforum* 19.4 (September–October 1999): 20–21.

—. "Reconceptualizing East German Popular Literature Via the Science Fiction Niche." *German Quarterly* 77.4 (2004): 443–461.

—. "'Sagen von Unirdischen': Romantic Elements in a Science Fiction Story by Anna Seghers." Unpublished essay, 1996.

Fulbrook, Mary. *Anatomy of a Dictatorship*. Oxford: Oxford University Press, 1995.

—. Retheorising 'state' and 'society' in the German Democratic Republic." *The Workers' and Peasants' State*. Ed. Patrick Major and Jonathan Osmond. Manchester: Manchester University Press, 2002.

Gaida, Edith. "Belletristische Heftreihenliteratur der DDR. Eine erste Bestandsaufnahme." *Weimarer Beiträge* 16.12 (1970): 158–176.

—. "Die Heftreihenliteratur der DDR." Diss. Potsdam Pädagogische Hochschule "Karl Liebknecht," 1973.

Gentikow, Barbara. "'Spannungs– und Unterhaltungsliteratur' der DDR oder Möglichkeiten und Grenzen der Umfunktionierung von 'Trivial-literatur.' *Text & Kontext* 10.1 (1982) 88–106.

Gerhard, Ute. "Die staatlich institutionalisierte 'Lösung' der Frauenfrage. Zur Geschichte der Geschlechterverhältnisse in der DDR." *Sozialgeschichte der DDR*. Ed. Hartmut Kaelble, Jürgen Kocka and Hartmut Zwahr. Stuttgart: Klett–Cotta, 1994. 383–403.

Germer, Dorothea. *Von Genossen und Gangstern*. Literaturwissenschaft in der Blauen Eule; 20. Essen: Verlag. Die Blaue Eule, 1998.

Gersdorf, Catrin. "The Digedags Go West: Images of America in an East German Comic Strip." *Journal of America Culture* 19.2 (Summer 1996): 35–45.

Gewerkschaft Unterricht und Erziehung, ed. *Kinder in Gefahr*. East Berlin: n.p., 1955.

Giese, Berthold. Rev. of *Professor Mittelzwerck's Geschöpfe*, by Johanna and Günter Braun. 33.4 *Science Fiction Times* 4 (1991): 20.

Goetz, Ursula. "Über den Zukunftsroman." Rev. of *Patent A.V.[W].*, by Laxar Fosifovich Lagin. *Bibliothekar* 4.5 (1950): 261–264.

Gottwald, Ulrike. *Science Fiction als Literatur in der Bundesrepublik der siebziger und achtziger Jahre.* Frankfurt am Main: Peter Lang, 1990.

Graaf, Vera. *Homo Futurus: Eine Analyse der modernen Science Fiction.* Hamburg; Claassen Verlag, 1971.

Graves, Peter. "Utopia in Mecklenburg: Peter Hacks' Play 'Moritz Tassow.'" *Modern Language Review* 75 (1990): 583–96.

"Grünes Licht der Utopie. Interview mit dem Leningrader Schriftsteller und Literaturkritiker Wladimir Ditrewski." *Jugend und Technik* 13.11 (1965): 963–964.

Gruhn, Werner. *Wissenschaft und Technik in deutschen Massenmedien.* Erlangen: Verlag Deutsche Gesellschaft für zeitgeschichtliche Fragen, 1979.

Habermas, Jürgen. *The Structural Transformation of the Public Sphere.* Trans. Thomas Burger. Cambridge, MA: The MIT Press, 1989.

Hacks, Peter. *Das Poetische.* Frankfurt am Main: Suhrkamp, 1972.

—. "Utopie und Realität. Vorwort zum Essai–Band 'Das Poetische/Ansätze zu einer postrevolutionarären Dramaturgie.'" *Essais.* Leipzig: Reclam, 1984.

Hager, Kurt. "Die entwickelte sozialistische Gesellschaft. Aufgaben der Gesellschaftswissenschaften nach dem VIII. Parteitag der SED." *Einheit* 11 (1972): 1212.

—. "Der IX. Parteitag und die Gesellschaftswissenschaften. Rede auf der Konferenz der Gesellschaftswissenschaftler der DDR am 25. und 26. November 1976." Berlin: Dietz Verlag, 1976.

—. *Zu Fragen der Kulturpolitik der SED.* Berlin: Dietz Verlag, 1972.

Haines, Gerd. "Aktennotiz: Gespräch mit Freunden der Wissenschaftlichen Phantastik am 31. Mai 1978." (31 May 1978) SAPMO–BArch DY 27/3543 Pages [Bl.] 1–4.

Hall, Stuart. "Encoding/decoding." *Culture. Media. Language.* Ed. Stuart Hall. London; Hutchinson; Birmingham, West Midlands: Center for Contemporary Cultural Studies, University of Birmingham, 1980. 128–138.

—. "The Problem of Ideology – Marxism without Guarantees." *Stuart Hall: Critical Dialogues in Cultural Studies.* Eds. David Morley and Kuan Hsing Chen. London; New York: Routledge, 1996. 28–43.

Handreichungen Jugend– und Kinderbuch. "Hinweise für die Diskussion der Themenpläne 1956 und der Perspektivpläne bis 1960 auf der

Planungsgemeinschaft Kinder und Jugendbuch Ende November 1954."
(1954) DR1/1265 Pages [Bl.] 1–2.

Hanke, Helmut. "Entwicklungsprobleme des kulturellen Lebensniveaus und des geistig–kulturellen Lebens in der DDR." (1980) SAPMO–BArch DY 30/IV B2/2.024/9 Pages [Bl.] 16a, 1–30.

Hansot, Elisabeth. *Perfection and Progress: Two Modes of Utopian Thought.* Cambridge, MA; London: The MIT Press, 1974.

Hartung, Thomas. *Die Science–fiction Literatur der DDR von 1980–90.* Magdeburg: Helmuth–Block–Verlag, 1992.

Haucke, Lutz. "Die Träume sozialistischer Massenunterhaltung in der DDR." *Weimarer Beiträge* 37.6 (1991): 805–819.

Hauswald, Gerd. "Propheten dringend gesucht. Eine Betrachtung über den Zukunftsroman." *Sonntag* 29 December 1957: 8.

—. "Eine Utopie ohne Hintergründe." *Sonntag* 15 September 1957: 8.

Hebdige, Rich. *Subculture. The Meaning of Style.* London: Methuen, 1979.

Heidtmann, Horst. "A Survey of Science Fiction in the German Democratic Republic." *Science Fiction Studies* 6 (1979): 92–99.

—. *Utopische–phantastische Literatur in der DDR.* Diss. Universität Hamburg, 1980. München [Munich]: Wilhelm Fink Verlag, 1982.

Hein, Herta and Karin Ludwig. "Die Aufnahme und Verbreitung der Wissenschaftlich-Phantastischen Literatur in der DDR." *Quarber Merkur* 7.1 (1969): 20–39.

Hell, Julia. *Post–Fascist Fantasies. Psychoanalysis, History, and the Literature of East Germany.* Durham; London: Duke University Press, 1997.

Hennig, Gerd. "'Mass Cultural Activity' in the GDR: On Cultural Politics in Bureaucratically Deformed Transitional Societies." Trans. Gunner Huettich. *New German Critique* 1.2 (Spring 1974): 38–57.

Hienger, Jörg, ed. *Unterhaltungsliteratur. Zu ihrer Theorie und Verteidigung.* Göttingen: Vandenhoeck and Ruprecht, 1976.

Hillich, Reinhard and Wolfgang Mittmann. *Die Kriminalliteratur der DDR 1949–1990.* Berlin: Akademie Verlag, 1991.

"Hinterm Horizont der Zeit." *Sputnik* 8.7 (1974): 141–145.

Hochmuth, Arno ed. *Literatur im Blickpunkt. Zum Menschenbild in der Literatur der beiden deutschen Staaten.* Berlin: Dietz Verlag, 1967.

Hochmuth, Arno and Hinnerk Einhorn. "Geschäft mit der Zukunftsangst. Zur Funktion der Science–Fiction–Massenliteratur im Imperialismus." *Einheit* 9 (1981): 932–939.

Höger, Alfons. "Die technologischen Heroen der germanischen Rasse: Zum Werk Hans Dominiks." *Text & Kontext* 8:2 (1980): 378–394.

Höpcke, Klaus. "'1984'? – 1984!" *Einheit* 39.2 (1984): 102–104.

Hoffmann, Michael; G.K. Lehmann and H–J. Ketzer. "Tendenzen und Widersprüche der Massenkultur und Medienentwicklung in der DDR." Karl–Marx–Universität, Sektion Kultur– und Kunstwissenschaften, Fachbereich Ästhetik, Leipzig. Analysematerial zur Vorbereitung des XII. Parteitages der SED. (1989) SAPMO–BArch DY 30/42224/1 Pages [Bl.] 1–20.

Hoggart, Richard. *Uses of Literacy: Changing patterns in English Mass Culture.* Fair Lawn, NJ: Essential Books, 1957.

Hohendahl, Peter. "Jürgen Habermas. 'The Public Sphere' (1964)." Trans. Sara Lennox and Frank Lennox. *New German Critique* 1.3 (Fall 1974): 45–55.

—. "Theorie und Praxis des Erbens: Untersuchungen zum Problem der litararischen Tradition in der DDR." Literatur der DDR in den siebziger Jahren. Eds. Peter Hohendahl and Patricia Herminghouse. Frankfurt am Main: Suhrkamp, 1976. 13–52.

Hohlfeld, Carsten and Thomas Braunstein. "Die beliebtesten DDR–SF– Bücher." *Info* 6 (Jan 27–28, 1990) n.p.; see Steinmüller, *Vorgriff* 17– 174. Ivo Gloss. Homepage. 26 January 2005. <http://home.t–online.de/home/ivo.gloss/andymon.htm>

Honecker, Erich. "Inhaltliche Tiefe und meisterhafte Gestaltung." *Neue Deutsche Literatur* 19.8 (1971) 3–6.

—. "Zu aktuellen Fragen bei der Verwirklichung der Beschlüsse unseres VIII. Parteitages." *Neues Deutschland* 18 Dec 1971: 3–5.

Horkheimer, Max and Theodor Adorno. "Kulturindustrie." *Adorno, Theodor W.: Gesammelte Schriften.* ed. Rolf Tiedemann. vol 3. Frankfurt am Main: Suhrkamp, 1969: 141–191.

Humble, Ronald. *The Soviet Space Programme.* London; New York: Routledge, 1988.

Hutschenreuther, Bernd. "Das Leben nach dem Tod." In Both, Neumann and Scheffler, *Berichte* 51–55.

Innerhofer, Roland. *Deutsche Science Fiction 1870–1914.* Literatur in der Geschichte Geschichte in der Literatur 38. Wien [Vienna]; Köln [Cologne]; Weimar: Böhlau Verlag, 1996.

"Interview mit Angela und Karlheinz Steinmüller." *Science Fiction Times* 28.9 (1986): 11–13.

Jäger, Manfred. *Kultur und Politik in der DDR.* Köln [Cologne]: Edition Deutschland Archiv, 1995.

James, Edward. *Science Fiction in the 20th Century.* Oxford, New York: Oxford University Press, 1994.

Jameson, Fredric. *The Political Unconscious.* Ithaca, New York: Cornell University Press, 1981.

—. "Progress vs. Utopia; or, Can We Imagine the Future?" *Science Fiction Studies* 9.2 (1982): 147–158.

—. "Reification and Utopia in Mass Culture." *Social Text* 1 (1979): 130–148.

—. "Science Fiction and the German Democratic Republic." *Science Fiction Studies* 11.2 (July 1984): 194–199.

Joho, Wolfgang. "Blick auf Unterhaltungsliteratur." *Neue Deutsche Literatur* 4.8 (1956): 141–144.

Jonas, Wolfgang. "Von der Leidenschaft utopischen Denkens. Zum 60. Todestag von Jules Verne." *Neues Deutschland* 25 March 1965: 4.

Jorgensen, Sven–Aage. "Valium des Volks? Die utopische Science–Fiction in der DDR." *Text and Kontext* 12.2 (1984): 225–243.

Junker, Harald and Udo Klotz. "Die Traummeister der DDR–SF. Ein Interview mit Angela und Karlheinz Steinmüller." *Der Golem* (1990): 65.

Kagarlizky, Yuli. *Was ist Phantastik?* Trans. Reinhard Fischer. Berlin: Verlag Das Neue Berlin, 1979.

Kagle, Steven. "Science Fiction as Simulation Game." *Many Futures, Many Worlds. Theme and Form in Science Fiction.* Ed. Thomas Clareson. Kent: Kent State University Press, 1977. 224–236.

Kaiser, Paul and Claudia Petzold. *Boheme und Diktatur in der DDR.* Catalog to the Exhibition at the Deutsches Historisches Museum September 4 – December 16, 1997. Berlin: Verlag Fannei & Walz, 1997.

"Kampf gegen die Schund– und Schmutzliteratur." *Bibliothekar* 9 (1955): 405–411.

Kannapin, Detlef. "Peace in Space – Die DEFA im Weltraum." *Zukunft im Film.* Ed. Herbert Hernecke; Frank Hörnlein. Magdeburg: Scriptum Verb, 2000. 55–70.

Kehrberg, Brigitte. *Der Kriminalroman in der DDR 1970–1990.* Poetica. Schriften zur Literaturwissenschaft 28. Hamburg: Verlag Kovac, 1998.

Keiner, Reinhold. *Thea von Harbou und der deutsche Film bis 1933.* Hildesheim; New York: Georg Olms Verlag, 1991.

Ketterer, Dave. *New Worlds for Old. The Apocalyptic Imagination, Science Fiction, and American Literature.* Bloomington; London: Indiana University Press, 1974.

Kettlitz, Hardy. Personal interview, 15 April 1999.

Klaus, Georg. *Kybernetik und Erkenntnistheorie.* Berlin: Deutscher Verlag der Wissenschaften, 1966.

Klaus, Walter. "Literarischer Dilettantismus oder Real–Phantastik?" *Sonntag* 40 (1967): 10.

Klotz, Udo and Michael Matzer. "Eine Blume im Sturm. Die Situation der DDR–Science Fiction nach der 'Wende.'" *Das Science Fiction Jahr* 6 (1991): 103–111.

Knietzsch, Horst. "Lob der technischen Phantasie." *Neues Deutschland* 28 February 1960: 4.

Köhler, Willi. "Alpträume oder Gewißheit menschlichen Glücks?" *Neues Deutschland* 17 April 1966: 5.

Kogan, L. "Ist die phantastische Literatur arm?" *Presse der Sowjetunion* 8 (1965): 5–6.

—. "Die phantastische Literatur muß reicher werden!" *Presse der Sowjetunion* 13 (1965): 6.

Krämer, Reinhold. *Die gekaufte "Zukunft."* Frankfurt/M: Buchhändler Vereinigung, 1990.

Krakauer, Siegfried. *From Caligari to Hitler. A Psychological History of the German Film.* Ed. Leonardo Quaresima. Princeton, NJ: Princeton University Press, 2004.

Kramer, Thomas. "Die DDR der fünfziger Jahre im Comic Mosaik: Einschienenbahn, Agenten, Chemieprogramm." *Akten. Eingaben. Schaufenster. Die DDR und ihre Texte Erkundungen zu Herrschaft und Alltag.* Eds. Alf Lüdtke and Peter Becker. Berlin: Akademie Verlag, 1997.

—. *Micky, Marx and Manitu. Zeit– und Kulturgeschichte im Spiegel eines DDR–Comics 1955–1990. "Mosaik" als Fokus von Medienerlebnissen im NS und in der DDR.* Berlin: Weidler Buchverlag, 2002.

Krauss, Werner. "Überblick über die französischen Utopien von Cyrano de Bergerac bis zu Etienne Cabet." *Reise nach Utopia.* Ed. Werner Krauss Berlin: Ruetten & Loening, 1961: 5–59.

Kreuzinger, Frederick A. *Apocalypse and Science Fiction. A Dialectic of Religious and Secular Soteriologies.* AAR Academy Series 40. Chico, CA: Scholars Press, 1982.

Kristeva, Julia. "Word, Dialogue, and Novel." *Desire in Language: A Semiotic Approach to Literature and Art.* By Julia Kristeva. Ed. Leon S. Roudiez. Trans. Thomas Gora, Alice Jardine, and Leon S. Roudiez. New York: Columbia University Press, 1980: 64–91.

Kroczeck, H. "Jahranalyse des Jahrganges 1958 *Jugend und Technik.*" (1958) SAPMO–Barch DY 30/IV 2/16/107 Page [Bl.] 98.

Kröber, Günter. "Wissenschaft als soziale Kraft." *Neues Deutschland* 17/18 April 1976: 10.

Kröger, Alexander [Helmut Routschek]. "100 Zeilen zur DDR–SF." *Lichtjahr* 7 (1999): 120–122.

Krupkat, Günter. "Beitrag." *VII. Schriftstellerkongreß der DDR. Protokoll. Arbeitsgruppe IV Literatur und Kritik (Berlin) 14.–16. Nov. 1973.* Berlin: VII. Schriftstellerkongreß der DDR, 1973. 203–206.

Kruschel, Karsten. *Spielwelten zwischen Wunschbild und Warnbild.* Passau: Erster Deutscher Fantasy Club, 1995.

—. "Zwischen Vision und Banalität. Die SF–Literatur der DDR – abgeschlossenes Gebiet? Ein Rückblick. Ein Countdown." *Das Science Fiction Jahr* 7 (1992): 152–173.

Kuhn, Anna K. *Christa Wolf's Utopian Vision: From Marxism to Feminism.* Cambridge, England: Cambridge University Press, 1988.

Kurze, Gottfried and Dieter Lange. "Intelligenz vom andren Stern." *Jugend und Technik* 14.9 (Sept 1966): 839–843.

Lange, Fritz. "Schund und Schmutz – ein Teil imperialistische psychologischer Kriegsführung." *Tägliche Rundschau* 18 May 1955: 3.

Lange, I.M. [Hans Friedrich Lange]. "Von Kolportage, Kriminalroman und Unterhaltungsliteratur." *Börsenblatt (*Leipzig) 22 (1947): 234–235.

Lem, Stanislaw. "Jeder Fortschritt fordert seinen Tribut. Gespräch mit dem polnischen Schriftsteller Stanislaw Lem." *Presse der Sowjetunion* 4 (1969): 18–20, 23.

—. *Microworlds. Writings on Science Fiction and Fantasy.* New York: Harcourt Brace Jovanovich, 1984.

—. *Phantastik und Futurologie.* Frankfurt/Main: Suhrkamp, 1984.

—. "Science Fiction: Ein hoffnungsloser Fall – mit Ausnahmen." *Polaris 1.* Ed. Franz Rottensteiner. Insel Taschenbuch 30. Frankfurt am Main: Insel Verlag, 1973.

Lewerenz, Walter. "Letter to Ministerium für Kultur, HV Verlage und Buchhandel, Hd. Genn. Eva Höltz re: Szameits's "Alarm in Tunnel Transterra." (21 July 1983) BArch DR 1/5440 Pages [Bl.] 1–2.

Lewerenz and Orthmann. "Wissenschaftliche Phantastik – Stiefkind der Literatur?" *Jugend und Technik* 16.1 (Jan 1968): 2–3.

Lindenberg, Bernd M. *Das Technikverständnis in der Philosophie der DDR.* Europäische Hochschulschriften Reihe XX Philosophie. Frankfurt am Main: Peter Lang, 1979.

Lindenstruth, Gerhard. "Suttner, Bertha von." *Bibliographisches Lexikon der utopisch–phantastischen Literatur.* Ed. Joachim Körber. 12 Vols. Meitingen: Corian, 2004.

Lukács, György. *Ész trónfosztása. The Destruction of Reason.* 1952. Trans. Peter Palmer. Atlantic Highlands, NJ: Humanities Press, 1981.

Mabee, Barbara. "Astronauts, Angels, and Time Machines: The Fantastic in Recent German Democratic Republic Literature." *The Celebration of the Fantastic*. Eds. Donald Morse, Marshal Tymn, and Csilla Bertha. Westport, CT: London: Greenwood Press, 1989. 221-235.

Mallinckrodt, Anita M. *Das kleine Massenmedium. Soziale Funktion und politische Rolle der Heftreihenliteratur in der DDR*. Köln [Cologne]:Verlag Wissenschaft und Politik, 1984.

Maltzan, Carlotta von. "Man musste ein Mann sein': Zur Frage der weiblichen Identität in Erzählungen von Kirsch, Morgner und Wolf." *Acta Germanica* 20 (1990): 141–155.

Manifest und Ansprachen bei der Gründungskundgebung des Kulturbundes am 4. Juli *1945 im Haus des Berliner Rundfunks*. Berlin, n.p., 1945.

Mannheim, Karl. *Ideology and Utopia*. 1936. Trans. Louis Wirth and Edward Shils. New York; London: Harcourt Brace Jovanovich, 1985.

Mechtel, Hartmut. "Die phantastische Methode." *Lichtjahr* 4 (1985): 102–116.

—. Rev. of *Lichtjahr 5*, ed. by Erik Simon. (January 1986) BArch DR 1/3634 Pages [Bl.] 1–6.

Merkel, Ina. "Leitbilder und Lebensweisen von Frauen in der DDR." *Sozialgeschichte der DDR*. Ed. Hartmut Kaelble, Jürgen Kocka, and Hartmut Zwahr. Stuttgart: Klett–Cotta, 1994. 359–382.

Modleski, Tania. *Studies in Entertainment: Critical Approaches to Mass Culture*. Bloomington, IN: Indiana University Press, 1986.

Moylan, Tom. *Demand the Impossible*. Methuen: New York and London: 1986.

—. *Scraps of the Untainted Sky. Science Fiction. Utopia. Dystopia*. Boulder, Colorado: Westview Press, 2000.

Müller–Enbergs, Helmut, Jan Wielgohs and Dieter Hoffmann, eds. *Wer war wer in der DDR. Ein biographisches Lexikon*. Berlin: Christoph Links Verlag – LinksDruck GmbH, 2000.

Myers, Michael. "Visions of Tomorrow: German Science Fiction and Socialist Utopian Novels of the Late Nineteenth Century." *Selecta* 14 (1993): 63–69.

Nägele, Rainer. "Trauer, Tropen und Phantasmen: Verrückte Geschichten aus der DDR." *Literatur der DDR in den siebziger Jahren*. Ed. Peter U. Hohendahl and Patricia Herminghouse. Frankfurt/Main: Suhrkamp, 1983. 193–222.

Nagl, Manfred. "Neu in der DDR." *Science Fiction Times* 28.10 (1986): 29.

—. *Science Fiction in Deutschland*. Tübingen: Tübinger Vereinigung für Volkskunde, 1972.

"Neuer Kurs." *DDR Handbuch* 3rd ed. Vol. 2, 1985.

"Neues Ökonomisches System." *DDR Handbuch* 3rd ed. Vol. 2, 1985.

Neumann, Hans–Peter. *Die grosse illustrierte Bibliographie der Science Fiction in der DDR.* Berlin: Shayol Verlag, 2002.

—. "Kröger – Tuschel – Frühauf. (Im Untergrund)." *Alien Contact* 8.26 (1997): 21–23.

—. Personal interview, 16 November 1998.

Nutz, Walter. *Trivialliteratur und Populärkultur.* Opladen/Wiesbaden: Westdeutscher Verlag GmbH, 1999.

—. *Der Trivialroman. Seine Formen und seine Hersteller.* Köln und Opladen: Westdeutscher Verlag, 1962.

Parrinder, Patrick. *Science Fiction. Its Criticism and Teaching.* Methuen: London and New York, 1980.

Pehlke, Michael and Norbert Lingfeld. *Roboter und Gartenlaube: Ideologie und Unterhaltung in der Science–Fiction–Literatur.* Reihe Hanser 56. München [Munich]: Carl Hanser Verlag, 1970.

Penley, Constance. "Feminism, Psychoanalysis, and the Study of Popular Culture." *Cultural Studies.* Eds. Lawrence Grossberg, Cary Nelson and Paula Treichler. New York; London: Routledge, 1992. 479–500.

"Protokoll der internen Besprechung über Verlags– und Buchhandelsfragen." (1947) Barch DR 2/1149 Pages [Bl.] 1–19.

"Protokoll der Präsidialratssitzung des Kulturbunds." (1951) BArch SAPMO DY 27/913 Pages [Bl.] 169–193.

"Protokoll zur Präsidialratsitzung des Kulturbunds am 2. April 1947." (1947) SAPMO BArch DY 27/909 Pages [Bl.] 157–184.

Radway, Janice. *Reading the Romance: Women, Patriarchy and Popular Literature.* Chapel Hill; London: University of North Carolina Press, 1994.

Rasch, Carlos. "DDR–SF abgewrackt oder noch aktuell?" *Lichtjahr* 7 (1999): 122–124.

—. "Fantastik hilft die Zukunft begreifen." *Thüringische Landeszeitung* 4 October 1968,Weekend insert [Wochenbeilage]: 2.

—. "Die utopische Literatur und die Gegenwart." *Börsenblatt für den Deutschen Buchhandel* [Leipzig] 17 Jan 1967: 55–56.

Redlin, Ekkehard. "Eberhardt Del Antonio – der literarischen Utopie verschrieben." *Börsenblatt für den Deutschen Buchhandel* [Leipzig] 21 June 1966: 428–429.

—. "Er liebte die Technik und die Menschen." *Alien Contact* 8.27 (1997): 5–6.

—. "Kairo's Geheimnis." Rev. of *Kairo*, by Rainer Fuhrmann. *Neues Deutschland* 25 October 1996: 12.

—. Rev. of *Gigantum*, by Eberhardt Del Antonio. (n.d.) BArch DR 1/3941 Pages [Bl.] 59–60.

—. Rev. of *Die Ohnmacht der Allmächtigen*, by Heiner Rank. (17 April 1972) BArch DR 1/3629 Pages [Bl.] 1–7.

—. Rev. of *Zeit der Sternschnuppen*, by Herbert Ziergiebel. (14 May 1971) BArch DR 1/3629 Pages [Bl.] 1–6.

—. "Ungewohnte Wirklichkeit. Über das Vergnügen an utopischer Literatur." *Sonntag* 23 April 1972: 6.

—. "Die utopische Dimension." *Neue Deutsche Literatur* 16.10 (1968): 166.

"Regelung der Tätigkeit von Verlagen und Druckereien und der Herausgabe von Druckschriften durch den Präsidenten der Deutschen Verwaltung für Volksbildung in der sowjetischen Besatzungszone." (1948) Barch DR 2/1149 Pages [Bl.] 1–19.

Reid, J.H. "En route to Utopia: Some Visions of the Future in East German Literature." *Renaissance and Modern Studies* 28 (1984) 114–128.

Richter, Karl–Ludwig. "Zu einigen Problemen der Rolle, Funktion und Gestaltung von Wissenschaft und Technik in der phantastischen Literatur, untersucht an ausgewählten Werken der sowjetischen Phantastik." Diss. Technische Universität? Dresden, 1971.

Rottensteiner, Franz. "Die 'wissenschaftliche Phantastik' der DDR." *Polaris 5*. Ed. Franz Rottensteiner. Phantastische Bibliothek Band 54. Frankfurt am Main: Suhrkamp, 1981. 91–118.

Rundell, Richard. "Individual and Community in East German Science Fiction." Unpublished essay, 1979.

—. "Socialist Technological Utopias: Notes on GDR Science Fiction." Unpublished essay, 1976.

Ryan, Judith. "Twilight Zones: Myth, Fairy Tale, and Utopia in No Place on Earth and Cassandra." *Responses to Christa Wolf. Critical Essays*. Ed. Marilyn Sibley Fries. Detroit: Wayne State University Press, 1989: 312–325.

Sargent, Lyman Tower. "The Three Faces of Utopianism Revisited." *Utopian Studies* 5.1 (1994) 1–37.

Schierlich, Walter. "Zur Problematik des Zukunftsromans." *Bibliothekar* 11.9 (1957): 925.

Schittly, Dagmar. *Zwischen Regie und Regime. Die Filmpolitik der SED im Spiegel der DEFA–Produktionen*. Berlin: Links, 2002.

Schlösser, Hans. Rev. of *Bis zum Nullpunkt des Seins*, by Kurd Lasswitz. (1982) BArch DR 1/5432 Pages [Bl.] 1–5.

Schmiedt, Helmut. *Ringo in Weimar. Begegnungen zwischen Hochliteratur und Popularkultur.* Würzburg: Königskausen and Neumann, 1996.

Scholes, Robert and Eric Rabkin. *Science Fiction: History. Science. Vision.* New York: Oxford University Press, 1977.

Schröder, Gustav ed. *Potsdamer Forschungen. Untersuchungen zur sozialistischen Unterhaltungsliteratur.* Gesellschaftswissenschaftliche Reihe A Heft 16. Pädagogische Hochschule "Karl Liebknecht," Potsdam 1975.

—. "Zur Geschichte der utopischen Literatur in der DDR." Schröder, *Potsdamer* 31–47.

Schubbe, Elimar, ed. *Dokumente zur Kunst–, Literatur– und Kulturpolitik der SED.* Stuttgart: Seewald, 1972.

Schulmeister, Karl–Heinz. "Bericht über die Verwirklichung des Beschlusses vom 17. Januar 1985." (10 February 1986) SAPMO–BArch DY 27/972 Pages [Bl.] 133–156.

Schulte–Sasse, Jochen. *Die Kritik an der Trivialliteratur seit der Aufklärung. Studien zur Geschichte des modernen Kitschbegriffs.* München [Munich]: W. Fink, 1971.

Schultz, Robert. "Blochs Philosophie der Hoffnung." *Ernst Blochs Revision des Marxismus.* Ed. Johannes Heinz Horn. Berlin: Deutscher Verlag der Wissenschaften, 1957. 51–70.

Schulz, Hans–Joachim. *Science Fiction.* Stuttgart: J.B. Metzlersche Verlagsbuchhandlung, 1986.

Science Fiction–Club Sondershausen, ed. *Besondere Zeiten. Informationsblatt für Science Fiction und Fantasy* 2 (1989).

Sckerl, Adolf. Rev. of *Unheimliche Erscheinungsformen auf Omega XI*, by Johanna and Günter Braun. (11.30.1972) BArch DR 1/3630 Pages [Bl.] 1–7.

—. "Wissenschaftliche–phantastische Literatur. Überlegungen zu einem literarischen Genre und Anmerkungen zu seiner Entwicklung in der DDR." Series Arbeitsmaterial für die literaturpropagandistische Arbeit im Kulturbund der DDR. Diss. Humboldt U. 1977.

Seelinger, Rolf. "Vorsicht! Marsmensch!" *Neue Deutsche Literatur* 8.9 (1960): 151–154.

Seghers, Anna, "Eröffnungsrede. VII Schriftstellerkongress der DDR." *Neue Deutsche Literatur* Berlin 22:2 (1974) 19.

Sielaff, Erich. "Zur Frage des Unterhaltungsromans." *Bibliothekar* 4.9 (1950): 457–464.

Simon, Erik. "Blütezeit und Fall des SLK." In Both, Neumann and Scheffler,*Berichte.* 44–46.

—. "Die Science–Fiction der DDR 1991–1998 (und davor)." *Das Science Fiction Jahr* 15 (2000): 616–629.

Simon, Erik and Olaf Spittel. *Die Science–fiction der DDR. Autoren und Werke.* Berlin: Verlag Das Neue Berlin, 1988.

Soldvieri, Stefan. "Socialists in Outer Space. East German Film's Venusian Adventure." *Film History* 3 (1998): 382–398.

Spittel, Olaf. Postscript. *Die Zeitinsel.* Ed. Olaf R. Spittel. Berlin: Verlag Neues Leben, 1991. 461–470.

—. Rev. of *Bis zum Nullpunkt des Seins,* by Kurt Lasswitz. (1978) BArch DR1/5432 Pages [Bl.] 1–7.

—. "Vier Jahre zu spät." *Science Fiction Times* 5 (1989): 4–7.

—. "Zur DDR–SF der 80er Jahre." *Das Science Fiction Jahr* 3 (1988): 552–564.

Startiz, Dietrich. *Geschichte der DDR.* Neue Folge Band 260. Frankfurt am Main: Suhrkamp, 1986.

Steinmüller, Angela and Karlheinz. *Vorgriff auf das Lichte Morgen. Studien zur DDR–SF.* Gelsenkirchen: Erster Deutscher Fantasy Club, 1995.

Steinmüller, Karlheinz. "Die biologische Zukunft des Menschen im Spiegel der Phantastik." *Temperamente* 1 (1980): 150–159.

—. "Das Ende der Utopischen Literatur: Ein themengeschichtlicher Nachruf auf die DDR–Science Fiction." *The Germanic Review* 67.4 (Fall 1992): 166–173.

—. "Die Maschinentheorie des Lebens. Philosophische Fragen des biologischen Mechanismus. " Diss. Humboldt University East Berlin, 1977.

—. "Die Positionsbestimmung der Seesternwesen. Zu Problemen des Realismus in der Science–fiction–Literatur." *Positionen* 3 (1987): 147–167.

—. "Über Science Fiction Literatur." Unpublished notes, 1984.

—. "Zukünfte, die nicht Geschichte wurden. Zum Gedankenexperiment in Zukunftsforschung und Geschichtswissenschaft." *Was wäre wenn.* Ed. Michael Salewski. HMRG–Beiheft 36. Stuttgart: Frank Steiner Verlag, 1999.

"Stenographische Niederschrift eines Gesprächs zu utopisch–phantastischer Literatur." (20 June 1973) SAPMO–BArch DY 27/3535. Pages [Bl.] 1–120.

Stephens, Anthony. "The Sun State and its Shadow: On the Condition of Utopian Writing." *Utopias.* Ed. Eugene Kamenka. Melbourne: Oxford University Press, 1987. 1-19.

Stites, Richard. *Revolutionary Dreams. Utopian Vision and Experimental Life in the Russian Revolution.* New York: Oxford, 1989.

Strugatsky, Arkadi and Boris. "Nein, die phantastische Literatur ist reicher! Antwort auf L. Kogan." *Presse der Sowjetunion* 11 (1965): 18.

Suvin, Darko. *Metamorphoses of Science Fiction. On the Poetics and History of a Literary Genre.* New Haven and London: Yale University Press, 1979.

—. "Playful Cognizing, or Technical Errors in Harmonyville: The Science Fiction of Johanna and Günter Braun." *Science Fiction Studies* 8.1 (1981): 72–79; *Polaris 5.* Ed. Franz Rottensteiner. Phantastische Bibliothek Band 54. Frankfurt am Main: Suhrkamp, 1981. 119–131.

Taut, Heinrich. "Das Bekannte ist nicht das Erkannte." *Sonntag* 30 December 1962: 10–11.

—. Rev. of "Carlos Rasch: Die Heloiden." BArch DR 1/5060a Pages [Bl.] 441–446.

—. "Träume, Träume, wo ist eure Wonne?" Wie soll unsere Zukunftsliteratur aussehen?" *Sonntag* 28 October 1962: 11.

Todorov, Tzvetan. *The Fantastic.* Ithaca: Cornell University Press, 1975.

Trommler, Frank. *Sozialistische Literatur in Deutschland.* Stuttgart: Alfred Kröner Verlag, 1976.

Turek, Ludwig. Postscript. Turek. *Die Goldene Kugel.* 170–171.

Tyman, Marshall B. *The Science Fiction Reference Book.* Mercer Island, WA: Starmont House, 1981.

Tzschaschel, Rolf. *Der Zukunftsroman der Weimarer Republik.* Schriften-reihe und Materialien der Phantastischen Bibliothek Wetzlar 30. Ed. Thomas Le Blanc. Wetzlar: Förderkreis Phantastik in Wetzlar e.V., 2002.

"...und Ihre Meinung?" *Jugend und Technik* 14.12 (Dec 1967): 1060.

Velberg, Steffi H. "Der Militärverlag." *Science Fiction Times* 30.9 (1988): 4.

Vollprecht, Sabine. *Science–Fiction für Kinder in der DDR.* Stuttgarter Arbeiten zur Germanistik; 285. Stuttgart: Heinz, 1994. Diss. Pädago-gische Hochschule "Karl Friedrich Wilhelm Wander" Dresden, 1992.

Walker, William. "Contemporary GDR Science Fiction: The Example of Johanna and Günter Braun." *Studies in GDR Society and Culture* 3 (1983): 137–148.

Weber, Hermann. *Kleine Geschichte der DDR.* Köln [Cologne]: Verlag Wissenschaft und Politik, 1980.

Weigand, Jörg. *Die triviale Phantasie.* Bonn; Bad Godesberg: Asgard–Verlag Dr. Werne Hippe KG, 1976.

Wiechmann, Gerhard. "Leit– und Feindbilder im Science–fiction–Film. Die DDR–Produktion. Der schweigende Stern." *Leit– und Feindbilder im*

Science–fiction–Film. Schriftenreihe Medienberatung 5. Bonn: Bundeszentral für politische Bildung, 1997. 9-27.

Wierling, Dorothee. "Three Generations of East German Women: Four Decades of the GDR and After." *Oral History Review* 21.2 (Winter 1993): 19–29.

Williams, Raymond. *Problems in Materialism and Culture.* London: Verso, 1980.

—. "Science Fiction." *Science Fiction Studies* 15 (1988): 356–360.

"Wir stellen ein Buch zur Diskussion. Turek, Ludwig: Die goldene Kugel." *Bibliothekar* 4.1 (1950): 46–47.

Wloch, Karl. Verlagsproduktionsplan 1956 – Stellungnahme zum Themenplan, Abteilung Literatur und Buchwesen, Sektor Schöne Literatur. (1955) Barch DR 1/1265 Pages [Bl.] 1–2.

"Zeit des Neubeginns. Gespräch mit Sergej Tulpanow." *Neue Deutsche Literatur* 9 (1979): 42.

Zetkin, Clara. Introduction. Bellamy 10–11.

Ziegfeld, Richard E. *Stanislaw Lem.* New York: Frederick Ungar Publishing Co., 1985.

Zipes, Jack. *Fairy Tales and the Art of Subversion.* New York: Wildman, 1983.

—. "Struggle for Grimm's Throne. Legacy in FRG and GDR." *The Reception of Grimms Fairy Tales.* Ed. Donald Haase. Detroit: Wayne State University, 1993. 167–206.

"Zu unserem Beitrag 'Grünes Licht der Utopie.'" *Jugend und Technik* 14.2 (1966) 98.

"Zur Entwicklung des Kulturniveaus der Arbeiterklasse und anderer werktätiger Schichten. Die Erhöhung des Einflusses der Arbeiterklasse auf die sozialistische Kultur und Kunst und die weitere Ausprägung ihres Bündnisses mit Künstlern und Kulturschaffenden." (October 31 1980) BArch IV B2/2.024/9 Pages [Bl.] 1–30.

"Zur Feder Gegriffen." *Jugend und Technik* 15.3 (March 1966): 194–195; 15.5 (May 1967): 386; 15.9 (Sept 1967): 770; 14.12 (Dec 1966): 105; 14.11 (Nov 1966): 962; 15.7 (July 1967): 579–582; 15.8 (Aug 1967): 674.

Index

Fanzines 79, 223–225
Feinstein, Joshua 51, 120
Feix, Gerhard 79
Fickelscherer , Helmut 174
Film, Science Fiction 15, 19, 44–45, 57,
    67, 113–114, 155, 174, 191, 232,
    243–245, 256
Fischer, Ludwig, 17
Fischer, William 40–44, 64
Fisher, Peter 45–47
Förster, Werner 17, 19, 174, 221
Foltin, Friedrich 18
Formalism
    Debates 68–69, 94
    Russian 30
Foucault, Michel 23, 33
Fox, Thomas 58
Franke, Herbert 177, 182
Free German Youth (*Freie Deutsche Ju-
    gend*, FDJ) 93, 99, 233
French Occupational Zone 53
Freud, Sigmund 201, 203–204
Fricke Hans, Werner 27, 67, 81, 88, 91
Frink, Helen 91
Fröhlich sein und singen 75, 100
Frühauf, Klaus 173, 287–288
Frye, Northrop 272
Fühmann, Franz 28, 89, 166, 191–192,
    217, 225–227
Fuhrmann, Rainer 174, 230, 287
Fulbrook, Mary 22–23
Future
    Alternate 25, 71, 81, 122–123
    Subversive potential of 25, 71, 81–
        83, 107–108
Futurology (*Prognostik*) 105, 108–109

Gagarin, Yuri 101
Gaida, Edith 78
Gebrüder Weiss Verlag 52–53
Geelhaar, Anne 146
"Gegenwartsroman" (Novel of the Pre-
    sent) 82, 105, 119, 186

Generation 101, 132–133, 179, 187, 196,
    207, 223, 225, 229, 231
Genre 21, 78, 84, 106
Gentikow, Barbara 17
German Writers' Union (DSV) 27–28,
    67, 92–93, 95, 105, 115, 124,
    174–175, 185, 198, 220, 241,
    255
    Committee on Utopian Literature
        (*Arbeitskreis Utopische Litera-
        tur*) 112, 183, 187–188
    Seventh German Writers' Confer-
        ence 168
Gernsback, Hugo 40
Gibson, William 232
Gigantum (Eberhardt Del Antonio) 91,
    93, 95–97, 134, 138, 144, 156
Gilliam, Terry 232
Glasnost 217, 233
Glenn, John 191
Gobsch, Hanns 45
Göhler, Olaf 180
Goetz, Ursula 74
Golden Sphere, The (Ludwig Turek) 56–
    62, 64, 89
Der Golem 222
Görlich, Günter 180
Gorbachev, Mikhail 217, 233, 238–239,
    259, 273
Graf, Oskar Maria 49
Graves, Peter 117
Grotesque 34, 122, 166

Habermas, Jürgen 188
Hacks, Peter 117–118
Häußler, Hubert 79
Hager, Kurt 165, 218–219
Haines, Gerd 221
Hall, Stuart 20, 86–87
Hanke, Helmut 217–218
Haraway, Donna 32
Harbou, Thea von 26, 44, 238
Hardel, Gerhard 75

Mabee, Barbara 17
Maetzig, Kurt 15, 110, 113, 146, 155
Malik Verlag 49, 56
Mallinckrodt, Anita 13, 18, 49–50, 55–56, 101, 115, 179
Manhattan Project 137
Mannheim, Karl 260
Mardicke, Fritz 53, 64
Marken, Wolfgang, pseudo. See Fritz Mardicke
Mars (planet) 40, 61, 110, 112, 127–128
Marx, Karl 71, 188
Marxism–Leninism 19–21, 34–36, 50–51, 59–60, 70–71, 76, 84, 103, 106, 117, 124, 132–133, 140, 143, 147, 164, 186, 189, 195, 214, 234
    Emancipation of Women 34, 147–156
Mass Culture 19–21, 39, 49, 52, 143, 165, 175, 181, 184, 218, 220
Mate, Rudolph 113
Matzer, Michael 14, 20, 93, 190, 224
May, Karl 19, 43, 65, 84, 114
McCaffrey, Anne 231, 244
Mechtel, Hartmut 28, 222, 228–229, 244
Memory 143, 245–246, 277–278, 280
Merkel, Ina 149, 154
Metropolis (Thea von Harbou) 44
Meyenburg, Anna 49
Michalz, Stefan 79
Mielke, Heinz 75
Mielke, Stasi Mielke 188
Militärverlag 93, 179
Miller, Walter 175
Ministry of Culture (Kulturministerium) 76, 93, 115, 124, 165, 183, 218, 220
Mitteldeutscher Verlag 94, 118
Modleski, Tania 21
Möckel, Klaus 28, 169
Moorcock, Michael 116

More, Sir Thomas 29–30, 55, 73, 120, 124, 249, 262
Morgner, Irmtraud 146, 155, 160
Mosaik (Hannes Hegen) 19, 85, 100, 282
Moylan, Thomas 30, 124
Müller, Heiner 22, 225
Müller, Horst 110–111, 138
Müller, Paul Alfred 53
Müller, Walter 46
Myth 29, 70, 168, 228, 238, 246, 272

Nagl, Manfred 17–18, 41–42, 44, 53, 64, 164
National Socialism 14, 26, 42, 44, 52–53, 58, 60, 64–65, 74, 88, 123, 127, 134, 200, 261, 283
Nationalism, East German 34, 43, 64, 68–69, 88, 101, 103, 116, 133–138, 166, 191, 227
Nesvadba, Josef 121, 126, 176
Neue Abenteuer, Das Series 55, 75, 113, 179
Neue Deutsche Literatur 80, 222
Neumann, Hans–Peter 15, 20, 56, 80, 115, 170, 179–180, 183, 223–225
New Course (NK) 76, 134, 136
New Economic System (NÖS/ NÖSPL) 103–104, 134, 136
Niche Mentality 28, 188–193, 220, 230
Nutz, Walter 19

Obrutchev, Vladimir 75
Office of Literature and Publishing (Amt für Literatur und Verlagswesen) 67, 93
Oppenheimer, Robert 137
Orthmann, Edwin 177
Orwell, George 226, 245, 278–279, 287
Ostalgia 277, 282, 287
Osten, Ludwig, pseudo. See Fritz Mardicke